Volume I

Stories of Eastern
Montana's Pioneers

As told to:
    Mrs. Morris (Gladys Mullet) Kauffman

Sweetgrass Books

Cover Logo
The logo used in the original "As I Remember" series
in the Glendive Ranger-Review

Rear Cover Photo
Sharon Kauffman

-Contact Information-
www.As-I-Remember.com
gmk311@hotmail.com

Printed in the United States of America

ISBN 1-59152-031-2

Sweetgrass Books
A Division of Far Country Press
Helena, Montana

Table of Contents

The first 29 Stories – 1964

Photo Section

Glossary
Complete List of Interviews

Loaned Photo Acknowledgements

Introduction

In 1964, during Montana's territorial centennial year, Mrs. Morris (Gladys Mullet) Kauffman of Glendive, Montana noticed the dwindling number of pioneers who had settled Eastern Montana. Too many of them were taking their stories to the grave. Surely someone should record those stories! Of course, there was no 'someone' so Mrs. Kauffman, despite having nine children at home, undertook the task.

During the next twelve years she interviewed over 160 of the early Eastern Montana pioneers and published their stories in Glendive's newspaper, the Ranger-Review, naming the column "As I Remember."

Mrs. Kauffman, herself the daughter of early settlers, reflects her love of history and her affection for Eastern Montana in her writing. She vividly brings to life the colorful pioneer era as she retells the heartaches, joys, laughter, and hardships of those hardy settlers.

As Mrs. Kauffman interviewed the old timers they related their experiences as they recalled them. Thus the name "As I Remember." The reader may notice variations in the different recollections, but we do not attempt to reconcile discrepancies. These stories are 'their' memories.

In 1964 the Ranger-Review printed the first twenty-nine interviews, most of which were fairly short. As Mrs. Kauffman continued the project, she began drawing more memories out of those pioneers, and many of the later stories are considerably longer. In the latter half of this book, we have grouped the first twenty-nine stories together in chronological order as they were published.

Although most of the stories were written by Mrs. Kauffman, a few were submitted in writing by others for inclusion in the original series. In this book we have not changed the original submissions to conform to our format. The same applies to other sources, such as newspapers. These entries appear in italics.

And now a note about language: The reader should keep in mind that these stories were recorded between 1964 and 1975 and reflect life experiences in the late 19th and early 20th century. These interviews are in the language of the time and no attempt has been made to 'update' the stories to conform to today's standards.

In the back of the book, a glossary explains some terms and locations that may be unfamiliar to the reader. These terms are marked by an asterisk* in the book to indicate their inclusion in the glossary.

Also in the back of the book is a list of all the interviews Mrs. Kauffman recorded between 1964 and 1975. Most of those stories not included in this book will appear in Volume II.

Let "As I Remember" take you back to another era and also help you appreciate the times in which you live!

Foreword

Ever since the "As I Remember" series began in 1964, people have encouraged me to get the stories compiled into a book. Over thirty years have passed since the last article was printed. Prospects for a book looked bleak, but I am blessed to have a supportive family.

This winter, my son Kent took the winter off to concentrate on the book project. Without his determination and persistence these stories would still be in boxes and binders. Together we typed, edited, proofread, and organized.

Considerable assistance with typing came from my daughter Twila. My son Vance was a big help with the website we created for the project (www.As-I-Remember.com) and with invaluable technical assistance. Daughter Vaughn was supportive with phone calls and brainstorming. Other family members contributed time as well.

We could not have done it without the help of many others. Cindy Mullet, reporter for the Ranger-Review, was an immense help in tracking down and copying articles we were missing. We would not have a complete collection without Cindy's contribution. The staff at the Ranger-Review in general have been most cooperative. Our friend Doris Gnagey in California spent hours proofreading the stories for us.

We are grateful to those who loaned us photos: Louise Cross, Jessie Evans, Bev Kelly, Agnes Kinney, Cindy Mullet, and Norma Jean Peterson, and also to Matt Yovich who provided technical assistance with the photos. We appreciate the many who helped us with information, particularly Don Welsh and Fred Dion.

A special thanks to Molly Holz from the Montana Historical Society and to Bob Rydell, Dean of the History Department at Montana State University for their suggestions and guidance.

A myriad of 'people connections' facilitated various aspects of the project and it was gratifying to see everything come together. We hope the book promotes both an appreciation of our past and a gratitude for our present. Enjoy!

Thank you to all!

Gladys Kauffman

Map of Dawson County, Montana and Surrounding Areas

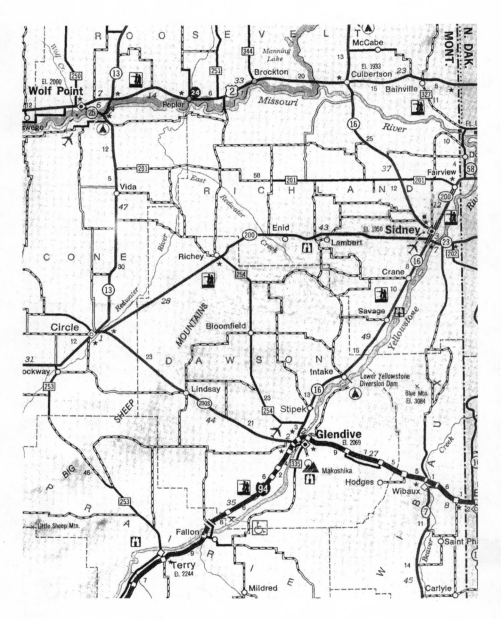

Map courtesy of Montana Department of Transportation

Mrs. Bailey (Lucy Armstrong) Fisher

October – November 1966

A dugout in a bank – a blanket for a door – a dirty table piled with dirty dishes – a sullen, uncommunicative squaw – what a reception for a new bride! Such was the reception for Mrs. Theodore Armstrong, mother of Sidney's Lucy Fisher.

Theodore Armstrong, a cowhand near Woodriver, Nebraska, had long harbored a hankering to go West, and in 1882 his chance came. The Wood Brothers, bankers in Woodriver, had heard about Eastern Montana's vast ranges with their lush grass so they bought a bunch of longhorns down in Texas and hired some cowboys, with Armstrong as herd foreman, to drive the cattle north to the Montana range.

The drive was long and hot and dry, part of it through hostile Indian territory, so cattle losses could be heavy, but they reached Montana with plenty of beef on the hoof to form a herd nucleus.

They chose a location on Hard Scrabble Creek south of the Missouri River in what later became Dawson County and still later Richland County. At that time, however, Montana wasn't even a state so the last thing to concern the Armstrong boys would have been what county might some day be formed there.

Comer Armstrong, brother of Theodore, also came in 1882, and in 1889 another brother joined them. Since all they had to do then to claim land was to 'squat'* on it, the brothers chose their locations carefully with the aim of controlling Hard Scrabble Creek from source to mouth.

The devastating winter of 1886-87 wrought havoc with the Wood Brothers' holdings, but they bought more cattle and kept on. In '84, '86, and '88 Armstrong was sent to Texas for more cattle. He would go down on a steamboat in the spring, pick up a bunch of young fellows who wanted to come to Montana, then return, driving the cattle overland. That drive would take all summer. In 1890 or '91 the Armstrong brothers bought out the Wood brothers so the Pothook became the Armstrong brand, and the Pothook cattle belonged to the Armstrong boys.

Back in Nebraska the Armstrong boys had a sister, Nettie. A young widow with a small boy was staying with Nettie, working in a print shop by day and sewing in the evening for Nettie to pay for her board and room and that of the little boy.

Theodore Armstrong and Lillian Chamber, the widow, began exchanging messages through Nettie, and in time they began a correspondence of their own. Finally they decided to get married and in 1889 Mrs. Chamber journeyed by steamboat to Fort Buford* where she was met by Theodore and a friend, Walter Kemmis.

Mrs. Chamber and Armstrong were married in Fort Buford by the army chaplain with Walter Kemmis as witness. That same day they started back

1

toward the ranch, going as far as the Kemmis Ranch (near Sidney's present location) where they spent the night. Next day with team and wagon they continued on to Hard Scrabble.

When they reached the ranch, the new Mrs. Armstrong looked in vain for a house. Plenty of corrals. Lots of cattle. But where was the house? Her husband pulled up to a dugout in the bank, fronted with logs and a blanket hanging over an opening, and stopped.

"Here we are," he told her and let her out of the wagon, then went on down to the barn to put his team away. When he came back, she was still standing outside the dugout where he had left her. He lifted the blanket and ducked through the opening into whatever was inside, but she stood rooted to the spot. When she didn't follow, he came back and asked her, "Aren't you coming in?"

She came then, but one look inside made her wonder why she did. Seated at a table stacked with dirty dishes were Comer Armstrong (her husband's brother) and his wife, Josephine. Comer had married an Indian woman, and they had been quarreling so Josephine was in anything but a congenial mood.

She offered no greeting, and when Theodore hinted, "We've come a long way and would like something to eat," Josephine merely pulled her blanket a little closer around her head and grunted, "Your squaw. She cook."

If the two-day wagon trip to the ranch could be called a honeymoon, the honeymoon was over. The city girl had to make some adjustments, and she had to begin right then.

Theodore cleared the table and helped her find something to prepare for a meal. The loaf of bread he brought out looked as though it had been made with sand instead of flour, and her appetite waned, but she struggled through.

The bedroom turned out to be another dugout room. Two poles had been driven into the dirt bank to support one end of the bed while the other end was propped up. Willow branches were laid across these poles, and a hay mattress topped it off. Little Ross, the small son she had brought with her, had to have a bed so some more branches were piled in a corner on the dirt floor and covered with her coat.

For many months Josephine maintained an unrelenting antagonism toward the new Mrs. Armstrong, and eventually the latter learned the real reason for the hostility. Josephine had two other sisters, one of them, Sarah, married to a cousin of the Armstrongs, the other still single. The three Indian sisters wanted Theodore to marry this third sister so when he, instead, brought a city girl to the ranch, they determined to drive her away. They tried all sorts of stunts, but Mrs. Armstrong held out against all their efforts.

Once Sarah invited her and Ross for a ride in a buckboard*, and as they followed a lonely trail through the badlands (all the trails were lonely then) two mounted Indians suddenly burst upon them. They were a fearsome sight in their war paint and headdress, yelling and firing their six-shooters. Little wonder that the horse pulling the buckboard started to run.

2

Sarah pretended to be scared, and Mrs. Armstrong pretended not to be. She put little Ross between her knees and held on for dear life as the buckboard careened through the coulees* and over the hills, the Indians in hot pursuit. Mrs. Armstrong grimly hid the terror she felt, and finally the Indians gave up the chase. Only later did she discover that, though the Indians were genuine enough, the wild warrior demonstration was a fake; Josephine and her youngest sister had dressed up like warriors and the chase had been rigged in an effort to drive out the unwelcome white woman.

The Armstrongs were married in October, and by the latter part of November they had a floorless log shack ready to move into on the Lone Butte Ranch. Mrs. Armstrong was in no way reluctant to leave the dugout they had shared with Comer and Josephine, even though their new dwelling left much to be desired.

They had no seasoned lumber with which to build so they had used green logs, and the cold weather that fall added complications. The plaster, which they used for chinking between the logs, would freeze before it could dry so there were gaps in the walls, but at least the gaps were private!

They just about froze that winter – a pan of water four feet from the little stove would freeze – but they endured it, and the next summer they, too, built a dugout. The dugout was built into the front of a bank. It had twelve rooms, all in a single line so they could share the front, which was faced with logs. The dugout proved warm in winter and cool in the summer.

Although Mrs. Armstrong's background in no way prepared her for ranch life, she helped with the cattle and horses and soon became a proficient ranch hand.

The Armstrongs' only child was born in 1892 – the first white child to be born in what later became McCone County. They didn't plan that she should be born in what was to become McCone County, but plans sometimes go awry.

Mrs. Armstrong planned to go to Poplar where the Fort doctor would deliver the baby, and to be on the safe side, she was going to stay the preceding month in Wolf Point with Miss Cogswell, a spinster who kept house for her brother, a Wolf Point trader.

They started for Wolf Point a month before the baby was due (they thought) but Mrs. Armstrong began getting sick on the way, and by the time they reached the Missouri River she was too sick to go any farther.

There was no bridge across the Missouri then – no ferry, nothing. The only means of crossing was by canoe, and crossing by canoe was out of the question.

An old woodcutter lived in a shack near the river – he cut wood for the steam-boats that came up the Missouri – so they managed to get to his shack, and there Lucy (now Mrs. Fisher of Sidney) was born. And that's why she was born on the south side of the river, the first white child born in what is now McCone County.

Harold Bawden, their neighbors' child, was born a few weeks before Lucy, but he was born in Poplar – as Lucy was supposed to be. By the time Lucy was born, Mrs. Bawden and her new baby were home again so Mrs. Armstrong was moved to the Bawden home until she could make the sixty-mile trip back to the ranch.

The Bawdens and Armstrongs were good friends (for a number of years they were just about the only 'all white' families in the area bordering the Missouri River). Ten years later Mrs. Bawden died suddenly after giving birth to her fourth child, Jimmy. Mrs. Armstrong and Lucy moved in with the Bawden family to take care of the newborn baby and the other three children until more permanent arrangements could be made.

Mrs. Fisher recalled the problem presented by little Irvin and his eating — rather it was his not eating that posed the problem. They couldn't get him to eat cereal — eggs — anything except pudding.

Since he would eat pudding Mrs. Armstrong would keep a kettle of pudding cooked and that was reserved for the little fellow. Because of his partiality for pudding Lucy and Harold dubbed him 'Pudding'. The name stuck to him, stuck so closely, though shortened to Pud, that in later years many of his acquaintances knew him only as 'Pud Bawden'.

By the time she was ten years old Lucy had already done a good bit of traveling. Her first trip came when she was six years old and her mother took her to Denver. Much of their traveling was by wagon, but for this trip they took the train from Glendive to Butte, on to Spokane for some visiting, then back to Salt Lake City and Denver.

In Denver Mrs. Armstrong told Lucy she was going to take her to see a 'friend'. As they talked the 'friend' kept passing her handkerchief close to Lucy's nose and telling her to "smell my nice perfume." The 'nice perfume' soon had Lucy sleeping and when she awoke she was enraged to find her hands and feet bandaged, enraged because she was sure she knew what the bandages meant.

Lucy was born with six fingers on each hand, six toes on each foot. Those bandages told her that while she slept the extra fingers and toes had been cut off, although her mother had said nothing about any such plans. She probably felt she had good reasons for keeping quiet on the subject remembering the smallpox epidemic a year or so before.

One of the sheepherders at the ranch had come down with the dread disease so a doctor was summoned all the way from Glendive to vaccinate any one who might be exposed. Little Lucy watched apprehensively as the vaccinations began — Ross, Mother, and Comer's three girls — all submitted while Lucy was left for the last. When time came for the 'last' she wasn't there.

A search was begun and at last they found her (her dog betrayed her whereabouts) hiding behind the doorsteps. The opening at the end of the steps was big enough for her to crawl through but it wasn't big enough for any of the others to follow her. Their orders and their threats (what could they threaten that would be as bad as having her arm jabbed with that needle?) had no effect upon her. Neither did their efforts to poke her with the broom and make her come out; she could get beyond reach of the broom.

She won that time and the doctor had to leave without immunizing her, but when it came to the fingers and toes they cut them off first and let her find out about it afterwards.

Lucy was as familiar with Indians as she was with whites, but on that trip she saw a Negro for the first time. She made friends with the porter and when he picked her up she mortified her mother by spitting on her finger and rubbing his face trying to get the black to come off.

Mrs. Fisher is well acquainted with the problems that pioneers faced to educate their children, since she was one of the children educated. The Culbertson School seemed the most feasible to attend, but even that was twenty-three miles from the Armstrong home so during the school term they moved to Pat Doyle's place, just across the river from Blair. Then every Monday morning Lucy would be taken to the Blair pump house*, seven miles west of Culbertson, to stay until Friday evening.

The pump house was run by Mrs. Armstrong's brother-in-law, and each morning he would take the school children to Culbertson on the speedcar*, then pick them up after school. The speedcar ride down the railroad track was fine in mild weather, but in severe weather they had to really bundle up to keep from freezing in the fresh-air conveyance.

In the Culbertson School, a little log house about four blocks from the depot, there were more Indian children than white, but that didn't bother Lucy. She was accustomed to Indians, and could talk better 'Indian' than English when she started to school.

Lucy's education involved just about as many schools as it did years. Mrs. Armstrong had her heart set on getting a school in their own area and rode miles and miles to get signers to petition a school, but her goal was not to be realized immediately even though they succeeded in getting the promise of a school.

By the time Lucy was ready for the third grade, the promised school had become a reality, and those first terms were held in a dugout. Lucy's uncle, John Curans, lived about a quarter of a mile from the dugout school. Two years after school was begun there he moved closer to the river to facilitate keeping water for the cattle so the school was moved to the house he vacated.

During the following summer Aunt Nettie (Father's sister with whom Mother had stayed back in Nebraska) came to visit the Armstrongs in their home on Gumbo Flats, directly south of Poplar. They decided to go to Great Falls so they fixed up a wagon with beds, a camp stove, and a cook box (mess box) and started on their trip. Mother drove the wagon and Darwin, the small grandson Aunt Nettie brought with her, rode beside her while Aunt Nettie and Lucy rode saddle horses. They spent the winter in Great Falls, and Lucy attended school in the city that term. Mother and Aunt Nettie both kept busy as seamstresses during the time they were in Great Falls.

When Lucy was in the seventh grade they made another trip to Denver, another wagon trip. This time her stepbrother, Ross, had come home, and they decided to go to Denver where Mrs. Armstrong's father, getting along in years, was living. Again Aunt Nettie and Lucy rode their saddle horses, and Ross helped his mother with the wagon driving. The trip to Denver took thirty-six days, two weeks of which were spent in the Black Hills. They lived with Mother's brother that winter, and Lucy attended the Fort Morgan School. The next summer they made the return trip to Gumbo Flats, and Lucy was ready for the eighth grade.

Harold Bawden, neighbor John Bawden's son, stayed with them that term to attend school because the distance from his home was prohibitive. He'd ride over on Monday morning and stay through the week, riding home again Friday after school. When the weather was 'reasonable' the scholars going from the Armstrong home rode their saddle horses to school, but when the weather was severe, they would drive in a single sleigh. Hot rocks in the bottom of the sled helped to keep their feet warm.

Lucy graduated from elementary school that year and that fall embarked on a secondary education as varied as the first eight years of formal schooling. Her high school career took in Kalispell, Tacoma, Glasgow, and Great Falls where she graduated in 1910. She still has the cup the Professor gave her for graduation.

During that school year she and her mother lived in the home of a Methodist minister, Reverend Edwards. Edwards had been active in starting Sunday Schools in developing areas, and it was he who had started the Sunday School at Nickwall.

The Nickwall community, though about sixteen miles from Armstrongs', was nevertheless in 'the neighborhood' so the Armstrongs attended the services there. Mrs. Fisher recalled that they would plan to assemble about noon, each bringing some food for a 'potluck' dinner. They would eat together, then have Sunday School in the afternoon.

It was through this Sunday School that the Armstrongs became acquainted with Rev. Edwards and so found themselves in his Great Falls home for Lucy's final year in high school. His home was across the street from Charlie Russell's studio, and Lucy loved to spend hours watching Russell paint. Rev. Edwards used to remark that he always knew where to find Lucy; she'd be across the street at Russell's.

Russell was rather rough, but he was nice, and Lucy could speak 'Indian' with him. That he was to become Montana's outstanding painter would not have concerned her; she spent time in his studio simply because she enjoyed watching him paint and enjoyed him.

That year while they were in Great Falls the Rainbow Hotel was being built. It was going up on the grounds where Lucy had picketed her horse when she attended grade school in Great Falls several years before. The contractor for the Rainbow was a distant relative of the family, and one of Mrs. Armstrong's jobs that winter was cooking for him.

Although the Armstrong ranch was near the Missouri River, they did most of their trading in Glendive, their county seat. They made the trip with a four-horse team and wagon, taking at least three days one way. Their first stop would

6

be at Bill Keeland's near Richey (only there was no Richey) for one night, then they would camp again between Keeland's and Glendive. The shopping list better be complete when they 'went to town' because there would be no running back for some forgotten item. It would be at least six months before they made the trip again.

Mr. Armstrong was much older than his wife, and when Lucy was ten years old he hired a young fellow, Bailey Fisher, to look after the ranch for him. Eleven years later, when she was twenty-one, Lucy married Fisher. Fisher was chairman of the school board when Lucy attended the Gumbo Flats School, and he was still chairman of the board when their youngest child went to school forty-four years later.

Even though he was working for Armstrong, Fisher had squatted* on a piece of land before it was surveyed, then filed on it when the land opened up for homesteads. The Fishers lived together on the ranch near Andes many years, rearing a family of thirteen children, before illness forced Mr. Fisher to retire in 1954. They moved into Sidney in March of that year.

Mrs. Fisher took a job in the City Hall right away. She had been Justice of the Peace since 1914. After moving into Sidney she spent seven-and-one-half years as police judge. She lives in Sidney's first jail so perhaps it was only natural she should spend some time as police judge. She remarked that she isn't sure just when the jail was built, but she knows people who were in it – as prisoners, not as houseguests – in 1908. Whenever the building was built, it was meant to stand. It is made of lumber from Frederickson's old sawmill, 2x6's laid up 'crib' fashion.

The two front rooms of her house were the jail, and since she has lived there she has had other rooms built onto the rear. They had to cut through those planks to make a door connecting the two parts, but when she suggested making a picture window in the front her sons told her nothing doing! It was just too much of a job sawing through those walls.

Through her long years as Justice of the Peace Mrs. Fisher has had many interesting experiences. It wasn't too unusual to perform a marriage ceremony for a couple, then years later do the same for a son or daughter, but in one case she accommodated three generations. She married a couple in 1919, then in the 40's she married their son. They moved to Libby, but in 1964 the granddaughter made arrangements to come all the way from Libby for her marriage so Mrs. Fisher could perform that ceremony, too.

Two years ago Mrs. Fisher had a stroke, and the doctors told her she would never walk again, but now, at seventy-four years, she gets around. She doesn't seem too confined, even though she does live in a jail!

Karl Hepperle

March 1968

"You will starve to death over there!" wailed his mother when Karl Hepperle, thousands of miles from the Plevna, Montana site that was to be his homestead, announced sixty years ago that he was going to America. She was much distressed.

In answer to her dire prediction Karl quoted an old Russian proverb, "The honest hand will go through the land." He felt sure that he could succeed in the new land. Little did his mother dream then that his determination to go to America would save her from starvation in the not-too-distant future.

The Hepperles in Russia owned a large farm and were well to do. They hired a number of workers to help with the farm, boys for the field work and girls for housework – and to milk the cow, as was customary there.

With Karl Hepperle it was not economic necessity, as it was with many emigrants, that compelled him to leave his native land, but an inner urge that would not be denied. He must go to America!

When his mother saw his determination, she told his father and his father, too, tried to dissuade him. He offered Karl his share of the inheritance at once if he would stay and farm, but Karl could think only of America.

He didn't want to leave without his parents' consent, but his mind was made up. "Voluntarily let me go," he told his parents, "or I will go anyway." In the face of such determination his parents decided they could only yield. "I don't know whether the ship will sink with him or whether he will discover a gold mine in America!" his father had exclaimed, but they let him go with their blessing.

So it was in 1908 his father bought his ticket for him, including ship passage and train fare to Eureka, South Dakota. Eureka was chosen as his destination because they knew some people there who had emigrated from Russia about two years earlier.

Before he started his ocean voyage Karl asked an old fellow who had crossed the ocean several times what would be good to prevent seasickness. The advice he received was, "Eat garlic or drink vodka." He didn't try the vodka, but as the ship plowed its way across the ocean he ate garlic until he couldn't eat any more. When he could down no more garlic he started eating lemon and hard sugar.

Whether that formula was responsible or whether he owed his feeling of well-being to some combination in his makeup that made him a sailor he didn't know, but he was thankful he didn't have a moment of seasickness the entire voyage. He watched plenty of others who did, however!

He arrived in Boston with just $25 to his name so he didn't linger long but continued on his way to Eureka. In Eureka he received a job offer almost immediately from a farmer who wanted him two months at $50 a month. With his finances in the condition they were he didn't hesitate but took the job at once.

They were a gracious couple who treated him right, and he did his best for them, too. But one thing he stipulated when he hired out to them: he would not milk cows. Back in Russia milking cows was strictly women's work. Hiring out to work for someone else was demeaning enough; hiring out to milk cows would have been too much!

They agreed to that condition, and after the day's field work was done he would take care of the horses and do the other barnyard chores. Then he would wait inside the fence where the cows were while his employer and wife did the milking. After the milking was done he would turn the crank of the cream separator and feed the milk to the calves.

He hadn't worked there long, though, until his ideas began to change. Customs just weren't the same here as in Russia so he began helping with the milking, too. Soon he started getting up earlier in the morning, and he would have two or three cows milked by the time the boss appeared. At the end of the two months his employer rented out his land. His wife told the renters, "We have thirteen hired men, but none as good as Karl" – the Russian-German boy who had learned to milk cows.

Karl Hepperle next took a job with a threshing crew for a couple weeks, and when that was finished, he started hauling hay and straw for another fellow. He got along fine with the hauling, but this family had a number of children, including a pair of small twins, and during the day those twins would play on his bed. That he couldn't take. His mother had always been particular about clean beds, and now Karl found himself homesick. He had hired out for a month, but at the end of two weeks he collected what he had coming and went to Aberdeen. He went to Aberdeen with the intention of enrolling in school, but when he went to the school a few boys about his age were standing around outside, talking and laughing! He felt that they were laughing at him, a foreigner who spoke very little English – and that broken. (He was, however, familiar with five other languages, having studied Russian, French, German, Greek, and Latin in school in Russia.) Discouraged, he changed his mind and went back to work.

He worked for a while in a grain elevator in Artas, a town just two-and-a-half miles from where he had worked before. Although he was given a raise later on, he started out at $33 per month with $20 taken out for room and board. But he thought this was an opportunity to learn something so he accepted the job. Later on he was to make good use of the experience gained in the elevator.

When homestead lands opened up in Montana, he decided he was going to have a homestead. His boss tried to talk him out of it, but he made up his mind he would not miss this chance. In 1909, a year after he came to America, Hepperle filed on a homestead eight miles south of Plevna, Montana. That summer he worked in Baker for the Milwaukee Railroad for a month, then for a carpenter. Meantime he worked at his homestead when he could, 'commuting' from Baker via saddle horse.

He started first to build a shack, and while he rode back and forth he carried his lunch and drank water from the creek. Carrying the lunch was fine, but he found out the hard way that it was a mistake to drink from the creek. He contracted typhoid fever and spent a month in the Miles City hospital.

When threshing time came around again, his former boss in Artas wrote and asked him to come help through the 'rush' season so he went back to South Dakota. He stayed three months, and when he went back to the homestead the first of March, he took with him his bride. On February 28, 1910, he had married Elizabeth Opp from Eureka.

The little 14'x24' shack which he had built served not only for living quarters but for a granary as well. Weather turned bad after they moved out onto the homestead and continued that way through April. The only building on the place was the shack in which they lived so there was nothing to protect their livestock from the elements. When they moved from Eureka (by immigrant car*), they brought four horses, three cows, one heifer, and two pigs.

When the bad weather came, he moved the wagon next to the shed to fashion some sort of windbreak for the animals. He was especially concerned for the horses because he was working them, depending on them for the farming – the very livelihood of the new homesteaders. In addition to the makeshift shelter, he covered the horses with sacks, even the overcoat he had brought with him from the Old Country, wrapping them with the harness lines and halter ropes to keep the wind from blowing them off.

After he started breaking sod the horses got tender* so the wet and cold was harder on them than ever, but now he had a solution for the shelter problem. He dug a one-foot depression about eight by ten feet, then built up walls from the sod chunks he had broken up. He had had some drop siding left over from the shack so he used that for the roof. What a happy day that was when he finished the little sod barn for his horses! However, this was by no means the end of all his problems. His horses were working, breaking sod, and should have had grain, but he had no grain to give them – and no money with which to buy grain. In spite of this handicap he managed to break sixty-five acres that first spring and planted ten acres of oats, four acres of corn, and fifty-one of flax.

Mr. Hepperle describes that first summer on the homestead as 'pretty tough'. Mrs. Hepperle's mother had given them four hams when they moved from South Dakota, and that was about the extent of their meat until late the next fall except for an occasional rabbit. Certainly there was no money to buy meat or much of anything else, for that matter. About all they had plenty of that summer of 1910 was hard work.

While the little 8'x10' sod barn had been a great help until something more adequate could be built, after he had his crop planted he decided the time had come to build the 'more adequate'. Again he built of sod, this time a structure

10

208'x64'. He made many trips out to the Pine Hills and chopped trees to use in holding up the roof and for other support, as well as for the mangers.

By the time he was ready for the roof he had harvested his crop and had some money so he bought lumber for the roof and tarpaper to cover it. He was glad the roof was on and the barn closed in when the weather turned bad.

His second spring on the homestead followed the same pattern as the first. He broke sixty-five acres of sod, had very little money, very little feed. The third spring, however, the pattern changed just a bit. He still had very little money and very little feed, but he had more acres ready to put into crop, and that spring, with some help, he was able to break about 100 acres of sod.

He had to finish his breaking with skinny horses because of his lack of grain, and sometimes he had to throw out his plow in the middle of the field because they couldn't pull any more. When a spinster on a nearby homestead asked him to put in some flax for her, he agreed so he could get a little cash with which to buy feed for his horses while he finished his breaking.

Her brother had broken the ground for her, and Hepperle contracted to disc the ground and plant the flax. The disking and drilling would give his horses a 'breather', he figured, and then there would be grain for them when he went back to breaking sod. He finished the job in good time, but then he had to 'earn the money all over again' trying to collect it.

Harvest that fall was the turning point in his homestead operations. His twenty-three acres of flax yielded ten bushels to the acre, and he harvested 1,800 bushels of wheat and some barley besides. From then on there was feed for his horses — and some money too.

The next fall (1913) he harvested another good crop so he went to South Dakota and bought more horses — four mares and one two-year-old colt. Two weeks after he returned home with them one of the $200 mares died.

Two more good crop years and he decided he was ready to leave the farm and venture into a new business. He harvested a bumper crop that fall of 1915 with over 5,000 bushels of wheat, 1,700 bushels of barley, and 500 of flax. After just five years on the farm he held an auction sale, which netted $4,500, and he had cash for his new enterprise.

He figured he had learned enough about the grain business to run an elevator so he went to Minneapolis where he got a blueprint and a contract to build an elevator. Building the elevator cost him a little over $5,000 in the second decade of this century.

He ran the elevator until 1928, then sold it and built a filling station and garage. Automobiles were coming into their own by this time, and he saw the opportunities in this field. In 1930 he also started selling implements, handling John Deere and Case machinery. Then in 1939 he took on the Buick and GMC dealerships.

Karl still runs his garage and filling station in Plevna and sells Buicks and GMC's, but he no longer sells Case or John Deere implements. As he reviewed his sixty years in the United States he contrasted his lot with that of his family in Russia.

In the years 1903-1906 he had attended school in Odessa, and it was during those years that he made his decision to leave his native land. A student from the University of Odessa would occasionally visit in the home where Karl boarded, and it was from this student that he learned that the Communists, working through the university students, were planning to overthrow the Czar government. His friend was not in favor of the revolution and avoided these meetings, but his warnings of what was ahead were responsible for Karl's determination to emigrate to America. And before many years those warnings proved all too accurate.

In 1917 the Communists overthrew the government, just nine years after Karl left Russia, and all private property was subject to seizure. His father's property was no exception. Looters ran wild through the land, carrying off whatever they could get their hands on. As Mr. Hepperle (Karl's father) watched them dragging away his possessions he saw among the looters a boy who had formerly worked for him. Calling the boy by name, he remonstrated with him, "You know that belongs to me; why are you taking it?" "But Uncle," the lad replied (he was not actually uncle; that was a term of respect), "if I don't take it, someone else will." Mr. Hepperle recognized the inevitable and conceded, "You are right; go ahead and take it."

Before long the real tragedy began to emerge; while the Communists had pitted the 'have-nots' against the 'haves', it soon became evident that many of those who had not managed before to provide for themselves could not or would not manage now that they had someone else's property. Food production dropped alarmingly, and by 1920 starvation was widespread, those who had become the 'haves' starving along with the dispossessed.

In 1920, Mr. Hepperle sought help from his son Karl in the United States – the same son who had been warned by his mother, "You will starve to death over there!" ('over there' referring to America). Karl was able to send food parcels to his parents through the American Food Administration. Then in 1923 Mr. Hepperle wrote to ask for help to get them to America.

Karl sent them tickets, but before the tickets could be used Hepperles had to sneak to Latvia. They succeeded in getting to the border, but there those who had helped them asked for another $100 to get them across the border so once more they wrote to Karl. When the $100 was paid and they were able to cross over into free territory it was, as they described it, like getting out of hell into paradise.

The horrors were now behind them, but multitudes, including many of their own family and kin, were not so fortunate. Only two of Karl's brothers came when his parents did. Another brother would have come, but his wife was not yet ready to leave her parents and relatives. Later she had no choice about leaving, but America was not her destination when she parted from them. The destination was Siberia. Brother, his wife, and some of their children, along with many other people were taken in boxcars over 2,000 miles.

The women were settled in barracks tall enough to stand upright, wide enough to stretch out. The men were taken 200 miles farther to work in the woods. They wrapped their legs with tree bark as they worked in snow crotch deep. Within thirty days more than a thousand had died.

When the brother was next heard from, about two or three months later, he was back in his home again where his wife and children, just skin and bones, had preceded him. He was still in danger there so he crossed over the Caspian Sea into Caucasus for several years.

Here there were American stores where he could buy if he had American money so Karl sent him some, but after several times he wrote to quit sending because "they were getting jealous and making him suffer for it." Little wonder that Karl Hepperle, in Montana, praised the Lord that he had reached freedom while freedom was within reach.

After World War II refugees from Russia streamed into Germany, and Mr. and Mrs. Hepperle began getting appeals for help, help they gladly supplied. Some of those writing were from the generation born after he left Russia. One family found his address on the street in Berlin and wrote for help.

They sent many dollars worth of food and clothing to those pleading for 'eleventh-hour' help. Mr. and Mrs. Hepperle cried over the letters of thanks they received realizing that it was only through God's mercy that they had been able to render assistance.

Karl's parents, too, were very active in sending relief to the refugees. They had lived in Plevna for awhile after coming to the United States, then moved to Missoula. They became naturalized citizens, and now from their position of blessing were eager to help those who were suffering as they had suffered.

Mr. Hepperle, Sr., was given a permit from Missoula city authorities to go from house to house to collect clothing and shoes for the destitute. He collected one-and-a-half tons which he shipped to Germany for those who had fled Russia after World War II.

Shoes that weren't good enough to send he repaired and made them good enough. A Missoula shoemaker donated the sewing Mr. Hepperle couldn't do himself, and two local stores gave him strings. They also gave new shoes that were out of style.

In the freedom and security of his new homeland Karl's father lived to be over ninety years of age, his mother eighty-six. Of their thirteen children, only three in America are still living.

As for Karl Hepperle, he is now seventy-nine (in 1968) and is in good health. When he was operated on a few years ago, the doctor assured him his condition was as good as that of many men in their fifties.

He is still active in operating his filling station, on hand to open shop at six o'clock in the morning. Mr. and Mrs. Hepperle have three children, two in eastern Montana and one in North Dakota. Mr. Hepperle observed that as he looks back to those years when he started out, it's been worth it all.

Mrs. A. J. (Catharine Calk) McCarty

August 1965

When Miss Catharine Calk invaded the Big Dry* country in (then) western Dawson County, the rancher was still king and the region was still rough and primitive, even though much of the eastern part of the state was becoming well settled. (Western Montana had been settled considerably earlier.) Just how rough and primitive it was, she didn't quite realize before her arrival. She had come from Kentucky to visit her aunt in Bozeman, where two of her brothers were attending college. One of these brothers had already located in the Jordan area, and urged her to do likewise so from Bozeman she headed for Jordan.

She fared fine as far as Sumatra because she could travel by train, but there her route left the railroad. She was obliged to spend the night in Sumatra and hope to catch a ride somehow to Sand Springs the next day. The only rooms for rent in town were located over a saloon, and she had to share one of those with a strange woman. Her enthusiasm at these arrangements was running at low ebb, but the sight of the bed completely dismayed her. Her exclamation, "Why, these sheets haven't been changed!" apparently fell on deaf ears. A closer look revealed that, not only were the sheets unchanged, the bed was already occupied – by bedbugs! Catharine spent the night sitting on a chair, and morning didn't come too soon.

The next day she caught a ride to Sand Springs in a Model T Ford with the man who carried the mail. The little Ford was no limousine, and the trail bore no resemblance to oiled highways, but she arrived intact. She was even more dismayed, if possible, with the arrangements that night than she had been the night before. Her room had no lock on the door! She had no idea what kind of barbarians might inhabit the town (if there was another woman within its limits, she was not in sight) so she dragged the dresser in front of the door for a barricade, and again, morning didn't come too soon.

A new day brought promise of better things when the same mailman who had given her a ride from Sumatra to Sand Springs took her on out to her brother's ranch. She soon realized she hadn't moved into a center of culture. That first day some of the cowboys lassoed a wolf up on the ridge and dragged it down to the house, convincing her that she must indeed be in uncivilized territory.

Catharine homesteaded a half-section* that joined her brother's place, staying with him until she could get her log house built. Her brother, James, had to be in Bozeman much of that summer so she was alone a good deal, her nearest neighbor two miles away. She had a dog with her and a few horses besides some cattle.

One morning she awoke early to find that a big herd of cattle had descended upon their (her brother's and her) hay field. She was depending upon that hay for winter feed so she saddled a horse, took a revolver, and rounded up those cattle, shooting into the air to encourage their speedy departure. She

14

chased them about ten miles, then came back home and ate her breakfast. This was repeated several mornings, and she was far from happy with the situation, but then it was brought to her attention that some others were not happy, either.

One forenoon three men rode into her yard. They explained that they were representing the local cattlemen and pointed out to her that shooting at cattle was illegal. She explained that she had shot above them, not at them, but they maintained that was illegal, too, and she must stop running their cattle. She protested, "But what can I do? They're eating our hay, and we're depending on that for winter feed!"

They didn't seem much moved with concern for her and her problem so she came up with a suggestion. "Let's eat dinner, and then after dinner you can bring your mower and horses and one of you can cut the hay for me while some of you put up a corral, and we'll get that hay out of the way." They didn't fall over themselves making promises, but they did eat the dinner she prepared for them. She doesn't remember what all she fixed, but she did make some lemon pies. They discussed the matter further and wound up cutting the hay and putting up a corral for her.

A few days later one of the big ranchers, the policy-maker for the group, sent for her to come see him. (He was ill and couldn't go to her.) She complied and found him, wrapped in a big robe, sitting in his chair. As he peered at her from under his big shaggy eyebrows, he explained, "I just wanted to see that red-headed woman who would get our delegation to cut that hay, using our own horses and machinery, and then get them to make a corral to put it in besides!"

While she was proving up* on her homestead she generally spent the summers on the claim to satisfy residence requirements and the winters in Bozeman – or in Helena, if the legislature was in session. Charlie Hoffman of Bozeman had suggested to her that she get a job as stenographer in the legislature so she applied and was hired. She taught herself typing and shorthand, and at one session she served as private secretary to both the Democratic and the Republican floor leaders. Mrs. McCarty mentioned that the only time a judge was impeached in Montana she wrote out the impeachment papers for the House.

During the winter of 1918 while Dr. Butler, head of the Livestock Sanitation Board, was in the Service she was clerk of the board which meant, in effect, that she was in charge of the office during his absence. She had proved up* on her homestead that year. That same year she assisted in the capitol post office. During the dread flu epidemic the postmaster was stricken, and there was no one to take over his duties because everyone was afraid to go into the post office so Governor Stewart asked her if she would do it. Her duties there included being on hand at 6:30 every morning to receive the mail.

During her second year on the homestead she decided to go back to Kentucky for a visit. Her brother James had to go to Sumatra to get seed wheat so that seemed like a good time to go. She accompanied him, he with four horses on a wagon, she on her saddle mount, 'Tramp'. It was sixty-five miles from the ranch to Sumatra so they took their bedrolls along and that night had to camp in the open. James hobbled one of his horses, and that was usually sufficient to keep all of them within reasonable distance of the camp, but that night they had a severe electrical storm and all the free horses started to run. James got on the other horse to round them up and spent most of the night chasing those horses.

Meanwhile back at the campsite beside 'Dead Horse Hole', the water hole where they had camped for the night, Catharine started thinking about wolves. There all alone, what would she – what could she – do if wolves should come, singly or in a pack? She concluded that she would be safer in the wagon so, first prudently arming herself with the carving knife from the 'grub box', she climbed into the wagon and wrapped her covers around herself again. Sleep was out of the question as she sat hunched in her blankets, tensely listening for any sound that might betray the approach of a wolf. There! What was that noise? Not the sound of the storm, but....

As she strained her eyes in the darkness to see what it might be, a sudden sheet of lightning clearly revealed a wolf at the water's edge, scarcely twenty feet from the wagon. Again the world about her was plunged into darkness so all she could do was listen and watch even more tensely than before, wondering where that wolf was and what he was doing. He did not molest her, and subsequent flashes of lightning disclosed no sign of him. Evidently he had slipped away again in the darkness that had covered his approach. The storm finally spent itself, and streaks of gray began lighting the eastern sky, another day when morning didn't come too soon. By that time she was feeling she needed that month's visit in Kentucky!

Complications had a way of besetting efforts to 'get around' in the Jordan country. The winter of 1916-17 was a hard one, and even before Christmas severe weather had besieged them. The state legislature was to meet the first Monday of January. Catharine Calk was determined to be in Helena by that date in order to get a much-needed job with that law-making body. To start her on her way a neighbor gave her a ride in an open wagon the twenty miles from the ranch to Jordan. There she found that she could ride to Miles City with a doctor, the only doctor in that part of the country – a bachelor, by the way – in his Model T coupe. But that night while she was in Jordan a big snowstorm dumped added inches on the snow that was already hindering travel. She and the doctor started out for Miles City the next morning in his Model T, but they had gone only about two miles when they got stuck in a snow bank. By the time they shoveled out they were convinced there was no use trying to go any place in a car but back to Jordan.

By this time she almost despaired of getting to Miles City to catch the train for Helena before the legislature convened, but then someone at the hotel told her that the Butz family was planning to go and that Mr. Butz was even mounting a sheep wagon on runners to get them there. She ran all the way to the livery stable through the snow and cold to where Mr. Butz was working, only to be told that he already had five passengers and couldn't take any more with his family. Desperate, she couldn't let this only chance slip through her fingers and pleaded with him to squeeze her in, too. He pondered a bit, then conceded, "Well, you don't weigh very much; I'll crowd you in." That was a trip she doesn't expect to forget.

The first day they got as far as Cohagen where they spent the night in the store, sleeping on the counters. At Cohagen one of the passengers bought some oranges but they froze before they could be eaten. There was a little stove in the wagon, but it was hardly adequate for the severe weather they were experiencing. They made some soup to eat for their noon meal but put the macaroni in too soon and the soup burned besides. So they had burned soup for Christmas dinner.

They stayed at a halfway house the second night and were adequately fed there, but the storm seemed to increase in intensity rather than abate as they continued on their way, and progress was slow. Even at midday a man had to walk with a lantern in front of the horses (four horses were pulling the wagon) to keep them on the trail. In spite of all precautions the horses would sometimes flounder into deep ditches and have to be shoveled out. They should have reached Miles City well before the third night, but they were hardly able to make it to a place called the Stone Shacks. Some of the passengers had almost given up hope of surviving the journey before they reached shelter.

An old roundup cook was wintering in the Stone Shacks, and his brother from Indiana had come to spend Christmas with him. Neither seemed to be hospitably disposed and the weary, freezing, hungry travelers began to wonder if they were going to be denied the shelter and food which by that time amounted to life itself. The old cook finally relented and let them in but made no move to give them anything to eat. They had reached the point where they weren't bashful about asking for food, but in response to their urgent questioning he set out only some murky coffee and dry bread. They were willing to pay for what they got, but they wanted to get something to pay for and besought him for something more so then he grudgingly produced what was supposed to be a pork roast but all it boasted was fat. Then Catharine noticed on a platter what appeared to be a cake with smooth white frosting and eagerly exclaimed, "Oh, Christmas cake!" But it wasn't. It turned out to be greasy headcheese and the 'frosting' was a coating of lard.

Somehow they managed to get through the night and the next day (the fourth) they struggled on into Miles City. And Miss Calk reached Helena in time to get a stenographic position with the legislature.

The man who was to become her husband had a homestead about six miles from hers. He had charge of the Smoky Butte Post Office and had wondered why so much mail was coming to this Miss Catharine Calk, observing that he had never met her. That deficiency was remedied one day when they both happened to be riding horseback and met on the range, but it wasn't until after they were both living in Glendive that they became really well acquainted.

At the beginning of World War I President Wilson ordered an inventory to determine the resources of the country. Every county had to appoint someone to take the inventory, and it was Catharine Calk who was appointed for Dawson County. That meant checking every store to report supplies on hand. While she was working at this inventory A.J. McCarty was working in the office of the county engineer. This gave them opportunity to get to know each other better. They were married in February 1921, in the Episcopal Church of Glendive with Rev. Durant, Brad Durant's father, performing the ceremony. Before that, though, Catharine spent some time in Helena.

She didn't finish the inventory job because that's when she was asked to go to Helena as clerk of the Livestock Sanitation Board. After the war the Honorable William Lindsay appointed her executive secretary of the Dawson County Red Cross. She had been interested in the Red Cross work for some time, helping when she could, so she came back to Glendive the first of January 1919, to assume this position. Her work had to do mostly with discharged veterans returning from the war.

Dawson County at that time still included the present counties of Garfield and McCone, and Mrs. McCarty mentioned that this 'old' Dawson County had the highest percentage of casualties according to population during World War I of any county in the United States. One out of every six servicemen from Dawson County was killed or wounded. The Dawson Chapter has individual files of 2,000 claims of World War I that have gone through the local Red Cross Home service office. During her several years as executive secretary she received a salary, but most of her affiliation with the Red Cross has been voluntary as Chairman of Home Service Office, now chairman of Service to the Military. While she has been able to help many through the Red Cross, she insists she has received the greatest blessing. She emphasizes that she has had wonderful cooperation from those who have assisted her.

Active in politics, Mrs. McCarty served two terms in the State Legislature, first in 1923 and again in 1925. She has been the Democratic State Committee woman from Montana for many years. Through her legislative affiliation she has met many colorful figures in Montana history. Numerous honors have been conferred upon her, both politically and for humanitarian service, but she suggested that it isn't necessary to mention all of those.

Mr. McCarty passed away October 27, 1964. Of her husband Mrs. McCarty says, "He was the most wonderful man possible." She added that he had a keen sense of humor and that he always 'stuck by' her in her various interests and endeavors. She continues to live in their Glendive home, traveling when she wants to travel (traveling is a little easier now than when she lived in the Jordan country fifty years ago), and still takes an active interest in current events.

Mrs. Nick (Elizabeth Raser) Scabad

August 1973

Elizabeth Raser Scabad came to the United States from Hungary in 1913. An aunt, Margaret Decker, had already been in the U.S. a number of years when Elizabeth came. Elizabeth's parents made arrangements for her to travel with one of her former schoolmates and with an older man and his wife who were their 'sponsors' or chaperones.

Before she left home her mother packed food such as home-cured ham sandwiches for her to eat on board ship so she wouldn't get sick from eating the ship's food. Mother had warned them, too, about the ship's water, so they drank beer while on board.

Mrs. Scabad and her daughter Eva laughed as they recalled a friend's introduction to bananas on his ocean trip to the United States. He had never seen bananas before (neither had Elizabeth), but when someone came around selling some he decided to try one.

Remember he had never seen a banana in his life so he tried eating the peeling, too. The effect wasn't at all pleasant so he threw the banana overboard. No point in trying to eat fruit that tasted like that! He noticed that others, however, continued to buy and eat, and finally someone showed him that the peeling was supposed to be removed. He tried again and this time decided bananas weren't so bad after all.

Elizabeth was a good sailor and didn't get sick at all on the ship, either from the ship's motion or the food. She was able to dance all the way! Others in her party didn't fare so well though. One boy on board, she recalls, became very ill, though probably neither the boat nor the food had anything to do with it. Elizabeth, using her mother's home remedy, rubbed his throat and chest with lard and garlic, and he was soon better. When the ship's doctor came to see him he commented, "I smell garlic," but the boy protested, "No, I haven't eaten any garlic." He was very grateful to Elizabeth and kept in touch with her for quite some time after they were in the States.

Her sponsors and the other girl accompanying her came only as far as Chicago so from then on she was on her own. Alone on the train from Chicago to Glendive she became more and more lonesome. The brakeman felt sorry for her so he bought her some fruit and filled her apron with it while she slept. She was surprised to waken and find her lap full of fruit.

She could speak no English so the lady next to her showed her that she was supposed to eat it. Elizabeth remembered her parent's instructions and explained, "No, my daddy told me not to eat anything anybody gave me," and put it on the seat. When the brakeman came through he also showed her that she was supposed to eat it, and finally she did – and suffered no ill effects.

From Chicago the train came straight through to Glendive, Montana, but she insisted, "I'm not going to Montana." Glendive, yes; Montana no. She did get off at Glendive, though, so she found herself in Montana.

19

By the time she reached Glendive she was really lonesome. Her godfather (Aunt Margaret's husband) met her at the train, and what a joy to hear him call, "Come on, Lizzie, come on!" She cried, "Oh, my God!" ran to him and grabbed him, she was so glad to see a familiar face and hear a familiar voice.

Elizabeth suffered much from homesickness the first weeks she was in Glendive before she had a chance to get acquainted. "Glendive," she observed succinctly, "was not much to look at in 1913."

She soon secured a job as dishwasher at the Jordan Hotel. She missed her parents and brothers and sisters, and at noon as she walked through the alley to the post office (the post office then was located on the corner of Towne and Kendrick) she would cry into her apron. How she cried! She remembers with appreciation the sympathy demonstrated by a man who worked at Douglas-Mead*. He always came out as she was going to the post office and was sorry for the young homesick Hungarian.

There were other people from Hungary in Glendive, however, and it wasn't long until she became acquainted and was less lonesome. Then Nick Scabad entered the picture. She went to a weekend party in New England, North Dakota – they danced three days and three nights – and there she met him for the first time.

It wasn't long until Nick came to Glendive to see her – and kept coming. In 1914 they were married in the Catholic Church in Glendive. They built a home at 219 N. Sargent where Mrs. Scabad and one of her daughters still live. Mr. Scabad passed away in 1964.

Nick had come from Hungary, too. His father died when Nick was a young boy. Later his mother married Peter Schultz who brought her and her three children to Richardton, North Dakota.

Nick was a tailor. He had gone to a private tailoring school in Germany and had received more training from Marx and Brown in Chicago. In Glendive he spent many years working in the Glendive Steam Laundry for the Healy Brothers (Grandma Healy owned it when he started).

Mrs. Scabad's oldest daughter, Eva Welsh, testifies that her mother was a very good cook. She has made many, many wedding cakes, but her specialty was snowballs. She used to make them for the Moose Lodge as well as for many private individuals.

Eva remembers the wonderful times the women and girls had when they gathered at the Feisthamel home to read. Feisthamels subscribed to a German newspaper (the language of the Scabads) so each week the German-speaking women gathered to read the paper. The women would take turns reading aloud from the paper – Mrs. Feisthamel, Mrs. Scabad, others of the neighbors. Sometimes Eva would get to read, too. These experiences and the warm fellowship helped build a sense of security for the young people.

As a girl in Hungary, Mrs. Scabad had learned to make lace, using a hook, and could make exquisite lace from just string. She also knits and has done much beautiful embroidery.

During both world wars she knit sweaters for the soldiers. Through this she acquired a new 'son'. She included her name and address with each sweater, and one of the boys who received a sweater began a correspondence. His mother had died when he was a baby so he had written to Mrs. Scabad, "I'm going to be your boy."

Mrs. Scabad's mother heart is big enough to include other 'sons' besides those born to her so she was willing to include him. The correspondence continued, and he brought his bride to visit Scabads on their honeymoon. She gave them some of her handwork for a wedding present – sheets, pillowcases, dresser scarves, chair-back sets.

Clyde Bower of Billings is another of her 'adopted' boys. She recalled the time when her oldest son, Wendell, asked her, "Do you want a boy?" She laughed as she told how she had protested, "I'm too old!" Wendell quickly explained that he just meant providing a home for a high school boy. She wasn't too old for that, so Clyde became one of her boys, too.

The Scabads had five children of their own: Eva, Wendell, Elizabeth, Pearl, and Raymond. Pearl died when she was three years old. Wendell was killed during World War II. He was stationed in Texas, a pilot ferrying planes. One day as he was taking off some kid soloing was off his flight pattern coming in for a landing and struck Wendell's plane. News of Wendell's death brought on Mr. Scabad's first heart attack.

In spite of her eighty-two years, Mrs. Scabad is still active, cooking and keeping house in the home Nick built for her almost sixty years ago.

Floyd Davis

December 1968 – January 1969

Cowboy – horsewrangler – broncpeeler* – rancher – homesteader – sheriff – Floyd 'Gobbler' Davis, has lived in three different counties, all in the same spot. When he homesteaded, after a colorful career as cowboy, his claim was located in Dawson County. Later, as chunks were lopped off Dawson to form other counties, he found himself and his farm in Richland until still another division put him in McCone.

Grasshoppers have figured more than once in eastern Montana's history, and they figured in bringing Floyd Davis to this part of the country. In 1902-03, they stripped the range on the foothills of Wyoming's Bighorn Mountains and forced stockmen to move their stock. Davis helped move some of that stock across into Montana north of Forsyth, then drifted north up Snow Creek.

He had reasons for drifting north, and most of his reasons could be spelled w-a-g-e-s. In Wyoming at the turn of the century a cowboy was paid $20 a month; on the Yellowstone range he could get $25, but between the Yellowstone and Missouri Rivers he could make $40 a month. His idea, he explained, was to come over and get rich quick, then go back and spend it. But he never did get back.

Floyd was born in Wyoming, not far from the Montana line, south of Custer's Battlefield*. His father was a freighter hauling from the head of the Burlington Railroad to towns farther on. His uncle, John Jacoby, was in partnership with his father, and the two hauled freight with team and wagons ahead of the railroad building crew.

The 'team' consisted of eight horses and two mules. They preferred to use mules for leaders because a mule forms habits better than a horse. Leading a long wagon train over the trails through rough country demanded exacting leadership. For example, rounding a bend at the head of a canyon required swinging wide enough so that the entire train would clear and not be pulled into the canyon. Mules are better at remembering such things and so made better leaders. Besides that, mules generally live longer than horses. Mr. Davis quoted an old saying, "They had to kill the first mule to start a mule graveyard!"

In the early 1890's, Floyd's father decided to quit freighting and settle down. He put in his own irrigating outfit and began raising hay. There was no school within miles so Floyd and his older brother, Arthur, didn't do much worrying about the Three R's.

It wasn't until 1894 that they started to school. That fall John Jacoby made the last freighting trip from Crow Agency to Junction (just across the river from the town of Custer) because the next spring the railroad connected and he settled down in Junction. Junction boasted a school so his sister's boys came to stay with him and his wife and get some book learning.

As he made that last freighting trip he picked up the boys and took them along to Junction. The trail led across the Indian reservation, and at his first sight of Indians Floyd ducked down inside the wagon. His precautions were too late because the Indians had already seen him, and one of them remarked to Uncle John, "Papoose, him afraid of Indians." He was so right.

With the Battle of the Little Bighorn less than twenty years history Floyd figured he had reason to be apprehensive. Along with the story of Custer's massacre he had heard tales of many other clashes with the Indians. His mother had passed away when he was only four years old, and she was buried near Wagon Box Massacre, so called because Indians killed about twenty soldiers there. The soldiers were buried there on private property, and later, as need arose, the owners gave permission for others to be buried there also. The soldiers were later moved to Custer's Battlefield, but a few other graves remain. Even though the Indians by this time were confined to reservations, little wonder that to a boy not yet ten years old they still posed a threat.

Shortly before Floyd and Arthur Davis went to stay with their uncle, John Jacoby, John's sister, Effie, had completed her normal school training and had written to him, asking about the chances for employment. He promptly wrote back that he was on the school board and told her to send in her application.

Teachers were not easy to secure – especially teachers with training – in that out-of-the-way place so teacher and patrons were both happy with the arrangement. Teacher was happy because it gave her an opportunity to really get acquainted with her brother and with her sister's boys; patrons were happy because they had a qualified teacher.

The Jacobys had come from Wisconsin. Floyd's mother, Susanna Jacoby, had married J.L. Davis and moved west, as did her brother John. Later both her parents passed away, leaving two small girls, Effie and Margery still in the home. Little Effie was only two years old when her mother passed away and four when her father died. Their mother's maiden sister, Sarah Jane Keller, took Effie and Margery and reared them.

In 1883 Sarah Jane saw her way clear to join her fiance, Frank Watkins, at Fort Benton so they could be married. Taking the little girls with her – they were by this time six and eight years old, respectively – they traveled by steamboat up the Missouri River. So it was that Effie and Margery (the latter to be the first school superintendent in Teton County) grew up in northern Montana, strangers to John and Susanna in southern Montana and northern Wyoming.

The teaching position gave Effie an opportunity to get acquainted with her brother, even though it was too late to get to know her oldest sister. But she learned to know her oldest sister's boys. The boys found that she made a wonderful teacher, too.

Floyd was assigned the task of harrowing the meadow with a team of stallions that had been kept in the barn all the time. Anyone familiar with horses knows what that meant; they just about ran his legs off as he followed them around the field, trying to keep up with them and the two-section harrow.

If that harrow had just been equipped with a seat perhaps he would have kept his job longer. As it was, he got to experimenting, climbed onto one of the horses, and found he could ride. From then on he rode that horse and drove the other. He thought it a fine arrangement, this eleven-year-old boy, but the 'boss' caught him at it and was of a different mind. Next day he was 'paid off' for driving the horses too hard.

The next summer he started riding for the U Cross (the Pioneer Cattle Company) whose land joined his father's holdings. From then on he was pretty much on his own, always riding. A boy became a man fast under those conditions – not quite fast enough, though, to go to Europe with Buffalo Bill Cody because no matter how you could ride, it didn't change your chronological age.

Cody was going to Europe with a show troupe (cowboys, bucking horses) and had come to Sheridan looking for horses and a few more men. Several other fellows from the outfit Floyd was with went in to 'try out', and Floyd signed up for a trial ride, too.

He got by the ride, all right, but when Cody started asking questions for the contract (anyone going over had to sign a contract that they would stay the whole time the troupe was in Europe), he asked, "Kid, how old are you?" "Seventeen."

"No use going any further." Buffalo Bill told him, "Unless you get consent from your parents." So it was no use going any further. By this time he had left home and preferred not to go get consent. At least he had the thrill of a personal interview with the famous frontiersman. One of the other fellows from this outfit did make the European tour.

Cody was also looking for more horses so Floyd's 'boss' took over some ornery, hard-bucking cayuses he had, but they didn't qualify. Oh, they bucked hard enough, all right; that was the trouble. They bucked so hard they were liable to put themselves right out of the show. What he needed was horses that would buck and bawl and put on a good performance, yet do it in a manner that was easy on themselves – and easier on the rider, too, for day after day 'entertaining'.

Floyd 'Gobbler' Davis rode in rodeos long before he was eligible to vote. He started when he was still in Wyoming, and considering that he was only seventeen when he migrated to the Treasure State*, he must have had an early start.

Rodeos were conducted in quite a different manner then from what they are now. There were no chutes in which to saddle your horse, put on a bronc halter, and mount. No gate to open, no ten men to help the rider from his horse when the ten seconds were up.

You just saddled in the open, and a couple fellows would hold the horse 'til you got the reins in your hand, your hand on the horn, and your foot in the stirrup. Then they'd let go and you were on your own, riding until you or the horse gave up – in other words, until he bucked you off or quit bucking.

Lucille Canfield of Richey has written a poem describing an 'old-time' rodeo. The poem, which appears in the January issue of "The Western Horseman," treats an era a little later than Davis's first rodeo participation

24

because he started before the time of cars. But she gives a vivid picture of the rodeo when it was non-commercial and strictly for 'fun'. She has graciously given permission to quote the poem, which follows:

THE HI LINE RODEO IN MONTANA

Up on the Hi Line years ago,
A rodeo was a big-time show;
The riders came in ten gallon hats,
Chaps of Angora, with wings like a bat's.
A cowboy then wore a bright silk shirt,
Of such violent hues, your eyes would hurt;
A neckerchief tied around his throat,
And just a vest, but not a coat.
No fancy grandstands or an arena then,
Just an open flat, and a holding pen.
The cars would park in a circle wide,
To try and keep buckers from getting outside.
People brought lunches and cold root beer,
And homemade ice cream the kids to cheer;
They always came from miles around,
Some set up camps right there on the ground.
You could tell the rider that came from afar,
For he strapped his saddle on the hood of his car.
They didn't rope calves, that wasn't part of the fun;
But rode horse after horse, until it was done.
The announcer was horseback and rode 'round the ring,
He yelled out their names and everything.
He got no money, he did it for fun,
Though he might share lunch with anyone.
Now saddle bronc riders got a very small purse,
And bareback riders got mount money or even worse.
These rode without riggin's, just loose-end ropes,
Or a mane and a tail holt, with laughter and hopes.
When they got tired of riding, they'd jab in the shoulder,
The bronc would set up and they'd step off, none bolder.
Then back to the holding pen to climb on another,
And the barebacks popped out, one after the other.
Now the saddle bronc rider had few rules on call,
He couldn't ride a form-fitting saddle was all.
He could fan with his hat or maybe a quirt,
And the crowd cheered him on with Klaxon's alert.
His horse was dragged out while having a fit,

They'd blindfold the bronc to calm him a bit.
Then on with the saddle and rider — good luck!
Off with the blindfold and let 'er buck.
The timing was done by the judge with a gun,
Who also was horseback so he had fun.
The bullets were real and the noise was loud,
If the judge's horse bucked, that pleased the crowd.
Then the bucker was roped 'fore he got away,
No flanking was done in that long-ago day;
No unsaddling chutes to help those men,
Often they threw them and unsaddled them then.
Sometimes a girl would want to ride,
So they'd hobble her stirrups and help her astride.
Then each cowboy would rush to mount his horse,
For to pick up a girl was more fun of course.
The girls were pretty and some were flirts,
And they wore long, divided riding skirts.
They'd ride or get thrown and they'd get teased,
But by this you know they'd all be pleased.
Afterwards was a dance and everyone came,
Even the riders that were bucked off and lame;
With a fiddle or two and a piano to play,
They danced all night until break of day.
Yes, rodeo then was laughter and fun,
Not lots of hard work to make it run.
Everyone helped and few got paid,
but for us old timers, those memories don't fade.

But the biggest share of Davis's bronc riding wasn't in rodeos. He recalls the sympathy he got when he was bucked off onto his head on a pile of rocks. He was riding for a horse rancher who, every now and then, would take horses to the sale ring in Sheridan, sell them, and often buy others.

Once when Floyd was along with him he decided to buy a horse for his own private mount. A horse from Oregon took his eye, and saddle marks indicated he was 'broke' so Floyd bought him and took him out to camp.

Next morning he saddled up his new steed and, with one of the older hands, started off to wrangle horses. About a hundred yards from camp, all of a sudden his horse blew up and Floyd landed on his head in a coulee* on some rocks. As he hung to the horse's reins, the older fellow rode up, surveyed the situation, and congratulated him, "Kid, you used good judgment; fell on your head to save your ankles."

The rancher paying his wages at that time lived in Montana but had more range across the line in Wyoming than in his own state. When the grasshoppers ate the grass off the range, he moved his horses north across the Yellowstone.

About twenty or twenty-five miles north of Forsyth he pitched a tent for Floyd (who had helped chase the horses), laid in a grub supply for him, then left him at the camp to ride line* while he went back to get his family.

A fellow came along late one afternoon and wanted to stay all night so Floyd, of course, let him. Range custom wouldn't have considered any alternative. Instead of just over night, he stayed two days with him – "to let his horse rest." Davis noticed the fellow seemed nervous and jumpy, but he had other things to do besides analyze a stranger's behavior pattern.

At four o'clock one morning the visitor got up and left. And he didn't bother to tell Floyd good-bye or say where he was going. He didn't even say thank you. But a couple days later two men, one of them a law officer, came looking for a fellow answering his description. Seems his guest was wanted for murder.

After the 'boss' got back and the horses were located on their permanent range a line-rider was no longer needed so Davis spent the winter in Rosebud, just doing odd jobs as they came up. They didn't come up very regularly. That winter of 1903-04 was a killing winter, and the latter part of April Davis headed north.

With fifty cents in his pocket, he took the first job he could get, which happened to be herding sheep. While he was on that job his horse got loose and took up with a wild bunch. He managed to get close enough to him to get a rope on him, but on foot he couldn't hold him so he and his horse parted company, and from then on he herded sheep on foot.

He stayed with the sheep outfit during shearing and made enough – all but one dollar – to buy another horse. Then Hank Cusker offered him a job on the roundup, and Davis wasn't slow to take it. It was Cusker who gave him the nickname 'Gobbler'.

When Floyd went to work for Cusker, Hank didn't ask his name and Floyd didn't volunteer it. On range land in those days a fellow was as likely to be known by a nickname as by his given name.

The stranger drifting in might be a fugitive from justice – or he might be a kid who had run away from home. In any event, if a man didn't tell you his name and nobody else had found one for him you just called him whatever came handy. As long as he did his job no questions were asked.

Floyd wasn't eager to bring along the name he had acquired when he was still in Wyoming. He was only about fourteen years old, but he was working on a ranch and somehow "got in bad with some guy." The fellow was getting kind of rough with him one morning so he grabbed up a picket pin* and threw it.

He missed his target, but his adversary seemed to consider the intention as good as delivery and before it was over had rammed Floyd's face with his elbow. From then on he carried the name 'Bad Eye' (his eye got a little black and swollen) so it's little wonder he wasn't eager to bring that name along.

About the first thing Floyd did when he joined Cusker's outfit was start breaking a colt. Some whim prompted him to call the colt 'Gobbler'. Davis was no fugitive from justice, but he hadn't been given any name so, for want of a better 'handle', Cusker dubbed the wrangler the same as the colt. From then on Floyd Davis was known as 'Gobbler' – so extensively that the first time he ran for sheriff of McCone County a friend told him that half the people didn't know who Floyd Davis was. After that he campaigned as Floyd 'Gobbler' Davis and won the election.

Cusker had a bunch of rough horses, and there was no chance to gentle them down any before roundup started so every day, riding circle, he had to break a new horse. They didn't have to wait until the Fourth of July to have a rodeo; they had one every morning as cowboys and horses battled to determine which was master.

Young Davis (he was only seventeen when he landed in Dawson County) covered much of the territory between the Yellowstone and the Missouri during his riding days, and his reputation as a bronc rider went even farther – although Mr. Davis isn't our source of information on that point.

Joe Kelly of Sidney declared, "If a horse threw Gobbler Davis, nobody else wanted to tackle him!" The late Billy Wood was another who attested to the riding skill of Davis. He had to chuckle as he recalled the time Gobbler, repping* for the HS with the XIT (a couple of area ranches), brought some butcher knives over to the Wood ranch to get them sharpened.

"He was always riding a horse that was only about half broke," Mr. Wood explained, "and here he came with a paper sack full of butcher knives. As he rode into the yard our dog started to bark and his horse started to buck, and I started hollering, 'Drop those knives!' They were sticking through the paper sack, but he just kept hanging onto them with one hand and his reins with the other until he finally got that bronc straightened out. Then he came on in and sharpened the knives for the roundup crew."

After Cusker, Davis rode for various outfits – among them the Pot Hound Pool on Charlie Creek south of Culbertson and the HS on the Redwater. The HS had just bought the remnants of the Butterfield hot bloods so they put Gobbler to work early in the spring breaking horses until roundup time.

About half-a-dozen of those hot bloods 'fizzled out' – just wouldn't break because they had been spoiled before. Even the broke horses ('broke' was a rather loose term meaning you didn't have to tie them down to saddle and bridle them!) could generally be counted on to put on a good performance when first mounted in the morning – especially on a rainy day.

The morning he left for the XIT roundup Jim (the boss) came down while he was packing his bedroll and suggested, "You'd better take along a couple gentle horses for night herding and rainy days." That was real thoughtful of him, but Gobbler pointed out that if a fellow took a couple gentle horses along with that string, you'd ride them to death.

He took twelve horses with him, but there wasn't enough work on that roundup for that many horses so he gave some away.

In 1908 Floyd 'Gobbler' Davis went to work for the '14' Ranch, northwest of Richey, east of Vida. Then in 1909 he married Clara Hilger, and that put a stop to his roundup career.

Clara Hilger had her first introduction to the Treasure State in 1898 when her father moved his family from Minnesota to Shelby. 'Brother Van' (W.W. Van Orsdel, famed pioneer Methodist preacher) was still very active in Montana while the Hilgers lived at Shelby, and Mrs. Davis well remembers his visits. He came once a month from Great Falls to hold services in the little town, and she considers it a real privilege to have played the piano for some of those services. 'Brother Van' was famous for his singing so little wonder that it made a deep impression upon her. Describing it she said, "He'd throw his head back and sing with all his heart while tears rolled down his cheeks."

In the summer of 1907 Clara visited the Redwater-Missouri River country and for the first time met cowboy Floyd Davis. She didn't stay long that year, but in September of 1908 she was back and worked in a hotel for a few months. That 'here again, there again' was all right for awhile, but when she came back the next fall Floyd evidently decided that was enough itinerancy. He didn't use his lariat, but he roped her for life and they were married November 6, that very fall.

For their fiftieth wedding anniversary their family and friends helped them celebrate, and J.K. Ralston of Billings sent them a crayon drawing of their 'wedding trip'. The sketch pictured an outlaw horse Floyd used to ride. J.K. (Ken), as a boy, would stand breathless and watch whenever Gobbler mounted that horse. Even though Ralston hadn't seen the horse for fifty-two years, there was no mistaking the identity.

In the drawing the horse was hitched to a buggy and half rearing as he ran while two wheels of the buggy were off the ground. The bride was pictured clinging to seat and side of the buggy, her veil streaming in the wind. Underneath the drawing was the caption, "I wasn't there, but knowing Floyd, it must have been something like this." Davis doesn't deny the aptness of the picture.

The wedding party had indeed gone by team and buggy as far as Poplar, but then they boarded the train to go on to Glasgow. There the Reverend White, formerly of Shelby and a friend of the Hilgers, performed the wedding ceremony.

When they got back to Poplar, they had to stay overnight and they thought they were in for a charivari*, but before it really got a good start the leaders of it called them out and told them to come on down to the dance hall. They complied and found a surprise dance planned for them.

The fellow who had planned to give their 'official' wedding dance had his house full of wheat so they had the dance in the schoolhouse instead. Cowboy friends gave them royal treatment. One got out the catalog and ordered them a cook stove (just about a luxury item, even though it wasn't gas or electric), and the others each chipped in $5 – quite a chunk out of a forty-dollar-a-month check. With this cash gift the newlyweds were able to buy their needed furniture.

Floyd was in partnership with Bill Bartley at the time so they moved into his log shanty. Together they were running cattle and two bands of sheep for the Williams ranch. Then in 1910 he filed on a homestead, and they moved onto his claim.

Maybe trading the roundup for a homestead wasn't such a bad deal. Novels and TV might glamorize the role of cowboy, but working ten, twelve, fifteen hours a day wasn't always glamorous. When your turn came for riding night herd, taking two hours out of a night that was already short was even less glamorous. No overtime for those extra hours, either! But a lot of people – people who haven't tried it – figure all a cowboy had to do was ride horses, and riding horses is a pleasure.

Floyd 'Gobbler' Davis located in Dawson County when he crossed over the Yellowstone in 1904, but when county-carving started a few years later he found his homestead in Richland County.

He was getting along fine in Richland County and was serving as the West End deputy sheriff when the legal knife carved away another chunk and put him in McCone County.

When McCone County was created, all officials were appointed until an election could be held. Hank Johnson, deputy sheriff for Dawson County located at Circle, was appointed sheriff of the new county, but he was a blacksmith and chose not to run for election so Davis ran and was elected.

It was during that campaign that a friend had advised him that "half the people don't know who Floyd Davis is" so he had let people know that it was 'Gobbler' Davis that was running.

The various candidates for offices were making a lot of promises so one night at a Nickwall dance the folks wanted him to make a speech. His speech was brief. "All the others," he declares he told them, "are telling you all the good things they're going to do if elected. All I will promise is that any time my pay check isn't good I'm going to quit!" That promise must have been enough; he was elected and took office January 1, 1921.

The sheriff was busier then. There was no police force and no highway patrol (no highway!) so the sheriff had to take the whole responsibility for law enforcement.

Since his terms as sheriff were served during the prohibition era, the moonshiners and bootleggers supplied him with a good share of his business. One moonshiner who was out on bond failed to appear as ordered by the court so Davis was sent a bench warrant to bring the fellow in.

First he had to find him – he was never home – so Davis asked a fellow he could trust (the prohibition law was unpopular and not everyone cooperated with attempts to enforce the law) where the fugitive was 'holed up'. He was hiding in a cabin along the river, the sheriff was informed, "but if you wait until dark he'll come out and go up to his own place."

With this advice the sheriff took up his watch, and sure enough, about dusk he saw his 'customer' coming out of the brush so Davis shouted, "Halt!" Instead of halting the fellow "took off like a scared rabbit. I hollered a couple times more," Mr. Davis explained, "but he kept going. I saw I wasn't gaining any so I fired a shot. That man stopped so fast he threw up a cloud of dust. I asked him why he didn't stop when I called halt, and he said he didn't hear." No question about hearing the shot, however, and seemingly he knew what the shot meant.

Another major item of business during his administration as sheriff was the posting of foreclosure notices. In most cases, Mr. Davis pointed out, these foreclosures weren't a matter of some struggling farmer losing his home. Rather, most were speculators who had filed on a claim, obtained a substantial loan, then abandoned the homestead. The loan companies would file suit, but often it would wind up with the county selling for taxes.

One winter between October 20 and April 4 he served notice of land foreclosure proceedings against 823 pieces of land, with three sets of notices against each piece. His car was tied up in the snow at John Bawden's that whole winter so he served all those notices on horseback.

One of Mr. Davis's neighbors urged, "Be sure to ask Gobbler about the four-buckle overshoes." Mr. Davis looked rather surprised at the request for details about the overshoes, but he did – a bit hesitantly – explain, "Well, one morning down at John Bawden's there was a young fellow afraid to get on his horse. He was walking around there with the buckles flapping on his overshoes. It was cold that morning like it was most of the mornings that winter. Saddle leather stiff. So were his rubber overshoes.

"I told him, 'Better buckle up those overshoes and get on and ride like a man.' He didn't want to so I said, 'I'll shoot the buckles off your overshoes.' He didn't move. It was time to get going so – I shot. Didn't want to shoot too close and hurt his legs so I just shot a buckle off. The fellow," he added succinctly, "got on and rode."

One of the most colorful periods of Gobbler Davis's duration as sheriff was during the building of the railroad into Circle. When the building crew moved in, the foreman stopped in to have a chat with the sheriff and ask for cooperation. He needed his men on the job, not locked up, if they were to get the road built, and he knew beforehand he would need the help of the law to keep them straight – and working.

A crew of 200 men camped on the Redwater just out of town was liable to keep things lively, but trouble was kept to a minimum. "The Circle jail was only big enough to hold about three people" (the same jail that's serving McCone County yet today) "so if we'd 'a locked those men up for every little thing we'd 'a had to build a pasture for them," commented Mr. Davis.

One night the sheriff had gone to a dance at the Redwater store (had to police the dances, too, he explained), and awhile after midnight a man from Circle came rushing in to call him back to town.

Seems the railroad men were in town and didn't want to leave the pool halls at midnight so they had been thrown out. Now about forty of them were organizing down on the flat and hard telling what was coming next.

"What are you going to do, Gobbler?" the summoner worriedly wanted to know. Not a man to waste words, Davis didn't outline the strategy he had in mind, but neither did he waste time – not even to organize a posse to help him deal with the mutineers.

Instead he hurried back to Circle, and as he approached the camp he turned off his headlights and sneaked up close. When he was almost upon them he suddenly turned on his lights and shouted, "Police officers!" The effect was all he could have desired. The whole bunch scattered – scattered in every direction. One man ran through three fences (he later declared) and got himself so lost he couldn't even find the camp when the scare was over.

Once the gang dispersed Davis returned to Redwater to pick up his wife. On the way home, as they neared Circle, they found the hapless fellow who had tangled with the fences, his shirt torn and his generally disheveled appearance lending credibility to his tale of woe.

Next morning Sheriff Davis found a hat in the area from which the gang had departed so precipitately the night before so he picked it up. As he looked around over the crew, hard at work, he noticed one fellow in the blistering heat (can you even think 'heat' with the frigid temperatures we've been having?) hard at work assembling bolts and nuts while the sun beat down upon his hatless head. Good Samaritan compassionately offered the hat, which was promptly clapped onto the bare head. It fit, as he had a hunch it would.

One day Superintendent Haley told Davis there was an agitator in town, working on his crew. "Not good for my men," he worried. Davis checked on the man and noticed he wasn't doing much.

After a few days he made an opportunity to visit with the fellow. As they talked he pointed out, sociably enough, "Busy time of the year. I've been watching you around here four or five days and haven't seen you do a thing except visit with these railroad men. I don't think you're going to like it around here much longer." That was the last sociable visit he or anyone else in those parts had with the stranger. Never saw him again.

When the railroad tracks were laid into Circle, and Haley was ready to remove his crew, he presented the sheriff with a Stetson hat. Evidently he was satisfied with the cooperation from the law enforcement officers.

Along with the bootleggers and moonshiners, the land foreclosure proceedings, and the railroad crew, there were plenty of other things to keep a sheriff busy. "Every once in awhile some fellow would get cattle or horses tangled up with his own and couldn't tell what brand to put on so I'd have to straighten that out," Davis explained.

The Davises lived in Circle during the time he served as sheriff, then moved back to the farm. One day little Charles, their oldest child, watched as Mrs. Davis's father sowed a little grain, broadcasting it by hand. A few days later as Mr. Davis came from the field he noticed Chuck running back and forth from granary to pasture. He thought that bore investigation so he went to check and found that his keg of staples, which he had been using as he fenced the pasture, was almost empty.

He demanded an explanation from his young son (probably about four years old) who explained, "Sowing staples like Grandpa...." "They never came up," Mr. Davis informs us dryly.

Floyd Gobbler Davis belongs to that breed of men who believed in working for what they got but were willing to share anything (as long as they could do it voluntarily) with anyone in need. He feels strongly that the 'something for nothing' complex so evident in American society today is cause for great concern. In his eighty plus years he's seen hard winters and has seen big outfits go broke. The men who settled and built this country didn't ask the government to use other people's money to help them; they relied on themselves, and when they were down, they got up and started over again.

He's gone through the same experience himself – for example, when he bought sheep at $16 and had to sell them for $1.50. He just doesn't countenance the government forcing people to get aid. He refused to take any social security until he was seventy-two, just on principle, but he'd paid into the fund so he finally decided to take it.

The Davises have three children: Charles in Three Forks, Susie in Vida, and Requel in Butte. They also have ten grandchildren and six great grandchildren.

Mr. and Mrs. Davis still live on the farm, and he still rides horses – but not the kind that earned him his reputation sixty years ago.

Winning Cowboys in the American Legion Rodeo, Glendive, July 1924
Billy Peoples, C. Powers, H.H. Shaffer, Red Kinney

Archie Hamilton

February 1965

Archie Hamilton began his career in Leon, Iowa, in 1883, but he did a 'heap' of traveling and tried a 'heap' of jobs before he settled in his present location with his present occupation. While he was taking care of his father's farm down in Missouri he learned what a 'heap' is. It means a whole lot. He had hardly reached Missouri before everyone in the area knew he was there. (That Missouri grapevine, he says, beats the telephone or any other means of communication for speed.) One old fellow soon had him collared and had told him all there was to tell about everybody up and down the 'holler'. At the conclusion he confided, "Some folks don't like me." Archie didn't quite know how to reply to that so he just said, "That so." The fellow continued, "I talk a heap." Pause. Then, "But there's a heap to talk about!" Archie figures, too, there's a heap to talk about and maybe that's one of the reasons he enjoys his insurance business.

As soon as Archie had graduated from the Davis City, Iowa, high school, he headed West and wound up in Wyoming, about thirty-five miles east of Sheridan, working for the Ucross, a big cattle outfit. Next was a session with the Monarch Coal Company west of Sheridan but a bout with pneumonia halted that job, and he went back to Iowa for a time. His father had bought a farm down on the Osage River (it's under ninety feet of water now) so in the spring of 1904 Archie went down to take care of it. That's when he got educated in the language of the Missourians. One thing he couldn't get used to was having someone tell him, "Y'all come over and see us." Archie would explain, "Nobody here but me." But they'd tell him "Y'all come anyway."

He went back to Wyoming that fall, and the next couple years divided his time between Missouri (his folks moved down there) and Wyoming. In the latter he worked variously at the Ucross; in the Burlington machine shops, for a construction outfit; in the Big Horn Canyon where the Burlington was building a railroad through to Casper and Denver; and for the Pitchfork Ranch at Meteetse.

Finally he decided to head for a good country, and he landed in Glendive in the fall of 1906 with fifty cents in his pocket. His brother-in-law, Arthur Patterson, had homesteaded out on Deer Creek and urged Archie to do likewise so that's how he found Dawson County. Archie observed that that winter started a good deal like this present one. Soon after he arrived he got a job at the Snyder Coal Mine near the present Clapp Mine, working there until Thanksgiving Day, when he quit and walked back to town. Snow started falling that day and just didn't know when to quit the rest of the winter.

Back in Glendive he got a job teaming for Edward and Johnny O'Neil. They supplied him with a four-horse team with the agreement that they'd feed the team, he'd feed himself, and they'd split his earnings fifty-fifty. The next few months were busy with hauling cement to the new dam being built at Intake: hay, coal – what have you.

Part of the winter he hauled ice from the river, off the bayou*, for storage. One cold morning he harnessed his team and headed for the bayou, but just as he arrived he found the cutting crew walking off – too cold to work. He put his team up, then walked over past the N.P. yard office where the thermometer hung and casually asked the yardmaster what the temperature was. "Sixty-three degrees below zero!" was the answer. Archie just about froze.

The consignment that stands out above all other that bitter winter was the trip to the Butterfield Ranch across the Divide* over Paxton way. Ranchers in those days customarily laid in enough supplies in the fall to carry them through the winter, but for some reason the Butterfield's supplies didn't carry through. By the end of January all they had left to eat was beans. Their situation was desperate so one of the Butterfield girls rode horseback to Glendive – no casual undertaking in the dead of a winter such as the winter of 1906-07 – to hire someone to go out with supplies. The prospect was not enticing, and she found no bidders eager for the hazardous journey. She had been in town almost two weeks when finally Archie and three other fellows agreed to go. They started out, each with a four-horse team and sled. The Butterfields kept racehorses and had nothing for them but hay, so they'd sent an order for oats, too. One sled started out loaded with oats, but by the time they reached the ranch they had only four or five sacks left.

The weather was cold and the snow was deep and treacherous. Coulees and creeks, blown full of snow so the country appeared level, were concealed until the lead outfit floundered in and buried team and sled. That called for a session with the shovels (they had even taken along a scraper* and long chain; needed it, too) until they had their caravan on its way again. They got to the Hollecker Ranch the first day, which wasn't too bad; they were acquainted with the country that far, but from there on the drivers were not familiar with the terrain so they never knew when the bottom might drop out from under them. The second day they only made about four miles. Besides having to shovel through creeks, etc., the sleds would tip over and have to be reloaded. Going was slow at best; at the worst....! That second day they had made so little progress that they left the sleds, took the teams back to Hollecker's, and stayed there that night, too. The third day took them to the Schaeffer Ranch, where they spent that night, and the fourth day again saw so little progress that, as before, they unhitched their horses and came back for another night. The fifth day finally took them to Butterfield's. By that time no offer could have induced them – any of them – to start out on another trip like that.

About the middle of February the weather finally 'broke' and caught Archie out at the Hollecker Ranch when it did. He had spent the night there, and when he got up the next morning, he found the whole country flooded. He had to drive all over those hills to get back into town, and that was the end of the sledding.

At that time there were only two houses in Glendive beyond the present Quanrad, Brink, & Riebold Auto Parts store*, but four more were in the planning stage so Archie hauled the gravel for those, then his job 'played out'. If that gravel hauling had just held out a little longer, he figures he'd still have his hand today, but it didn't so when he heard that the Northern Pacific was hiring, he applied. They needed a brakeman, but he was told they were hiring only experienced men. He assured them he was experienced, so they hired him and sent him out to Forsyth that very night. He was not experienced, but he soon learned. He was getting along fine until July when he met with the accident that cost him his hand, caught in a coupling. There was no N.P. hospital here at that time so they sent him to Brainard, Minnesota where he spent three weeks in the hospital. When he was discharged he went to St. Paul to settle up with the company, then remained to attend business college so it was December before he returned to Glendive. He worked as call boy for a couple years, but the spring of 1908 found him in the hospital again, this time with eye trouble, so he spent another summer in St. Paul. Back in Glendive in September he learned that N.P. Superintendent John Rapplje had been transferred to Missoula so he went to Missoula, too. Rapplje called the chief dispatcher, who put him on at Garrison as a telegraph operator. He stayed with that until 1911, but he had filed on a homestead in the spring of 1907, and now there was talk of contesting his claim because he hadn't spent much time there so he laid off the railroad to come make some improvements on his homestead. So far as the railroad is concerned, he's still 'laying off'.

His homestead was adjacent to Arthur Patterson's out on Deer Creek beyond the Hollecker Ranch. During one of the spells of bad weather while he was out on the homestead, he wasn't able to get to town for a considerable length of time, and by the time he could, he had quite a few eggs collected, as did his folks (they had moved to Montana, too). When the weather cleared, they loaded the eggs into his dad's new Model T and headed for town. The melting snow had pretty well punctuated the road with ruts and washouts, from a few inches to a couple feet deep, and the eggs began bouncing around. Archie began hollering, "Slow up Dad; slow up!" but his dad hadn't handled the new fangled thing very much so the Model T went faster and the eggs bounced higher. Archie climbed into the back seat to try to hold them down, but he didn't have much luck, and most of the eggs that didn't bounce clear out were pretty well scrambled by the time they got to the Yellowstone Bridge. They decided they'd better stop and clean out the eggs before they came on into town. Presently a fellow who had come in behind them stopped, noted their operations, and observed, "So you're the fellows with the eggs. I followed your trail all the way from Bamber Hill*!"

Getting used to that Model T proved to be quite different from handling horses. Soon after they got it his dad was over at Archie's place with it, and when he got in it to leave, Archie told him, "Hold it Dad; I'll get the gate." Too late he realized he should have started for the gate before his dad got into the car because once he started he couldn't stop. He started pulling back on the steering wheel and yelling, "Whoa, Whoa!" but he got to the gate before Archie did and went right through it – brand new board gate, too, all freshly painted. When he did get it stopped, he ruefully remarked to Archie, "Don't pay no attention to a 'whoa', does it." And Archie made a new gate.

There were still plenty of old timers around when Archie came and one of the most colorful was old Jim Seeds, an Indian scout who had come in with the first railroad survey party. Jim loved nothing more than to spin yarns, and one day as he and Archie were standing together in front of Hollecker's store (now Anderson's) a stranger came along. Noting Jim's long gray hair (he wore it shoulder length and longer) and general appearance, the stranger asked, "Say Mister, are you an old timer here?" Pointing to Hungry Joe*, Jim asked him, "See that pile of dirt up there? Well, Old Charley Krug and I wheeled that up there with a wheelbarrow out of this channel they call the Yellowstone."

That was a little too much for even an Easterner to swallow, and he just turned and walked off. Jim gazed after him, then grunted, "He didn't have to be so umpish about it! He ought to know that pile of dirt couldn't be hauled up there in a few months, or a few days, or a few years."

He tried farming for ten years, but it must have been the wrong ten, and by 1921 he had decided that whoever it was that said, "You can't go wrong with land," didn't know what he was talking about. Archie was not only broke, but deeply in debt as well when he came back to Glendive and started selling Fuller brushes. After a few years of that he decided to run for county treasurer, but the Democratic central committee seemed to think that was a joke and gave him no support whatever. He won anyway. His campaign strategy, he explains, was simple. He called on every home in the county, taking his brushes with him, and warned the housewife she'd better vote for him or he'd be back with his brushes next year. A couple weeks before election he visited every house in Glendive again taking his brushes and using the same speech. Election day came, and he had his post by a big majority.

After serving two terms as county treasurer Archie began selling insurance for the Montana Life, now Western Life, Insurance Company. At last he'd found the work he really liked. He's been in the business now for thirty-eight years and is Western Life's oldest active agent. He doesn't 'Push it' very hard anymore, he explains, but he still keeps his hand in. It's great to be in love with your job!

Ole Helvik

January 1968

Wibaux was a lively town when Ole Helvik, fresh from Norway, came to live there in 1909, and cowboys from surrounding ranches helped to make it so. Long after the cowboys were gone, holes in the roof of the old harness shop where Helvik spent his first working days – first years – were mute reminders of the occasions when some hilarious cowboy let off steam by shooting at the roof.

Over in the 'Old Country' Ole had learned the trade of shoe making, specializing in the making of lady's shoes. The entire shoe, from start to finish, was made by hand. He had a good trade, but two of his brothers had come to America, and he believed there was a better chance for work here so he crossed the ocean, too.

His brother, Louie, had located in Hamilton so Ole went there for a few months first, then came back to the eastern part of the state where his other brother, Mons, had settled near Hodges. Ole promptly went to work for Frank Stipek in his Wibaux harness shop and worked for him the next five years.

Stipek's harness shop was located in a large shack where the courthouse now stands. The making and repairing of harnesses was big business in 1909. Here again the entire process was by hand. He had a special stool – kind of like the seats on the old grindstones – on which he sat while he worked.

The stool was divided so that the front could be opened and the tug* inserted, then closed to secure the tug while he sewed on it. He used a stitching awl to do the sewing, waxing the thread to make it strong and rubbing it with bee's wax to make it slick.

Along with the making and repairing of harnesses, Helvik also repaired saddles and shoes. Although skilled in making shoes, in Montana he only repaired them. He was so busy with harnesses and saddles that he didn't have much time to spend on shoes.

He started out at $45 a month, working until seven or eight o'clock in the evening. His board and room cost him $25 a month, and his needs and wants were few (no car to consume his earnings) so even then he was able to save a little each month. He was soon given a raise, and before many months he was getting $85 a month. "Frank Stipek," Mr. Helvik commented, "was a good fellow to work for and always paid promptly."

Often as he worked away in the old harness shop he could hear by the shooting and shouting outside that cowboys had come to town. One day he saw a cowboy go past the shop, shooting as he went up the street, but he thought the fellow was just having some fun and paid no attention. A moment later, however, a shot at the livery stable took the life of a young fellow who worked there. It seems the day was bitterly cold, and the livery owner had sent the boy to get a horse which the cowboy had left tied on the street for what the livery man figured was too long. The furious cowboy, who had been drinking, decided the boy had stolen the horse so he followed him to the stable and fatally shot him.

Mr. Helvik recalled that the best restaurant in town during that period, located where the Silver Dollar Bar now stands, was run by a Chinaman named Lu Fong. Customers sometimes had to wait an hour to get in because so many people wanted to eat there.

Helvik worked for Stipek until 1914, then bought a place over by the bridge and started in business for himself — still in the harness business. He was kept very busy with harnesses in those days. However, as mechanization moved in and horses moved out, the harness business inevitably slowed so Mr. Helvik started a shoe store.

In the meantime, in 1917, he married Edith Anderson of Hodges. Edith's father, Charley Anderson, was one of the first settlers in the Hodges area. He first came to Montana in 1882, working on the Northern Pacific Railroad.

Mr. Anderson, a native of Sweden, had come to St. Paul where he had a sister living and had secured employment with the N.P. He helped lay the railroad tracks as far as Huntley, Montana. The ties were put in by hand, the grading done with horses and scrapers* — scrapers that would carry only a fraction of the dirt handled by the modern earthmovers.

After five years in the states Mr. Anderson went back to Sweden and married Christina Danielson, then returned to this country and spent about a year at Antelope, North Dakota before settling at Hodges.

Again Mr. Anderson started working for the Northern Pacific, this time as section foreman, and continued with them another nine years. During this time he started a ranch near Hodges but did not immediately move out there.

The land at that time had not yet been surveyed so he had no way of knowing that the spot he had picked for his ranch buildings was railroad land. By the time this fact was established he had lived there so long he was allowed to keep it. He homesteaded 160 acres and also bought surrounding acreage.

Mr. Anderson's mother came to this country and lived in her son's home the last ten years of her life. She was the first person dying of natural causes to be buried in the Wibaux cemetery.

Mr. Anderson was a progressive rancher and built the first dam in the area, using horses and scrapers. Daughters Edith (Mrs. Helvik) and Olga (Mrs. Presthus) drove the teams while their father handled the full scrapers, their brother the empties. This was not the only experience the girls had in helping with the ranch work. Mrs. Helvik recalled many instances where they 'filled in', helping with the sheep and with other chores.

Mr. and Mrs. Anderson lived in the Hodges community until they died, Mr. Anderson in 1934 and she in 1938. As is the way with families, their children scattered to homes of their own, Edith to Wibaux as Mrs. Ole Helvik.

In the disastrous flood of 1929 five feet of water in the Helvik's shoe store soaked a good part of their merchandise. Much of their inventory had to be sold for little or nothing. The wall of water had reached the little town about seven o'clock in the morning, and people had little warning of the danger. Water on the main street reached heights of six to eight feet. Three lives were lost so even though the Helviks were hard hit – it could have been worse.

In 1938 they went into the grocery business. The store was on the main floor of their building and their living quarters were on the second floor. Disaster struck again in 1962 when fire destroyed both store and home. By this time one of their sons was active in the store so he used the insurance money to purchase their present facilities at 111 W. Orgain Ave., and restocked. "There used to be six grocery stores in Wibaux," Mr. Helvik observed. "Now there are two."

The Sr. Helviks now live in an apartment at the rear of the store and leave the managing of the grocery business to son Alf. Their other son, Arley, is with Wibaux's First National Bank. Mr. Helvik still does occasional shoe repairing when someone has a need.

In Ole Helvik's almost sixty years in Montana he has seen periods of depression and periods of prosperity. In spite of two business disasters he could conclude, "I've been pretty lucky since I came to this country; I haven't gone broke yet!"

Dave 'Prince' Anderson

April 1972

Although he has been known as Prince most of this century, Dave Anderson doesn't really claim any royal blood. In a day when men on the range were more likely to be known by a nickname than by their given name, when politeness – or prudence – deterred even the curious from asking that name, this Scotchman from England was dubbed 'Prince'. And 'Prince' he remains to present day.

Dave Anderson, though his people were Scotch, lived in England until he was seventeen. He, with his family, did spend some time in Scotland, too. There were ten in his family, and he didn't see much prospect of getting any place in England so he left for the 'New World'.

He went to Saskatchewan in 1897 and contracted to work for a big farmer there. Terms: $100 for the year (yes, one hundred dollars a year) plus room and board. Later he found that ranchers around there were paying $20 a month, and even $20 a month sounded good compared to his contract, so the next year he went to work on a ranch.

While he was working on the ranch he met a couple cowboys from Culbertson who were up in Saskatchewan hunting cattle that had strayed from their outfits down in the States. They told him wages were a handsome $40 a month in Montana so the next year (1900) he came down to Culbertson. For a while he broke horses for the Diamond G and several other ranches around there. Then in the fall two cowboys from the CK south of Oswego were repping* in that area. They had gathered fifty to sixty head of cattle, and when they were ready to go back, they suggested to Anderson that he come with them, and he did.

At Oswego they swam the cattle across the river, then went on to the CK headquarters. At the ranch the foreman told him where the roundup wagons were – twenty-five or thirty miles away. He also said they were short handed so Dave rode over, and Dave Clair took him on right away. He worked the roundup that fall, beginning his ten years with the CK.

The next year he rode for the CK from the Musselshell to the forks of the Yellowstone–Missouri; from Forsyth, down the Yellowstone to the Missouri, back up the Missouri to Redwater. In those days a man's cattle weren't confined to a fenced pasture!

They gathered the cattle onto Redwater, then drifted a bunch of them west onto Hell Creek and Snow Creek where they turned them loose to winter. That country was so rough that a wagon couldn't get in there so the next spring when it was time to round up the cattle, the wagons stayed out on Box Creek, and four men – Prince Anderson was one of them – went into that jungle with a pack outfit to round them up. Talk about rough country – that was it! They got the cattle out, though, and branded a good bunch of calves.

Prince remembers the spring of 1902 as a bad one for the roundup all the way around. Seven outfits — he didn't take time to name all of them, but he mentioned the L7 — the LU Bar — the CK — the W Bar — the XIT — met at Muggins Corral down on the Musselshell to start the roundup, but the rain started first. Rained for a week straight.

Each outfit had ten or twelve men, and besides those, there were reps from other spreads (the CK would send a rep from their outfit to other parts of the country, and other outfits would send a rep to work with them). All told, there were probably 100 cowboys with the wagons: 100 cowboys strung twenty miles up the creek with nothing to do but play poker and shoot craps.

And wet! So wet they couldn't turn a wheel until the twenty-second of May. That roundup was a mere seventy years ago (1902), but as Prince Anderson talked about it, he seemed to feel the cold, wet weather yet.

When the cattle were rounded up for shipping, they were trailed to the nearest shipping point. Since all the shipping points were on the other side of the river, and there were no bridges across the Missouri — no ferry yet, either — they had to swim the cattle across.

There was a bridge across the Yellowstone at Glendive, but it was a wooden structure, and the livestock allowed on it at any one time was strictly limited so even at this end of the county they'd swim the cattle rather than cross the bridge. Oswego on the Missouri, and Fallon or Terry on the Yellowstone were the main points for crossing.

During the time Anderson was with the CK they never lost a man, but later on a CK man did drown. He went into the river with his chaps* on and went down before they could rescue him. Every man was supposed to put on a life belt before going into the river, but he didn't do it, and his chaps were certainly no substitute.

At shipping time they usually went for the mail about every day. This meant crossing the Missouri every day, and George Clark manned the rowboat to take the mail carrier — a cowboy from the ranch, not a government employee — across the river. Prince knew how to row a boat so first time he went for the mail he offered to row the boat across. Clark replied, "I'm admiral of this fleet." And he did the rowing.

He was a big, powerful man. "Pretty good fellow, Clark was," Anderson reflected. He had frozen his feet some years before when he got lost up on Prairie Elk. He was wearing tight boots at the time, which didn't help his circulation any, and had lost both feet as a result of that experience. He had bought artificial feet; cost a hundred dollars.

One morning at the CK Clark was just getting up when Prince came in. Clark had his feet off and couldn't get off the bed, so Prince took advantage of the situation to rough him up a little — planted his knee on him and tousled his hair. It was all in good humor, and Clark warned him, "Mr. Scotchman, I'll get you." A few days later he hid behind the dining room door, and as Prince came through, Clark hit him in the chest, knocking him back through the door again and evening the score to Clark's satisfaction.

"About all the entertainment we had in those days," Mr. Anderson recalls, "was telling lies about each other." George (Clark) had staked his brother Ray to a team of horses so after a time Prince told him he'd seen Ray headed west and added, "You won't see him back for a while." Unperturbed, George replied, "He's been trying to break into the pen, and I'll help him." They could give and take lots of joshing.

Prince Anderson was with the CK for ten years. He started out as a $40 a month cowboy, ended up as foreman at $100 a month. The CK (Conrad Kore of Helena was the owner and used his initials for the brand) was a big outfit in the early 1900's. They bought Texas steers and shipped them up here, 7-8,000 at a time. Besides that, from their own cows they'd sometimes brand 4-5,000 calves between the Yellowstone and Missouri Rivers.

One year a cowboy who came up with the cattle from Texas was quite a roper, and he stayed on to ride for the CK. Mr. Anderson recalls that Bill Davis once remarked, a bit sarcastically, "Four Eyes is a professional roper. When we round up cattle, he just pulls the papers out of his pocket, puts them under a rock on a hill and goes in and shows what he can do." "But Four Eyes," Mr. Anderson declares, "could deliver the goods."

Prince Anderson remembers the first organized rodeo in Wolf Point about fifty years ago. Hank Cusker was a judge, Steve Mormon helping. In those days it was strictly local talent. They knew all the riders, knew all the helpers. The real test of riding skill, however, came in those informal contests out on some ranch fifty miles from anywhere or wherever a bunch of cowboys might be together. There were some tremendous exhibitions of riding on such occasions. No eight second time limit on those rides. They rode until the horse stopped.

As Mr. Anderson and Sig Cusker reviewed some of those impromptu demonstrations, they especially noted Ned Quin's ride on a mottled gray at the CK horse camp. Hank Cusker brought out the horse, and Prince asked who would ride him. Hank replied, "You'll see this Indian in the middle of him in a minute or two." Ned Quin got on him, and that horse – both Cusker and Anderson verify – bucked as high as ten feet. When the horse's feet hit the ground again Quin, still in the saddle, swung down to where he could grab a hand full of grass and threw it in that gray's face!

Another rider these two old timers agreed was outstanding was Vern Hubbard. Vern worked for Hank Cusker – broke horses, gathered them, and so forth. A horse couldn't buck him off, they say. Seems his brother was quite a rider too. He could step off a horse any time. Vern couldn't do that and had to stay with the horse 'till he stopped. But he could stay with him!

A few years after Prince started riding for the CK he made a trip back to England and spent the winter foxhunting. When he returned to the CK, the wagon boss told him he was foolish to ride. Just as well stop at the ranch and work there. Anderson decided he'd do that. They irrigated several hundred acres of hay land. Took off as high as 300 tons while he was there. Sagebrush in some of that country was as high as three feet. When the roundup wagons came in he didn't let a man go; just handed him a hoe and let him start grubbing. Prince and another fellow hauled off the brush in a wagon.

The winter of 1906-07 was a bad one. CK lost quite a little in this eastern part of the range. It wasn't as bad as it was claimed, however. When the wagons pulled in for the winter, they would bring some cows and calves. They'd use some dry cows for beef, winter the others.

They had 300 or so cows around the ranch, but that was just a drop in the bucket to what they had on the range. They had put up lots of hay and had also bought probably 200 tons on the reservation – $3 a ton for blue joint. They drove four horses and broke roads to get the hay to the cattle; just had one sleigh, and they hauled hay all winter. The CK had two line camps, two or three men at each camp besides seven or eight at the ranch. They also had a horse camp on Sun Creek where they kept two or three men so they had a sizeable crew even during the winter.

In 1910 Dave 'Prince' Anderson left the CK to start ranching for himself on Prairie Elk. He got a bunch of horses first, then cattle. He stayed on the ranch until his arthritis got so bad he couldn't saddle a horse. As the arthritis became an increasing problem, a friend sent him a gentle horse he thought he could saddle. When he couldn't manage it, he just walked to the house and told his wife, "We're through. Let's buy a house in Wolf Point." And they did.

After his wife passed away he sold the house in town – the ranch, everything – and moved to the rest home in Wolf Point where he has resided since. He has two daughters, one on the ranch on Prairie Elk, one at Livingston. Each daughter has three children so he has six grandchildren.

Mrs. Andrew (Grace Kelly) Larson

February – March 1968

The year that Mrs. Andrew Larson graduated from high school back in Sleepy Eye, Minnesota, (she was Grace Kelly then) their class rings were made of Black Hills gold, and the numerals '97' (for the class of 1897) were cleverly formed instead of some jeweled set. She paid $2.50 for the ring when she bought it seventy-one years ago, but it cost $3.00 to have it repaired recently when it separated between the '9' and the '7'.

After her high school graduation she attended Mankato Normal for one year, then began teaching the sixth and seventh grades in her hometown of Sleepy Eye. In 1904 her family decided to move to Glendive, but since Grace was teaching she did not come when the rest of the family did. Dennis, the youngest member of the family and only son, was still in high school so he and Grace finished out their school terms, then joined their family in the Gate City*.

A number of years before (about 1896) her father's twin brother, Bill Kelly, had moved to Montana with his family (including five-year-old Mary, who later became Mrs. C.A. Banker), and it was through them that Grace's family was drawn to the Treasure State*.

They rented a house in Glendive from Jack Martin (where the Congregational Church* now stands). While there, Mrs. Kelly, one daughter (later Mrs. Stanley Felt), and Dennis took homesteads, all in the Lindsay area. Though living in Glendive they spent enough time on their homesteads to meet residency requirements.

Douglas Mead* was the main store in Glendive when the J.J. Kellys came, and there you could buy just about anything – groceries, dry goods, wagons, or buggies! Anything, that is, that was available in a frontier town.

Grace continued with her teaching, first in Glendive in the school that stood where the First National Bank* is now located. She taught the first three grades, and among her pupils were the late Paul Hagan, Clarence Harpster, and Bill Dion.

The following year, however, she took a rural school near Sidney. She knew she had to ride the stagecoach to get to Sidney and took that in stride. What she didn't realize until she reported for duty was that to get to the school she had to cross the river – by boat! Mr. O'Brien, owner of the only grocery store in Sidney, took her across, and she was scared to death – almost. Fortunately for her they didn't have a full nine-month term because she determined not to cross in that boat again until she had to. She knew she would have to cross again at the end of the term, but in the meantime she made no unnecessary trips. She 'stayed put' until school was out.

'Staying put' also had its drawbacks. She boarded in one of the nearby homes, and in this house the ceiling was just muslin cloth – typical of the ranch houses of the day. (Some of the log houses then had 'walls', too, of muslin – strips of cloth hung inside the logs, fastened at the top and bottom, then

45

whitewashed). Grace didn't mind the muslin ceiling; what bothered her was the rats that ran back and forth across the muslin while she was trying to sleep! She was glad for more reasons than one when she was safely back across the river again.

The next year she went back to teaching in Glendive, again grades one through three in the building which later housed the Bismarck Grocery*. She continued teaching there until her marriage in 1908 to Andrew Larson, Glendive pioneer.

Andrew Larson's first reaction to Eastern Montana as he traveled through on a train in 1885, headed for California was, "A man must really have a grudge against himself to live in this kind of country." Little did he guess that seven years later he would return and spend the next sixty-seven years in Glendive.

Larson was born in Norway in 1865 and came to the United States when he was only a year-and-a-half old. Needless to say, he didn't remember much about the fifty-four-day ship journey. He lived in Wisconsin, then Minnesota until he was twenty-five years old, but when he visited his sister in Glendive, he changed his mind about this part of the country and settled down here in 1892.

Beginning as a common teamster and ranch laborer, the pioneer worked his way to the offices of undersheriff, sheriff, county commissioner, city alderman, and the board of directors of the Building and Loan Association.

While he was working on a ranch in the summer of 1894 Larson made seven trips to Canada, selling work horses. The Canadians, in his opinion, were more honest to deal with than Americans. To illustrate he told about a Canadian farmer to whom he sold a horse. The man signed a promissory note and did not consider buying a chicken without Larson's consent. A native of Winnipeg once told Larson, "We just make our people honest," and he always found it so.

The keen rivalry between Miles City and Glendive dates back to the early 1890's, according to the early settler. It seems that at a Miles City horse race a Custer entry was favored to win, but the race had a surprise ending. A Dawson runner, which Larson jokingly described as looking more like a cow than a horse, won the race, and the competition between the two towns, which lasts to this day, began.

The very next Sunday Miles City, determined to prove its superiority, challenged Glendive to a cowboy foot race in the Gate City. Again Miles City was unanimously favored to win, but there was another surprise ending. The Glendive cowboy was just a few paces behind in the last lap when a Dawson fan fired a gun.

The town's racer took off as though it had been he that was shot from the gun and saved the day by reaching the finish line first. Miles City lost $5,000 in betting money that afternoon, and according to a statement from Larson, "They even had to borrow cash to get home!"

Larson died in 1959 at the age of ninety-three, but we are fortunate that he recorded some of his experiences and recollections while he was still living. (The Dawson County Pictorial, Thursday, July 12, 1956) For example, he pointed out that in 1906, 400 Indians camped in Glendive with their

46

headquarters where the high school now stands. The government paid the ferry fee for fifty-nine wagons to come from the Wolf Point vicinity to Glendive during fair time.

Larson had been their supervisor in 1904 so he knew their way of life first-hand. Since he was acquainted with Old Jerome (the tribe's chief, a college graduate of Carlyle) Larson was allowed to enter their council tent and smoke the 'pipe of peace' with the Indian members. It was quite an occasion for white men to watch the Indians slaughter their cattle at an open pit where Ames Wye is now located. They never wasted a portion of the cow; the squaws contributed to the conservation by drinking the blood!

According to the old timer, five houses and a milk house situated near the present post office can easily describe Glendive's north side at one time.

Appointed County Commissioner in 1912, Larson played an important part in constructing many of Dawson County's roads. Mrs. Larson pointed out that building roads was a job he loved.

The road graders of his day were of far different design from the present day models, and Mr. Larson found the jolts and jars almost more than he could take by the end of the day. He remedied the situation by placing a car seat with a board over it on the platform and standing on that. Then the jolts didn't bother him.

The road builder made three predictions while he was in office: that the day would come when there would be a transcontinental road through Glendive; paved streets in the city; and a road through Makoshika State Park. All three predictions came true before he laid down his tools.

Andrew Larson was active in promoting the local badlands park as a scenic center. When a suitable title for the park was being sought, Larson did some research and learned after many inquiries that 'Makoshika' is the Sioux word for badlands. He recommended that it be adopted as the park's name, and his recommendation was followed.

There has been much controversy over the pronunciation and spelling of Makoshika for many years, but the park promoter said that the present choice is the original way. He and his wife spent many hours walking through the badlands and showing tourists interesting locations.

The DAWSON COUNTY REVIEW for October 3, 1946, carried an article on the appreciation of a party from Western Reserve University, Cleveland, Ohio for Mr. Larson. The article said in part:

"Andrew Larson, virtual father of the Maco Sica Park, recently received a warm letter of appreciation and a box of man-size linen handkerchiefs from Professor Henry F. Donner, head of the department of geology and geography at Western Reserve University, Cleveland, Ohio, for Mr. Larson's courtesy and generosity in guiding Mr. Donner and a travel group of 16 Western Reserve University students through Badlands Park when the group stopped in Glendive on August 3, on a geology field trip.

"The group was vociferous in their praises of the Bad Lands area and bewailed the fact that their itinerary could not be changed to permit them to spend several days in this area while they prospected the badlands via saddle horse. One of the group was a graduate student who had traveled extensively in Europe, and it was her definite opinion, as expressed to Mr. Larson, that the scenic attractions of the Badlands Park are second to none."

Mr. Larson expressed the opinion that "the city has always been on the conservative side, making progress slowly but safely." He pointed out that "No Glendive bank or concern went broke during the depression years." But then on the other side he made a prediction for which taxpayers now will probably hail him as a true prophet. He warned, "Glendive's sudden influx of population will eventually need many community improvements, which will be a heavy burden on the taxpayers."

Another community service performed by Mr. Larson was his work on the cemetery records. Some lots had been sold more than once, and there was much confusion in the records that he was able to straighten out.

When cars began coming into practical use, the Larsons, along with other Glendivians, enjoyed taking motor trips. In the early years of cars, because of the fickleness of autos and uncertainties of the road – and because they enjoyed company – travelers generally found it advisable to travel in groups. Then if something happened to one car, they could be sure of help nearby. Otherwise help could be far away and long in coming. One such 'caravan' set out for Denver from Glendive and included four different cars: Larsons, Herricks, Mullendores, and Lowes. When they reached Denver, they were a dusty group, but they had a great time on the trip.

After Mr. Larson's death in 1959 Mrs. Larson continued to live in their North Kendrick home for a time, but two years ago she moved up to Badlands Home Sweet Home. She likes living in the Home and declares she doesn't know how any arrangement could improve on it.

The Larson story has a unique sequel. When Dale Dalbey, manager of local radio station KGLE, began reading the first installment of Mrs. Larson's story in Sunday's "As I Remember," he noticed the name 'Kelly' from Sleepy Eye, Minnesota, and brought it to the attention of his wife, whose grandfather was Pete Kelly from Sleepy Eye.

Mrs. Dalbey didn't know anything about her grandfather's family, but she lost no time contacting someone who did. A telephone call to Mrs. C.A. Banker, cousin of Mrs. Larson mentioned in the story, revealed that Pete Kelly was a brother to Bill (Mrs. Banker's father) and Jack (Mrs. Larson's father) Kelly.

The two older ladies well remembered Mrs. Dalbey's grandfather and were able to tell her much that she had never known about her family background. The Jack and Bill Kelly families had moved from Sleepy Eye before Mrs. Dalbey's father, Perry (youngest of Pete's family) was even married. Perry, in turn, moved from Sleepy Eye to Mankato when Candace, youngest of his children, was just a small child, so she knew nothing about her grandfather's brothers.

After her marriage to Dale Dalbey they left Minnesota for North Dakota, then moved to western Montana in 1946, to Wyoming in '53, and back to Montana – to Glendive, to be exact, in 1963. Sleepy Eye seemed far away and long ago to Mrs. Dalbey and so did any cousins her father might have had – until she read 'As I Remember' in the February 25 Ranger-Review.

The relatives lost no time getting acquainted, and Mrs. Dalbey could only exclaim, "It is really thrilling! I've never had anything like that happen to me before!"

Joe Kelly

July – August 1966

When someone asks Joe Kelly from Sidney, "Are you really Irish?" Joe replies, "Well my mother's name was Bridgette Dougherty, and she came directly from Ireland to Glendive. My father's name was Michael Kelly, and he came from Ireland, too. Besides that I was born on the seventeenth of March so if that doesn't make me Irish, I don't know what would." The only reason he isn't Pat is that Pat was here before he was. Joe was the third child of Michael and Bridgette Kelly. Pat was the first.

Michael Kelly had made his way to the New World in the 1870's. Three of his brothers were already in this country, working in the mines at Butte, but mining evidently didn't appeal to Michael. He chose tailoring instead, and upon his arrival in the U.S. he located in Chicago where he learned the tailoring trade. The West must have been beckoning, even though he didn't go to Butte, because he left Chicago for Denver, then sought out a little town just beginning to sprout at the western terminus of the Northern Pacific Railroad. There he set up shop in the back of Gallagher's general store and began tailoring in Glendive, Montana.

The Gallagher's were from Ireland, too, and that fall Mrs. Gallagher wrote to her sister back in 'The Old Country' and asked her to come help out in the Gallagher home. In December of that year her sister arrived, and that's how Michael Kelly and Bridgette Dougherty met each other.

Miss Dougherty, coming from the mild Emerald Isle where snow never fell, was greeted in Glendive by a foot of it. When she stepped off the train and saw what lay before her she exclaimed, "If this is Glendive, God help me!"

As she stood on the depot platform, looking about her uncertainly at the few scattered shacks and houses, the conductor came to her rescue and graciously offered to take her to the Gallaghers. With so few people in the town she no doubt would have become acquainted with the tailor even if his shop hadn't been in her brother-in-law's store. Acquaintance soon ripened into friendship and more. A year after her arrival in Glendive, Bridgette Dougherty and Michael were married.

Their first two children were born in Glendive. Then when Mary (later Mrs. Paul Obergfell) was just three weeks old, seventy-nine years ago this July, they moved to Ft. Buford where Mr. Kelly accepted the position of tailor for the soldiers stationed there. The end of July was hardly the ideal time to move a family over a hot, dusty trail, especially when a tiny baby was involved, but they managed. They traveled by government ambulance – a covered wagon drawn by four horses. In 1887 there were no towns between Glendive and Ft. Buford and very few houses. When they could manage it, they stopped overnight at a ranch, but when the ranches didn't come in the right place, they had to just camp out. (And that tiny baby!)

When the Kellys first moved to the Fort, a detachment of colored soldiers was stationed there. Later they were transferred and replaced by white soldiers. For colored soldiers or white, the making of uniforms was the same, and making uniforms was Mr. Kelly's business. Basting, padding, stitching – much work went into each of those uniforms.

Mr. Kelly stayed at Ft. Buford until it was closed and the soldiers transferred to points east. The tailor was asked to retain his position and accompany them when they moved, but by this time several more children had been added to the family, and the Kellys felt that a fort was not the best place to bring up a family. He declined the offer, and instead of following the soldiers, Mr. Kelly homesteaded a mile-and-a-half northwest of what is now Sidney.

When Mr. Kelly chose his homestead site, he didn't know they were going to be living so close to town. The family lived on the homestead several years before there was anything at all where Sidney was built up. Two brothers, Jack and Dave Stewart, had given $5 an acre for the section* that later spawned Sidney, and early in the 1900's they built a store on it, Sidney's first store.

There was a little store at Newlon (south of Sidney's present location) when the Kellys moved to the homestead, but Glendive was the nearest shopping center so twice a year the Kellys went to get supplies. The trip was made with team and wagon and took two days each way. The first day they would go as far as Bill Arkle's where they would stay overnight, then the next day they would go on to Glendive. They purchased their supplies at the Douglas-Mead general store – enough to last six months, and then began the two-day journey homeward.

Michael Kelly had never farmed in his life when he filed on that homestead, but he learned. Mrs. Kelly had lived on a farm in Ireland and knew something of the rudiments of farming, and neighbors were helpful. There was much exchange of labor among farmers then. Farming was a little simpler in those days, too. Along with tilling the soil, Kellys also raised cattle and horses.

As might be expected, the daughters of the tailor were taught to sew and all learned to make their own clothes. One of the girls, Agnes (Mrs. Wiebler) is a professional seamstress. Mrs. Wiebler now lives in Yakima. Four of the Kelly's eight children are still living. Mrs. Obergfell (Mary) lives in Denver, Mrs. Niehenke (Julia) lives in Sidney, and Joe also lives in Sidney, making his home with his sister.

Growing up in the Sidney area, Joe learned first hand what hard times are. He joked that he learned to write in the bank – signing his name on the bottom of a note. He can laugh about it now, but the hard times were no laughing matter when they were going through them. Joe recalled the time in his own experience when, he says, one of Sidney's bankers could have taken everything he had and set him out into the street – but he didn't.

Joe usually did his business at Sidney's other bank, but in this case he had borrowed eleven hundred dollars from an individual who later sold the note to the bank. The note came due, and Joe had nothing with which to pay. He walked into the bank that morning feeling just about as cheerful as a man facing the hangman's noose. If it had been the bank where he customarily did his business, he might have hoped for leniency because of past satisfactory relationships, but this was the competing bank.

The banker greeted him and asked, "What can I do for you, Joe?" (Everyone in town was acquainted with everyone else). Joe's Irish optimism was hard pressed as he replied, "I sure hope you can do something. I have an eleven hundred dollar note due, and I don't have the money to pay it." The banker thought a moment. "Just what can you do?" he asked, "I can pay the interest," Joe replied. It seemed to him that his future was hanging in the balance. Then, without any further discussion, the banker reached for a blank and made out another note.

Borrowing and lending practices were different in pioneer days, Mr. Kelly reflected. Everyone knew everyone else and their reputations, too, so security was seldom expected for a loan. He recalled another time he needed some extra cash to tide him over and figured he could get it from a man at the courthouse so he went to see him. When he got to the courthouse he found the object of his call talking with a couple of the women employees.

He didn't feel that he wanted to make a public announcement regarding the purpose of his visit so he asked the fellow if he could talk to him, to which the fellow replied, "Well, you're talking, aren't you?" He finally got the idea across that he wanted to talk privately so the prospective lender joined him in a corner, and Joe explained his mission. Money-man promptly wrote out a check for $500, the desired amount, and handed it to him. "But – aren't you going to make out a note or something?" Joe asked him. "You're going to pay it back, aren't you?" "Well of course!" "Then what do I want with a note?"

In his younger days, when eastern Montana was still largely ranch country, Joe worked on ranches a good deal and rode in many roundups. One year as they were gathering cattle on Burns Creek, he and a couple other cowboys spotted a pack of wolves, so for a few hours they let themselves be sidetracked from the business of collecting cattle and concentrated on wolves.

They chased the pack until they succeeded in getting one wolf cut out. After running about two hours, the wolf, tongue hanging out and thoroughly fagged, dodged into a plum thicket. You can't very well rope a wolf in a plum thicket so Johnny suggested to Joe, "You go in and run him out." The wolf may have been on the verge of exhaustion, but Joe wasn't interested in getting chummy with him in a plum thicket and told Johnny he could have the privilege himself. Put that way, the idea didn't sound so good to Johnny either. After considerable maneuvering they managed to get the wolf back out into the open where they could rope him so they killed him and skinned him and turned in the hide for a $10 bounty.

On Ren Mathew's spread the cook (at the house, not on the roundup wagon) was very much interested in seeing a rattlesnake, so one morning when Matt Obergfell found one in the course of his riding he captured it and took it along to the house. He carried that rattler all the way home on his saddle horse and when he went in for dinner, carried it into the kitchen to display his prize.

Right then the cook discovered she just thought she wanted to see a rattler. Joe sententiously concluded, "Dinner was just about ready, but what wasn't we had to finish ourselves."

Joe knows old timers from one end of the county to the other – and beyond, so as he was thinking of old times he was naturally reminded of the old timers and some of the stories connected with them. A stockman would think of Glendive's stockyards, the only shipping yards in the area and of course, Hank Neuman. According to Mr. Kelly, someone asked Hank, "What would you do if you'd freeze your nose?" and Hank's answer was, "I'd rub snow on it as far as I could reach and throw snowballs at the rest."

Any cowboy around eastern Montana at the turn of the century knew about Floyd Davis and his prowess as a rider. Joe summed up his riding reputation with a sentence. "Any horse that bucked Floyd Davis off, the other fellows stayed off!"

Recently Joe met Mrs. Hedley Robinson, but Mrs. Robinson didn't recognize him until he told her, "You used to sell me candy at Douglas-Meade years ago." Mrs. Robinson took another look and decided, "You must be one of those Kelly kids."

Pioneers in the Sidney area would remember ranchers Meadors and Kemmis, two of lower Yellowstone Valley's earliest settlers. Mr. Kelly recalls that as a boy living at the Fort, he looked forward to the marketing trips of these gentlemen. They would bring eggs, butter, and cream to deliver to the soldiers there, and as they made their rounds, some of the Kelly boys would invariably be in the buggy, enjoying the ride. And wouldn't a boy or girl of today enjoy it, too?

Mr. Kelly still enjoys visiting with friends, new and old. Recently he spent a few days in the hospital with plural pneumonia, but he's up and around again, always ready with a greeting and his friendly Irish grin.

Frank W. Kinney & Sons – Harold & Red

March – April 1965

Horace F. 'Red' Kinney was one of the names on our list of old timers for many months, but this 'old time' winter kept him so busy with cattle and like work that he just couldn't seem to find time for a visit.

Two weeks to the day before the day of his death a conversation with his wife disclosed that he was busy as ever, and the roads were blocked most of the time besides. (Their children had been staying with 'Grandma' Kennedy in Glendive so they could get to school).

No choice, it seemed, but to wait for spring. But the Grim Reaper doesn't consult our time schedule, and on February 19, 1965 Red Kinney very suddenly departed this life as a result of a heart attack while he was feeding cattle.

Brought here from his Idaho home by the sad occasion, Red's older brother Harold graciously shared his reminiscence as Red's passing brought back a flood of memories.

Their father, Frank Kinney, came to Montana from Amboy, Minnesota, in 1881. Some of Montana's early settlers came to the new country with money to invest, but when Frank Kinney landed in Glendive, his material resources consisted of a ten-dollar bill (borrowed money) and an extra pair of socks. He came as far as he could on the railroad – the Northern Pacific tracks reached Wibaux that spring of 1881 – then horse power brought him on to Glendive. At Wibaux he was greeted by the sight of buffalo hides, stacked as high as a man could reach, piled for a quarter of a mile along each side of the railroad track.

Kinney's first meal in Glendive was, to him, a memorable one. When he sat down at the counter in a restaurant, a big, red-faced fellow who was hashing came over to him, planted his hands on the counter, thrust his face close to Kinney's and barked, "What'll you have – beef or buffalo?"

Kinney's first job in Glendive was in the new brickyard. He seemed to just naturally gravitate toward horses, though, and much of his activity was on ranches in the area, punching cattle and breaking horses. He began his career on a cattle ranch by working for Charles Krug, and later worked five years for the Griffin Brothers.

One spring while riding for Griffin they found some horses that had strayed from the Wibaux Ranch. A twenty-five dollar reward was offered for their return, and he undertook to deliver them. He thought it would be just twenty-five miles, but when he reached the ranch, Mr. Wibaux was gone and the horses had to be taken to their camp down on the Little Missouri.

By the time he got back, he had ridden two hundred miles instead of fifty for the round trip. A light snow had fallen and the sun shone so dazzlingly on the snow that by the time he delivered the horses he was snow blind, a most painful experience. The Kinneys still have the twenty-four-page letter, written in the 1880's, which he wrote home, describing those events.

54

While he worked for DeMores, at Medora, it was Kinney's lot to ride with Teddy Roosevelt on the roundup. Years later after Kinney had a family, Roosevelt came through Glendive and made a train stop. Kinney himself was unable to get to the train (he had heard that Roosevelt never forgot a face so he'd have liked to meet him again), but son Harold had the privilege of shaking hands with the distinguished visitor.

Kinney helped wage war on coyotes. One winter day as he rode down the river he found two that he had poisoned, but it was so bitterly cold he didn't take time to skin them; he just tied them on his horse and started back to camp. On the way he met some Indians. The Indians couldn't talk much English, but they finally made Kinney understand that they would skin the coyotes if they could have the meat. Kinney was more than happy to make the deal.

Kinney was great at saving his money – didn't drink or squander his money – so he hadn't been here many years before he decided he was ready to start his own herd of cattle. The idea was sound, but the time was wrong; he came through the winter of 1886 with one lone buckskin cow, and that spring she fell through the ice and drowned. Next he tried sheep, but another hard winter cleaned him out again so he turned to horses, running them on the present Charlie Frizzle place. In 1887 he began working for the ferry company at Glendive and three years later he bought the interest of the owners and ran the ferry until the bridge was built. He ran it again later when the bridge washed out. However, he continued raising horses and became one of the leading horse breeders in eastern Montana, owning as many as five hundred head at a time. He specialized in Percherons and accumulated a fine bunch of blooded stock.

While Kinney was in the west he kept in touch with the 'home folk', including visits to his parental home. So it was that he met the school ma'am at the Kinney School back in Minnesota and in 1895 he married her. They returned to Glendive to make their home. After a few years they bought the '71' Ranch, five miles straight west of Glendive, from Jimmy Livingstone.

Buying a ranch at that time usually didn't include buying the land because in all probability it didn't include much land. Instead he just chose the location he wanted, put up the buildings he considered necessary, and let his stock range over the countryside. So when Kinney bought the ranch, he actually bought the improvements and used the land.

When the Homestead Act came into effect, Kinney filed on his 'own' ranch. Later he bought and leased additional land so that at one time he had as much as seven sections. The Kinneys also owned considerable Glendive property, including their winter home.

By the time the Kinneys moved to the ranch in 1902 they had three children, a girl and two boys. Baby Horace (Red) made the trip in his basket. There were two log houses, connected by a porch or a breezeway, on the ranch when they bought it so they lived in these until 1911 when they built the present ranch house.

These log houses had dirt roofs. To keep the water from soaking through during a rain they stretched a heavy canvas under the dirt roof for a ceiling.

They usually spent their winters in town, but pack rats spent their winters at the ranch so each spring when the family was ready to move out, they'd have to remove the stones and cacti and other odd objects the rats had stowed away between the canvas and the roof and tack up the canvas again.

Another annual spring job was the filling of cracks between the logs. A mixture of lime and sand with water was used to plaster the cracks on the inside, gumbo* and water to 'chink' the cracks on the outside.

At best that canvas-covered roof was none too good, and at worst – well, they had a long, oil cloth-covered table that would seat about thirty people; at worst they moved their beds under the table to sleep to keep the rain off themselves. At the other extreme if they slammed the door too hard it was dirt that fell.

In the spring of 1908, so much snow was dumped on the dirt roof of their ranch house by a late snowstorm that Harold and Red had to shovel it off before it started to melt so it wouldn't leak through. When they had completed their job, they jumped down into the snow bank and sank in so far they couldn't get out until the hired man heard their yells and came to their rescue.

In 1911 they replaced the log house with a ten-room cement block house, from blocks made on the ranch. They also built a new 40'x100' barn, the lower part of cement, the upper of lumber. They bought a water tank and pump from Lowe Brothers and piped water into the yard but not into the house.

About that same time they planted some apple trees (which still bear fruit) and some strawberries. When the latter were growing nicely, Kinney sent a couple cowhands to hoe the strawberries. After they had the plants all hoed out they asked Kinney, "Which trees do the strawberries grow on?"

One year a flash flood sent the water rushing down with such force that it took all the topsoil, as deep as it had been plowed, from the potato patch and washed out all their potatoes. The water rose so high that after the flood they picked potatoes off the vines right out of the trees.

During the spring break-up on the Yellowstone one year they saw a horse coming down the river on an ice cake. When the ice jammed near Sawyer's Island, Kinney and another man took an axe for chopping the horse loose and some oats to coax him to be led and rescued him from his icy confines.

At one end of the ranch house porch was a room used to store feed and at the other end was a room for parking buggies. During the winter while the Kinneys were living in town, the long-horned range cattle would 'take over' at the ranch. To find shelter from the cold they would crowd onto that porch and as they crowded, push into those end rooms. That meant that each spring there was repairing and cleaning to be done on the porch and even removing frozen cattle.

Some of those Texas longhorns had such a wide horn spread that they had to tip their heads to get through a stock car door. They were notorious fence climbers. The most effective way to keep them from going through a fence was to hang a tin can containing several rocks to the wire so they'd 'spook' when they heard the rattle. Harold recalls when the CK outfit rounded up all their

56

longhorns and threw them together at the old 'Lemmly Camp' before starting the trail to the Big Dry* because of the lack of open range here.

Life was anything but dull on a ranch where there were three lively children – especially when two of them were boys. Red's earliest interest pointed to a career as a rider and all-around rodeo man. If his parents were considering it at all, they would have considered him too small when he decided to start his career (he probably wasn't a day over three years) but Red didn't consult them.

A cowboy had tied his saddle horse to the corral fence, and Red somehow managed to loosen him and clamber aboard. The first his mother noticed his activities was when she saw him gallop past the house to the tune of a triumphant shout, "I've got him alopin'," while he kept time with the quirt. His mother just about had a heart attack then and there, but she lost no time getting to the spring, whence the miniature cowboy had taken his steed for water, and jerking him from the saddle.

He wasn't very much older – hadn't started to school yet – when he roped his first calf. He probably would have fared all right if he had been content to just rope the calf, but for some reason he tied the other end of the rope around his own middle. As could be expected, the calf took off, and Red had no choice but to take off with him.

Around the house they went, Red stretching his steps as long as he could stretch, bouncing along behind that calf, when one of the older members of the family noticed his plight. His mother and Agnes and Harold immediately gave chase and managed to catch the calf the fourth or fifth time around the house and released the budding roper.

It was about that same time that he decided to go to work for the CK outfit. The CK's roundup wagon was camped by a spring near their place so Mrs. Kinney and the children visited the camp. They were invited to stay for dinner, and the foreman jestingly asked little Red to work for him. Red quickly consented, but stipulated that he would have to go get his clothes first.

Sufficient to say that he never did join the crew, but after that when things didn't suit him at home, he'd run away to 'join the CK'. He never got more than a quarter of a mile from home, but he'd put some of his belongings in his little red wagon and start out. He was always careful to take his 'horses' along with him. To anyone else they might look like a bunch of sticks, but to Red each was an individual horse with an individual name: Shorty, Cricket, and Roany, to name a few – all 'minem horses'. When he'd decide to go, he'd carry as many as he could and the rest he would tie in a bundle and haul in his wagon.

When Red was a little fellow, their mother viewed with trepidation the approach of spring because she just never knew what to expect to find in Red's pockets when she'd undress him for bed. He'd stuff into his pockets anything from rocks to bugs, toads to water snakes.

The boys had a variety of pets on the ranch, including two toads. When they wanted the toads to come out of their holes, they'd sprinkle a little sugar on the ground nearby to attract flies, and as soon as the flies started collecting, the toads were out of their holes, catching their prey.

Their winter home in Glendive was located where Guelff's Lumber Yard* is now. One day a hobo came and asked for something to eat so Mrs. Kinney fixed him a sandwich. When she gave it to him, he started cursing and tried to get in. Mrs. Kinney couldn't get the screen door locked so she grabbed the broom and started wielding it. Then it was the hobo that tried to shut the door. Unnoticed by him, Mr. Kinney had driven up during the fracas. He reached the door in short order, grabbed that tramp by the collar and trouser seat, and pitched him over his shoulder. Harold reflected that to a small boy watching this was a mighty feat, and unmindful of the advantage that his dad, on ground level, had over the tramp on the step, his estimation of Dad's prowess soared immensely.

The boys early tried to imitate anything they saw the cowboys do, and of course, any cowboy should be able to rope so they started practicing. Anything they would find on a saddle or any place else, they'd 'borrow'. This could be inconvenient for the unintentional 'lender' so finally their dad bought a throw rope for each of them. These ropes were to be exclusively theirs, and they were to keep hands off other ropes.

Came a day when Arnold Holling, hauling hay for them, noticed his brake rope was missing (the boys were innocent this time) so he took one of theirs. They discovered it before he left, however, and recovered their property, so when Arnold had gone some distance and started down a hill, he found himself without a brake. That could have been a calamity so Arnold came fuming back in a mood to thrash 'those kids', but since this was not within his jurisdiction, he insisted Kinney whip them.

This time, though, Mr. Kinney figured the youngsters were within their rights so he refused and Arnold quit. Arnold packed his clothes, but then Kinney soothingly protested, "Oh, you don't want to quit over a little thing like that." Holling finally relented and stayed on, but he wouldn't speak to the boys for three or four days.... He quit several times on account of the boys during the twenty years that he worked for Kinney, but he never 'quit' long enough to get to town.

The two boys were great helpers, their mother (harassed woman!) discovered on numerous occasions. One of their jobs was gathering the eggs each day. They decided they'd surprise her sometime when she was ready to go to town by bringing her a whole bunch of eggs so they dug a hole about the size of an apple box, with which they covered it, and each time they gathered eggs they'd slip a few into this hole. Finally they accumulated a goodly number of eggs and decided one day (one very hot day) when their mother was ready to go to town that the time was ripe (unknown to them, so were the eggs) to 'spring' their surprise. They lifted the box off the cache, only to find that some hornets had made a nest under the box. Poor little Red, intercepting one of those piercing stingers, quite forgot to watch his step and fell right into the middle of that hole full of rotten eggs!

Corn shelling was another of their jobs; one they couldn't have liked less. They had an old wooden washing machine, and each Saturday they were supposed to shell enough corn to fill that tub. Who can think of a more tedious job than shelling corn? Two animated boys couldn't so one Saturday they decided on a short cut; they filled the bottom half of the tub with cobs, then finished filling it with the shelled corn. They escaped the drudgery, but all their activities were overshadowed by the certainty that they would inevitably be 'found out'. All went well the first few days, but about Wednesday, Mother got to the cobs – then the reckoning. They didn't try that dodge again.

Fruit was hard to 'come by' in those days so when there was a good crop of buffalo berries (which might not be more than once in three or four years) their mother canned all she could. She'd cook the berries, squeeze out the juice, and discard the pulp, canning gallons of the juice in a good year. Harold and Red threw the discarded pulp, a bright red, to the chickens and soon had them coming whenever they threw out something red.

The boys had some red firecrackers, which they had carefully hoarded since the Fourth of July, and they discovered that if they threw out some pulp, then a firecracker, the hens would grab the firecracker just as eagerly. A merry chase would follow with a dozen hens chasing the celebrated holder of the firecracker. Finally the firecracker would explode, and the boys would almost explode with hilarity at the ensuing squawking and dust raising. Their hilarity was abruptly quenched when their mother noticed the commotion and discovered what they were doing, fortunately before they blew a chicken's head off.

That wasn't their only adventure with fireworks. However innocent their intentions, they always seemed to precipitate some sort of cataclysm. One year they got hold of a device that would explode in a ball of fire when struck. One night after the boys had gone to bed they figured out that if they'd break the things in two their supply would last longer so they proceeded to break them.

They managed all right with the first few, but then one exploded – and another. Their mother came charging in to see what was happening, saw the balls of fire, and began beating them with the broom to extinguish the fire. The more she beat, the more they exploded until balls of fire were dancing all over the bed and all over the floor.

Another time when they were herding horses over on Seven Mile, they had some torpedoes that would explode when thrown. There were always a few mares that were hard to get started home so they'd toss one of these torpedoes behind them and the mares would start in a hurry.

Red was prepared to start them with three or four of these in his back pocket, and it was just about time to go home. While they waited, Red kept teasing until Harold lost his patience and as Red ran past, Harold gave him a kick. The torpedoes exploded, and for a while Red thought he had exploded, too, but it was soon evident that only his back pocket had been blown off.

Another of the boys' escapades involved their mother's prize gobbler. Her sister had sent them this registered gobbler (he weighed about forty pounds) but after a time he got mean, and every time the boys tried to go through the barn door, the gobbler would jump on them. That was rough on the boys. Finally they hit upon a plan to break him of the habit. They got hold of some 'soup', a concoction to smear on bucking horses before they left the chute to make sure they'd put on a good performance, then watched their chance.

The next time the gobbler jumped on one of the boys, they caught him and rubbed him thoroughly with the 'soup'. What a performance that gobbler did put on! As soon as they turned him loose he tried to gobble, but instead of gobbling he started turning somersets. He'd get himself straightened out and stretch his neck to start to gobble, only to start turning somersets again. By the time he got over the effects of the 'soup' he was a chastened gobbler, and that was the last time he jumped on one of the boys.

Loving brothers that they were, Harold and Red sometimes included sister Agnes in their fun. (Agnes was two years older than Harold; Harold two years older than Red.) So it was they let her go duck hunting with them. It wasn't a matter of shooting the ducks, but rather of capturing them alive from the pond about a mile and a half from the ranch house.

Though young, the ducks were able to do some flying, but when the youngsters surrounded the pond, the ducks submerged with just their bills sticking out. Those bills were enough to betray their whereabouts so the boys waded in after them and were able to catch three of them – but how to get them home?

The boys had ridden horseback, so they weren't about to try to take those ducks aboard with them and scare their horses. Agnes had walked, so for the privilege of going along with them, she was permitted to grab those wet, slippery, hard to carry ducks by the legs and lug them the mile and a half home.

They kept those ducks all summer and that fall entered them in the county fair. They won a prize, too, and were rewarded with a dollar and a half for the trouble of catching and caring for those ducks – and letting Agnes carry them home.

Agnes, as well as the boys, early took to the saddle, and she had her share of mishaps. The most serious occurred while she was riding alone. Her horse, Ginger, bucked her off and she broke her collarbone. With the bone broken she was unable to remount so, with no help at hand she had to walk home and lead her horse.

She fared a little better the time she was unseated in town. When her horse pitched and dislodged her from the saddle, he bucked right out from under her so she landed upright on her feet, just behind him, as though she might have been trying a circus trick. Nice to be able to land gracefully when there are spectators!

After high school Agnes taught country school for a while to pay her way through college. After college, she worked a number of years on the Minneapolis Tribune before moving to Seattle in 1941. There she lived until her death a little more than two years ago.

Educating the children required real effort on the part of Mrs. Kinney. She'd drive back and forth from the ranch for about two months in the fall and one in the spring, moving to Glendive during the winter months. They moved to town no less than seventeen times to get the children through school. The

60

commuting wasn't a matter of slipping into a comfortable, powerful car, and buzzing into town in a few minutes time. It meant driving a team and buggy, sometimes through mud, sometimes through dust.

One spring after they had moved out, the rains just kept coming until finally one morning the wheels sank so deeply into the mud that the bed of the buggy rested on the mud. The little team of Indian ponies which their mother was driving just couldn't cope with that kind of pulling so Mr. Kinney had to come with their Percherons. The big team had to be used from then on while the mud lasted.

One day when Kinney was taking them, they were a bit late starting and forgot to grease the buggy wheels. Coming up Surprise Mountain the wheels got so hot they locked, so Kinney scraped the butter off their sandwiches to grease the wheels and they were on their way again.

Their mother would get excited when things went wrong, but she'd manage to keep control – even the time one of the horses, switching his tail, caught the lines and pinched them under his tail. He kicked until he had kicked the leather dash out of the front of the buggy, but Mrs. Kinney held on until she had him quieted down again.

Harold's first day of school stands out yet in his memory. A blank had to be filled out for each child, stating birthday and nationality. Most of the children had a single nationality – Norwegian, Swede, Irish, what have you. But the Kinneys? They were a mixture of English, Irish, Scotch, and Holland Dutch! Naming that list seemed to him completely out of the question; he'd probably be branded for life. So he said he didn't know. The teacher gave him a note to take home, but he threw it away and next day told her he'd lost it. She gave him another so he threw that one away, too.

The third day the teacher told him "Just wait after school, and I'll go home with you." This was it! He just about sweat blood while he waited. Not only was the information to be obtained; he bid fair to be spanked for not bringing the notes. It was a long wait and a long walk home (they were living in town then). When his mother and the teacher met, they 'hit it off' so well they forgot all about him while they visited. Teacher remembered before she left, however, why she had come so, although he escaped punishment, the authorities did learn his nationality.

Neighboring Henrys kept their perishables in their well, and one morning the boys upset the butter into the water. They fished for it, without success, until they were almost late for school, then after school invited Harold to come along and help them retrieve it. They got the butter, but Harold almost fell into the well in the process.

In the Kinney's town house the chimney was in the boys' bedroom, and their bed was in front of the chimney, leaving a space between the bed and the wall. That night in his dreams he was fishing for that butter again and this time did 'fall in'. His shouts for help roused his dad, who came and pulled him out from between the bed and the wall.

In 1914, they bought their first car, a Ford. By that time Harold was old enough to learn to drive (he was the first one in the family to learn) so he drove it back and forth to high school. One morning he had backed it out, then left it parked toward the barn while he got out to shut the gate. His dad got into it and drove it right into the side of the barn before he got it stopped. The only damage to the car was a bent crank so they straightened that with a crow bar and went on their way.

Agnes damaged it more thoroughly when she was learning to drive. Driving along a narrow road, she came up behind a fellow driving a high-wheeled wagon. She honked the horn, but he wouldn't give way so she rammed into the back of the wagon and knocked a hole in the Ford's radiator.

Cars were still rare and very much a curiosity so there were many interested, both in driving it and riding in it. When Harold tried to teach Ruth Swanson to drive (out of town, where there was plenty of room), she was wearing a big, wide-brimmed hat. About the time they turned the first corner, the wind caught her hat so she grabbed for the hat and forgot about the steering wheel.

The car veered from the lane, mowing down some fence posts before they got it straightened out again. The Winkler girls, whose dad owned the Ford agency, knew some 'tricks of the trade' and gave him a bad time by using a hairpin for a key and 'swiping' the Ford while he was in school. When he'd come out of the schoolhouse, ready to go home, he'd find no car.

When Harold was in high school the furnace was fueled with coal and the ashes dumped in the back yard. When another student kept pestering him, Harold finally grabbed him and held him over the hot ashes which the janitor had just dumped. The fellow struggled and kicked so hard Harold couldn't hold him and was forced to drop him – onto that hot ash pile. He fairly bounced, then tore across the yard to the outside sink to cool off. Harold had no further trouble with him,

Harold's temper was prone to flare quickly, but the time he knocked Red cold was a turning point. He thought he had killed him and hurriedly summoned his mother. They soon restored Red to consciousness, but that night Harold dreamed he really had killed him and woke up 'bawling and crying', to use his words, and it was some time before they could convince him that Red was still alive. That experience was enough. Clearly, fighting was just no good. How easy it would be to put out someone's eye, for instance, or worse still, even kill him, as he thought he had done. Then and there he made up his mind that from that time on he was going to hold that temper.

If losing his temper didn't pay, neither, he concluded, did 'showing off'. One summer afternoon Agnes was entertaining some girls on the porch when he rode in from the range. Mindful of spectators, he galloped up to the gate, stopped his horse with a few stiff-legged jumps, and sprang from the saddle. Unfortunately, his chaps* were new and stiff, and his stirrup bolt was a little too long.

The chaps caught on the bolt, and his horse took off, dragging Harold across the sagebrush and kicking at him with every jump. The stirrup finally turned and the chaps unhooked, releasing him, just about the time he was in front of the porch. The clothes on his back were pretty well in tatters from the rough 'sledding' and the alacrity with which he had jumped from the saddle was conspicuous by its absence as he got to his feet after that demonstration, resolving, "No more showing off!"

They had a snow white horse named Stockings, and one spring day while Kinney and the hired man, Elias Bamber, were working around the buildings, a fellow came riding in on that same white horse. He asked for a match, then after some exchange of small talk, Kinney asked where he got the horse. Fellow claimed he bought him in Ekalaka.

Kinney's horses ranged from the home ranch to points as far as Terry, Circle, and Savage, with some straying farther, but that didn't give anyone license to appropriate them, so Kinney requested that he leave the horse in the barn. There was a pick handle leaning against the side of the house, and when Elias saw that the discussion was waxing hot, he began edging toward that handle. By the time their visitor started to reach for his back pocket (they didn't know if he was packing a gun or not) Elias was able to grab the pick handle, and the stranger's hand came back empty.

He left the horse in the barn and left his saddle, too, for the simple reason it was too heavy to carry sans a horse, and started down the road with his bridle over his arm. Elias started for the sheriff, but he didn't have to go far; the sheriff was already on the way. The rider of the white horse had galloped his steed across the Yellowstone Bridge, and that was against the law, so the sheriff was on his trail. He was apprehended and sentenced to three years in the penitentiary for horse stealing.

Among their hundreds of horses there were certain to be a few oddities. They had one horse that actually sat down to graze. His back legs would stick straight out in front of him, while with his front feet he'd work himself around in a circle until he had the grass all eaten, then he'd move to another spot and 'sit down' again. He had the hair all worn off the top of his tail.

They had only one pair of twin colts, and only one colt was pure white at birth. Two white mares each had manes that dragged on the ground. Each spring after they'd round up the horses, they'd comb out those 'witch's tails'. When they found one of the mares with her mane hooked over a fence post so she couldn't get loose, they decided it was time to cut both manes.

When the mother of one little colt died, four geldings (former colts of the same mare) took charge of it. They'd push that orphan to a mare that another colt was sucking and make her let it feed, too — or else. Those four geldings raised that colt that way.

One spring their stock got the 'itch'. The only cure seemed to be a mixture of kerosene, sulfur, and lard, liberally applied with a broom. Unfortunately, human beings could get it, too, and Harold did, from working with the stock. He began to find out what a miserable time the cattle must be having! The doctor gave him some ointment to rub on himself, but it didn't help any.

Finally in desperation, Harold decided to use the remedy that worked for the stock. He applied a generous layer all over himself, then put on some long woolen underwear so the stuff would stay put. He was hot, and the fumes burned his eyes, but it worked on the stock and it worked on him; he had no more trouble with the itch.

If there was one thing their folks tried to drill into them, it was that they should tell the truth. They might accidentally kill a horse or a calf or break a window, but tell the truth about it and they wouldn't be punished. One day while Harold was fishing with Bill Dion at Intake, Scribers caught a fish, the likes of which none of them had ever seen. They tied the huge catch onto the side of their Model T to bring it home, and the snout hung over the fender while the tail dragged behind. When Harold got home he excitedly reported Scriber's catch to his dad, but Dad was unimpressed. He merely cautioned, "Now don't tell a lie!" Harold insisted, but Kinney reminded him, "I've run the ferry across that river three different times" (probably seven or eight seasons, altogether); "I've fished that river all summer long and I know there is no such thing in it!"

Harold was hurt that his dad would so flatly reject his story, even though it was a fish story and without precedent, and determined to catch a fish like it to produce as proof. He offered Bill $5 to take him to Intake, but halfway there they remembered they had to play baseball so they had to come back. He didn't catch a paddlefish, and his dad passed away before the recent influx so he never did get to prove that his 'fish story' was true.

Mr. Kinney remained active, herding sheep, riding horseback, riding for the cattle, almost until his death. The horse he rode, Dinky, could be turned loose any place, and he'd wait for his rider. One afternoon, though, when Kinney had gone after cows, Dinky came home without him. Red found his father by Spring Coulee, where he had had a stroke, and carried him in. After that he lived in town with Harold for a short time, but he passed away in January 1942.

It was Kinney's practice to give a mare and colt to each of his children at birth. Harold's first colt was named Wildfire. He was a small horse – only weighed about 700 lb. – but tough enough that a grown man could ride him all day. He was so well trained at rounding up horses that he didn't have to be guided. He'd head for the highest hill, look until he'd spot some horses, then gallop to them. If the horses stood still, Wildfire would slow down to give his rider a chance to look them over, but if they started to run, Wildfire was after them until his rider could check them. About three o'clock in the afternoon, though, he'd head for home, and then you needed a bridle!

He never did get over the disconcerting practice of unseating his rider when he got the notion. When he was twenty-three years old, Harold had ridden into town and Wildfire caught his foot in some chicken wire. He started to pitch, and deposited Harold on the ground. It seemed that Harold was always getting caught off guard so he decided to show Wildfire he could ride him. He remounted, quirt in hand, and dug in his spurs. Off he went again! This time he climbed on, grimly determined nothing would dislodge him — and Wildfire trotted off home.

Quite the last straw, Harold figured, was the time Wildfire sent him 'spread-eagling' into a gooseberry bush. He had ridden into a clump of plum trees, but the ripe plums were all in the tops of the trees so he stood up in his saddle and stretched to reach those plums. His horse took a step. Harold lost his balance, and before he could get 'set' in the saddle, Wildfire started to buck. At the first jump the saddle horn gouged him below the belt and made a furrow all the way to his neck as he sailed through the air.

As Wildfire left the grove Harold extracted himself from the gooseberry bush, grabbed a big ash club, and followed; this time he was going to kill that horse. When he emerged from the grove Wildfire was meekly standing there waiting for him and even whinnied softly at his approach. Harold threw the club away and rode on home. He speculated that he's probably been bucked off on every hill between Glendive and the ranch!

Both boys, as soon as they were old enough (maybe sooner) followed rodeos, and three different years Red had his own show, traveling with it through North Dakota, Minnesota, and Wisconsin, presenting two shows a day. A special feature was Red's Roman Team. With one foot on the back of one horse and one foot on the back of the other horse, he'd ride, standing up, at a full gallop.

Nowadays you might hear people complain about unexpected company just at dinner time, but Mrs. Kinney took that in stride. Harold says he recalls more than once when his mother had the table set for dinner that a bunch rode in, and by the time they sat down to the table there'd be fifteen or twenty people to be fed. Sometimes they fed them horse meat, although they always tried to have other meat too, if they knew someone else was going to be there. They never killed a horse just for eating but when one of their young horses broke a leg they tried a hind quarter and found it made good eating.

One Sunday some friends dropped in just as they were ready to eat, and the only meat they had prepared was — horse meat. During the meal the guests asked what kind of meat they were eating, but the host tactfully evaded the issue (some folks might be squeamish).

The next time the friends dropped in, again the only meat on the menu was horse meat. The Kinneys asked how they had liked the meat last time, then explained, "We always try to have some other kind of meat when we know we're having company, but you ate horse meat." They asked, "What kind do you have today?" "Horse meat," was the reply. "Let's go eat!"

Harold with his family moved to Idaho about four years ago. His mother died in 1930 so Red's recent passing leaves Harold the only living member of the family of pioneer Frank W. Kinney.

Following is a letter written about eighty years ago by Frank Kinney, Montana pioneer, to his mother in Minnesota (his father had passed away earlier).

Dear Mother and all,

I received your letter some time ago and was out in the badlands and the opportunities were rather poor for writing. I am very happy to hear of your gaining and only hope it may continue and hope you will be careful not to over do yourself.

We are having some nice rains now and grass is growing fine. Frank Griffin is rebuilding. I done most all of the chopping. We went back in the hills where there was some pines about 6 miles. Took our tent and grubstake and I stayed, done the chopping and he hauled home. I did all the hewing, the first I ever done. The house is 12 × 36, divided in three rooms and a bedroom on one side 9 × 12 and are busy to get it done before the roundup, which begins the first of June.

Suppose the boys are about planting corn by this time. Will have to tell you of the long ride I had the first of March. There was 5 head of western horses that were shipped in here last fall and were taken down on the Little Missouri about fifty miles from the RR track, got away and strayed back this way and I found them (or rather F.G.) and as there was $25 reward offered for them, thought I would undertake to deliver them. But I supposed I had to take them only about 25 miles from here. So I caught the best horse in the lot I have to ride. Frank was with me the first half day and he left me after we had got about half way and pulled for home and I kept on across the country keeping my direction the best I could but as the day was kind of hazy and there being no road I soon lost sight of the 'Camels hump' (or the Blue Mountain) and had to go by guess and my horses were wild and I had to drive them on the run most of the time to get them where I wanted them.

About 5 o'clock I struck the creek where the home ranch was but about 10 miles too high up so I headed them down the creek on a good round trot and hardly let them stop until I came up to the ranch where I expected to get rid of my horses. But on going in I found no one home but the man's wife and servants. As he is quite wealthy he lives in a fine house and she keeps one girl to cook and one to look after family affairs but they have only one child, and that is less than one year old and an old Frenchman to look after the wood and a few chores around the barn. The men folks stay down at the lower ranch some 50 miles from there. Mr. Wibaux, the owner of the stock, was down below to spend a couple of weeks and as they had so little hay the woman (Note: This would have been Mrs. Wibaux) did not want to take the horses and so I was in a fine pickle. But after hard thinking, concluded to start below in the morning. So went out to corral the horses and after running them for half an hour succeeded in getting them in.

After taking care of my horse with the help of the old Frenchman we went to the house and I was taken into the kitchen and allowed the same fare as the servants. As it was after supper hour I was given an abundance of fried potatoes and venison, bread and coffee. It was served on a rude table without table cloth, and a bench to sit on. And the most interesting part of it was neither the old man or the cook could understand a word of English. But the serving maid could talk a little but she was in but little. When supper was over the old man beckoned for me to follow and we went up stairs.

He began to strip his linen for bed and so I followed suit. As I was tired from my long ride I was soon fast asleep and was awakened by the crowing of a rooster about ten feet from our bed. The old Frenchman had taken in some frozen-toed chickens and one of them was reminding us of morn.

As I was in somewhat of a hurry I was the first one out and as soon as I got breakfast was off. The servant had a big time trying to find out if I wanted a lunch and some oats to take for my saddle horse. Two of them could not understand white man's talk and the other but little and I guess if it had not been for Mrs. Wibaux we would have been jabbering back and forth now. That was the first private house that I ever stayed that the work folks had to eat in the kitchen and I was with the W.F. But as anything goes I did not complain.

I got started about 8 o'clock and had 50 miles before me. Most of the way there was but little trail and there had been three or four inches of light snow, but the morning was bright and I started with the intention of driving all the way through in one day. I knew the first 10 miles but after that had never been over the trail. The snow was kind of frosty and the sun sparkled so it hurt my eyes considerable and before noon they were giving me some pain. As near noon as I could guess I stopped to let my horse graze and to eat my lunch. By this time I had made about 20 miles. The trail was dimmer all the time. After giving them half of an hour's rest I saddled up and started. Felt quite sure of getting through that night but soon came to forks in the road and then I was bothered to decide which one to take. Finally took the wrong one, of course.

It was now about 2 o'clock and the sky began to cloud over and soon shut me into a circle of about one mile with myself in the middle and the only moving object. I got on well till I came to a Prairie Dog town and lost the trail as the dogs always keep the grass all eaten off — had a hard time to find it.

But after half hours circling found where it left and you can hardly realize how I made those broncos throw snowballs as it was thawing a little. But soon came into the badlands and had to go slower as the north hillsides were a perfect sheet of ice and this light snow had covered it up and made it all the worse. As my horse was barefoot had to be very careful or I would find myself and horse down in some little coulee where I would be likely to stay.

After winding around through the hills for two hours or more I began to find cattle so with the hopes of soon striking the river, 'The Little Missouri River', I hurried on.

Now I had got down into the bottom of the coulee that was from four to ten rods wide and pretty good going and when the sun was about an hour high as it showed through the clouds once in awhile so I could tell the direction I was going to some extent I came in sight of some timber and thought it a little strange as I had not calculated I could make the ranch before dark at best. On coming into the timber to my surprise found it was the Beaver Creek, the same I left in the morning, but I thought it must be a small creek on which Wibaux was located and soon came to a broke road and looked down the creek.

I could see some men working on a house then I felt sure it was the right place as I knew they were building. Until I had got clear up to the shack builders and all of the faces were strange did I begin to realize but what I had got to my journey's end.

When one Howard Eaton came out of the shack and shook hands did I fully know where I really had strayed. Had met him in the spring and fall roundup and had been to this very shack. It all came to me so sudden I never was so surprised in my life as then. Of course as one of my horses had a bell on they thought they were stray horses and asked whose they were so I told them, and where I wanted to go. Never once let on that I had been such a long way round. I had made 30 miles down the creek and probably had traveled over 40. So Mr. Eaton proposed I go down and stay with him five miles further on at the mouth of the Beaver on the L.M.R. (Little Missouri River) as he had good corrals and plenty of hay and at this ranch there was neither. It belonged to his brother Charley Eaton and he had come up to help on the house with his man.

They turned in and helped me down and I was very thankful to have them as my horse was getting very tired and I did not feel very fresh myself. We got them down and corralled with but little trouble. I believe I was as tired that night as I ever was and when supper was over as there was lots of papers handy thought I would read a little but my eyes would not admit of it so I took a back seat and held my face till bedtime. Even then did not bring relief and till long into the night did I get to sleep.

But morning came soon enough when I got to sleep. We got up in good season and when breakfast was over I asked Mr. Eaton what my bill was and he told me it was $22.50. I noticed some of the bystanders direct their attention to me to see how I would bite at it. I remarked as dryly as I could that I thought that very reasonable and if it ever came in my way, would be glad to accommodate him. He remarked that I was perfectly welcome and to stop on my way back. I thanked him for his hospitality and but a few weeks ago we had the satisfaction of being the cause of his men finding two of his horses. They came along and Frank dropped him a line and made mention of it in Glendive. He probably thinks he has got pay for keeping the poor tramp of a cowboy.

But now back to the broncs. The morning was pretty frosty and the sun was pretty bright. The worst kind of a day for snow blindness. But again luck was on my side. There was a cowboy up from a ranch a few miles below the one I was going to. There is no wagon road down the river from here and but a poor bridle trail in the summer and still more treacherous in the winter. He was mounted on a small mule and shod so he had considerable the advantage of me as safety from slipping down the hillsides.

We got on well for about one third of the way and we lost the trail he had made the day before, it being the only track made since the snow. Finally we brought up out on a high point that over looked a large scope of the worst kind of badlands.

We had calculated to make to a high table land but a big coulee had swung round to our front and completely headed us off. So we had to back track. To shorten our way back on to the river bottom we picked our way down through a cedar thicket. As they grow on the north and east sides of the buttes there was some snow but not ice. After we got on to the river we were content to pick our way through the brush consisting of willow, ash, bullberries, and rose bushes for a couple of miles and then we came to a trail that led across the hills and cut off a big bend in the river.

Where we struck the river it was at an old Indian camp now vacated with the exception of an old Frenchman hunting for a living. His only companion was his horse and dog. The broncs got scared at the sight of a man on foot and made a dash up an icy hillside. Was too slippery for me to ride so had to tie and head back afoot.

Before they got back to the trail they had several falls. At one time three of them were in one pile and if they had been any but wild bronchoes half of them would have come out with broken legs or crooked necks. My partner had to stop and beg a chew of tobacco but soon joined me and all went lovely so far as horse driving was concerned but my eyes felt as though they'd burst. We reached camp about 2 o'clock and a happier mortal never lived. We corralled the horses and stabled our own with the aid of the boys at the ranch who were glad to see them come back. After a short chat we were to go in and the boys got us dinner after which our 'or rather my' friend and helper bid us good day.

The afternoon went quick and as one of my eyes had to have a handkerchief over it to quiet it now I had to hold my hand over it and then it seemed as though it would jump between my fingers. The evening was long but bedtime came at last and I thought it would bring me relief. But instead it seemed as everything got quiet it just got ready to ache and it gave the other one an invitation to join which it willing did. I think that night was the longest one I ever experienced. But I held it all to myself without a murmur and was almost morning when I fell asleep.

"Having one's girl go back on them was nothing in the way of tears. I think I shed a thousand to one. For the next morning my coat that I had for a pillow was wet with tears." When I got up and it got fairly daylight, I found it would be impossible for me to trail that day for to step out doors it would send sharp pains darting through my eyes that would almost stagger one. But as my horse was getting pretty well worn out did not care to start til the next morning anyway. So I laid my case before the house and the boys rustled out their goggles and one had some smoked glass ones that he offered which I thankfully received and kept them on all day out doors or in and by night they felt quite easy.

By the next morning felt quite comfortable but would not stand sunlight. But I had made up my mind to go so with the goggled eyes I got ready. When almost ready to start Mr. Wibaux said if I would wait for him to get ready he would go up with me. I was only too glad to wait and about seven o'clock we pulled out for his home ranch, by the ridge road over fifty miles and not a ranch on it. He had two horses, led one and rode the other and changed every 12 or 15 miles. I expected to get left on the trail, but my horse being one of the best of its kind that I ever saw, stayed with the Frenchman to the end which we found about four o'clock making the ride in about 8 hours for we stopped and let our horses graze at noon. After caring for our horses we went to the house and a supper was soon served. But in quite a different style. Instead of benches and cook table and servants it was filled with easy chairs, nice tables, china dishes, and everything to compare. But I must say the change was so great that I felt a little awkward.

Of course my former reception was all right. I could not expect one in her situation to do anything different, I being a perfect stranger and making no other pretentions than a cowboy. One could see on entering that the house was furnished to a different taste than a 'simon pure' American. One of the oddities was a fire place but as this is out of line will not bother you with more.

When bedtime came I was shown to a well furnished room where I had the best night's rest I had had since starting from home. That was some difference from the stubby little Frenchman's that slept with his cap on and bed about a foot too short and a hen coop to perfume the room. As soon as breakfast was over Mr. Wibaux settled with me and thanking him for his kindness I saddled up and directed my horse 'which started off as nimble as ever' through the hills for home some 30 miles due west.

When I left Frank the Thursday before had made arrangements to meet him the next Saturday at noon at a ranch about one mile back from where we separated, so I stopped to learn that he had made his round and was quite anxious to find out what had become of me. We were going to look up some cattle and take back on to our range. But he had to return without any satisfaction, and the next day but one was back again and heard from someone that had been there that Wibaux had gone below so he returned to await my coming, thinking that perhaps I had to take the horse down. It was dinner time when I got there so when dinner was over and I got back into the saddle it was quite a consolation to think that this afternoon's ride would bring me home. Just as the twilight was fading I brought up at our ranch, thankful that the ride was over.

(And if you blunder and stumble in reading this as I have in writing I think you will be lamer than I was over the long ride of most 200 miles.) This being my first attempt will please escuse. (Note: At this point Mr. Kinney drew a picture of a long-horned steer and inscribed it 'Headed Off').

Sunday, May 23 — I calculate to start on the roundup one week from tomorrow. We have more territory to work over this year than last and at the best will take about six weeks. The wolves are killing some calves. Frank and his wife were out riding on the range today and found one little calf badly torn with the wolves but not *dead yet. That makes four we have found this spring that we charge up to wolves, more than all we have found before.*

As it is getting late will close for now. I think for so long a letter as this you had ought some of you to send me a letter every day for the next two months.

Wishing you all good health through these hot days, will close.

From your affectionate son,

F.W.K

Frank Kinney Ranch Barn, 110' x 40' x 40'

The Kinney Ferry in the Yellowstone River at Glendive

Frank & Ella Kinney

Little Red Kinney in typical dress

Red Kinney standing on horses

Red Kinney and the Big Barn

Mrs. John (Meta Hafele) Sura

February – March 1969

Aloysius Hafele was no farmer, but the lure of free land and his brother-in-law's urging persuaded him he could be one so in the spring of 1909 he loaded his family onto the Northern Pacific train and headed for Montana. His family and their clothes were all he brought. Since they had lived in town (Worthington, Minnesota) they had no machinery or equipment so all they had to sell was their household furnishings and they were ready to move.

Pete Russ had brought his wife (Hafele's sister) and only daughter, Florence (now Mrs. Mike Guelff) to Montana in 1906, and it was his influence that brought the Hafeles. He met them at Beach with team and buggy when they came and took them to his home. The 'women folk' – Mrs. Hafele and the two girls, Meta and Gertrude – stayed with the Russ family until a homestead site could be selected and some kind of shelter erected on it.

Meta was of school age when they made the move to the Treasure State so she continued her schooling at Yates while they waited to move to the homestead. The Yates School at that time was held in a little shack, but it was school nevertheless.

By the end of May a combination barn and granary had been put up on the homestead southwest of Glendive – many miles from Yates. No house was built yet; the plan was to live in the granary end of the building temporarily so Mrs. Hafele and the girls moved to the homestead. That first summer while they lived in the granary end of the building, the livestock lived on the other side of the partition. That arrangement is common enough in Europe, but not so general in the United States. The Hafeles weren't very enthusiastic about it (those flies!) but they endured it as an emergency measure. When you have to 'start from scratch' – when there's absolutely nothing and you have to do everything, the necessary has to wait for the imperative.

1909 was a year of ample rainfall, and the newcomers – the two girls, anyway, were thrilled with the oceans of flowers that spring. The grass was a lush green carpet and flowers bloomed everywhere. Although there was plenty of rain it didn't mean a crop for them that first year. In the first place, Mr. Hafele just didn't have time to get much ground broken to plant a crop, and then a severe hail storm came along and wiped out what crop he had planted.

When the hailstorm struck, Mr. Hafele was gone with team and wagon to Yates for some supplies so the girls and their mother were home alone. The granary-barn had a tin roof, and the hail pounding against it made a frightful din. The windows were small, but they were big enough for the hailstones to find and shatter. Mrs. Sura recalls that her mother held a washboard to a window to keep out the hail.

That storm was bad enough, but a few years later they had one even worse. By that time they had much more ground under cultivation, and the oats crop stood so tall that when Mr. Hafele walked into the field they couldn't even see him. After the hailstorm the oats field looked like a plowed field instead.

This storm covered a wide area, including the town of Glendive, and did wide spread damage. So many windows were broken in town that by the time farmers such as Hafeles were able to get to town there was no glass to be bought. All the windows in the house were broken (they weren't in the granary then) so they had to tack cloth over the opening or board them up for a couple weeks until glass was available.

New settlers, of course, were warned about rattlesnakes so Hafeles – the girls, especially – were on the lookout. Mrs. Sura well remembers the first one she saw. It was her job to bring in the cows at milking time, and she always walked after them. There was no such thing then as pasture fences so, even though the cows were kept hobbled (they had been bought from someone near Glendive, and whenever they could they'd head back where they had come from) sometimes they'd hide themselves and she'd have to hunt.

One afternoon she started out to look for them, and her little sister, about four-years-old, went along with her. Leaving Gertrude on top of a little knoll, Meta started down through a coulee* to look on the other side when suddenly there it was – a rattlesnake!

Although it was the first time in her life she had seen one she had heard aplenty and recognized it without question. That rattle carried a warning that sent her scurrying, scared, back up the hill to Gertrude, but she refused to leave the scene until she had seen the rattler. Her curiosity satisfied, the two girls hurried back to the house and fetched their dad to come and deal with the snake. It was still there when they returned, and Mr. Hafele killed it with a black snake (whip, not reptile).

Meta Hafele's first encounter with a rattlesnake after she came to Montana gave her a scare, but when she saw a blow snake the encounter was terrifying. She was thankful she wasn't alone. Wood was scarce in most parts of the country, except along some of the creeks. They used to go down along Seven-Mile Creek sometimes to get kindling, and it was on one of these trips that she saw her first, last, and only blow snake.

They had loaded the wagon – Meta and her father – and were ready to start home when the horses started acting up. Instead of proceeding, they reared and snorted while at the same time the dog, perhaps fifty yards away, had set up a furious barking.

Checking on the dog, they found the reason for the horses' fright, too. A huge snake – the biggest she ever saw – was blowing at the dog, blowing so loudly they could hear it almost half-a-block away. Not only was the snake the longest she had ever seen; he was also puffed out with his blowing until, to her nine-year-old eyes, he almost resembled the dragons of myths she had heard. Mr. Hafele killed the snake, but not before it had blown poison into the dog's eyes so that later the dog, too, had to be killed.

The fall of 1909, after some of the most pressing tasks had been taken care of, Hafeles built their house. As was customary then, neighbors all pitched in and helped so it really didn't take long to have it ready for occupancy. They moved into it just before Thanksgiving.

Unlike many of the little shacks that went up on the homesteads, their home had four rooms on the main floor and two rooms upstairs. It had a full basement, too, which had been dug with team and scraper*. While many 'first shacks' had only heavy building paper tacked to the two-by-fours on the inside for finishing, they were happy to have their house interior plastered. But this house, of course, was not the 'temporary'. The granary had been that, so when they built the house they built it for permanent use, and they lived in that house as long as they were on the homestead. The lumber from their house is still 'lived in'. After they left the farm the house was torn down and the lumber reused for a residence in West Glendive.

Two other houses in the community at that time were also finished with plaster. They were fortunate that Jim Seeds, a plasterer (plastering was by no means his only talent) was available to do the work. One of the other plastered houses belonged to Fosters, early Glendive photographer. With a professional photographer as their nearest neighbor, the Hafeles were well supplied with pictures of their developing farm and the community. Mrs. Sura still has many of those pictures.

Their first year on Pleasantview they hauled their water for household use in a barrel on a stoneboat* from a spring almost half-a-mile from the house. When the men came in from the fields with their teams, they'd take the horses to the spring to water them.

In the spring of 1910 they dug a well close to the house. Can one accustomed to getting water at the turn of a faucet appreciate the convenience of having a well close to the house? The well was dug by hand, and pulleys were used to haul the water buckets to the surface. This well did much more than just furnish the water supply. It also served as cooler. Milk, cream, food – all were lowered in their containers by rope into the well, then the other end of the rope was secured to one of the nails for that purpose around the top edge of the curbing.

So efficiently did the well serve as refrigerator that later when they sold sweet cream to a dairy in Glendive, they could keep it sweet delivering only twice a week. By the time they started selling cream to the dairy they had installed a pump in the well and had covered the opening with a hinged lid that could be opened to lower things into the well.

Although Meta was of school age when the family moved to Montana she didn't attend school on Pleasantview because as yet there was no school. Her parents were concerned enough about education to send her to Yates where she stayed with her aunt and uncle, Mr. and Mrs. Pete Russ, and went to school.

However, in the spring of 1911 school was started in their home community with a three-month term. School was held in a one-room homestead shack, the owners of which had proved up and left the area. Miss Ora Chaney (Mrs. Menno Mullet) was the first teacher.

They were a little short on pupils to meet the minimum required for opening a school so Meta's younger sister, Gertrude, was allowed to go. She really wasn't old enough, and neither was one of the other pupils, but they went. Mrs. Sura recalls that the teacher let them take naps at school because they were so little and got so tired.

Mrs. Bolsen boarded the teacher the first year, but the next year the teacher stayed at Hafeles and did each year from then on until Meta took up where her mother left off. Meta had married and was living in the same community so she boarded the teacher from 1928 to 1941.

Her four children all attended the same school she had attended, and all but the last one graduated from the eighth grade from that school. Suras moved from the community to a location just west of Glendive when their youngest son, Jim, was ready for the eighth grade so he broke the tradition and graduated from the Washington School in Glendive.

Although Aloysius Hafele (Mrs. Sura's father) was not a farmer before he came to Montana, he learned fast – fast enough to help make (yes, make) the threshing machine with which he threshed his first crop. He and a couple neighbors worked together to build it. The machine was not elaborate, but it did the job. Neighbors worked together much more then than is generally the case now.

Watching all the farm operations – from breaking new ground, drilling the seed, and cutting the grain with the binder, to the threshing – was fascinating to the girls who had known nothing but city life before coming to the Treasure State.

They especially liked to watch the little colts. As the horses pulled the implements around the fields they had to be rested periodically. Then the colts that had been following their mothers would hurry to take advantage of the pause. After filling their stomachs they would often lie down in the shade of the horses and rest until action was resumed. Meta quickly learned to love the farm and the farm animals, even though they represented an entirely new way of life. Along with the cattle and horses they usually had a few bum lambs* to raise.

One summer they noticed that the lambs, which always grazed with the cattle, took to running home in the middle of the afternoon. Mr. Hafele decided the matter bore investigating and as he hunted he found a coyote den in the hill near the spring where the stock watered.

He and a couple of the neighbors decided the best way to get rid of the coyotes would be to flush them out so they packed water up the hill and poured it into the hole until the coyotes emerged. There were four pups in the den so Hafeles kept three of them. They penned them up in the granary, which worked fine while the pups were small. However, when they grew bigger, they got so they could get over the partitions between the bins and out into the hallway. This development carried the threat that the coyotes might escape sometime when the door was opened so Mr. Hafele killed them.

Fosters, living only about a quarter-of-a-mile from Hafeles, were the first in the community to own a car. It was equipped with kerosene lights for night driving. Mrs. Sura remembers a couple times when something happened to these lights so they hung a kerosene lantern on each side of the car and went anyway.

Mr. Foster's mother and his sister, Clemmie, had an interesting arrangement for proving up* on their homesteads. Their claims were adjoining quarters, and their houses were built just across the line from each other. The two women lived together, first in one house a few days, then in the other house a few days. Thus they were both able to establish residence, yet live together.

In 1916 John Sura, who had been working up around Forsyth, came to the Glendive area and hired out to Pete Russ. (Russ had moved to Pleasantview some years before.) He wasn't long getting acquainted with Meta, and in 1917 they were married.

After their marriage they lived first on 'the Gleason place'. They were the first in the community to be stricken with the dread flu in 1918 – not a 'first' to covet! The flu's reputation had arrived ahead of it so everyone was afraid of it and afraid to come near Suras. When John came down with it, Mike Guelff came daily to do their chores – take care of the livestock, carry in water and coal and carry out ashes. He was afraid to come into the house so he just set things inside. He had a weakness for candy, though, and Mrs. Sura kidded him for years afterwards because she had made some before the flu caught up with her, and he ate the candy even though he was afraid to come in.

Of that first house they lived in Mr. Sura facetiously observed that when they lived there, they didn't have to sweep the floor because the wind blew all the dirt over to one side of the room. They were 'hailed out' at Gleasons so they moved into Glendive, and John went to work for the railroad. When the railroad workers went out on strike a few years later, they moved back to the farm and stayed with the farm – although not the same one – until retirement.

They had three children when they went back to the farm: Ervin, five years; Imogene, two years; and Elaine, just a baby. Mrs. Sura hauled a lot of grain with team and wagon to Glendive that first fall. In her absence Ervin would watch the two little girls while his dad worked around the place. He was a reliable little fellow for his age and also looked after the little ones when she would walk out to the pasture to get the milk cows. They rented several different places on Pleasantview before they bought a place of their own on the Buffalo Rapids Project and moved a few miles west of Glendive in 1942.

One fall when Elaine was big enough to help her pick corn – and big enough to handle a gun – the two of them went to the field to get roasting ears for dinner. They glimpsed what they thought was a skunk in the corn patch so Elaine hurried home and got the 22. When she got back with it, Mrs. Sura shot and shot but all her shots hit it in the stomach and didn't seem to faze it. Finally Elaine shot it in the head, and the skunk turned out to be a porcupine.

After they moved to the farm, they started a dairy and for six of those years delivered dairy products on a route. They spent twenty-three years there before they retired in 1965. Upon retirement they bought a house in Forest Park where they now live.

Mr. and Mrs. Sura celebrated their golden wedding anniversary in 1957. Their children are scattered from here to Oregon, but they were all home for the celebration. A young priest whom they have known since he was a boy, now serving in Mexico, also came for the occasion.

In contrast to the very rigid schedule which the dairy demanded, they are now free to come and go as they please. They've decided not to keep even a cat or dog or bird because of the problem when they want to take off on a trip – a couple days or a couple weeks. They enjoy that freedom and take advantage of it to visit children or do any of the other things that were on the 'waiting list' when they were tied to the farm.

Gene Hoffstot

April 1967

As Gene Hoffstot reflected upon his first few years in Montana, he observed that in those days he knew every man in and around Sidney and still didn't know very much. There weren't very many people in the Valley when he found his way to the Treasure State, and it didn't take long to get acquainted.

He was only a seventeen-year-old kid trailing his older brother when he came here sixty years ago. His brother (Marion) had been in the Valley the year before, working on the Big Ditch*, but had contracted typhoid fever and returned to their Iowa home to recuperate. When he started out the next year, Gene went with him.

They struck out for Colorado first, then after a short time, made their way to Butte. Mr. Hoffstot explained that they weren't exactly tramps because whenever they were broke they got a job and worked until they had money to go some place else.

After a month in Butte they hit the trail again and this time landed in Glendive – May 20, 1907. His brother was confident they could both get jobs on the Ditch (and they were needing jobs again by this time) so they caught a ride on a freight wagon to the La Mesa camp, headquarters for the Reclamation Service.

Gene started at the La Mesa camp as a roustabout* but was soon sent to the Newlon camp – to haul hay. Saturday night the teamster for the survey crew got drunk and didn't show up for work Monday morning, so the survey boss called La Mesa to get permission to put Gene on as teamster. So it was that, though he had no civil engineer training (he didn't need that kind of training to drive horses), he became a part of the survey crew. He stayed with that crew all the while they were building the Ditch and in time he was promoted to rodman*. During this time he worked under Bailey and R.T. Hurdle, chief engineer for the project.

After the Ditch was completed he went to work for Fred Barker, rancher on Burns Creek. In the meantime his former boss on the survey crew had been transferred to Browning where work was being started on Two Medicine Lake Dam on the Blackfeet Reservation. He wrote and offered Gene a job with the crew there so the summer of 1910, after shearing was finished on the ranch, young Hoffstot left for Indian Country.

That fall he returned to Dawson County and began building his homestead shack. As soon as he was old enough he had filed on a claim on Burns Creek, within sight of the old Chimney Rock landmark. It was he who later opened and started operation of the Chimney Rock coal mine, still in use today. His chief source of income now was freighting. Brooks and Patterson had built a general store in Savage in 1910, and he did a good bit of freighting for them as well as for various homesteaders, using a wagon with a four or six horse team.

Occasionally the blacksmith in Savage would ask him to bring three or four sacks of hard coal along for his forge. Mr. Hoffstot recalls that when he did Brooks would grumble "that coal dust gets into everything on the wagon – even the canned goods!"

The Northern Pacific Rails reached Savage in the fall of 1911, and with the coming of the steel, the need for the old freighting wagons was greatly reduced. Even the farmers in the surrounding area were helped a good deal because with the railroad in Savage their hauls to market were shortened by about thirty miles – a long, hard day with a loaded wagon and team.

Mr. Hoffstot hauled the last wagonload of freight out of Glendive for the Brooks-Patterson store just a short time before the steel reached Savage. They knew it wouldn't be long so they didn't stock up much, but they had to have enough to keep them supplied until the first railroad cars could come in.

In addition to the Brooks-Patterson General Store and the blacksmith shop, Savage at this time boasted a hardware store, a drug store, two of the inevitable saloons, and even two hotels.

The little town had grown rapidly in the few brief years Hoffstot had been in Montana. At the time of his arrival there was not even a post office on the site. The post office serving the area was located instead at Tokna, about a mile northwest of Savage, and August Frederickson was postmaster.

Hoffstot started on his homestead with high hopes, but it didn't take many years for the high hopes to dwindle. The money just didn't seem to roll in as fast as it rolled out. Roy Kinsey, old time rancher in the area, succinctly pinpointed the problem one day when Hoffstot met him on the street and asked how he was getting along.

"Oh, I'm all right," the old rancher told him. "When I started out, I thought I was going to get rich, but I saw I couldn't do that so I decided to just make a living. Since I started that I'm doing pretty well."

Hoffstot found that on his homestead he wasn't doing too well, even making a living so he decided to take up roadwork. He bought a grading outfit and started building roads. Before he quit, he put in many miles of grade for Dawson and Richland Counties.

He recalled with amusement that when they built a road along what is now the Sidney-Circle highway, they thought they were putting in quite a grade, but now as you look down on it from the highway, "It looks pretty small."

Hoffstot's road work, of course, was done entirely with horse power and fresnoes*, years before the introduction of today's big diesel-powered earth-moving machines. It took a lot longer, but they got the job done.

His crew was camped just across the road from the Sidney fairgrounds when one of the first air shows was exhibited there. The roof of their cook tent provided a 'grandstand seat' from which to watch the daring exploits of young Charles Lindberg and his fellow pilots.

Construction had begun on some of the buildings at the fairgrounds, so the pilots anchored their planes to one of these for the night. During the night a severe storm struck and demolished the building. It did a fairly good job of the same to one of the airplanes, leaving only the motor.

The same wind upset a load of hay which Hoffstot had parked next to his cook tent and to which he had tied a couple broncs the night before, one on each side.

When he went out to investigate, he found the bronc that had been tied to the west side (the direction from which the wind had come) was on the east side of the overturned rack. He evidently had jumped when the wagon flipped and landed on the other side. He couldn't get his head down because his rope was still attached to the side of the rack that was up, and the other horse couldn't get his head up because he was still tied to the side that was down. That was one air show with quite a climax.

By 1923 Hoffstot was persuaded that road work wasn't the most profitable business, either, so when Dick Nutt offered him a job looking after his cattle on Indian reservation land he had leased in South Dakota, he went back to ranch work. That decision wasn't hard to make because he always did prefer that kind of work. Hoffstot remarked that if he hadn't always wanted to be a cowboy, maybe he would have made faster progress.

He spent two years in South Dakota, then came back to Montana and worked for the Frye Cattle Company at Poplar. During the two years he worked for the company he saw the 'boss' just once.

After the Poplar job, they went back to the homestead. They didn't attempt much farming but rather raised cattle. With the 'dry thirties' coming up, cattlemen had a tough time ahead. He has the returns yet showing he sold cattle to Rice Brothers Commission House in Chicago for as low as one-and-six-tenths cents per pound.

He found running cattle for Balthauser and Moyer, Glendive butchers, paid a little better, but after eight years of this arrangement Moyer moved to Fargo. Fortunately, carrying mail three times a week on a route from the old Burns post office gave Hoffstot opportunity to supplement their income the years between 1929 and 1938.

In 1938 he had thirty days accumulated leave so they went fishing on the Madison River. About three days was enough fishing for him so he spent the remainder of his vacation haying on a nearby ranch. At the close of his vacation, the foreman offered him a permanent job so he came back to Dawson County and gave notice to the postal department, then returned and worked three years on the Madison.

In the fall of 1940, Moyer offered Hoffstot a job in his Fargo feed lot so he tried it a month, but that was enough. He declares he just about got killed (he broke his back) in that feed lot work so he quit but Moyer had another job to offer him: buying lambs and calves.

Hoffstot confided that his wife's aunt had warned her she shouldn't marry a cowboy because they never stay in one place very long, and by this time evidence was indicating that the aunt was a prophet. They had already done a good bit of moving, but nothing compared to the moving during the two years he was engaged as buyer for Moyer. They were on the go all the time.

In 1943 he put an ad in the Billings Gazette for a ranch job, and as a result he soon found himself working for the Mackey Sheep Company. Only instead of taking care of sheep he worked with cattle.

He thoroughly enjoyed his job on the ranch, and couldn't speak highly enough of Mackey. "There just aren't any better people living than Mr. Mackey," he declared.

They stayed there until he retired in 1954 when they moved to Washington where one of their daughters lives. Washington couldn't keep them, however, and in 1960 they moved back to Glendive. Their other daughter, Mrs. Slim Graves, lives in this vicinity. And here they are going to stay the rest of their days, Mrs. Hoffstot asserted.

Hoffstot explained, "When my wife gets to talking, if you folks weren't natives you'd think this was paradise." And she left no room for doubt that she considered this part of the country "the best place in the world to live."

Construction on the 'Big Ditch' – Lower Yellowstone Irrigation Project starting at the diversion dam at Intake, Montana

Mrs. Ella Lineweaver

March 1965

In Iowa in 1909, there was a great deal of talk about available homestead land in Montana, and Mr. Lineweaver and I decided to make a trip to Glendive to look over the situation.

We owned a one-seated Overland car with top and a small storage space in the rear. After packing bedding, clothing, numerous cooking utensils and dishes, we started on our trip to the Big Sky Country on September 17, 1909, knowing that we would encounter some strange experiences on our journey from Brooklyn, Iowa.

It was our plan to travel very leisurely. We made many stops on our way, traveling on some good roads, through some beautiful country, but we didn't escape some Iowa mud. We followed prairie trails through North and South Dakota, and with the heat and dust and rocks, some days were not very enjoyable.

We stopped on the wild prairie for our meals with not a soul in sight, but in the far distance could be seen what appeared to be a small shack, and on October 2, we arrived in Bismarck.

We crossed the Missouri River by ferryboat to Mandan. We were advised there not to attempt to cross the Bad Lands by automobile, and so we reluctantly shipped the Overland, and after a rest, left by train for our destination.

We arrived in Glendive on October 4, 1909, stopping at the Jordan Hotel. While we were eating dinner, to our happy surprise, in came Bert Phillips and Harvey Read, both formerly of Brooklyn, now land agents in Montana.

The next day our Iowa friends took Mr. Lineweaver out to look over the country, and he chose a homestead in the Thirteen Mile Valley and made arrangements with some nearby neighbors to help him build a shack. Eight days later, after purchasing a bed, stove, two chairs and some staples, we moved into our homestead, and enjoyed our first meal in our new home using a box for a table.

Within a short time, my husband had built a cupboard, table, washstand, shelves and we began to keep house. He also built a roughly constructed addition at the northeast end of the shack which served as a garage and storage area for my washboard, tub, pails, and other things. It also served as a windbreak for our east door entrance. With shades at each of the four windows and sash curtains made by hand, I felt quite dressed up in my home in Dawson County.

We had a number of bachelor friends who called at the homestead. Lester Brown, who at one time taught country school, Alfred Doane, Isaiah Kauffman, Frank Magers, Ed Peterson and Albert Larson stopped by often. Quite often, one or more would come to spend the evening playing games. More often, they would come by to purchase a pound of butter for 40 cents or a dozen eggs for 30 cents, and we would always invite them to stay and eat with us. Quite often, I managed to add a quart of fresh buttermilk or some homemade cookies to their purchase.

We received mail twice a week, with Mr. Coryell bringing it out from Glendive to our little town of Bloomfield, which then consisted of a large country store operated by the Albrights who lived in the back part of the store. Mail days were gala days when a letter came from far away or the old hometown paper so eagerly watched for came.

It was the day of the free range and in order to keep the horses and cows from coming too near us, we built a large fence. Not only did the range stock annoy us often, but even more often did the howl of the coyote.

Prairie fires were quite numerous and could be seen a great distance away. Many times, my husband would get into the Overland and drive great distances to help fight the fires, sometimes being gone the greater part of a day, returning home tired and hungry and with his clothes filled with smoke.

I recall upon arising one morning, we found the shack unusually dark as well as all of the outdoors. It was necessary to keep a lamp burning all day. The cows and horses were standing near the fence and the chickens were uneasy. At sunrise, the sky was a brilliant yellow, unlike any I had ever seen. We learned that the darkness was from forest fires burning in western Montana. We were aware of the smoke for several days before it gradually drifted away.

We were saddened one day to see Isaiah and Lizzie Kauffman's shacks on fire. Isaiah and Lizzie were our closest neighbors. We immediately had become friends and enjoyed visiting and helping each other. I became very fond of Edna, Lizzie's little daughter, and she afforded me much company. Mr. Lineweaver hurried over to help but they were able to save only a few belongings.

They lived with us for a few days, and then Lizzie and Edna went to Mrs. Miller's home to stay until the shacks could be rebuilt.

As good friends and neighbors do, there were donations of money, clothing, food and many necessary items, and everyone pitched in and their new shacks were ready in just a few weeks.

Isaiah and Lizzie had adopted a unique manner of living on their claims. Each had his shack on his own claim, but they were only a short distance apart so that they could help each other and yet each be on his own homestead.

Much later, Mose Mullet's house burned to the ground and they lost all their possessions. They too, spent some time with us. Again, help came from relatives, neighbors, and friends, for even though far apart, we were all neighbors and the miles didn't seem to separate us in those early homestead days.

We had many unexpected callers at the homestead. About nine one evening, Mrs. Roy Reed and her daughter, Hazel, and her mother, Mrs. Lease, strangers to us, knocked on our door asking if we could keep them overnight. It seems they were returning home from Glendive when it began to drizzle, grew dark, and she became lost. Seeing a light in our window, they found their way to our shack. They were wet and cold, and so after hot coffee and a lunch, and a night's sleep, they were on their way after breakfast.

Another time, a rider by the name of Rich rode in and asked if we could give a meal and keep him overnight, as he'd been in the saddle all day. Both he and his pony were fed and bedded, and after breakfast the next morning, he was on his way to bring in the range horses.

Emmet Andes, called 'Slim', would walk five or six miles to visit us. Today, it would be too long a distance to even consider walking, but in those days it seemed nothing at all.

A few days preceding our first Thanksgiving in the shack, Lester Brown drove in bringing a live turkey that he had won and asking me if I would roast it and ask some of the bachelors for Thanksgiving dinner.

I had never cleaned, or even roasted a turkey, but I agreed. With the help of my husband, I was able to serve a good Thanksgiving dinner to Lester Brown, Alfred Doane and Frank Magers who seemed to thoroughly enjoy the meal.

The summers were very hot and dry, and the seemingly constant wind was so annoying, although there were many pleasant days too. Our garden yielded plentiful quantities of potatoes, carrots and onions, but things such as radishes, lettuce and other vegetables just didn't thrive too well.

The winter of 1910-11 was severe with huge snowdrifts and plenty of wind, with the temperatures dropping at one time to forty degrees below zero. One could dig his own coal from the not-too-distant coalmines, and it was the custom to lay in a good supply for the cold winter months. Quite often, a chinook wind would come, and it was surprising how fast some of the snow could disappear.

The Northern Lights were beautiful, and the moon never shone with more beauty. The moonlit nights were the lightest nights I have ever seen. The wind blew furiously almost every day. Indeed, it was a land where "the coyotes howl and the wind blows free."

As we settled in our 12'x14' homestead, we made two rooms by hanging curtains on a smooth wire stretched across the width. One room became our bedroom, and the other was our living room and kitchen. We had a cot with folding sides in the kitchen, and thus were able to have friends and strangers as overnight guests. This 'kitchen-bedroom' afforded accommodations to a great many people. Another addition to our homestead was the well that Ezra Borntrager 'witched' for us.

There was no church in those days in the neighborhood, and so often on Sunday, we would take long walks, climbing the buttes looking for agates. I have still a ring and pin made from agates I found in those days.

We eventually purchased an adjoining section of land, and my husband began fencing, breaking the sod and working the new land. The neighbors often exchanged work and occasionally would borrow a team and wagon. I recall Alfred Doane taking a large load of hay to Glendive for us.

I remember worrying whether or not he would be able to get up and down the hills and over the little streams with his four horses without upsetting. It was a two-day trip to Glendive by wagon, one day each way. Mr. Lineweaver made numerous trips with the Overland. One time he took Lizzie to Glendive, and she commented later that that was the fastest trip she'd ever made to Glendive.

When we left Iowa, it was not our intention to make our home in Montana. In the spring of 1911, we had proved up on our homestead. It had been a happy and wonderful year and a half, although hard work. We had made many good friends among the homesteaders, but after careful consideration, we decided to return to Iowa.

We were not long in disposing of our belongings. We made many final visits and enjoyed goodbye meals with our neighbors and good friends, the bachelors. It was hard to say goodbye to these good people, especially my dear friend, Edna. On March 29, 1911, we arrived in Brooklyn.

My husband died in 1952, and my daughter, Esther and her husband, Joe Billick now handle the affairs of the Montana homestead. Through Mr. Senner, who rents the land, my memories of those early days are often stirred as he sends reports of the weather, the crops and the news of the area. I find satisfaction that the early day memory of mine is still 'proved up' and is a fine producing farm.

John Syversen

July 1965

John Syversen, one of Montana's 'old timers', celebrated his 90th birthday last Sunday, July 25, with an open house, at the home of his son, Bill, northwest of Intake. Mr. Syversen still walks erectly, reads without glasses, has his own teeth, his mind is keen, and he said Sunday that he felt real good.

Many old friends called throughout the afternoon to wish him well. Four of his five children, Esther (Mrs. George Devier), Rowdy, Jordis (Mrs. Peg Lease), and Bill, all of Dawson County, were able to be with him. One other daughter, Nell (Mrs. Bob Chaney), could not be present. Mrs. Bill Syversen showed the visitors a silver spoon which the honored guest and his wife had received as a wedding gift in Norway sixty-six years ago on their wedding date, July 4, 1899, and is one of several spoons of the set still in the family's possession.

When John Syversen homesteaded near Burns Creek, some of Dawson County (Thirteen Mile Valley, for example) was getting pretty well settled by farmers, but other areas, Burns Creek among them, were still ranch country. Mr. Syversen had emigrated from Norway to Faribault, Minnesota, in 1901. In Minnesota he had had so much of cutting trees and grubbing roots that when he moved to Montana he chose land that was free of trees – except for a clump of chokecherry bushes, that is; they liked chokecherry syrup so he made that concession. The rest of the family would have liked to have trees, and Burns Creek was one of the few areas where there were trees, but he chose open land up on the table.

Mr. Syversen's sister Caroline (later Mrs. Herman Greiman) and his wife's sister with her husband, the John Twedts, had come to Montana the year before and had homesteaded. His sister Sophie was also here, and the prospects sounded inviting so Mr. Syversen and his brother, Matt, came to look over the land in the fall of 1910. Matt had followed the Trail of '98 at the time of the Alaskan Gold Rush, but now he was ready to settle down. Upon reaching Glendive the two brothers set out afoot for the Twedt farm, thirty miles north of Glendive. They selected their home sites and each built a one-room frame house (about 12'x24') with loft, reached by a ladder.

Once the house was built, Mr. Syversen was ready for his family to join him. They came by train and moved their farm equipment, livestock, and household goods by immigrant car*. The freight train was sometimes left for a time on a siding, and some place between Minnesota and Glendive some of the farm equipment disappeared; a six-section drag* was one of the items that was 'lifted'.

Soon after the family arrived, their nearest neighbor, Mrs. William Graves, (mother of Slim and Mike Graves) came calling to welcome them, riding 'Clover', a little strawberry roan. She lived about a mile and a half from them and was their first woman visitor.

Mr. Syversen started his farming on his half-section homestead but over the years added more acreage. The hard years challenged him, just as they did many another homesteader, but he managed to weather them. When others began buying tractors and other new-fangled machinery, going heavily into debt to do so, Mr. Syversen stuck to his horses and credits the horses with carrying him through the hard times when so many farmers went broke and lost their places.

Drought wasn't their only foe; the mustard weed, among others, would have liked to take over the plowed fields so the children would go through the flax fields, careful not to trample the grain, and pull out the mustard stalks.

Sunday morning routine in the Syversen home followed a definite pattern. After the breakfast dishes were washed and the necessary chores completed, the family gathered for Sunday School in their living room. Those first years there was no organized church or Sunday School in the neighborhood. Dad would read a Scripture and then they would discuss the passage together, all without benefit of Clergy. They'd sing some hymns together, too. After their Sunday School session Mr. Syversen (during the growing season) would walk through the fields, looking at the crops, while dinner was prepared, then the noon meal was eaten.

Later a church house was built on land donated by Matt Syversen. A few years ago it was moved onto land John gave so that it is more accessible.

The second year they were in Montana they built a sod addition along the north side (the long side) of the house. This addition then served as kitchen and utility room, nice and cool in the summer.

The children slept in the loft, and each fall the straw ticks which served as mattresses would be filled with fresh clean straw. Several times during the winter as the straw would pack down and begin to lose its resiliency they would take advantage of a nice 'spell' of weather to go to the straw stacks for a fresh filling for the ticks.

At first they got their mail at the Marco Post Office (near Intake's present location), then at Burns, and later on a route from Intake. Joe Balison was their first mailman.

As the neighborhood became more populated a Ladies' Aid was organized. This Ladies' Aid was rather unique as it was pretty much a family affair. The ladies did the sewing – making patchwork quilts and such items – but the men furnished them with transportation so the children had to come along too. Each family in the community took its turn at being host. The hostess prepared a sumptuous lunch and as a fund-raising gesture the 'collection plate' was passed. Whenever weather would permit, the men and boys would go out to the barnyard where the host (thoughtfully) had rounded up some of his livestock, and they would proceed to put on a rodeo of sorts. Thus it was that from such a mild-sounding affair as Ladies' Aid, one of the young fellows came home with a broken collarbone. When Mrs. Graves entertained the group, Slim had rounded up some 'tough ones', and Hank Hansen's bronc wouldn't turn out for the tree that was in front of them. As a rule the casualties were light, however. Following the rodeo, the men that were too old to ride would play horseshoe.

During the winter months these meetings proved rather dull for the restless youths. At one meeting some of the older boys grew tired of listening to 'chit-chat' so they congregated in the back bedroom to play 'Penny-Ante'. They used the bed for a card table and sat around the edge. They kept the game very quiet, as the lady of the house was a devout woman who took a dim view of gambling in any shape or form and certainly would not have approved of such 'goings on' in her house. It came time for the usual collection and the hostess started making the rounds of the various rooms where little groups were clustered, visiting. As she approached the back bedroom one of the boys artfully flipped a blanket over the evidence. The hostess took one long look at the guilty faces, picked up the corner of the blanket, and with a majestic sweep of her long arm, yanked the blanket off. Behold! There lay the cards and the cash! Calmly announcing in her stentorian voice, "I'll take the pot, boys!" she scooped up the pennies with her strong, bony hands, and continued her rounds.

When daughter Nell was in Glendive for the 1900-1930 reunion, she recalled some of their early school days at the little country school. Three months of school in the spring and three months in the fall was their norm. Nell commented that she had never attended a nine-month school term until she went to high school. They had a different teacher for each term because some of the older boys (there were some big ones in grade school in those days) were so rough and unruly no teacher cared to come back for a second term. Nell's first teacher was Olive Brooks. Some of the other early day teachers at the Burns Creek School were Flora Schroeder, Hazel Kennedy and Mae E. Cummings.

Syversens lived four miles from the school and walked that distance morning and evening. Long-horned cattle still roamed the range, and some morning it would be eleven o'clock before the children would get to school because those cattle, unaccustomed to seeing a human being on foot, would chase them. The youngsters would scurry for the nearest coulee where there was a little brush, perhaps just a little old buckbrush, then lie there hiding until the cattle would finally go away.

They had to cross the creek a number of times between their home and the school so one morning during the spring thaw their dad decided to take them in the lumber wagon because of the high water. The water was rising steadily with big chunks of ice coming down stream, and the water was so high when they reached one of the crossings that Mr. Syversen was dubious about trying it. Yet he could see fresh tracks indicating that a buggy had just crossed so he should be able to do it with the wagon, and they plunged in. When the full force of the current caught them, it lifted the box right off the wagon frame. They might have been able to use the box for a boat for a few minutes, but they had all been sitting on a bench along one side so as soon as the box detached from the frame, it tipped over, spilling them into the icy water. They were close enough to the bank that the older children and the horses were able to scramble out of the water, but Nell and her sister just older, Jordis, had to be carried by their father. The current carried them downstream and across to the opposite bank from the others before they could get ashore. So now the creek was between them and home.

Slim Graves came along just then, and seeing their plight, attempted to rescue them. He had crossed a scarce half-hour before (those fresh buggy tracks) so thought he could surely make it again. The sight of those dripping, shivering children on the bank spurred him on, and he started to cross. But the water was too powerful. His buggy tipped over and both his horses drowned. Mr. Syversen took the children to McPharlands where they were put to bed while their clothes dried, then walked to Jack Martin's bridge (six or eight miles) to cross the creek and get back home.

Little wonder, with such obstacles to attending school that Nell decided to quit. As she put it, "I was a school dropout, but then the compulsory school attendance law was passed so I had to start again." This time she kept on, not only through grade school, but through high school as well, then on to Normal School (teacher-training institute) and kept right on in school as a teacher. After her marriage to Bob Chaney she quit teaching for a time and raised her family, but now their children are grown and she's teaching school again, in the Helena school system.

An annual treat while attending Burns Creek School was the pilgrimage of an Indian tribe going north, returning from wintering farther south with their kinsfolk, as was their custom. They would camp on Burns Creek about an eighth of a mile from the schoolhouse, staying usually two or three days. During the noon hour the teacher would go with the children down to the creek to watch them. The Indian children were timid, but the squaws would giggle and chatter as they sat in the creek with their clothes on, rubbing sand in place of soap on the most soiled parts of their dress (namely the stomach). The children couldn't understand what they said, but it was very interesting to watch them go about their daily tasks amidst smoking campfires, colorful tents, and dogs. It seemed there were almost as many dogs, of all descriptions, as there were Indians.

Dolls weren't so plentiful when she was a little girl as they are now, and Nell was thirteen years old before she had a real, complete 'store-bought' doll. Their mother used to buy little china doll heads (white faces and shiny black hair painted on) and make bodies for them. She was artistic, and even the little stick dolls she made for them were fun. Using a forked stick for the legs and body, she'd nail on other little sticks for arms, paint features on the stuffed cloth heads, and use yarn for hair, then dress them.

But perhaps their 'live dolls' were the most fun of all. Nell and Jord would go down to the slough and catch frogs, then dress them up. They may not have been the most beautiful dolls, but they certainly did have action. At night the girls would undress their 'dolls' and put them into a bucket of water, keeping it up in the loft where the children slept. One night, however, the frogs came to a tragic end – an end that put an end to all frogs in the house. Their house did not yet have wallboard on the inside, just the bare two-by-fours. Consequently where the upstairs flooring joined the two-by-fours there was a gap between the edge of the floor and the outside wall. One night the frogs jumped out of their bucket of water and fell down between the flooring and the outside wall to the room below where the parents slept. Not only into the room where their parents slept, but into the bed. Two smashed frogs brought the uncompromising edict – No more frogs in the house!

The Syversens milked several cows and sold the cream, at first in Savage, then in Bloomfield. They got most of their groceries in Savage and Mr. Syversen did his banking there also. About once a year they made the three-day trip to Glendive (one day to go in, one day to shop, the third day to return home) to 'stock-up'.

On the South Fork of Burns Creek the boys made a nice swimming hole. Saturday evenings they would go for a swim and be cleaned up for Sunday.

The Syversen homestead now stands empty, but the two sons, Rowdy and Bill, still farm it. Mr. Syversen has retired and has lived in town the last few years, but just now is again out in the country, staying with his son Bill and wife, near the old home place.

Mrs. Andreas Kalmbach

May 1965

Andreas Kalmbach's ill health in South Russia caused him to turn hopeful eyes toward America. Already a number of his relatives had emigrated to the New World, and perhaps such a change would improve his physical condition.

With this hope in view he and his wife, with their three children, made plans to join the trek toward new horizons. They were accompanied on the journey by two of his brothers, one of whom had a wife and a two-month-old baby. Other members of the party found the eight-day ocean voyage an upsetting experience – upsetting to the stomachs, that is – and battled seasickness all the way, but Mr. Kalmbach felt fine.

By the time they docked in New York Harbor his old symptoms had disappeared, never to return, and in his new homeland he lived to within a few weeks of his seventy-fifth birthday.

Memorial Day that spring of 1910 was spent with relatives in North Dakota. Then they continued on to Montana as they looked for a new home. Mr. Kalmbach had a great uncle living in Fallon so they sought in that direction and found homestead land available near the present site of Marsh (Marsh hadn't been built up yet) on Cabin Creek. The family stayed with relatives in Fallon until a house could be built.

The transition from the Old Country to the new was made much easier for them because they settled in a German-speaking community, easing the language problem. This fostered a language problem for the children, however. Since German was spoken throughout the community, the children didn't learn English until they started school. This meant that they had to go to school a year to learn to speak English before they could start in the first grade.

They were located in good cattle country so, although they did a little farming, their main interest was cattle. Life was not without excitement, even in their quiet little community. Range cattle roamed at will when the Kalmbachs settled on their homestead and had a way of making life difficult for the newcomers at times. Fences had to be built to keep the wild cattle out, but while they were building the fence the longhorns would sometimes meander around and, finding a man on foot, give chase, sending the hapless fence-builder scrambling up a tree where he stayed until the steer found something else to interest him.

In Cabin Creek the water depth varied. Once Kalmbach had chased some cattle across the creek when the water was fairly low, but when he was in midstream a sudden rush of water swept the horse he was riding off its feet, spilling Kalmbach into the creek. The horse struggled to the shore, but Kalmbach was left floundering in the water. He succeeded in grasping a tree that jutted out over the water and pulling himself up onto the bank, but it was the wrong bank.

His horse was on the opposite bank, the homeward side, and Kalmbach had no way of crossing the torrent. When he didn't come home in a reasonable length of time, Mrs. Kalmbach went searching for him and found him stranded on the other side of the creek. She went home for aid and his brother brought a rope which he was able to throw across the stream to Kalmbach who grabbed it and was towed ashore.

Four more children were born to the family after they moved to the United States, making a total of six girls and one boy. The son was the only one in the family who learned to drive a car. Kalmbach tried once to drive, but he wasn't very happy with the results. The car lunged forward, heading straight for a fence post. He managed to swerve in time to miss the post but then found he had swung directly toward the house. With a desperate effort he succeeded in stopping the car before it hit the house, but from then on he left the driving to his son.

When daughter Dorothea was about ten years old, the family attended a church conference thirteen miles from their home. One of the neighbor girls had just learned to drive a car, and during an intermission she decided to display her newly acquired skill. Someone started the car for her but then, instead of going out through the gate right in front of her, she drove around the church house, then panicked when she realized she was driving directly toward a group of people standing outside.

As she plowed toward them the car struck Dorothea, running over her, and also struck her younger sister, but Mr. Kalmbach was able to jerk the younger one out of its path before it ran over her. As he did so, the car ran over his foot. The frightened driver finally got the car stopped at the fence before more serious damage was done. Dorothea, though knocked unconscious, sustained only a slight shoulder injury.

Dorothea mentioned that as children they enjoyed playing in the hills and rocks. They didn't have elaborate toys, but what fun they had with the wooden dolls that their father made for them! He had been a wagon maker in the Old Country, and was skilled in the use of the carpenter's tools, making cupboards and many other items as well. One of the girls was slow learning to walk so he designed a stroller on little wheels to help her learn.

Kalmbach received his citizenship papers in 1916. The law then provided that his wife automatically became a citizen when he did. About six years later another change brought new meaning to their lives when they learned to know the Lord in a way they had not known Him before. Their faith helped to sustain them through the hard years as well as the good.

In 1930, they traded their Marsh homestead for a farm east of Circle where they would have more pasture. They loaded machinery into the header box, their furniture onto trucks, and trailed the cattle the seventy-seven miles to the new location. They stayed there for fourteen years, then spent a summer near Froid before returning to Marsh.

Two years after their return to Marsh, their only son died. Although he was married and had one child they had all lived in one household. The entire family keenly felt this loss of son and brother, as well as husband and father.

In 1953, Mr. Kalmbach died. All of the children have married and have families of their own except for two girls. One daughter lives in Miles City; one in Glendive and one in Circle. Dorothea cares for their eighty-three year old mother and her sister who is in ill health. Mrs. Kalmbach, the eldest of twelve children, is the only one left of her family.

Dorothea comments that living in town was a hard adjustment to make at first because they had always made their home in the country, but she does say that life is a little easier now. Water is available at the turn of a faucet instead of pulling a bucket from the well with a windlass*.... a refrigerator replaces the root cellar for keeping their milk and perishables cool.... Yes, it's easier, but there's something about the country....

Steve Douglass

November 1965

Some of Montana's early settlers came by train, some came by covered wagon, and some – Steve Douglass, for example – came by horseback. When asked about the early days of settlement in eastern Montana (he came in 1904) Mr. Douglass hesitated, explaining that he "just wouldn't know what there'd be to tell." Until he was nineteen years old Steve had lived in the Black Hills country, but when cattle became too numerous for the range in that area, some of the cattlemen decided to move northwest. Young Steve joined the migration.

Steve's father was born in Scotland, but he had come to the United States as a young man and settled in Iowa. He was in the States in time to fight in the Civil War and after the war had moved on west, homesteading near Rapid City in 1865.

Steve's mother died when he was only five years old so he practically 'raised himself', although an older couple – and a dog – took care of him much of the time until he was thirteen. Mr. Douglass reflected that he wasn't always the best boy and sometimes needed correction. One day the lady was going to whip him for something he had done, but the dog bit her and she had to change her mind. Nobody could lay a hand on him when that dog was around.

He received his elementary schooling in a little country school, the Douglass School, located just half-a-mile from his father's homestead. (Now there's a $360,000 structure, still known as Douglass School, on that site.) Spelling was always one of his favorite subjects so the spelling bees each Friday afternoon were a highlight of the week for him. He particularly recalls one contest when the county superintendent of schools, Mrs. R.E. Talent (author of a history of the Black Hills) was visiting school. The winner for one week would have to start out at the foot of the line the next week so that's where he was when the word 'amateur' was pronounced. Who can measure the thrill of a young lad's triumph at 'spelling down' the entire school?

When most youngsters now days would be (at least should be) in high school, Steve was punching cows or roaming the Black Hills with a team and wagon, mining gold (placer mining).

The exodus of cattlemen from that part of the country brought him to Montana. He helped trail a herd of cattle to the lower Yellowstone where seven or eight families from South Dakota 'squatted'*. They spent eight days on the trip, mainly living off the land, shooting a few prairie chickens and the like. Now and then they would come to a sheep wagon where they were treated to a meal.

They found plenty of range for their cattle east of the Yellowstone in the general area across from the site that was later to be Sidney. Dan Gossett was one of the ranchers who had moved, and Steve went to work for him June 6, 1904, for $25 a month.

Once down on their chosen range, he didn't get back to town again for a year and a half – principally because there was no town to which he could go! O'Brian had a store at Newlon, but to get to it they had to come down to the river and row a boat across. Once a week someone would ride the twenty miles to pick up the mail.

About 1906 Ferris and Lord built a store. The Yellowstone Mercantile building went up about the same time to get Sidney on the map. Even then the unbridged river discouraged any unnecessary trips. Sometimes, though, trips were necessary – urgently necessary whether the river cooperated or not. Mr. Douglass recalled one night particularly, when, he declares, he wouldn't have crossed that river for a thousand dollars – but he crossed it. It was after Sidney had a hospital, and one of the neighbor women expecting a baby had to be taken across. He had to wade water on top of the ice, but the ice was solid so there was no great danger from that angle. The real threat lay in the possibility of stepping into an air hole in the ice. But he stayed on solid ice and they reached the hospital all of fifteen minutes before the baby was born.

During the ice-free season a ferry plied the river, making crossing a little easier. But even the ferry offered no immunity to peril and tragedy, as Mr. Douglass witnessed. He and some other fellows had gone to Fairview that day (this was back in 1905) and were returning home. They had just crossed on the ferry with their horses and had ridden up the hill when Steve stopped to straighten his saddle blanket.

While he was straightening it he heard a yell as the ferry cable broke. He whirled in time to see the ferry swing around and the team pulling the ferry jerked into the water. He and his companions raced back down the hill, but the ferryman had been knocked into the water, and they were unable to save him. One of the horses also drowned.

Steve worked for Gossett four years. During that time he managed to save enough from his $25 a month so he could start on his own. A homestead helped him get a start. He had filed in 1906 on a claim close to the North Dakota line. A couple years after he filed on his homestead, another character entered the scene – a character who was to have a decided bearing on the story.

When Maggie Porter was two years old, she had come from Minnesota to Dickinson in a covered wagon drawn by oxen. Her father supplied deer and antelope for the Northern Pacific Railroad crews as they pushed westward, laying track through North Dakota and into Montana in the early 1880's. He'd shoot thirty deer a day for them.

She was about seven years old – old enough to remember – when they had the last Indian scare. She recalled how her mother covered their windows with heavy material at night to prevent any telltale ray of light beckoning to the Indians. She remembers, too, how very quiet the children had to be. Before long her father took mother and children back to Minnesota, again in the covered wagon, until the uprising was over, and they would be safe on the plains again.

96

Later the family moved to Miles City. Here the older ones were able to attend high school. Mr. Porter seemed always 'looking for new horizons'. He had left home when he was only nineteen and apparently felt as though he was obligated to keep moving with the frontier. It wasn't until after he had homesteaded in the Sidney valley in 1906 that his family finally managed to apply the brakes and keep him 'settled'.

Mr. Porter and his boys made the move from Miles City to Sidney by wagon train, but the women folk traveled on the Northern Pacific as far as Glendive. There was no track beyond the Gate City* in 1906 so Mr. Porter met them there with the buckboard* to take them the rest of the way to Sidney.

Maggie had graduated from high school by that time and had been teaching school south of Wibaux. She was the first teacher for that district, and no schoolhouse had been built so she taught that first term at one of the homes in a lean-to that had been used for a storage room. The next year they built a little school. The weather and roads were so uncooperative that they had school only in the fall and spring.

After her folks moved to Sidney Maggie moved closer home and taught west of Sidney. That was their first term of school, too. Mrs. Douglass observed that most of her pupils were bigger than she was. She also filed on a homestead and began proving up* on that. Fairview had a land office and her father had driven her there with a team and buggy so she could file.

Schoolteachers of that day didn't stand much chance of staying single long in bachelor-dominated Montana, and Miss Porter was no exception. In 1908, she accepted a position in the Gossett School (for $35 a month) and there she met Steve Douglass. In 1909 they were married. At that time Sidney was five years short of being a county seat so they hooked up a team and buggy and drove to Glendive to get married.

Speaking of their trip to the county seat reminded Mr. Douglass of Sidney's battle for that position when Richland was carved out of Dawson in 1914. Lambert and Fairview were in the newly formed county, but Lambert lacked facilities so the real contest was between Sidney and Fairview. As with many towns, each of the two towns had opposing factions within them, Mr. Douglass explained, but when it came to fighting to get the county seat, Sidney's citizens forgot their differences and all worked together. He cited as an example two men who had not spoken to each other for ten years who were put on the same committee. As long as the issue was before them they worked together like a perfectly matched team, but when the job was done and Sidney had the prize, they picked up their feud where they had left it. He figures it was because Fairview's residents wouldn't unite their efforts that Sidney was the victor.

After Steve and Maggie were married they decided to relinquish his claim because his homestead was so far from town. Hers was more accessible and also closer to her folks so they let his go and moved to hers. They went in largely for cattle raising rather than farming. In 1912 they moved closer to Sidney – still across the river – on Bennie Peer Creek. Mr. Douglass noted that most of the creeks were named after old timers. In 1921 they moved into Sidney.

Mr. and Mrs. Douglass had five children but only raised four. Their eleven-year-old boy was killed when his horse fell on him. The cattle he was chasing became entangled in some wire, pulling it across the road. His galloping horse's foot caught in the wire and fell. The lad was crushed underneath and only lived until evening.

When their oldest boy was born they were living on the homestead on the east side of the river, but he was born in a little hospital in Sidney. When Mrs. Douglass was ready to go home from the hospital, a man took her by car as far as the river where Mr. Douglass was waiting for her with a rowboat. Crossing the Yellowstone, Mr. Douglass rowed while a friend who had accompanied him pushed the ice out of the way. Their team was tied and waiting on the opposite bank so they continued their journey home in the buggy.

No central heating system warmed houses in those days so they had a cold reception when they reached home. That new baby had to stay wrapped in his blankets a long time on his first trip.

Once when Mrs. Douglass was sick and had to get to the doctor, the only way they could get her across the river was on a hand sled because the ice was too thick for a boat but too thin for taking her any other way. Mr. Douglass exclaimed, "We had a time with that river! Sometimes we had to cross thin ice, sometimes the wind was blowing so we couldn't cross it at all; other times there would be water on top of the ice." To those of us who have always crossed on a bridge, perhaps the Yellowstone seems tame, but those who have had to grapple with it 'barehanded', so to speak, know how vicious and capricious it can be.

But Mr. Douglass "just wouldn't quite know what there'd be to tell" about the early days. They "just went through the usual routine of the early settlers!"

Mrs. H.L. (Gertrude Weyer) Finkle

October – November 1968

From the crowds of St. Cloud, Minnesota, to the emptiness of the vast Montana prairies; from a school of 900 to no school at all; Gertrude Weyer experienced quite an upheaval in her young life when she came with her parents to Wibaux County (of course, it was still Dawson County then) in 1908.

Gertrude's father George Weyer, came ahead of the family to locate a homestead and get a place ready for them to live. He hired a team and wagon from Dan Sutherland's livery stable and hauled out lumber for a shack on the claim he had chosen some thirty miles northwest of Wibaux, west of the Blue Mountains.

Darkness overtook him before he reached his destination so he used the stars to keep himself headed in the direction he wanted to go. When he reached the spot he had chosen on the open prairie, he unhitched the team from the wagon load of lumber and hobbled the horses, then spread out his bedroll under the Big Sky.

Next morning Mr. Weyer awoke to find himself afoot miles from anyone or anything – except his wagon load of lumber. His horses had departed during the night. He set out after them, and found them eighteen miles closer to Wibaux than they were when he had camped for the night. One of the horses had got his hobbles off, and the other, with his still on, had hobbled along with him as they started back whence they had come. After recapturing his team, Mr. Weyer had to go back to his campsite for the wagon before he could accommodate the horses' urge to get back to their livery stable.

As soon as he had a place ready for them to live, his family joined him on the homestead. Mrs. Weyer was in poor health, and it was their doctor's advice to try a change of climate that had motivated the family to seek a new home on the frontier.

Their closest neighbor was rancher Ab Owens who gave them an Indian pony, their only means of transportation – except walking – when they first moved onto their claim. The pony still bore its Indian brand. That pony was the greatest labor saving device on the homestead. Besides providing their transportation, the pony was used for a variety of jobs needing power around the farm, including hauling cedars from the nearby badlands for firewood.

The pony also came in handy when they were cutting posts. Mr. Weyer and two of his neighbors worked together during the winter, cutting cedar posts for some ready cash. Each day they would go about three miles to the hills where the cedars grew in abundance and cut posts, then use the pony to drag the posts to a central pile. In an unfenced land just opening up to homesteaders they found a good market for posts and had one order alone for 1,500 posts. They cut and piled the posts, but when they went to get them to deliver, they found that someone else had been there and helped himself so their 1,500 posts – and all the labor they represented – were gone.

Unlike the ranchers in some areas when homesteaders came in, the ranchers in that locale helped the homesteaders who were starting up. G.L. Pope let Mr. Weyer have a team of horses and a cow, then Weyer put up hay for Pope to pay for them. They got a dozen chickens from him, too. To make a shelter for the chickens they dug a hole – deep enough they had to have steps to go down into it – then covered it with two storm windows. It was a rather rude chicken coop, but they got a dozen eggs daily from the dozen hens – fed just on table scraps and the like – so the chickens must have been satisfied. But then, maybe even chickens expected less in those days.

When summer came and Mr. Weyer began putting up hay, Gertrude helped, with tramping the hay her special responsibility. The prairie hay was so full of needles that she had to wear overalls (not quite so common for girls then) to protect her legs while she tramped. One day she forgot her overalls when she went back to the field at noon, but there was a denim jacket on the hay rack so she pulled the arms of that jacket over her legs and buttoned it around her to give her some protection. Wouldn't you know, that was the very day a man picked to come to the field to see her father! Gertrude, well aware of the spectacle she presented in her makeshift uniform, scrambled to the other end of the stack trying to keep out of sight, but he saw her anyway.

Fortunate were the homesteaders who could build close to a spring of water. Most of them, however, were not fortunate in that respect, and many had to haul their water considerable distances until they could dig a well. The Weyers, thirty miles northwest of Wibaux, were in the latter category. They started digging a well soon after they moved into their little shack on the Montana plains, digging with a shovel and hauling the dirt up with a bucket on a windlass.

When they had dug down about thirty feet a little water began seeping into the hole, and he thought his task was about done, but then he hit a coal vein. He hit something else, too. When he reached the surface, he sat fanning himself, trying to get his breath. Next morning before anyone went down into the well they lowered a lighted lantern on a rope. Sixteen feet down the flame was snuffed out. Experimenting a little further, they tied a rope around the older boy and let him down into the well, too. He soon gave the signal to pull him to the surface because of the presence of gas so they hauled him out and abandoned the attempt to get water.

In the absence of a well they had to haul their water in barrels about six miles. Mr. Weyer was working in Beach at the time, coming home only weekends so the two barrels of water he hauled then had to last all week.

One day during the cattle roundup Mrs. Weyer saw some of the cowboys galloping toward the shack, riding hard. With her husband gone, she had no idea what to expect – after all, back in Minnesota she had heard all about the wild cowboys of the West – so she went to the door with a revolver under her apron, but all they wanted was a drink of water.

Two Larson brothers owned a well-drilling outfit so when other efforts failed, Mr. Weyer hired them to dig a well. They put up a windmill so they could have all the water they wanted without even having to man the pump. Of course, they still had to carry the water up the hill, carry it in and carry it out, but who didn't?

When sparks from Larson's big steam engine started a prairie fire in the thick, tall grass, they were glad for a water supply close at hand. So few people lived in the country then that even when everyone turned out to fight fire (and everyone did) the force still wasn't very big. A big herd of sheep was right in the path of the fire so someone was hastily dispatched to warn the herder. He had seen the smoke but didn't know which way to go. With the help, he did get the sheep out of the way.

Each farmer, seeing the smoke, grabbed all the sacks he could get his hands on, soaked them in water, and hurried to beat at the blaze. A nearby rancher joined them, too. He split a critter, tied each half to a saddle horse and dragged it across the fire line. They stopped the fire just before it got into the deep draws of the Blue Mountains.

Later the Larson brothers came back and invited all the fire fighters to help consume a keg of beer. Not many came, however, so they had more beer than they knew what to do with. They even gave the chickens some with the result that the chickens acted just as foolishly as human beings who've had too much.

There was no mail service when Weyers moved to the homestead because hitherto there had been very few patrons, but as other farmers moved in, they organized and got a man from Burns to bring the mail across the river to them once a week.

Anything they wanted done in those early days was a do-it-yourself project, and that went for a school, too. There was no school the first few years, but the settlers decided their children must have an education so again they worked together to get what they needed.

The residents of a community had to provide a three-month term of school themselves before a district could be formed so they secured a teacher – a spinster from Redwing, Minnesota – and school was started in Al Thompson's granary. In the absence of any piano, Gertrude Weyer provided the instrumental accompaniment with her mouth harp.

On the homestead even 'Santa' was a do-it-yourself project. Gertrude had several younger brothers and a sister so one Christmas she donned her dad's sheepskin coat (turned wrong side out), put on a mask, and gamboled into the room with a sack full of candy, nuts, and mysterious packages – one a little too mysterious, it turned out.

Littlest brother didn't appreciate 'Santa' and was frankly scared. Little bigger brother was a bit dubious about 'Santa', too, when he opened his package and found yeast foam! Mr. Weyer had brought the Christmas things from town along with the groceries, and unsuspecting 'Santa' inadvertently got hold of the wrong package.

The cook at Pope's ranch found the isolated ranch life lonesome and was glad to have some neighbors to visit. She used to walk three miles, pulling her two smallest children in a little wagon while the oldest one trotted at her side, to visit with Gertrude.

The cook's husband was a cowboy on the ranch. His life was suddenly snuffed out when the boat in which he was crossing the Yellowstone capsized near Savage. He was dressed in typical cowboy attire, including chaps*, which quickly became waterlogged and dragged him under. After his death his widow moved west and Gertrude lost track of her.

Near the Weyer homestead two brothers, Al and Gilbert Thompson, farmed together. With their big Pioneer Tractor they broke many acres of sod for the farmers rapidly settling the country. Their tractor was even equipped with big head lights so they could work day and night. Gertrude had one older brother, Joe, who went to work for the Thompson brothers. Later Gertrude did, too – for one of them, that is. She was still in her teens when she married Alfred Thompson, but she was probably more accustomed to taking responsibilities than most girls several years older now.

Once when his sister from Minnesota was visiting them, the men were moving the big tractor and the eight-bottom plow, while the two women followed with horse and buggy. They didn't attempt to follow a trail – not many trails to follow – as they skirted the edge of the badlands.

They had built a platform over the plow to haul their fuel barrels, and as they jolted over the rough terrain one of the barrels bounced off the platform and rolled down a deep coulee. The women could only watch as the barrel rolled away. It was easy enough for the barrel to get to the bottom of that gully, but it was not so easy to drag the thirty gallons of fuel to the top again.

The newlyweds made a trip to Minnesota for their honeymoon. After their trip they settled down on the farm. When the new school was built, it was close to the Thompson home (not quite as close as the granary in which the first term of school was held) so Gertrude boarded the schoolteacher.

Miss Thompson, the teacher, was staying at their home when their first baby was born. Although the baby was due in April, Gertrude was wary about the chance of a snow storm just about the time she'd have to go to town so she played it safe and went in four days early. Sure enough! The night her first baby arrived a blizzard hit the area and blocked all roads. One man who started out of Wibaux with his Model T hit a big snowdrift about a quarter-of-a-mile from town and had to leave his car in the snow while he walked back to town. Gertrude was glad she was already in town or she surely wouldn't have been able to get there. The nurse, right in Wibaux, had to walk from the hospital to the doctor's residence to get him because the telephone lines were down.

One time after her children started to school Gertrude almost shot their teacher – but not because of too much homework or discipline problems. Thieves had stolen some chickens a couple nights before so when the dog started barking she grabbed the shotgun and hurried out, determined her other chickens weren't going the same way. However, the dogs quit barking and all was quiet at the chicken house so she put the gun away. Later she found out that the teacher had slipped through the field to hang a May basket for the children on the door. Good thing she didn't come past the chicken house!

Life wasn't always easy for the Thompsons. In 1932 their house burned to the ground, and they lost everything in it – everything. It was in the fall, and she had dressed a bunch of chickens to take to Beach to sell and buy winter clothes for the children. Already that afternoon the snow was falling, and it was time to buy overshoes as well as other warm items.

Mrs. Thompson had just bought a new winter coat but, taking the chickens in and all, she decided to wear her old one instead. When they returned home, they found their house burned down. A brass bedstead was still burning, but everything else was finished. A fire is heart breaking at any time, but for it to come just then.... They had just painted the house, bought new furniture, bought new dishes. The fall canning – and she had canned a lot that fall – was gone, too. So was a big trunk of embroidery and other fancy work.

They went to a neighbor's for the night, then began the task of starting over. They had bought the 'Yates farm' so they moved into the house on that place, but replacing the furniture, clothing, and all their other household goods was not simple. And insurance to pick up the tab wasn't so common then.

It was about that same time that Mr. Thompson suffered a near-fatal accident while he was plowing with the old steel-lug tractor. As he attempted to throw the plow lays out of the ground, the lever somehow flipped forward and pinned him against the lugs of the rear tractor wheel. The lever held him there while the wheel kept going around. After seeming ages he managed to shut off the tractor, then fell to the ground. Mrs. Thompson found him there when she came from town.

He survived that but later became ill with leukemia and passed away in 1934. They had bought more land, but it wasn't quite all paid for at the time of his death. She had had to borrow money for medical expenses so she wrote to the woman from whom they were buying – herself a widow – telling her what had happened. The comforting letter she received in reply was much appreciated and so was the generosity. She was told to make the payments as she could. Gratefully she made the last payment when she sold the cattle.

In 1937 she married again, Hugh Chaffee, but he was killed instantly in a car accident in 1950. A young fellow from Lisbon, North Dakota had been to Glendive to get a load of hay with truck and trailer. In Wibaux he had attempted to get no-doze pills but wasn't able so had gone on. Someone had reported him so the highway patrol had dispatched a man to intercept him. The patrolman was just moments too late; he was right behind the Chaffee car when the truck struck it.

In 1954 Gertrude married Howard Finkle but was again left a widow when he died of a heart attack in 1964. In the fall of 1965, Mrs. Finkle moved into Wibaux and has lived there since. She rents her basement to a teacher and often has one of her children or stepchildren or grandchildren with her. Although she had only two children of her own, she reared six. In spite of hardship and tragedy, she has lived a full life and still has a full life.

Arcy DeLapp

October – November 1969

Last summer, little guessing time was so short, we asked Arcy DeLapp of Eureka (formerly of Circle and uncle of Mrs. Harold Waller) to share with us some of his experiences during his homestead years. He graciously complied, then hardly a month later suffered a stroke which claimed his life soon after. Though his voice is silenced, his typewritten memoirs remain and we'll pass them on as he wrote them down for us.

Having been asked by Mrs. Morris Kauffman from Glendive to write up a few items that happened years ago in my homestead days, I will do the best I can, although it's years ago, and lots has been forgotten, and the dates are not always given – just the main topics.

I think we'll start with about the year 1919. That was a crop failure year, and myself and two other men went to Dakota for harvesting and threshing, and then we shucked corn for a little while afterward. I finished up my job a little while before the other boys and went home. Happened to get into Brockway the 4th day of November and run into a foot of new snow.

Cars were scarce in those days and I tried my best to get somebody to take me on from Brockway up to my folks on Horse Creek – about twenty miles. Couldn't get anybody to go so I started out afoot. I walked part way and stopped at a place. A man lived there by the name of Wellman. That night he wasn't there so I found that there were a few groceries there. In those times anybody was welcome to stop, provided they washed up the dishes when they left.

Then I walked on home the next morning, and my folks were surprised to see me. They were pretty busy trying to get ready to feed the stock and things, and then there's a space in there where I just don't remember what we did, but snow got deeper and deeper, and I saw where my father was going to be quite short of feed although in an ordinary winter he had plenty of feed to carry his few head of stock through. So he had me start to haul baled hay and grain from Richey, which was forty-five miles one way. Hay was about $35 a ton to start with and oats was $60 a ton.

I hauled the biggest part of the winter and had a hard time hauling it as fast as I could feed it. My father lost several head of stock during the winter, and before the spring hay was sixty some dollars a ton, I think as near as I can remember, and we came out of the winter with about half as much stock as he had in the beginning of the winter. He was lucky he had any left because a lot of people lost all they had and had a big feed bill besides. He got through the winter some ways, but he was heavily in debt.

This item is about a band of horses that was bought from different people around the country. A man by the name of Mickel bought these horses cheap and wanted to

104

trail them some place. The people that bought them got ahold of one that they thought was a saddle horse. He was about half spoiled and whether they got afraid of him or what, they wanted to trade.

My nephew, Vincent Strecker, had a very nice gentle pony that they wanted real bad. So they finally made the trade, and they didn't want him to ride the horse home, or try to ride it home, so he led the horse home. When he got home he rode it, and had only a little trouble. He could ride it OK. When they found out that he could ride it they wanted to trade it back again.

Finally, when they began to trail this band of horses, they went down towards Miles City. I think in this Centennial book it says that we helped 'em to Miles City, but I recollect we only went down between, some distance south of Brockway. In the meantime some man came along and took a picture of the horses and us, and we went back home.

Before we left they offered to trade horses with the boy and give him his pick of any horse in the bunch. But he didn't make the trade, and I really don't know whatever did become of the horse. Too many years ago to remember all those things. But Vincent kept the horse as long as he was around the country – he finally joined the army in 1925. That's about all the special items about that so we'll try another place.

I forget years and all that, but in the meantime I started hauling grain a little. I remember one load of flax that I hauled when the elevator paid me. My check for hauling was a little more than the man that raised the flax. Grain was very cheap that fall. I only got seventy-five cents a hundred for hauling. I don't remember what he got per bushel. I asked the elevator man if there wasn't some mistake, but he said they were right. That's the way it figured out.

One time I was coming back from a trip to Richey empty. I met a man stuck in the mud, a neighbor not far from where I lived, name of Red Kimberly. He asked me if I would hook on and help pull him out. I told him I would pull him out, but he'd have to take his 4 horses off and I'd put my 4 horses on. He got mad because he thought that I thought his horses were no good. But I'd have had to pull his horses and his load, too, because his horses had been pulling until they couldn't pull together anymore. He finally agreed to take his horses off, and I had no trouble pulling his load out."

One fall my father and I hauled two loads of grain to Oswego. We got to the Missouri River bank with the expectation of crossing the river. When we got there, the river was full of slush ice and the ferry couldn't cross. There were several loads there ahead of us. We had to make camp and wait for the ice to go down.

Several of the loads were from close around and thought they'd make the trip in one day and they had nothing else to eat along. It would have been easier for them to go back home and wait. We were there two days and a half. Us fellows from farther away had our own grub but not enough to divide up with them. One man had a few navy beans sacked up to sell. They finally bought some of the beans from him and cooked them up in the pails we had been feeding our horses out of. So far as I know, the beans were cooked without salt.

Soon the slush ice went down. We all got busy and cleared off the landing so we could get on the ferry boat. That day we got across the river and back on our side. That was about the coldest experience I had while freighting, except the night when I slept in the barn, which I will tell you about later.

I found out one thing. You can't stay warm around a campfire. One side gets warm and the other stays cold. If you want to get warm all over you crawl into your camp bed, if you've got a good bed.

I think that's all there is to that item. We're going to make this short and sweet because it's too long ago. I can't remember all of those things, but we'll do the best we can. Some things may be right, and some things wrong, but some things happened. Just so it doesn't make it look as if I'm just telling my own life's pedigree.

I finally started hauling grain with six horses and two wagons. I hauled fairly steady, but I never did get a picture of the six-horse spread which I wished lots of times I'd had since.

One trip I made was in the fall of the year. The weather was real cold during the day, and I decided to camp inside. There wasn't any snow on the ground. There was a little town called Paxton, and I was gonna camp there. I usually camped out and slept on the ground — done my own cooking. But that time I thought it would be better if I slept inside.

There was a little hotel at Paxton, and I thought I'd get in there, but by the time I got there, why, it was filled up. They had no hay for the horses, and there was quite a few of 'em — so we had a little grain (we always carried our own grain) and tied our horse up.

I was out of luck for a bed, but I had my own camp bed along so I rolled it out finally in the haymow on a bare floor. The next morning, why, it was nearly 40 below zero. I didn't get cold because I had a good, warm bed, but the harnesses were stiff as a board.

We hooked up and started to Richey with our loads that morning, and about the only way we could keep from freezing was to let our horses go down the road and walk behind the loads. I don't know how many miles I walked, but I played dog most of the day. But we finally made it and got into Richey, and things were different.

A few days later the railroad came in to Circle. I think that was about 1929, if I remember, and the freighting was all over.

Lots of people asked me how I trained my horses to stay in camp the way they did. I don't know how they did it. I didn't train those four; they did it themselves. Any time I turned them loose I would tie up the green horses that weren't trained to the lead team's tails. In the morning I'd call them by name and slap on a bucket, and they'd all come right to camp.

My dad had two old mares that he couldn't keep in camp at all. We always had to go back four or five miles or farther the next morning to get them. He finally told me that if I could break them to stay at camp like mine, I could use them to freight with. So I took them.

When I turned them loose, I hobbled them a little tight with twine and turned them loose with the others, and they would start right up the camp road toward home. I'd let them get half to three-quarters of a mile from camp, and then I'd take a saddle horse and a whip and go whip them back to camp. As I remember I had to do this two nights in a row. From then on they stayed with the rest. It wasn't long until I could turn them loose and they'd stay right with the rest.

Some of my horses got so they would follow the rig home. When I got my load unloaded and ready to start home, I only used two horses on my drive home, and turned the other four loose. They would follow the outfit and feed along. As they fed, they would get out of sight once in awhile. Then they'd whinny and hurry up and catch the wagons. They would never let the wagons out of sight very long at a time. They'd always make it into camp for their grain and never missed a feed. That's the only outfit I knew of that turned their horses loose instead of leading them.

I forget the first year that I hauled wool, but I remember the man's name. I hauled wool for L.A. Dreyer. The first year we had good luck. He didn't want me to haul a six-horse load. He said I'd have enough trouble keeping the load in place. I and my nephew, Vincent Strecker, each hauled four-horse loads of wool, which is shown in the Centennial book.

The next year I insisted on a six-horse load and two wagons. I don't remember whether we had bad luck that year or the next year. There were two of Dreyer's hired men — one of them was Butch Wildon and the other was Olaf Jensen — who each had a four-horse load. We started out at noon and drove that afternoon.

We were just getting into camp when it looked pretty stormy. A man close to the place where we camped, named Leonard Boise, told us we could turn the horses in his pasture. So my nephew and I was taking the horses to the pasture when the others were setting up a tent and getting ready for supper.

It started to rain, and they built a fire in the opening of the tent. Then we rolled our beds out in the tent, thinking it might help some. During the night we felt ourselves getting wet. When I felt the wet, I reached out and found we were camped on the flat in about two inches of water. It was too wet then to move. We had to camp there for three days and a half.

That afternoon when we started out, we only pulled about three miles. The lead load started to cut in and tip over. I put my four horses on instead of theirs. Mine were used to work, and worked steady. By all of us standing on the high side of the load, we managed to get it pulled up on solid ground without tipping over. But we didn't have such good luck with the next four-horse load.

We started to haul it across and it did tip over. It all had to be reloaded. It was night so we camped. Vincent's four-horse load and my six-horse load had to stand all night. The next morning we reloaded the tipped load and pulled our own across without difficulty. But one of Dreyer's loads tipped over twice more before we got to Terry. It took us nine days and a half to make the trip, where we ordinarily made the trip in six.

Mr. Dreyer has three sons. I saw an ad in the Great Falls paper that two of the boys are running the ranch which has greatly expanded. They were rather small when I was hauling wool.

I started carrying mail in 1930 from Circle to Weldon, and I carried mail eight years. That was before they had roads in that country like they have now. But I made the eight years — only missed three trips. I got what they call an Arp's snowmobile. It fit on the Model A Ford. It broke down on me, and I missed three trips before I could get repairs. Otherwise, I made the trip all the time in the car. But I came out in the spring badly broke.

Then another man underbid me on the mail route so I moved back to the homestead, which I'd filed on in 1929. Then we made up our minds to move, and sold the homestead — very cheap at that time, and moved out here to the western part of the state — to Rexford, Montana.

I worked for the railroad, worked in the woods — skidding logs and falling timber. I put in a little time working for the Forest Service and finished up working on a ranch. Then my health gave out and forced me to retire.

We lived at Rexford until two years ago last fall. We had to sell out to the government on account of they were going to build a dam across the river and flood the town of Rexford, so we moved to Eureka.

Time and happenings may not be exactly right, but they're the best I can make it. If I was a writer there are lots of things I could add.

Many, many of our old timers have taken their stories to the grave with them. We feel privileged to share with you these experiences from Arcy DeLapp, even though he did not live to see them in print.

Mrs. Paul (Marie Maschera) Jarvis

February 1968

Mrs. Paul Jarvis isn't sure just when her grandfather first came to Montana, but it was early enough so that he could leave here (temporarily) in 1904. Joe Novasia, Sr. had come to America, leaving his wife and two small children in his native Italy before his first child, born in 1882, was old enough to remember him.

He went first to St. Louis where his older brother lived and worked in his brother's restaurant. His brother had done well enough in this new land that he was able to launch the newcomer in a business of his own. This business didn't last long, perhaps because he was his own best customer. The business was a bar, and Joe not only liked his product; he liked to 'treat' his customers so it wasn't long until he went broke.

Somehow Joe learned about a little town springing up along the newly completed Northern Pacific Railroad, and he decided that Glendive would be a good place to start over. Since he had no money he rode the rails and arrived in town just about as hungry and as dirty as he could get.

As soon as he could get out of the railroad yards he went to a house and asked for something to eat. He was so dirty that the girl who responded to his knock was frightened and told him, "You get out of here or I'll turn the dogs on you." To this threat he replied, "Go ahead, I'm so hungry I'll eat the dogs!" She gave him some food.

Before the turn of the century eastern Montana was ranch country – cattle, sheep, horses – and Novasia soon found a job herding sheep. He started out for Jack Martin on Burns Creek, just as many a later newcomer did.

In 1904 he received word from his family back in Italy that his daughter, Ercolena, was planning to be married to John Maschera so he made the trip back across the ocean for the wedding, his first visit since his departure in the 1880's.

Poverty was the rule in rural Italy, and anyone going any place walked – anyone, that is, except someone who had been to America. If the local people saw someone riding in a buggy their conclusion was, "He must be from America."

Ercolena and some companions, walking along the dusty road a short while before her wedding, noticed a stranger riding in a buggy, and she remarked, "Wouldn't it be funny if that was my dad?" She reached home and there sat the stranger – her dad.

He stayed in Italy to visit, and as he visited he told of the opportunities in the New World. His son, Joe Jr. had joined him in Montana before the Italy visit, and by the time his visit was concluded he had convinced a number of his friends and relatives that the brightest future was in the States.

His new son-in-law, John Maschera, returned with him when he came back to this country – "to make his fortune." John planned that as soon as he had enough money he would bring his bride to Murphy Table, too. He started herding sheep and within a year was able to send for Ercolena.

When Ercolena arrived, John was working for Dupliseas. To her children in later years Mrs. Maschera described Mrs. Duplisea as a wonderful person, kind and understanding. It was well that she was, for the young immigrant found many rough places that needed smoothing. The language problem was the biggest hurdle.

When they sat down to the table to eat, everyone would start visiting — talking and laughing, having a good time. Ercolena, of course, couldn't understand what was being said so she would start crying and leave the table thinking they were laughing at her, a stranger in a strange land. Then Mrs. Duplisea would talk with her, reassuring and explaining.

Sympathy and understanding can be communicated without words, but sometimes words were needed, too. Mrs. Maschera had an English – Italian dictionary with the English words on one side and the Italian on the other. It was by means of 'the little book' that the two women were able to talk with one another.

When the Dupliseas started ranching on Redwater, Indians were commonplace in the area, and the ranchers had learned how to get along with them. Mrs. Duplisea instructed the young Italian, who had heard plenty of 'horror stories' about the Indians before she left her native land, that if Indians should come they were to have plenty of food and then they wouldn't bother the settlers.

Ranchers from many miles around had to come to Glendive to get their supplies, and so it was with the Dupliseas on Redwater. The trip to Glendive and back required at least three days and wasn't made very often. One of these trips was necessary while the young Italian couple, Mr. and Mrs. John Maschera, was working at the ranch so they were left in charge of home quarters while the Dupliseas were gone. Then came the Indians.

Mrs. Maschera heard a rap at the door and saw that a big Indian was doing the rapping so instead of going to the door, she pulled the shades and hoped he would go away. But he kept knocking. When it became evident that he didn't intend to give up, she finally, with heart in her mouth, opened the door. He held out his hand to shake hands, but instead of shaking hands she started backing away, backing until she could retreat no farther.

Remembering Mrs. Duplisea's instructions, she gave him food — ham, bacon, potatoes — everything she could find. By the time she was through giving, there wasn't enough food left in the house for the children! The Indians made no trouble, of course, but even so, it was a greatly relieved young woman who welcomed the rancher and his wife back home.

By the time the Mascheras' first child was born in 1906 they were working for Jack Martin on Burns Creek, the same Jack Martin for whom Mrs. Maschera's father, Joe Novasia, Sr., had worked when he first came to Montana. During this time they lived in the sheepwagon, which could be moved easily as the sheep were moved to new grazing grounds.

110

Because of her father's drinking habits, her husband had forbidden Ercolena (Mrs. Maschera) to go to town with him, but one day when John was far from the wagon with the sheep, Joe came and wanted his daughter to go to Glendive with him. "If you go to town with me, Lena, I'll buy you a new pair of shoes," he told her.

Lena refused, reminding him of her husband's wishes in the matter, but he pleaded so hard and promised so faithfully that he would not take a drink that finally (she certainly could use the shoes!) she gave in and accompanied him on the condition that they have the same hotel room so she could 'keep an eye' on him.

Upon their arrival in town they got the room, and all went well that evening as she kept watchful guard. On through the night and into the early morning hours she continued to watch, but about four o'clock she dropped off to sleep. When she awoke, she found herself alone in the hotel room – alone in the world, it seemed to her! The town was completely strange to her, and she had no idea where to find her father or where she could get help.

For three days she stayed alone in that hotel room. Finally the third day, as she watched the street from her hotel window, she saw her father on the street below so she hurried down and caught him by the arms. One place in town she could locate; she knew where the livery stable was in which they had left the horses so she escorted him there. The attendant hitched the team to the wagon for her, tied the lines around the brake lever, and assured her the horses would take her home. Since she knew nothing about driving and her father wasn't able, she could only hope the attendant was right.

In later years she told her children that it was a terrible trip. She cried and prayed, and the horses kept plodding on. Finally they reached familiar surroundings again. As the attendant had told her, the horses took them home. She didn't have her new shoes, and she didn't go to town with him again.

In 1907 John bought a well-drilling outfit, and in the next few years he drilled many wells. Maschera made a practice of 'witching' for water and never failed to strike water, but a tragedy brought an end to his well-drilling career. Gas was always present in greater or lesser amounts when a shaft was sunk so before allowing a man to go down into a well, he always lowered a lighted lantern by means of a rope. If the lantern went out, they knew the well was not yet safe to work in.

In this particular well the lantern test had revealed that gas was present in dangerous amounts so orders were given that no one should go into the hole, then the crew went to Glendive to get supplies. When they returned they found that, contrary to orders, a young Italian boy staying in the community had gone down into the well. It was with difficulty that they removed his body, and though they worked long to revive him, all efforts failed. It was this misfortune that prompted Maschera's decision to sell his rig.

Mrs. Maschera's brother, Joe Novasia, Jr., had joined his father in Montana well before his sister's marriage and had chosen to be a cowboy rather than a sheepherder. He had never done any 'bronc' riding before he came to Montana, but he became quite proficient at it after he was over here, and it was this that brought about his death.

In 1908 the big cattle outfits, the CK and the XIT, staged their last roundup. A number of local ranchers sent out a wagon, too. As 'Pinote' (the nickname everyone used for Joe, Jr.) was picking out his string of horses for the roundup he set his heart on one of Chet Murphy's that had the reputation of being an outlaw.

Chet was reluctant to have him take the horse, but Pinote begged until he gave in. The roundup progressed smoothly – so smoothly that one morning as the fellows saddled their mounts they decided they wanted a little excitement. They agreed that each would ride his worst horse that day. Pinote, of course, picked the 'outlaw'. That morning he seemed to have turned over a new leaf and he wouldn't even buck.

Pinote fanned him with his hat to get him going, and the horse took off, running blindly. At that time there were few fences in the country, but there was one near Burns Creek, the only one between Murphy Table and Glendive. Straight into this fence the bronc ran. When he hit the fence, he threw his young rider into a pile of rocks. For sixteen days Pinote lay unconscious from his injuries in the Grace Hospital in Glendive, then passed away.

Pinote left his homestead to his father Joe, Sr. They had built a little log shack on the claim, and there Joe lived when he was not out in a sheep wagon. One evening an electrical storm broke so he went out to get some wood before it got wet. While he was at the woodpile lightning struck the shack, and later in the evening, after he had gone back into the shack, lightning struck the woodpile.

Everything, it seemed, happened to 'Grandpa'. One day while Pinote was still living his father was herding sheep on the flat above Burns Creek when he saw a rattlesnake. Before he could kill it the snake crawled into its hole. He reached in after it to pull it out, not realizing that a rattler turns in its hole so its head was where he expected the tail to be, and the snake bit him.

He managed to get back to his sheep wagon, and there, knowing that a rattlesnake bite is fatal, he wrote a note to his son: "Joe Mafraw to his son Pinote. Bit by a rattlesnake. That's how he died." (Although his last name was Novasia, Jack Martin had dubbed him 'Mafraw' because he could never remember his correct name.)

But 'Joe Mafraw' didn't die from a rattlesnake bite. A couple of Cavanaugh's cowboys happened along and found him so they took him to the ranch, loaded him into a wagon, and headed for Glendive. As they went they kept pouring whiskey down him to counteract the snake poison, and when they reached the hospital, the wound was drained. In spite of the time that had elapsed, he recovered. Later when someone asked him why he had reached into that hole he replied, "He no ring-a-da bell!" (The snake didn't rattle!)

In 1912 John Maschera and his wife decided to go back to Italy for a visit so they left Montana in November and spent a year in their native country. By this time they had two daughters, but during the year in Italy the younger, then four years old, contracted pneumonia and died.

On that trip, they were also accompanied by Mrs. Maschera's father, Joe Novasia, Sr. and her cousin, Felix Andorno. Felix went over to get married and stayed only briefly before returning to America with his bride, but Novasia ('Joe Mafraw') didn't return at all. He felt that he was too old to come back so he spent the remainder of his days in Italy. Since Joe did not plan to return to this country he turned Pinote's homestead over to his daughter and her husband.

Upon their return to the States in November of 1913 Mascheras moved in with the Andornos while the 'men folk' started building a house for Johns. John had earlier filed on a homestead, but his claim had been successfully contested because he was not yet a citizen. Since he had no homestead they built a house on Pinote's place. After it was completed in 1914, the original log homestead shack was used as a chicken coop for many years.

Mrs. John Maschera, mother of Mrs. Paul Jarvis, vividly remembered and often described to her children her first experience with a major prairie fire. At the time they were living in a house along Burns Creek, and although their dwelling was not in the line of the fire, it was the closest for men to come for food, and come they did, black and charred.

Mrs. Maschera had been in the States for only three years, and it was still much easier for her to cook Italian style than American. What do you feed a bunch of men when they come at all hours for a quick lunch before they dash back to the job? She couldn't help a feeling of panic at the responsibility suddenly thrust upon her, and she was ever grateful to Bob Kennedy who realized her predicament and gave a hand with food preparation. She later told how he "baked biscuits and baked biscuits" to feed the fire fighters as they came.

John Maschera was the first farmer on Murphy Table to own a tractor – a Nesson with huge wheels after the manner of the early models. Daughter Rose fell off the tractor, and the wheel ran over her foot. Though her back was injured her foot was unhurt – probably because the shoes she was wearing had been given to her and were much too big so it was just the shoe that was run over rather than the foot.

When John Maschera left Italy in 1904 for the 'New World' he expected – as did many an immigrant – to make his fortune, but he probably didn't realize how long it would take. Prosperity was preceded by a long, hard struggle against drought and hail and grasshoppers.

Daughter Marie (Mrs. Jarvis), born a few weeks after they moved into the new house, remembers helping in the battle against grasshoppers. She and her sisters would sit in the wagon and hold pails of poison between their legs, scattering the poison as their father drove through the field.

In later years Mr. Maschera designed a more efficient method of spreading the poison. He rigged up a barrel on an old Ford rear end and equipped it with propellers so that as he pulled it through the fields with a wagon the propellers scattered the poison – sawdust mixed with banana oil.

In order to provide an education for their children the Mascheras built a house in Glendive at 623 E. Benham – still almost out in the country, seemed like, because of the distance between neighbors in that section* then. Mrs. Maschera took in washing, scrubbing the clothes on a board, to help pay expenses so the girls could go to school.

The 'New Depot' was under construction at the time so some of the men who were working there were among her customers. 'Pick up and delivery' service was provided by Marie with a little wagon. She started in the first grade when the family moved to town and continued through sixth grade at Lincoln School. They were back in the country for her seventh and eighth grades, but were in town again for high school.

She noted that when they moved to town, many of the townspeople still kept cows. During the summer months boys would gather the cows and take them to the area where the Jarvis town house is now – East Dodge Street – and let them graze throughout the day, then take them back home in the evening.

When the girls were through high school, the family moved back out to the farm the year 'round again. In 1943 her parents retired and moved into Glendive, and Marie and her husband Paul Jarvis (they had married in 1932) took over the farming of 'the home place'. Mrs. Maschera passed away in 1951, Mr. Maschera in 1957.

Although the 'homestead' has had a number of owners it has never been bought or sold. From the original owner, Joe Novasia Jr. it went to his father, who left it to their daughter, Mrs. (Ercolena) Maschera. After her death John Maschera was the legal owner. When he passed away he left it to his daughter, Marie Jarvis, leaving other property to daughters Rose of Sidney and Josephine in California. Although Mr. and Mrs. Jarvis move to Glendive during the winter months when it isn't feasible to drive back and forth to bring their son to school, 'home' is still on the farm, Uncle Pinote's old homestead.

John Nadwornick

October – November 1967

"Now they push buttons; then everything we did we used our two hands." John Nadwornick's 'then' referred to his early days in the farming business – days that go back to the turn of the century.

When Nadwornick came to Montana in 1911, he wasn't eligible to homestead because he had already used his homestead rights in North Dakota. He had come to America from the Crimea as a boy of fourteen in 1897 and settled with his family near Dickinson.

They had been farmers back in the Crimea (an island belonging to Russia in the Black Sea) too, but the island was becoming too crowded to accommodate more farmers. After Russia had acquired the island from Turkey, settlers from all around had flocked there. The government gave to each settler a portion of land, not only for the head of the family but for each boy also. That was fine as long as unoccupied land was available, but by the time John's father began considering his boys' futures, the land was mostly taken.

Others faced the same dilemma, so five families from the village where the Nadwornicks lived, hearing of the abundant land in America, decided to emigrate. The Russian government would not grant passports for emigration, but they would for visits so some left on a 'visit' and never went back.

The fourteen-day ocean voyage was an exciting adventure for fourteen-year-old John, and so was the land trip across the North American continent to North Dakota. Some relatives of the Nadwornicks were already settled in the Dickinson area so that influenced the newcomers in their choice of location.

John's father immediately filed on a homestead. As soon as John was eligible he also filed. He farmed there for several years but 160 acres wasn't very much land to make a living in this part of the country so he sold his homestead and moved on farther west where it was easier to find acreage to buy, and where the acreage was also cheaper.

He found what he wanted in the Pleasantview community, fourteen miles southwest of Glendive, and bought two quarters there. He put up a little shed for some temporary shelter while he built their permanent house. They piled straw on the grass and gravel floor of their shack for beds.

By the time he moved to Glendive he had a wife and four children. Elizabeth Roller had come to the U.S. on the same ship that he had, coming from the same village. Their parental families settled in the same area near Dickinson, and in 1903 John and Elizabeth married. As soon as he was married, even though he was only twenty, he was allowed to file on a homestead.

The small children meant that getting a more substantial dwelling ready was even more important, so he gave full priority to building a house. He was able to buy used railroad ties in Glendive, and these made a substantial house indeed. Except for two days when he hired a man to help him put the shingles on the roof, he did all the building of the house himself.

In 1911 he didn't buy a tractor to put in his first crop, but he did pay $400 for a team of horses. Mrs. Nadwornick drove the team on a disc, working the breaking, while he followed behind, broadcasting the seed by hand. Flaxseed was so fine he had to scatter it with just three fingers, rather than by the handful.

One of his neighbors saw him seeding his flax in this manner and bluntly declared that no crop could grow from seed planted in such fashion. He kept on scattering the seed in spite of their skepticism and watched with amusement their amazement as his crop came up.

As the grain headed out his neighbor came over almost every day to see how the flax was doing, shaking his head in wonder that such a nice crop of flax could grow from that kind of planting. Later crops that he put in with a drill didn't always turn out as well as that first crop he put in by hand.

During World War I John Nadwornick bought his first car, a Model T. When he bought it the salesman took him for a ride to demonstrate the handling of the new-fangled machine, but as they went around a corner on the demonstration drive he broke off one of the front wheels when he hit the curb.

The Ford proved to be a great asset in his bond-selling drives. He could whiz down the road twenty-five miles an hour and really cover territory. The new car was put to many other uses, too, including the role of substitute hearse.

One morning about daybreak a pounding on his door jarred him out of his sleep. Answering the summons he found a Miles City man, almost incoherent as he tried to explain that his car had tipped over and had killed his wife.

At that time there was no oiled highway between Glendive and Miles City. The old Red Trail had been graded and served as the connecting link between the two cities, but in places it was rather difficult to distinguish between it and other grades, and in this case the travelers had wandered onto the wrong road.

Considerable rain had fallen, and the ungraveled road was slick. When he hit a rut, the car's front wheels slipped over the bank, and it tipped over. He was able to get out, but his wife was pinned under the chair back, the weight of the car on her. He could see Nadwornick's house from the wreckage so he hurried over to get help.

Cars in those days didn't have self-starters – not many of them, anyway – but had to be cranked. The Ford, at best, didn't have a reputation for easy starting and in wet weather it took longer yet, but this morning when they turned the crank, it started promptly.

Just at that time Nadwornick had a man plowing for him so he called the plowman to go along and also picked up another neighbor. When they reached the site of the accident they found the car with the four wheels in the air. All that was visible of the woman were her feet sticking out from under the edge of the car.

The car was a Studebaker, much heavier than the little Model T, but the four men managed to tip it back and free its victim who was indeed dead by this time. The rescuers could only lament their helplessness at arriving too late, yet thankful that coyotes had not attacked to add gruesomeness to tragedy.

116

At the same time they felt disgust for the man who attempted to drive while drinking and had allowed his brain to become so befuddled by liquor that he couldn't see how simply his wife could have been saved by removing the few screws that held the car seat in place. "She kept hollering," he told them, "get that car off my neck," but now she had choked to death.

They wanted to get the sheriff before moving her to avoid possible legal complications, but the husband insisted on taking her on into Glendive, so they put the body into the back seat. They thought he ought to sit in the seat to hold the body, but he flatly refused so the hired man did.

About halfway to Glendive he pulled out a pint of whiskey and handed it to Nadwornick who firmly refused with the explanation, "I don't drink when I'm driving." So he passed it to the neighbor instead, and by the time they reached town they had emptied the bottle.

The road was still so slippery that they slid in the ditch a couple times but reached Glendive safely and went immediately to the courthouse and woke the sheriff. He in turn got the coroner and they began the routine investigation. It was noon before they were able to return home.

The widower had asked Nadwornicks to pull the car over into their yard, but Mrs. Nadwornick couldn't stand the sight of it, thinking of that poor woman, so they pulled it on into Haskell's garage in Glendive.

About a year later the woman's sister and husband came and wanted to view the scene of the tragedy. Later they visited at the Nadwornicks' home to learn all the details possible. In preparation for a basket social that evening Mrs. Nadwornick had decorated a box with blue crepe paper. As they visited, the sister suddenly caught sight of that box and cried out, "Didn't I tell you we would be in a house with a blue basket in the corner?" and burst into fresh tears, all of which added an eerie touch to the whole affair.

His discovery of another accident victim led Mr. Nadwornick to observe that he must have been the undertaker out there. As he was returning home from Glendive late one evening, this time in the dead of winter, he came upon another over-turned car. He thought he saw feet sticking out from under it, and as he came closer he heard a faint call. There he found one of the neighbor's daughters, pinned under the car and almost frozen to death.

As she had struggled to get free she had kicked off her shoes so her feet were frozen, but she was wearing a long coat which had helped to protect her body from the bitter cold. He was able to free her, and as he put her into the car she feebly informed him, "My brother is dead." He went back to look and found that the brother, thrown from the car, had been struck on the back of the neck by the running board and was dead so Nadwornick concentrated on getting the girl to shelter as quickly as possible.

He took her to the nearest neighbors, got them awake, and got her into the house. She was still alive so they started rubbing her with snow and were finally rewarded with signs of life. The girl not only recovered but is still living, married and has a nice family. Since the brother was beyond help, all they could do was go lift the car off him, then go for the sheriff to take care of the body.

Mr. Nadwornick noted that he drove an automobile fifty years without an accident, but the last time he took his driver's test his license was quite restrictive. At first they were going to limit his driving to the city of Glendive only, but he protested that that kind of license was no good to him because his farm was fourteen miles out in the country.

They made a little further concession then – stamped on his license that he was allowed to also drive to his farm, fourteen miles out in the country. He says they insisted that an eighty-year-old man should have glasses to drive, but he insisted he didn't need glasses. Even now, at eighty-four, he can see to thread a needle and doesn't have glasses yet. But he did quit driving; sold his car and doesn't drive at all anymore.

Mr. Nadwornick continued to farm with horses until after World War I, but in the twenties he had to give in and buy a tractor. By that time his boys were big enough to help farm, and they figured they had to have a tractor. He started out with an International 15-30, and at first the boys kept it going around the clock – the horses under that hood didn't have to rest so one of the boys ran it during the day, another at night, but that, Mr. Nadwornick explains, "soon wore off."

For forty years he owned a threshing machine and threshed all around the country. During World War I he went to Aberdeen, South Dakota to help in the harvest. He saw an ad in the paper asking for harvest help. They needed 1,500 men so he borrowed fifty dollars to get him there and went to Aberdeen.

During those years there was very little to harvest in this area and times were hard. While he was in South Dakota he caught his sleeve in the separator belt*. He managed to jerk his arm free, but the belt tore off his sleeve up to the shoulder.

During the twenties and thirties many of the farmers in their community, as well as in other parts of the county, left the farm because of poor crops and low prices for wheat and cattle. Nadwornicks were among those who 'stuck it out' and after three decades were able to pay off their debts accumulated over the years. They realized that you just couldn't 'make it' on half-a-section so when lands were sold for taxes, he added two more quarters to the half-section he bought in 1911.

When he decided to retire, he turned the farm over to one of his boys, bought a house in Glendive, and moved to town. Their eight children (four boys and four girls) are pretty well scattered now: one in Alaska, two in Washington, three in California, and two in Dawson County.

Mr. Nadwornick reports that as he talked with an acquaintance recently the fellow boasted that he used to drive a mile twice a day to water his cattle, but now all he has to do is push a couple buttons. Sixty years ago they didn't push buttons; they did everything with their two hands.

Mrs. Ed (Olive Clement) Garfield

April – May 1968

Mrs. Olive Garfield was born in Ontario in 1897, but she has lived in Montana for sixty-two years. She and her younger sister, Margaret, came with their parents, Mr. and Mrs. Adolphus Clement, to Sidney – that is, to the area where Sidney later developed – in 1902. Her maternal grandparents, as well as three uncles and two aunts, had already settled in eastern Montana when her family arrived.

They arrived in February and although little Olive was only five years old, the bitter cold made an indelible impression upon her, as did the deep snow. Mrs. Garfield well remembers it yet. They had come on the Great Northern to Mondak, and were met there by one of her uncles with a team and bobsled. Little wonder she remembers the snow and cold! But the bottom of the sled was covered with straw, and heated bricks had been placed there to help a little in counteracting the cold. By the time they had snuggled down under blankets and robes they were much better equipped to cope with the weather than the modern motorist whose car stalls when he has not thought to carry along so much as an overcoat.

The new arrivals were taken first to 'Uncle Joe's' – Joe Stubb, who lived at Dore, North Dakota. By this time the Stubbs were well established in the Yellowstone Valley, having settled there in 1900.

During the trip west Mrs. Clement became ill and passed away soon after reaching the Treasure State*. Fortunate indeed it was for the little family that loved ones had preceded them to this frontier settlement and now were in a position to offer a home to the widower and his two little motherless girls. They lived with 'Grandma' Moore for almost six years until Mr. Clement remarried to Ada Messing. Of her father's second wife Mrs. Garfield comments, "She wasn't a 'stepmother' – not in the sense people often think of stepmothers; she was a real mother to us."

Mr. Clement was ahead of the homesteads and just 'squatted' on the land he farmed. He did not, however, depend upon the farm only for a living. He was a carpenter and had a hand in the building of much of early Sidney. When he arrived on the Montana scene, there was only one building on the town's site – a log structure belonging to Eddie Kenoyer and serving as combination residence, general store, and post office, so there was plenty of room for growth. The Yellowstone Mercantile and Sidney's first grain elevator were among the projects he worked on.

The French-Canadian immigrant from Ontario must have liked what he found in the Yellowstone Valley because he spent the rest of his life there. He passed away in 1940 so he watched Sidney grow from one log building to a thriving business center.

Mrs. Clement (Mrs. Garfield's stepmother) had preceded her husband in death in December 1927. Even Mrs. Garfield's son, Dick, remembers that occasion although he was only six years old at the time. The weather was bitterly cold (fifty-six degrees below zero) at the time of her death, and Mrs. Garfield made the trip to Sidney on the 'dinky'* – the combination freight and passenger train. Because of the snow and cold the fifty-mile trip took the entire day, but they arrived safely, and even the baby was none the worse for the experience.

In 1912 Olive married Earl Lamb. Earl was born on the Tongue River, but his father, Eldon J. Lamb, was a contractor on the 'Big Ditch'* so they had moved to Sidney. Lamb, Sr., had only one hand because the other had been blown off by a firecracker while they were still in southeast Montana. His wife had to drive thirty miles with a team and wagon to get him to the doctor.

After the irrigation project was completed, Mr. E.J. Lamb homesteaded on Burns Creek and spent the remainder of his days ranching there instead of returning to the Tongue River country.

During the railroad strike of 1916 Earl and Olive moved to Glendive where Earl, as well as his two brothers, went to work for the railroad. By this time they had a little Lamb, Clyde, who later distinguished himself as a cartoonist. Two years after the three Lamb brothers started working for the Northern Pacific Railroad, Archie Lamb was killed in an accident. Earl accompanied the body to California, where their parents then lived, and Olive went to Sidney with her relatives who had come for the funeral.

The funeral was just at the time the annual June rise had sent the Yellowstone well beyond its banks. Out-of-town relatives driving to Glendive (and they weren't coming in on an oiled highway) were met by high water as far out as Bamber Hill*. The road at that time followed right along the river instead of its present route. George Muxlow ran a livery stable in town so they got him to pull the cars through the water with his mule team.

On the return trip, after the funeral, they drove through water from the Yellowstone bridge to about where the service station, recently owned by the late Garfield Trulock*, is now located. From there they turned and went up over the hill to the right, on across the flat which now boasts Jefferson School (there was no road to follow) and so on back to join the Sidney road where it reached higher ground.

That wasn't their only experience with high water as far out as Bamber Hill. Several years later, after Earl Lamb had passed from her life and Olive had married Ed Garfield, they had gone to Sidney on a beautiful spring morning and returned that evening after dark to be flagged down – at Bamber Hill. Mrs. Garfield declares she was scared to death (almost), thinking it was a holdup.

Instead of a holdup, however, they found that the ice in the river had gone out that day and had flooded the road, not with water only but with huge ice chunks as well. There was no going through that night so they turned around and went back to Stipek. Stipek then consisted of quite a bit more than a couple elevators and a residence or two. At that time it had a lumberyard, rooming house and hotel combination, post office, harness shop, butcher shop, two

120

livery barns, and a grocery store that handled a good many other things besides groceries.

Fortunate it was for the travelers that Stipek had a rooming house then. The Garfields were not alone in seeking accommodations at the hotel that night; several other stranded travelers came too. Soon after the Garfields' arrival at Stipek a fellow was brought in, soaking wet. He had ignored the flagman who had tried to stop him (maybe he thought it was a holdup, too) and had driven into the icy water.

He was given prompt attention and hustled into dry clothes while hot coffee helped to get him warmed up. Thanks to the quick work, he suffered no ill effects from his impromptu bath.

Next morning the Garfields headed for Glendive again, but this time they met with complications at Deer Creek. Water from the flooding river had backed up into the creek during the night, and now cars were lined up at the bank as drivers hesitated to venture into the high water.

Mr. Garfield, however, had had enough of delay, so he removed the fan belt from his Model T, covered the motor with an old wool army blanket they had in the car, and plunged in with it. After his successful crossing, other drivers followed suit and all proceeded on toward Glendive. By the time they reached Bamber Hill a path had been cut through the ice chunks and water across the road (that road, remember, turned right from the bridge, following a course between the present Buttreys* site and the river) had receded enough to allow them to get into town. During the height of the water, people had been launching boats from the Yellowstone Bridge to get to points west.

At the time of her marriage to Ed Garfield, Olive Lamb was working for Little Lee, a little Chinaman, in the New York Cafe*. Ed was working in Dick Stathams garage at the time, and both of them worked nights.

The Garfields' Glendive residence dates back to 1890 when Ed's father, E.B. Garfield, came to Glendive as a conductor for the Northern Pacific Railroad. Some old pictures still in the family's possession testify that there wasn't much to Glendive when E.B. Garfield came!

Interestingly, the caboose, which Garfield used, is still in Glendive. It is owned by Marvin Graves and has been incorporated into a house in the rear of 1211 North Meade.

Edwin Garfield was just ten years old when his father, Northern Pacific conductor E.B. Garfield, brought his family to live in Glendive. The Gate City in 1890 was a fledgling town on the newly constructed Northern Pacific line, the rails into the Treasure State not even ten years old.

New though the town was, it was developed enough to have an elementary school so even frontier boys had to submit to education. The process didn't last as long for most of them then, however, as it does for most young people now, and when Ed was in his mid-teens he started working as callboy* for the Northern Pacific.

Next they took him on as fireman, but he only made a few trips in that capacity. He was on the Forsyth run, and after several trips he decided firing was too much work so he climbed off the train at Forsyth and went to punching cattle for the XIT, a Texas cattle outfit and one of the world's largest.

The life of a cowboy could hardly be considered an easy life, but it was a different kind of work. While he was riding for the XIT an incident occurred which affected Ed for life. He and another cowboy were caught in an electrical storm while riding, and the fellow was killed when struck by a bolt of lightning. For the rest of his life Ed Garfield was mortally afraid of lightning.

Along with the XIT Ed rode for a number of other cattle ranches – the CS – the N-N – the LU Bar – all through the Big Dry Country* and the Little Dry, the Big Porcupine, the Little Porcupine, and the Milk River. They called him 'The Kid' in those days.

Jack McNaney recalls that his dad for a time rode for the same outfit that Ed did. Mr. McNaney as a cowboy rode circle (checking on the cattle) so seven-year-old Jack couldn't trail along with him, but at that time Ed was horse wrangler, and a seven-year-old boy got along fine with him.

Jack was too short to reach the stirrup to mount his horse (no little pony for him, just because he was only seven) so Ed would boost him into the saddle every morning. But there were always times he'd have to dismount and get back on when Ed wasn't around so for such contingency Jack had tied to the saddle horn a rope with which he could slide down to the ground or could climb up to get back into the saddle.

Ed wasn't, Jack reflected, what you'd call a 'top' rider, but on the other hand, he could ride horses that a lot of other fellows preferred not to try. As a man, though, and as a friend Ed was tops, with no reservations to that statement.

When homestead lands opened up, Ed filed on a claim near Lindsay. He ranched and farmed there until 1912, but then his wife died, and Ed lost all interest in the place. He walked off and left everything – horses, furniture – all, and came to Glendive to work. When he went back later, he discovered that everything he'd left had been stolen.

Ed went to work for Dick Statham in Dick's garage, and in 1919 he married Olive Lamb. In the years following their marriage they continued to live in or near Glendive. Whether they were 'in' or 'near', excitement seemed to be able to find them. Mrs. Garfield especially remembers the dark, rainy night when the posse came looking for a fellow accused of murder.

He had been working in Glendive, but when he was found out, he attempted to get out of the country before the law caught up with him. He had stopped a young man in town and had ordered him, at the point of a gun, to drive for him. The Dry Creek Bridge was washed out, so when they reached that point, they had to stop the car because Dry Creek that night, with all the rain that had been falling, was not dry and couldn't be crossed.

Garfields were living west of Glendive, not far from the washed out bridge, and the outlaw fled through their yard – but they didn't realize who he was. A short time later the law followed so Mr. Garfield, not knowing who was pounding on his door, answered the knock with his shotgun in his hands.

It was the highway patrolman who identified himself and explained that they were searching for the fugitive. By that time he had left those parts but a posse was formed in Garfield's yard and followed him across country. They found him in a barn over along the Bloomfield road, and as the posse closed in on him he shot himself.

When Ed and Olive Garfield were first married, they lived in the Fowler Rooming House (an old landmark that could give plenty of history if it could speak), then they moved into a little green house where the new telephone annex is presently being constructed.

In those days houses weren't commonly equipped with central heating systems, and in this one the bedroom was very cold when the weather outside was cold so they moved the bed into the living room.

Mrs. Garfield wasn't feeling well one evening and had gone to bed early, and Mr. Garfield was playing the phonograph (it would be an antique now, no doubt) when suddenly the door was flung open, and a man, all covered with blood, burst into the room.

He had been in a fight over in the roundhouse and was running to get away from the police. Mrs. Garfield was terrified by the sudden apparition, but the intruder's consternation was hardly less than hers when he caught sight of her. He whirled about and departed as abruptly as he had entered.

They lived for a number of years in a duplex in the building which now accommodates the Cloverleaf Cafe*. There, too, Mrs. Garfield was frightened a couple times by intruders. She managed to put up a brave front, but she was glad they couldn't see how she was quaking inwardly.

One of the intruders walked in while she was standing in her doorway, saying good-bye to two women who had been visiting her. The fellow had one arm in a sling and walked in in such matter-of-fact manner that the departing guests thought he had the right and were not at first alarmed. Mrs. Garfield was alarmed but had no intention of letting him know it.

She demanded of him, "What do you want?" He mumbled in reply, "I saw a pretty girl come in here." "You didn't," she bluntly contradicted him. There were no girls in the house so she knew he hadn't seen anyone – not that she'd have let him in if he had.

She ordered him to leave, but he insolently replied, "Try and make me." By this time it was clear to the two women just leaving that his entrance was unauthorized, and they shared Mrs. Garfield's apprehension. However, Mrs. Garfield summoned Jack McNaney (the McNaneys at that time lived in the other part of the duplex), and Jack did the persuading. It turned out that the fellow had mental problems.

Another time a man walked in and grabbed little Margaret, Garfield's daughter who was then about two years old. That did scare Mrs. Garfield, but he released her unhurt and finally left.

Not all unannounced guests were of the unwelcome variety. One evening Mrs. Garfield was astonished to see her two younger half-brothers from Sidney ride up to her door – not in a car, not even horseback. George, the older of the two, was competing in a Boy Scout endurance contest so he had ridden his bike all the way from Sidney.

That was in the pre-oiled era, and besides pedaling the fifty-some miles over the gravel road, he had hauled his younger brother, Don, on the handlebars. He won his endurance medal, and Don who probably should have had an endurance medal, too, asked Olive to patch the seat of his trousers – which hadn't had enough endurance for the journey on the handle bars.

Besides Margaret, who now lives in Portland, Oregon, the Garfields had two other children: Dick and Donna, both of West Glendive. After sixty-one years in the Treasure State, Mr. Garfield passed away in 1951 following an operation. Mrs. Garfield continues to live in West Glendive, not far from her oldest and youngest offspring.

R.R. Durfey

March – April 1969

If you are planning on building a house and don't like the idea of that long waiting period before you can move into it, perhaps you'd like to ask Bob Durfey how it's done in a hurry. The first houses he helped build in Montana were ready for occupancy in about three days!

You might throw that up to your contractor if you've already waited months and are beginning to think you'll never get in. But then of course, he might throw back, "You want to live in a sod house with no plumbing, no wiring, no....?"

R.R. Durfey came to Montana in 1910. He and another fellow considered the possibilities in homesteading, and in March they decided to come out and have a look.

They went to Poplar that trip and found there was plenty of free land available to the north toward Scobey. Not bothering to file, they went back to Iowa to work for the summer. In August they loaded an immigrant car* and headed for Poplar again, but now they found that in just those few months since spring, all the best land north of the Missouri had been snapped up.

They turned their attention south of the river instead and found that, with the exception of a few ranchers, hardly anyone lived in the vast territory that stretched from the Missouri to Richey (even Richey wasn't there then). Section after section was just waiting for someone to settle on it so they promptly obliged.

There were five in the party eligible to homestead so they chose adjacent claims – might as well have a few neighbors. Durfey's was two miles east of the present town of Vida.

In fact, it was this little group that gave Vida its name. The nearest post office at that time was Wolf Point so before they had been settled six months, one of the other members of the group, August Nefzger, made application for a post office in his home. The application was granted, and he named it Vida, after his daughter – who, incidentally, had also homesteaded.

To say they homesteaded that fall isn't quite accurate. The land had not yet been surveyed so they 'squatted', then filed for homestead rights two or three years later when the survey was completed.

Once claims were located their most pressing concern was housing. They had set up tents for temporary quarters, which was all right in August but hardly suitable for wintering. There were four men in the party (besides Durfey and Nefzger, the latter's two sons, Clyde and Clarence, were also squatting) and they all worked together until they had a house built on each claim – about two or three weeks.

The only building material available in abundance in that prairie land was sod. There was plenty of that so they built all four houses of sod. They plowed the tough sod into chunks about two feet long and four inches thick, then hauled the strips to the building site with team and wagon. There they laid it up like brick, breaking joints and sealing them with mud made out of gumbo* — which was also abundant. They plastered the whole inside.

The walls of the cabin were about thirty inches thick at the bottom, sloping to about twenty inches at the top. The inside of the wall was straight with the slope on the outside. The ridgepole was mounted on the sod gables. Twelve-inch boards were bent over the ridge pole (he used sixteen-foot boards for his twelve-foot wide cabin) to form a base for the sod roof, then the sod was piled on six to eight inches deep.

His little sod shanty boasted three windows — one double and two halves. The homemade wooden door also had a glass in it. The windows in opposite walls made good cross-ventilation in the summer months when it was needed. It was about two years before the cabin boasted anything for floor but the ground over which it was built. The other cabins had twelve-inch boards laid on the ground for floors, but they soon warped and the dirt came up through the cracks so they might as well have been dirt. They were a little easier to sweep, though.

The only stove in the shanty was a little sheep-wagon stove, serving double-duty for both cooking and heating. They lived in the sod house four years. Even in the coldest weather that little stove provided adequate heat. After they built their frame house they just about froze. They wished a good many times in the cold of winter that they were back in the little old sod shanty. The same sod that had insulated the house against the cold had also kept it cool in summer.

Just five days before he left Iowa Bob Durfey had married, but his wife waited a couple weeks before joining him in Montana. By that time the sod house was ready for occupancy, and the immigrant car had been unloaded. Since they were just setting up housekeeping they didn't have much furniture to bring. But then, young couples setting up housekeeping on the frontier generally didn't start out with as much furniture as young couples consider necessary now. Certainly there was no electric range or refrigerator or freezer or TV. No hi-fi set — no electric anything. Not even a radio, difficult as it is for the modern to think of pre-radio days. Back somewhere near the stone age maybe?

They did bring a little farm machinery — not much, though; it didn't take as much machinery to start up then, either, and Bob didn't even have much of what it did take. He brought a cow and calf, too. As soon as the little sod house was made as comfortable as possible he built a barn for the stock, just big enough for the two. The barn was dug into the bank with the sides and front sodded up.

That first winter on the prairies the new settlers didn't have much going for entertainment — nor, for that matter, even work. When they got tired twiddling thumbs one way, Mr. Durfey explained, they twiddled the other way!

There was no sign of a road when they first built on the prairies so they'd just start off towards town. They'd get lost every once in awhile, but not so bad but what they'd get out all right. It was especially difficult if darkness overtook them before they reached home. Because the summer and fall had been so dry, tracks showed up all right, but after snow fell, tracks were liable to drift shut before you could retrace your route. The shifting snow could make keeping your directions even more difficult.

When they first came to Montana their post office was Poplar. They had unloaded the immigrant car there because of the ferry. Wolf Point would have been closer, but the only way to cross the Missouri there was with a rowboat. Then somebody built a flat boat about 8'x12' at Wolf Point that was propelled by two oars. It pulled hard, but with a man on each oar you could get across the river – if you had nerve enough to ride.

Before long they had their mail changed to Wolf Point. When the cold and snow of their first winter came, they couldn't get into either town very regularly. After one period of about two months without mail or supplies August Nefzger asked Durfey to walk to Wolf Point with him.

The weather was cold, and the crusted snow lay eight to ten inches deep on the level, and in the coulees – well, they avoided the coulees. That made their walk longer but considerably easier and less hazardous.

They didn't make very good time at first, dodging the coulees and trying to find their way in that dazzling white world. After about twelve miles they reached a homestead and found a sled track. They were too late for a ride in the sled that the track represented, but it gave them something to follow and made walking easier.

They covered about twenty miles that first day and spent the night at a ranch. Next day they walked on into town and filled their sack, which they had brought along for that purpose, with groceries and supplies – and mail, then walked back to Heser's homestead. The track was still open so they made good time – considering. The third day saw them home again. Although the distance to Wolf Point from their claims by the present highway is about twenty-two miles it was closer to thirty miles the way they went.

Before much longer, Mr. Nefzger decided they needed a shopping center closer home so he set up a kind of store in his house. He had built his cabin considerably larger than Durfeys and could spare the room. He'd get supplies out of Wolf Point, and other settlers in the area could buy there instead of having to make the long trip to Wolf Point. Although they found open country when they came in the summer of 1910 the land was taken up fast. Soon there were a number of homesteaders (to be when the land was surveyed) in the area.

Mr. Nefzger always had a sack of hard cane sugar under the counter and invited every child who came into the store to come behind the counter and break off a piece.

It was in March of 1911 that Mr. Nefzger inaugurated a post office (Vida) in his home along with the store. His son, Clyde, became mail carrier, picking up the mail in Wolf Point and delivering it at the Vida post office. There were no specifications as to how often he must get the mail, but he usually brought it out at least once a week. The government didn't pay him much – only three or four dollars a trip. His mail hauling was more an accommodation deal than financial asset. He also hauled freight for his father's store.

That first spring Durfey was on his claim in Montana, he broke up a little patch of ground for a garden, but it wasn't until the third spring he broke up any amount. The first few years he worked out mostly, picking up what jobs he could for ranchers or other farmers.

One of the places he worked was on a cattle and horse ranch up the creek a few miles. In the spring of 1912 the rancher let him use a team to break up some sod for flax. After the ground was broken he rented it to another farmer because he didn't have enough farm machinery yet to handle it. He rented it for cash and never did find out just how many bushels to the acre the flax made, but it was one of the best stands he's seen.

In the fall of 1911 he went back to Minnesota for harvest "and came back with a whole pocketful of money – $50!" But that took them through the winter. Produce from their garden helped stretch the fifty dollars. He didn't know the country then and hadn't plowed up a very good piece of ground.

In Iowa where he came from creek bottomland was the best, but he found that was not so in Montana. That's how it happened he chose a patch of gumbo that first spring. But in spite of that they raised a few potatoes – some carrots – rutabagas – beets.

He came back from Minnesota just in time to clean the garden before it froze up. The CK roundup wagon was camped about a fourth of a mile down the creek (Durfey's claim was on Wolf Creek) so in the evening after he was through cleaning the garden he took a pail of carrots and rutabagas over to them.

When he was ready to go back home, the cook told him, "Just wait a minute. I'll get you some meat." With that he cut the ribs off a front quarter of beef, then gave the rest of the quarter to Durfey. A roundup cook didn't often have fresh vegetables to offer on his menu so he was tickled to get some – and Durfey was tickled to get the fresh meat. It isn't every day that a fellow gets a quarter of beef for a pail of vegetables. But of course it wasn't a trade. It was just an example of pioneer spirit.

Durfey, as one of the first squatters, saw the influx of homesteaders as they hopefully rushed for free land. Then he saw the gradual exodus of many of those same homesteaders as successive years of drought, hail, and grasshoppers drained away those hopes.

Durfey himself sold out and left the farm in 1929; "went broke with all the banks." He moved into Wolf Point where he got a truck and started hauling. After about a year he moved back to the Vida country, doing any job he could get, mostly carpentering.

His four children grew up and scattered, as is the way of children. One boy now lives in Richey, one in Livingston, and the other in Washington. His lone daughter is the only one still in 'home territory'. She lives two miles north of Vida.

He lived with her for a time, but ten or eleven years ago some folks in Vida asked him to take care of their house a couple weeks while they were gone. They aren't back yet, so he's still taking care of it.

Mrs. John (Nancy Smith) Hollenbeck

February – March 1970

A washtub, a wash board, a boiler, a mop, broom, bedstead with a feather tick, table, six plates, cups, and saucers, and a frying pan. How does that sound for a wedding present to set up housekeeping? Nancy Hollenbeck's mother considered herself well equipped when her mother supplied her with such a generous dowry. But then, Nancy is ninety-two years old, and it was almost 100 years ago that her mother set up housekeeping. Nancy still has that frying pan.

For those of us born a little later, it's easy to forget how new the West is. Then someone like Mrs. Hollenbeck casually observes that she helped settle up two frontiers, and her mother helped settle up three! Surely the land in which we live is hardly past its infancy.

Mrs. Hollenbeck, who lives now in the Beach Golden Valley Manor, first came to Golden Valley County in 1902. "Father got hungry for free land," she explained, so they came to western North Dakota and looked over the land. However, the land was not surveyed yet so they just stayed a few days. Then in 1903 they came back and filed on homesteads. Nancy, too, filed on a homestead, as did one of her sisters.

Two different parties of homesteaders, four in each, came at the same time – her father with his two daughters and a nephew, Sam Smith; the other a group of four men. Nancy and the others in her group selected their homestead sites and filed their claims at the land office in Sentinel Butte. They were practically the first to file on homesteads in all that wide, open country so there were plenty of sites from which to choose. There were plenty of sites for the other group, too. Yet, after the Smiths filed in Sentinel Butte, three of the other men decided on the same sites, boarded a train for Bismarck, and filed their claims with the land office in Bismarck so their claims were registered in the state land office before the filings from Sentinel Butte came in. When the Smiths returned in 1904, they had to file again.

This time Nancy homesteaded about twelve miles from Sentinel Butte, while her father and sister filed near Sentinel Butte, along what is now Interstate 94. Her father built on the side of a hill so he became known as 'Side Hill Smith' to distinguish him from the many other Smiths in the area.

When Nancy and her father came to Sentinel Butte in 1902, the town had no hotel, so they stayed in the ranch home of Mr. and Mrs. Henry Gilbert. Mr. Gilbert had worked on the Northern Pacific Railroad when the tracks were being laid in 1881 and had made his home there from that time on.

When the Smith party came back in October 1903, Jack Snyder was running a hotel so this time they stayed in the hotel. Mrs. Hollenbeck remembers yet a lunch served to them in the Blodgett home – buttermilk biscuits, fresh butter, and tea.

Mr. Gilbert was running the land office in Sentinel Butte so he took them around in his buckboard as they looked for homesteads, and it was he who filed their claims for them – the claims that were preempted by men filing at Bismarck. It was in June, 1904, that they returned and filed on other homesteads, still in the Sentinel Butte area. Mrs. Hollenbeck observes that the land was better around Beach, but they didn't know that then.

That same June, 1904, lightening killed a sheepherder during a big storm. J.B. Stoddard had a herder out with a big band of sheep, and the lightening killed both man and horse. When found, the dogs were lying by the dead herder, and the sheep were scattered. Nancy's father and A.L. Martin took the body to Sentinel Butte and shipped it home. Smiths went back to Minnesota for the summer months, then moved out in October. Mrs. Hollenbeck has lived in the area ever since.

Since she was 'here to stay', she had to get a shack built. They hired a team from Frank Stone, and her dad helped her haul the lumber out. They happened to hit a rainy spell so they found hard going. Leaving Sentinel Butte about four o'clock in the morning, they kept to the top of the hills as much as possible – there was no road to follow, anyway – but even so, it took them 'til sundown to cover the twelve miles to her homestead. The team would pull until they couldn't pull any more, then have to rest.

When they reached the site she had chosen for her house, rain was still pouring down. They couldn't go back to town that night so they sat under their load of lumber. Father tied each horse to the others tail. That way they could eat, but they couldn't run off.

Although the wagon kept the rain off them, to a measure at least, the ground was as wet as any place else, so Nancy tried crawling up on the wagon reach*. But that was too hard so she had to go back to the ground. It was a miserable night, but there was nothing to do but stick it out.

They had only taken lunch for noon with them so they had no supper and no breakfast the next morning. Nevertheless, they went ahead and framed up the shack before they went back into town. They stayed in the hotel until the shack was ready for occupancy – which was a lot sooner than would be considered 'ready' now!

Nancy Hollenbeck's (she was Smith then) house on the homestead measured 10'x14' on the outside. To save space, she had a bed frame nailed against the wall. The 'spring' was a straw tick, the 'mattress' a feather tick. Not much room for any excess furniture in her little shack.

She dug her well, eighteen feet deep, with a posthole digger. Since she didn't have money for a pump, she just dipped her water out. Her 'dipper' was a tomato can with a wire for a bail and a burr on the top edge to make it tip so the water would run in when it hit the water surface. It was slow work, lowering the can with a clothesline rope and pulling the water can to the top of the well, but she got by. That well is there yet.

Homestead regulations did not require that she live on the homestead the year 'round so she 'worked out' some. While she was working in the Sentinel Butte hotel she served some distinguished guests. She cooked two meals for the Marquis de Mores' wife and their crew of twelve.

Alice Roosevelt DeLong was another guest she served. Mrs. Hollenbeck even remembers that the meal ordered by Mrs. DeLong and her party was beef steak smothered with onions. Bob Burnett, owner of the hotel, had just butchered a beef. White soda biscuits accompanied the meal but no dessert.

While she was working at the hotel she rode Teddy Roosevelt's private saddle horse. Burnett was taking care of the horse, which by that time was more than thirty years old. The horse had been a darker color in its earlier years but by this time was gray. He was getting rather feeble, and she only rode it about ten feet, she explains, but it was enough so she could tell her grandchildren and great grandchildren that she rode Teddy Roosevelt's saddle horse.

Before settling down permanently on the homestead she also worked for Dr. Stickney in Dickinson. Besides doing general housework she milked the cow and took care of the doctor's horses. Dr. Stickney was very particular about his horses, and no one but he or Nancy took care of them. And well he might be particular. Many a time the horses brought him home when the storm was too thick for the doctor to find the way – or when the doctor was just plain too tired to stay awake. Nancy was reluctant to leave Dr. Stickney's employ, but if she didn't get back to her homestead someone might contest her rights, so she moved back out on the claim.

When Nancy moved to Golden Valley County in 1904, Sentinel Butte was a thriving little town. She remembers there were two general stores, a hotel, three lumber yards, two banks, a restaurant, a saddle shop – a very good saddle shop; the inevitable saloons, of course – three of them; a butcher shop – the butcher, S.B. Kellogg, pedaled his meat by wagon; and a livery barn. The livery barn was later converted into a garage when horsepower under the hood replaced horsepower in the harness.

One of the storekeepers was A.L. Martin. Martin was an early rancher in the area, but instead of fighting the encroaching 'honyockers'* as did the ranchers in many parts of the west, Mr. Martin recognized the inevitable. He went into the lumber business, capitalizing on the homesteaders' trade. He also sold implements and machinery.

When Nancy left Minnesota, her uncle had given her a mare which had two colts. One of her horses had to be killed, though, or so she thought at the time. They were using him at the coal mine when the scraper slipped and hit him on the rump. He kicked against the edge of the blade and cut off his leg so they shot him. Later, however, she saw a horse with an artificial leg. A woman mail carrier used him on her run. In another case, a fellow from the Black Hills who came up to thresh had a team of horses, each of which had one leg cut off. He used those three-legged horses on the bundle wagon. If she had to do it over she would not be so hasty in disposing of a horse so injured.

In 1906 Nancy married John Hollenbeck. John had come to western North Dakota in 1895. There wasn't much of anything but ranches when he came – and since each ranch required thousands of acres, there weren't many of those.

During those early years in the West he had worked on ranches and as a teamster, hauling winter supplies and other essentials from the stores to the ranches. His ranch experiences included working as a roundup cook. Mrs. Hollenbeck described some of his culinary methods and equipment. For his 'stove' he dug a hole in the ground, just a size to fit his kettle, then built a fire in the hole. When the fire was reduced to just red coals, he'd put a little dirt on it, then he'd set his kettle of potatoes down in the hole and let them cook.

To bake biscuits, he'd use a kettle too, but for an 'oven' he'd also cover the kettle with dirt, sealing in the heat. The sourdough biscuits were standard fare for the cowboys. And of course, beans were standard fare too.

For breakfast it was none of this juice and toast; it was more probably beans boiled with pork bacon and ham. Beans would cook all night in their kettle over the coals and be ready for breakfast in the wee hours of the morning. Sourdough pancakes frequently appeared on the menu too.

To make coffee, he piled the dirt higher around the hole, then laid a grate across the top of it and set his coffee pot on that. For dinner or supper he often served 'black beef steak'. Mrs. Hollenbeck doesn't know just how this was prepared except that he burned it some way and cooked it on this grate. He served wieners too, sometimes. The crew generally consisted of about twelve men, though extras weren't unusual. As cook, he drove the mess wagon, which carried not only his cooking supplies, but also the bed rolls for the roundup men. As the crew moved from one location to another they had to camp near water so to find springs, they'd follow a cow trail.

John Hollenbeck was hauling mail when Nancy Smith married him in 1906. He used a buckboard for his transportation. The buckboard, pulled by two horses, was a light vehicle, yet it could haul heavy loads behind the seats. Mr. Hollenbeck hauled mail from 1900 to 1908.

In the first years after the homesteaders began coming in to the ranch country they found they had no market for selling stock. There was no local market, certainly no trucking, and the only way they could ship on the railroad was with a rancher. If he happened to be short a few head on a carload and would let them 'fill in', well and good. Otherwise they didn't ship. Later, though, an enterprising farmer gathered enough cattle from other farmers to make up a carload so they could ship independently of the ranchers. Although they had no formal organization, they demonstrated to themselves even then that they could accomplish things working together that they could not do alone.

Where Nancy came from in Minnesota there had been plenty of wood to burn, but on the North Dakota prairies fuel of any kind was scarce. There was some coal, but it was green and hard to burn. Even the ashes seemed different. Ashes apparently dead could start a fire hours later if put into a wooden pail. Often the settlers would go out where the range horses were and pick up droppings to be used for fuel. That burned better than green coal.

One time someone gave her an old building to burn for kindling. After they had chopped some of it and piled it behind the stove, they found that it was full of bedbugs! This happened after her husband had passed away and her family was grown and gone. Her only son was living with her at that time so she took a trip while he got rid of the bugs. After she left he filled the house with formaldehyde, then he stayed out of the house entirely, sleeping outside, until the gas had time to do its work.

Sometimes 'foreigners' coming in would have lice on their heads and bodies. She recalls one family with fourteen children who had that problem. And they shared the problem with anyone they could. They would pick lice off themselves, put them into a bottle, then shake them onto children who tried to keep clean. When her children took off their clothes in the evening, she'd wash the children and iron the clothes with a hot iron. Next morning she would iron the clothes again. She'd also carefully and frequently comb their hair with a fine comb. Not all of the experiences in the 'good old days' were so good!

In 1932 her husband passed away, leaving her to battle the drought and the depression alone with their four children. She had to mortgage the farm to keep going, then when she had the mortgage balance down to the last thousand (her taxes all paid up), she couldn't make a payment on time and the Bank of North Dakota foreclosed.

She had one year to redeem the farm. That possibility looked nigh hopeless because she couldn't borrow money from a bank, but then a friend loaned her the money just before the year was up. She immediately took the train to Bismarck. When she arrived at the bank, the 'boss' was out so a new clerk transacted the deal for her. By the time she had finished at the bank she had twenty-five cents left and had missed her train. That meant staying overnight in Bismarck so she used her twenty-five cents to get a bed. She had no dinner, no supper, and next morning she had no breakfast.

As soon as she got back to Beach she felt compelled – she explains that the Lord led her – to go to the courthouse and record those papers right away. That taken care of, she went to the hotel cafe. When she ordered her dinner, she told the waitress she had no money, but she had already missed three meals. The waitress explained to the hotel owner, who promptly sent the meal in to Mrs. Hollenbeck. The lady who ran the hotel and proved to be a benefactor that day still lives in Beach – and still has the gratitude of the widow to whom she extended credit that day.

After Mrs. Hollenbeck had eaten her dinner, a neighbor gave her a ride out to her farm – the farm she had almost lost but now was hers again. The next day an angry banker came storming to Beach, only to find the deed duly recorded in the courthouse. He had planned to charge her another $40 per acre but was foiled by a new clerk. And there was nothing he could do about it. Mrs. Hollenbeck owns the farm yet – 800 acres near Rocky Butte.

Western North Dakota was the second frontier Mrs. Hollenbeck helped tame. At ninety-two years of age she can look back and trace almost a century of progress, particularly in the development of farm machinery. Since most of those developments have taken place in the last hundred years, she has seen most of them herself – and what she didn't see, her grandmother told her.

Her grandparents came to the United States from the Highlands of Scotland. The ocean voyage took six weeks. Their first son was born in New

York, but he lived only a short time. They went on to Dubuque, Iowa, where they settled for a time but then moved on to Goodhue County in Minnesota.

During their sojourn in Iowa they bought a team of horses and two teams of oxen. When they moved to Minnesota in 1850, they made the trip by wagon, oxen pulling it. They took along their horses, a milk cow, a few chickens, and a couple pigs. Their arrival brought to four the number of white families in the county. And they had the first team of horses in the settlement. Grandfather cut trees from the Minnesota woods, then two men on a hand saw sawed the trees lengthwise to make slabs with which to build their house in the wilderness.

Nails are so commonplace to us that it's hard to think of them as 'modern', yet when he built his home on the frontier only some homemade nails were available. He used a few such, but for the most part the buildings were 'pegged' rather than nailed. A hole had to be drilled – with a hand drill, then a hardwood peg driven into it. All of the original buildings were constructed that way, but Mrs. Hollenbeck is not sure whether or not any of those buildings are still standing. The pegged cow barn was still there two years ago, but she doesn't know whether or not it is now. Her uncle built a big stone barn about 1904 so from then on it was used instead of the pegged barn.

Nancy's mother was the fourth of five children, the only girl. When the fifth child was born, Grandpa went with the team and wagon to bring a neighbor woman, Mrs. Lee, a midwife. After he returned he slipped and fell, breaking his back on a wagon wheel. He died one hour after the baby was born.

So Grandma was left a widow in the wilderness, a widow with four small children. Her brother, then seventeen or eighteen years old, came from Scotland to stay with her, but the government drafted him for a soldier in the Civil War, so she was again without help on the farm.

The nearest town was Redwing, thirty-five to forty miles away. More than once Grandma walked that distance, taking her butter and eggs to exchange for groceries. Not long after Grandpa's death, two of the other white neighbors moved away, afraid because of an Indian massacre which had occurred in another part of the state. Grandma stayed however, as did the Lees.

Although the other white families moved for fear of the Indians, Grandma continued friends with the natives. She was not a doctor, but she had learned a good deal about caring for the sick and often she 'doctored' the Indians. They, in turn, frequently brought her game which they hunted in the woods.

The skunk was especially useful to her. She used the pelt for making clothing, just as she used the pelts of deer, weasels, rabbits, and fox; but even more important from the skunk was the fat. She especially used it for medicine – to break fever, rubbing it on the chest or making a poultice.

Some of her other standbys were ginger plasters and onion plasters, especially for pneumonia. For cough syrup she baked an onion slowly in the oven in a covered pan, then used the juice. But when Mrs. Hollenbeck was raising her family, she was 'modern' and bought her plaster and cough syrups from traveling peddlers.

134

Skunk fat was an important ingredient in making soap also. Other fats could be used, but Grandma preferred the skunk if she could get it. She made leach by putting all her hardwood ashes (their chief fuel was wood) into a box, like a wagon box only smaller, which sloped at one end. When it would rain, the water would run out of the hole in the sloped corner of the box into a keg. Thus she made her lye, which in turn was used to make soap in combination with the fat. She also used the fat to make candles, some of which she gave to the Indians and some of which she used herself.

Years later, after the Indians had been moved to reservations by the government, some of them came back to Goodhue County while Nancy was staying with her grandmother. Some of the younger men had brought the older men to bathe for their rheumatism in 'Muddy Spring', one of their medicine springs. About fifty of them made the trip in wagons. (How else in 1899?) These older Indians remembered Grandma and came to visit her. When they left, they shook hands, and Nancy was deeply impressed at seeing her grandmother cry at the parting.

From the Indians Nancy Hollenbeck's grandmother learned the art of tanning animal furs, which she then used for making clothes, robes or rugs. In the tanning process they used the bark of some kind of tree; salt; water; and alum. Mrs. Hollenbeck still has the pelt of a timber wolf which her uncle killed, then tanned, using the Indian method. The pelt is older than she is – and she's ninety-two – yet it is still soft and in good condition.

She stressed that in sewing animal skins it is important to use yarn rather than thread. Thread will cut the skin, but yarn will not – and the timber wolf pelt bore out her statement. In a few places the yarn has broken, but in no place has it cut the skin.

Grandmother raised her own sheep, sheared them, carded the wool, and made it into yarn. From the yarn she knitted the underclothing for the family as well as mittens, blankets, and other items of apparel. A neighboring German family made their own linen, but she didn't.

In case you want to try your hand at it, they pulled the flax when it was in the green stage, tall and blossomed. They soaked it until the inside was rotten, then they whipped it against a log to get the insides out of it. The long skins that remained were then spun into thread, and the thread was woven into cloth from which men's clothing was made. To combine linen and wool they used the woolen threads in one direction, the linen threads the other. They made toweling, too, out of the linen.

Grandma did many other things for herself that we of a later era never think of doing – although some of them might be interesting to try. For example, instead of buying your cornstarch at the grocery store, perhaps you'd like to make your own, although you'll have to wait until summer to do it.

She'd gather the ears of corn when they were right for roasting (which is why you could hardly do it in February or March), but she didn't roast them. Instead she'd run them through a thing that grated the kernels off the cob and drop the kernels into water. After soaking for a time the skins would float and the starch would sink to the bottom. Then she would pour the water off and spread the starch out to dry. Once it was dry, she had a product like the cornstarch we buy in the super market today. Want to start planning now to make your next year's supply?

She made potato starch in a similar manner. She'd select big potatoes which she would peel and grate, drop into water, pour off and dry, just as with the corn. The starch would lift out in big chunks. She used it in the same way as cornstarch – for pudding, and thickening other things. She liked to have the potato starch on hand in case the potatoes froze.

Grandma's garden played a big part in feeding her family. Drying the fruit and vegetables was her chief method of preservation. Squash and pumpkin she'd cut into strips, apples into rings, then string them and hang them to dry. After they were thoroughly dried, she'd put the pieces into the oven and heat them to kill any bacteria – she might not have explained she was killing bacteria, but she knew she was killing 'whatever might make it spoil'. After the heating she put the pieces into bags.

Other fruit and berries she'd dry on a rack, which she had made. She'd cover the rack with cheesecloth, put her fruit on that, and cover it with another piece of cheesecloth. She'd keep it in the sun during the day, stirring it occasionally to insure even drying, and keep it in the house at night.

She made her own sorghum, also, from the cane she raised. (Maybe that's one of the reasons for problems in our day; plenty of people are willing to raise cane, but who makes sorghum?) To get back to Grandma's cane, she'd strip the leaves, squeeze the juice out with wooden rollers, then boil it down.

Of course, as her children grew older, they helped her with the work. From the maple tree they'd make sugar and syrup and candy. They'd bleed the tree and boil the juice down. From the hard maple they made syrup and brown sugar, from the soft maple, they made syrup and candy. To make the candy, they'd drop a string into the syrup as it was boiling, and the syrup would cling to the string, hardening into candy. Syrup from the soft maple was clear as water and made clear candy. Hard maple syrup was brown.

Mrs. Hollenbeck notes that in her grandmother's day they relied upon drying food to preserve it; in her mother's day they canned in open jars, making the fruit into a kind of jam which they stored in a big jar with a plate over it; then in her own day canning in sealed jars came into practice.

To preserve meat mother would salt pork thoroughly, pack it into a crock or pork barrel, then place over the top of it a board that Father had cut to fit. When she was ready to use the meat, she parboiled it to remove the salt, then rolled it in flour, and fried it slowly. She also salted beef, then dried it.

Nancy sometimes preserved meat by salting it down, too. She remembers that she used nine parts salt to one part sugar to rub into the meat. Some folks, she explained, added saltpeter to make the meat hold its color, but she didn't.

She did use saltpeter for curing ham, though. For years home-cured ham was her specialty when she hosted the Ladies Aid. If you'd like to try her specialty her recipe called for nine tablespoons salt, one tablespoon sugar (she preferred brown) and a little saltpeter in one gallon of boiling water. Then she'd add one teaspoon each of pepper, allspice, and ground cloves for each pound of meat.

Pour this brine over the ham in a crock, and leave it for six weeks or so in a cool place (she dug a hole on the north side of the house and set it in there). Then when you're ready to use it, boil it and serve.

Most things, though, Nancy canned – even fish. Late in the winter when the fish on the market would start to thaw, she could buy all the fish on the counter for $1. With no refrigeration facilities, a merchant was glad to get rid of it for anything he could get out of it. More than once she has stayed up far into the night – or morning – canning fish she thus purchased.

She'd fry the fish in butter, insert into wide mouth jars, cover with grease, and seal. She'd have as much as fifty quarts of canned fish in her root cellar sometimes – convenient insurance when unexpected company dropped in.

Nancy's grandmother, left a widow an hour after the birth of her fifth child, had to be a hardy woman to carry on by herself on the little frontier farm. She had none of the timesaving, back-saving machinery that has so revolutionized farming in the twentieth century. Instead she plowed her fields with a walking plow, broadcast the grain, harvested with a scythe, and threshed with a flail.

The walking plow had wooden moldboards and was pulled by one of the oxen. Grandmother and her oldest son worked together, one of them leading the ox, the other holding the plow handles. The wooden moldboard, rather than turning the ground, rooted the ground like a pig rooting with its nose.

Mrs. Hollenbeck declares that Grandmother, broadcasting her seed, could sow as evenly as a drill. Before the drill, as we know it today, a seeder was developed. The seeder had shovels like a corn cultivator, and the grain dropped down onto a small round plate that scattered the seed in the furrow made by the shovels. Then a drag* was pulled behind to cover the grain, but the drag had to be pulled by another team.

Grandmother used a scythe to cut hay, laying it in even windrows. Then her oldest son piled it in a pile for winter. When she cut wheat and oats, she used a scythe with a basket on it. She was a small woman, but she knew how to handle the scythe and could make the most of her strength.

To thresh the grain she laid it between sheets and flailed it. When the wheat was separated from the chaff, she'd hold it up and pour it from a height, letting the wind blow the chaff away.

After the wheat was threshed Grandmother would take some of the wheat to Cannon Falls where she'd have it ground into flour at the gristmill. The gristmill was built along a fast-flowing stream of water with the water furnishing the power. The wheat was ground between big stones, then another operation removed the bran and shorts. They could also have corn ground at the mill, but it had to be sifted when they took it home.

Mrs. Hollenbeck's parents saw a number of improvements in farm machinery during their lifetime. They used steel moldboards on the plows and saw the first reaper. That first reaper had sweeps to push the grain against the

137

sickle. While Father drove the horses, Mother walked behind the reaper with a fork and raked the grain off the platform. Next an improved reaper featured one more sweep – a longer one – that swept the grain off the platform and onto the ground.

Then the reaper came with a canvas on rollers that elevated the grain against two aprons which directed the grain into a single row on the ground, rather than a row the width of the reaper. At night when the dew was on, they picked up the grain from the ground and tied it, tying the grain itself into a knot instead of using twine or wire as was done later.

With this model of the reaper Nancy's parents did some improving on their own. They fixed a place for mother to stand, and she'd tie the grain (tie the stalks into a knot) as it came from the aprons instead of letting it fall to the ground to be picked up later. Mother would tie three bundles, then Nancy, standing beside her, would pull a lever which dropped the three bundles together. So, with a little ingenuity of their own, they considerably improved the efficiency of the reaper.

While today's combines work best in hot, dry weather, they did their cutting with the reaper at night when the straw was tough so it wouldn't break. Their first binder – reaper that did its own tying into bundles – used wire for tying the bundles. At first some of the horses and cows were lost because fine pieces of wire remained in the grain. Wire was unsatisfactory in several ways and was used only one year with the binder. After that twine was introduced and it is still used with the binder. Mrs. Hollenbeck observed that at least two features from the binder have been carried over to the combine and are still in use – the reel and the sickle.

Their first threshing machine – this, too, came in father and mother's day, not grandmother's – was run by horsepower. A tumbling rod connected the horses to the machine, and the horses would plod around and around. How some of the horses, Mrs. Hollenbeck reflected, hated to step over that rod!

One man would stand and feed the bundles into the machine, while others brought the bundles to the machine. Those first threshers didn't have blowers to blow the straw away so it had to be bucked or pushed away from the back of the thresher.

When Mrs. Hollenbeck's grandparents settled in Goodhue County, they had 'squatted' (she and her sisters still own that land, claimed 120 years ago), but her parents bought their land – 160 acres at $1 per acre. Later they added a 120-acre tree claim. They got title to that by planting trees on it – similar to the procedure by which homesteaders became landowners. They lived in prairie, marshy country, and trees did very well.

Those first years they burned hay and flax straw for fuel. When mother married, grandmother had given her a wash boiler with no handles. They would tramp the straw into the wash boiler, then set it, bottom side up, over the two front stove holes. They had an iron hearth stove (no ash box so they'd rake the ashes out onto the hearth) with four lids so they'd remove the two front lids and put the boiler over the holes. They couldn't have done that with later boilers because they would have melted. Mother used her dishpan for a wash boiler because the boiler was blackened.

Growing up on the frontier provided limited educational opportunities. For three years, when she was fifteen, sixteen and seventeen, Nancy was able to go to school from Christmas until the end of March when spring's work started. She wasn't placed in a grade then but just studied and moved along at her own pace with the teachers helping as needed. She learned the multiplication table on her fingers while she rode the sulky* plow.

In her younger days Mrs. Hollenbeck broke many horses, but she never had one that bucked. "Because," she explained, "I never used a saddle with cinches pulled up tight. I always rode them bareback. No bridle, either. I'd just use a small whip and hang onto the mane. At the water trough I would slide from my saddle horse onto a 'new' horse, then ride him until he was tired."

She went on to explain that while the horse was still tired she'd take him to the corral and work with him, putting on a halter and tying him, then mounting and dismounting. She never had a puller on the halter, either, she declared. "They always led up good and weren't afraid." She added that she worked with horses the way her mother told her the Indians did. They didn't use horses the way the white man did.

She didn't limit her riding to horses. When she and her sister herded cows, they'd climb onto the back of the last cow and ride her home. And they even rode pigs – but not when they wanted to go some place. The worst bump she ever got, she declared, was when she was riding a pig. (As you talk with a sedate ninety-two-year-old woman, you might have a little difficulty visualizing her doing such stunts as riding pigs – until you see the sparkle in her eyes. That sparkle is still young!) Seems that while she was riding the pig, a cousin hit him on the rump. That pig just sat down on his haunches with his front feet up and nothing, but nothing, for her to hang onto, and she hit the ground, hard.

Looking back on ninety-two years in this old world, Mrs. Hollenbeck states simply, "Everything I've done – anything I've made – God was at my back; He helped me through it all." And there was plenty to go through, plenty of hardship, trials, and sorrow. Yet she can declare, "Life was wonderful." Wonderful or not, she philosophized, "You never get anywhere asking for pity."

Many times when the going was hard, especially after her husband passed away, she was challenged by the memory of her grandmother and an aunt, each of whom had to raise her family alone when she lost her husband. Grandmother had four children to rear, the aunt, twelve. She would remind herself, "They made it so you can too." And she did.

Her only son was killed in a tractor accident a few years ago, but her four daughters are still living. She has two sisters living, too. The three of them have made their home in the Golden Valley Manor for several years, but one is now in the hospital. Mrs. Hollenbeck's daughter-in-law, Joanna Hollenbeck, is manager of the Manor and does a good job of keeping 'her' senior citizens comfortable and content.

Louie Elliot

December 1967

There is no man living today who came to Glendive before Louie Elliot (there never have been very many who could claim that distinction), long-time resident of Glendive now in the Holy Rosary Rest Home in Miles City. Louie was born in 1881 and came to Glendive when he was only a year old.

His mother had come from her home in Luray, Virginia, to Deadwood, South Dakota, where her older sister lived. In Deadwood she met and married a mine operator, a man by the name of Lou Elliot. When Elliot began to suffer from ill health, he sought medical help in Illinois, but three weeks before their first child, a son, was born Elliot passed away.

The young widow went back to her former home in Virginia until after the birth of her baby but later rejoined the Snyders (her sister and husband) in Deadwood. Snyder had been a buffalo hunter, but with the passing of the buffalo he had switched to the butcher trade.

When the Snyders moved to Glendive, Mrs. Elliot and her little boy moved with them. The party traveled by wagon train from Deadwood to Miles City, then took advantage of the new Northern Pacific Railroad (it had reached Glendive on July 4, 1881) to travel on to Glendive. They arrived here May 1, 1882.

The town's population in 1882 was strictly limited, but the coming of the railroad the year before was bringing more settlers in all the time. One of the few settlers who had preceded the railroad was Henry Dion, a former freighter between Bismarck and Deadwood.

Mrs. Elliot and Mr. Dion soon became acquainted (it didn't take long to get to know everyone in the town!) and later married. Louie recalls his stepfather telling about a trip he had made to this area in 1879. He had come up the Yellowstone on a steamboat and found Joe Allen camped at the mouth of Glendive Creek. Mr. Dion did not locate in Glendive on this trip, but it was either later that year or in 1880 that he did settle here. In 1882 he was appointed first sheriff of Dawson County by territorial governor Potts.

After coming to Glendive Louie's uncle, Mr. Snyder, started the town's first butcher shop in partnership with a fellow by name of Hodson. The shop was located across from where City Hall is now, about where the Vet's Club is. Snyder also ranched southwest of Glendive (now we'd say along Marsh road), with his buildings about half-a-mile from town.

In 1899 the disastrous flood which struck the Glendive area inundated their home site and Louie's aunt and uncle as well as several young people visiting them, were drowned. The river was late going out that year; didn't break up until April 7. When it did break up, the ice jammed, causing the water to rise very precipitately, deluging the Snyders' place in a very short time. They attempted to reach the railroad embankment which was high enough to offer sanctuary from the angry waters, but they were drowned before they were able to reach it.

One of the young fellows had escaped by climbing a tree and had attempted to help his companions, but the ice chunks churning in the torrents knocked over trees like tooth picks, and the flood claimed all the others. Later their bodies were recovered only two or three hundred yards from where they drowned.

Across the river in the general area of the present Buttreys* Store an entire family – the Sullivans – drowned. The bridge spanning the Yellowstone had been in use only a couple of years, but it was used no more after that flood because it was washed out.

The Dion home was on the corner of what later became Bell and Douglas. It started out as a two-bedroom home, but as the family grew they built more rooms until the house reached its present size. The house has since been moved to Towne Street, next to the river.

Mr. Dion was responsible for considerable building in the Gate City. In 1886 he built the former Exchange State Bank building (now Ruth's Style Shop) on the corner of Merrill and Bell, using brick from his own brickyard across Caines Coulee. 1886 was a year of much building activity in Glendive.

Louie Elliot explains that he was too young during Glendive's building boom of 1886 to remember much about that. The Phoenix block*, where Coast to Coast, Montgomery Ward, etc., are located now, was built up that year, but there's been very little building in the town since then that he doesn't know about.

He remembers seeing Hank Day lay the cornerstone for the Masonic building, the first building in that entire block. This structure also housed Day's hardware and a drug store

Two recent projects, however, that he would like to see but hasn't because they were undertaken after he left Glendive are the Safeway Store and the Towne Street Bridge presently under construction across the Yellowstone.

Ranches and cowboys played a prominent role in this area during Louie's boyhood days. It was a big day for the boys when the cowboys (that they didn't see on TV) came to town, especially when they bought marbles from the boys, then played a game with them – played for keeps.

The boys, of course, were in their element, but the cowboys, well, their skill in shooting usually was not with marbles so when the game was over, the boys would have most of their marbles back, the money they had received when they sold the marbles, and the thrill of a game with the cowboy besides. No wonder it was a big day for them when the big cow outfits came to town!

Unfortunately, not all diversion sought by the punchers was that innocent. Frequently the bars claimed a good share of the hard-earned wages, and the fellows, when drunk, would sometimes shoot up the signs – "Great habit of theirs," Louie explained.

He recalls that one time a W Bar cowboy (if you want to know his name, check with Louie) tried to ride his horse into a saloon. He was so persistent they had to send for the sheriff to dissuade him – which he finally accomplished by pulling him from his horse.

Lee B. stirred up some excitement in the little frontier town when he got the drop on a fellow and marched him up Front Street at the point of a revolver. Just as they reached the end of the street the fellow broke away and ducked into a house.

Lee started in after him, but he was met by the landlady with a business-like six-shooter. She told him not to come in. And he didn't. When Lee had left Belle Fourche, he had taken the other man's wife with him. When the deserted husband showed up in the Gate City, Lee figured it was to kill him so he reasoned that the fellow who got to his gun first had the best chance.

Boys nowadays may find excitement reading about cattle rustlers or watching them on the screen, but how would it feel to suddenly find yourself alone on a ferryboat with two real live rustlers? Louie knows!

He did a lot of swimming and fishing when he was a boy, and since there was no bridge across the Yellowstone then, he had to cross the river on the ferry. One day when Louie had finished his fishing and boarded the ferry to return home, he had to wait for Kinney, the operator, to get back to the boat. Kinney had just brought an elderly lady across from town and had carried her purchases to her home, not far away, for her.

Louie knew he wouldn't be gone long so he just waited on the ferry for Kinney to return. But while he waited with his fishing rod, he was suddenly joined by two other customers – customers he quickly recognized as two cattle rustlers that the law officers were pursuing even then.

Mr. Elliot frankly confesses that he was just about scared to death. He was strongly considering jumping off the boat and swimming to the island when one of the rustlers causally asked him, "Haven' any luck, Kid?"

That eased the tension and Louie decided not to jump overboard after all. When Kinney returned he ferried the trio across the river (if he was scared the little boy aboard couldn't detect it), and the two bandits headed on toward Wibaux. Billy Smith, the stock detective, caught up with them on a ranch near Wibaux, and the leader of the pair was killed.

During the years Louie Elliot was growing up in Glendive, he had opportunity to become acquainted with many of the ranchers in Dawson County (many in this case indicating percentage rather than number). Dawson County at that time, of course, took in a good part of eastern Montana. Glendive was the sole trading center between the Missouri River and Terry, from the Dakota line to – how far west did one have to go to find a town? – so sooner or later the ranchers would come to town.

Some of the big outfits of the day were the Circle Ranch with Modescy Carter the head of it; Carter had come to Montana from Chattanooga and met sudden death when he returned to that city – shot down right on the street.

The HS Ranch was started by a Boston capitalist, and Ed Moran, with whom Louie was well acquainted, was the foreman. Moran is buried in the Glendive cemetery.

The DT was owned by Hank Day, a town dweller, and Louie's stepfather, Henry Dion, also owned a ranch (in the area where Sidney later sprouted) but lived in Glendive.

C.A. Dole, owner of the Bar X was another rancher Elliot knew very well. The ranch foreman had a kid going to school in Glendive, and the two boys became good friends so Louie was invited to spend the summer (1894) on the ranch. He saw the Bar X's last roundup start from the ranch that summer.

Since he was only thirteen he had nothing to do with the roundup (he didn't even realize that this last roundup marked the beginning of the end of an era), but when he was older, he did work on the cattle ranches around the area.

Most of the Indian trouble in eastern Montana was behind when the two Elliots came with Snyders to Glendive, but Louie remembers one scare that they 'got in on'. He doesn't remember the date for sure, but it was at the time Sitting Bull was killed so it must have been about 1890.

The Fort Peck Indians had started their war dancing and were moving to join the Sioux on the Standing Rock Reservation in South Dakota where the uprising had started. Their route took them right through Glendive so the alarm had been spread throughout the surrounding country, and some of the scattered ranchers had moved into Glendive to await the outcome. The big cattle outfits, Mr. Elliot noted, stayed out on their ranches.

Louie's aunt and uncle from south of town (Mr. and Mrs. Snyder) came in to Dions; others put up where they could. Fort Keogh at Miles City had soldiers ready to dispatch to Glendive in case of need, but no hostilities broke out so the soldiers weren't needed, and various refugees returned to their own homes.

Troops actually were moved into Glendive in 1894 during the nationwide A.R.U. strike which tied up the railroads. A detachment of Negro soldiers was sent in from Fort Buford* at Mondak to ward off trouble, and again no trouble developed.

Glendive, during Louie's boyhood, was a typical frontier town. Most of its inhabitants and those of the surrounding area were law-abiding citizens, but violence was not uncommon. Besides the sudden demise of McPeet, Mr. Elliot told of others whose lives had ended without due process of law – the cowpuncher in the caboose; N Bar N's Negro cook at Fallon; the man who killed the cook, killed in turn by a bartender in Saco, the bartender then killed in Colorado.

But that was different from the murder of Sheriff Dominic Cavanaugh and the subsequent conviction of a young, local man of that murder. To have one of your schoolmates killed in an automobile accident can be a traumatic experience; how much more when a young fellow with whom you have attended school, even though it be a few years later, is hanged for murder! Little wonder Glendive was shaken.

Elliot spent some time working for the Reclamation Service during the building of the Lower Yellowstone Canal. While he was on this job he became acquainted with Captain Marsh, pilot of the steamboat Expansion. Captain Marsh had a steamboat line up the Missouri River to Bismarck.

During the building of the Canal the government contracted with Marsh to haul the cement, which had been brought to Glendive by train, from Glendive to the dam by boat. As Louie unloaded cement he became well acquainted with the captain, and listened with fascination to his stories — stories of his experiences with the steamer, the Far West which he was piloting at the time of Custer's Massacre.

It was Captain Marsh who brought out the wounded in the battles with the Indians that followed Custer's defeat. Mr. Elliot regrets that he didn't realize at the time he listened to those tales how significant they were historically.

Elliot was also acquainted with Charley Scerlie, under Reno's command, and with Morrie Caine (for whom Caine's Coulee is named), who was under Captain Benteen. Reno and Benteen were both under Custer, and all three were under General Alfred Terry. Terry had split them at the mouth of the Powder River and sent Custer up Rosebud Creek. Just over on the Little Big Horn Custer was killed.

Louie Elliot's first job was that of timekeeper for the extra gang on the Northern Pacific Railroad. He held other positions with the Northern Pacific also — in the freight depot, then as ticket and express agent, working for the railroad a number of years.

Later he became interested in politics and was elected to the office of Dawson County Clerk and Recorder. He spent thirty-eight years in the courthouse before his retirement. Mr. Elliot is now in the Holy Rosary Rest Home in Miles City where he has lived for the past several years.

Mrs. Harold (Lucille Strecker) Waller

September – October 1969

Mrs. Harold Waller came to Montana as a small child in 1910 and still lives within a mile of the first home she knew in the Treasure State. First on her father's homestead, then on her grandfather's homestead, she has spent almost sixty years on one or the other of the two places northwest of Circle.

Her father, Sam Strecker, came from Edgerton, Minnesota to Montana in 1909 and homesteaded, then in 1910 he brought his wife and three children to live on the Montana prairies. Lucille was the youngest of the three children.

Her very earliest recollection is of seeing huge clouds of dust and hearing the bawling of cattle – the CK roundup. She remembers how scared she and the other two children were and how they would run for cover at the sight and sound.

She can't remember much else of those first years in their new home on the frontier, but the next scene stamped on her memory was the death of her mother. Lucille was only five years old when her Mother passed away. Just a few months prior to this event in 1914 her mother's parents had also come from Minnesota and had filed on a homestead only a mile from their daughter's home. After her passing the children stayed with their grandparents a good deal of the time.

Lucille started to school when she was only five years old. One day before that she had gone to school to visit and had promised her sister that she would stay at school for the day, but while she was outside she changed her mind. She saw her father riding past on a saddle horse so she skipped out and rode home with him.

Another vivid scene on her memory's panorama is that of a horseback rider coming as hard as a horse could run. A cousin was bringing the news of her father's death, just nine months after her mother's. Mrs. Waller says she can see that horse coming yet, so fast. Although the children were not immediately given the message, that was the news the rider brought. From then on their home was with their grandparents.

On September 6, 1912, her father had started the Horse Creek Post Office in their home. Later the post office was moved to the DeLapp home (her grandparents). Her aunt, Gladys DeLapp, was postmistress until she married in 1916.

People came from twenty-five and thirty miles away to pick up their mail. They always stayed for a meal or two and perhaps they'd stay overnight. Mrs. Waller remembers several of the cowboys and ranchers that used to come, but she particularly remembers one special cowboy, 'Old' Jim Karney. Looking back she doubts that he was really old, but to the children he was. He always had candy along for them and always took time to play with them. They loved him for it.

She remembers, too, the time a lady tied her horse to the clothesline post. She doesn't recall all of the details of what followed, but she does recall that something scared the horse and the horse took off. He took the clothesline with him and also the clothes. Somehow he also managed to rip up a brand new mackinaw that the lady was wearing.

The home in which the Wallers now live was the DeLapp homestead, and that post office was in what is now their living room. Since those days the house has been moved onto another foundation, has been 'built onto', and remodeled, but the original house is still a part of the present home.

After their father's death following their mother's by just nine months, the three little Strecker orphans made their home with their grandparents, the DeLapps. Mrs. Lucille Waller, youngest of the three, observes, "Grandma tried so very hard to raise us up to be good kids."

No playing cards were ever allowed in their home; if any showed up (as they generally did when Uncle came home after being away for any length of time) Grandma would burn them. Somehow Lucille and her brother got some of Floyd Davis's campaign cards and made a deck of cards to play rummy. That was all right, as were such games as Rook, Flinch, or Pit.

Grandma wouldn't allow any swearing either. One morning Lucille's brother was out wrangling horses in the early hours when sounds carry far, and the horses thwarted all his efforts to get them in. He resorted to cursing and a neighbor lady who heard him decided it was her duty to report the incident to Grandma. So Vincent got a licking with a razor strap. A word such as bull was never used in the children's hearing (a bull was a 'gentleman cow'), nor did they know anything about such things as the breeding of the livestock.

Lucille and Vincent played a lot together. They didn't have any expensive toys or equipment, but she's sure they had as much fun using their imaginations as any modern youngsters have. They often pretended they were men, imitating two older cousins, even calling each other by the cousins' names.

One Fourth of July, Mrs. Waller remembers, Grandpa took all of them to Circle for some kind of celebration. They went in his lumber wagon with the long box, and it was an occasion to be remembered because the children had probably been to town only two or three times since they came to Montana. But that wasn't the part of the day Lucille remembered most.

The children were thrilled when one of the grown-up cousins gave each of them fifty cents. That was a lot of money, and they began envisioning what fifty cents could do, but — tragedy of tragedies — before Lucille spent any of it, she LOST HERS.

She was broken hearted the rest of the day — and probably for some days to come. She doesn't remember much of the celebration except that there were firecrackers, but there's no forgetting the heartbreak of that lost fifty cents.

Lucille experienced homesickness more than once when she was away from home, but perhaps never to the extent that she did the time the horse fell through the roof. She had gone to stay with a girlfriend for a week, but her visit was cut short when homesickness overtook her. The friend's house was built into the side of a hill, and one night a horse walked onto the dirt roof of the house and fell through.

A lot of dirt came down and some dishes were broken, but she was sleeping in a different part of the house and it didn't really affect her. She isn't sure whether the horse's unorthodox entry had anything to do with her homesickness or not, but homesick she was. She spent a good part of the night crying, and the next day they took her home with a team and buggy.

Even as a child she liked helping with chickens and it became her work to take care of the eggs, set the hens, look after the baby chicks. After her marriage she still liked chickens, and she also raised turkeys and ducks — or tried it. She had some turkeys half grown one time when she looked out the window early one morning to see a coyote killing them. He wasn't eating them — he'd just kill one and go on to the next. Before she could get to the rescue, he had killed all but three.

Her duck raising wasn't very successful either. She didn't know much about it and always found the eggs down in the water because that's where the ducks laid. Needless to say, she didn't raise any ducklings.

Mrs. Waller still thinks of her grandfather as a great horseman (although some of his practices were a source of keen distress to her). He had a fast driving team, Fred and Deck, of which he was very proud. (Fifty years ago the emphasis was on fast horses, rather than on fast cars.)

"I really think they were about the fastest team around," Mrs. Waller concedes, "but at that time all of us resented them because he was so proud of them, and no one else was allowed to drive them. He had a private saddle horse too, that we felt the same way about."

Grandpa DeLapp never tired of telling about the time Mr. Daily couldn't pass him on the way to town. Mr. Daily owned a car and cars were 'mighty scarce' in those days. Grandpa, telling about it, freely admitted that he wouldn't "give him the road." Since the road was just a pair of tracks cut into the prairie by wagon wheels, then more wagon wheels, and the ground beside the tracks was rough, the car driver had to be desperate before he turned from the tracks. But there was no denying the horses were fast.

Grandpa was very particular and no one else could harness a horse to suit him. If a strap was the least bit crooked he always had to take time to change it and make it perfect. It took him a long time, she remembers, to get a team harnessed, hitched, and off to the field.

He had good horses and was proud of them, but he could also be rough with the broncs that 'acted up'. Mrs. Waller observed that she especially hated his 'war bridle', as did the rest of the family. She remembers seeing him put it on a horse that, for example, wouldn't come in when wrangled in the morning and yank it around until its mouth was bleeding. From the time she was a child until she was grown that war bridle made her furious. Once, when she was grown up, she went out and tried to stop him and nearly got whipped herself.

At threshing time, with the bundle wagons, there would be many teams around, but Grandpa wouldn't allow the men to feed their own horses. He said

147

the men would waste hay or not take it out of the stack just right. Some of the men fed their own horses anyway and were 'cussed out' for it next morning.

Mrs. Harold Waller, reminiscent of the days that she and her brother and sister spent in the home of their grandparents, noted that Grandpa DeLapp farmed with horses until he quit farming and moved to Terry in 1929. All around him farmers switched to tractors, but Grandpa stuck to his horses. And what tractor could have shown the sensitivity of horses.

One time he was plowing with six horses on a gangplow*. The horses were fighting flies and somehow tipped the plow over. His arm was broken – crushed – in the accident, but somehow he managed to get the team unhooked and headed for home. The team walked beside him all the way but never touched his arm. It seemed to him they knew he was hurt. He was far from young at that time, but in spite of his age the arm healed and was hardly stiff.

Finally one of the younger generation represented in his household, either son or grandson, got an old Hart-Parr tractor from some place, but as Mrs. Waller remembers, it was always broken down or at best, wouldn't start. To this day she harbors a skepticism where tractors are concerned, never quite sure they will start when needed.

Grandpa never did learn to drive a car – probably the last man in the area to drive a team every place he went. His son finally bought a car, but horses were good enough for Grandpa. Grandma, too, drove a team, and most of their going was in a two-seated buggy, which for some years had a top on it. When Grandpa went he usually insisted on using his lumber wagon, with its extra-long box. They had a light bobsled which they used in the winter. It was a classy little sled, and they especially enjoyed riding in it when Grandpa used his sleigh bells.

Some Sundays during the summer months a minister would conduct church services at a school house about ten miles from the homestead. The whole family would load up in the wagon – or now and then, the buggy – and make the twenty-mile round trip. They had to allow a little more time to get places in those days.

For some pioneers, good water was a perennial problem. Some, it's true, were fortunate to have a supply of good water close at hand, but many others, far from having it on tap in the house, hauled their water for several miles. The DeLapps found themselves in the latter category, where soft water was concerned, anyway.

Every Sunday morning Grandpa loaded a barrel onto the stoneboat*, then filled it with soft water at a neighbor's about three miles away. This water was used for washing and was used very sparingly. In the winter they melted snow – always had a barrel in the kitchen for soft water.

Water for other uses they carried up the hill from the well. (Why were houses so often up the hill from the well?) They carried it in, then carried it out again in the slop pail. Mrs. Waller facetiously explained, "That's the kind of running water we had then, only we had to do the running."

She remembers that her grandmother tried hard to get some trees started around the house but with little success. She faithfully carried her wash water

148

onto them every week, but a few years seemed to be the limit they would live. How she would have loved the beautiful shade trees that now grace the same yard!

Prosperity wasn't the norm during most of the years Lucille and her siblings were growing up in their grandparent's home. Mrs. Waller remembers the crop failures and the hard times, but notes that they always had enough to eat and clothes to wear. The clothes might be second hand, but we used everything.

She especially remembers a pair of dark red button shoes that her paternal grandmother sent out from Minnesota. She hated those shoes, but wore them, even when she started to high school.

One winter following an especially barren harvest, they lived mostly on corn and dried beans. Even potatoes that year had been a failure, but they raised enough beans for their winter supply and also some corn. Grandma made the corn edible by putting it through some lye process followed by long cooking. So, while meals didn't have much variety, the family didn't go hungry.

One fall snow came very early, and the threshing wasn't done. They threshed grain most of the winter with a horse-powered machine which Grandpa hand fed. Twelve horses were attached to the machine and they went 'round and 'round all day.

Two years after Lucille went to live with her grandparents, she felt her world was utterly shattered – her aunt Gladys married and left the home. When she saw Gladys and a friend who lived close by making pink crepe paper roses, she had no inkling of their purpose. Inquisitive children couldn't get any satisfactory answer as to what the roses were for. Instead of telling the truth, the 'big' girls would make up some story. But it turned out that they were for her wedding.

'Auntie' was married in the very house in which the Wallers now live. The living room was beautifully decorated with the crepe paper roses. Roses covered the arch, and the little flower girls (Lucille was one of them) carried baskets of them. The bride's wedding dress was beautiful, too.

It was a lovely wedding, but to Lucille it meant only that Auntie was leaving home. She was always very good to the little orphans, her sister's children, and they loved her. As soon as she could get away after the wedding, Lucille fled to the upstairs and cried all the rest of the day.

After the newlyweds moved to their new home – it was made of logs, but it was a real nice house, not just a cabin – she liked to go visit them as often as she could and stay as long as she was allowed to.

Mrs. Waller feels that she was fortunate to get a high school education in a day when a high school education for every eighth grade graduate wasn't taken for granted. Students from the farm, especially, faced problems in continuing their schooling because of the distance to the high school. No bus service then to round up the scholars.

However, Grandma DeLapp was determined that the children should have a high school education. Some money was made available from their parents' estate to help with high school expenses, and by working for her room and board, Lucille was able to further her education.

She had passed her eighth grade exams in mid-winter and had gone right on to high school. The high school in Circle was still very new and the professor was so eager to increase enrollment that he urged her and another girl who had graduated at the same time to enter high school immediately. They did, but now Mrs. Waller feels that it was a mistake to start then. It was harder for them later and they were 'mixed up'. The other girl didn't graduate, but Lucille, the youngest in her class, did. She was the class salutatorian.

Mrs. Waller laughed as she recalled a slumber party of high school days. Her uncle happened to be in Circle with team and wagon so when he was ready to go home, fifteen or twenty young folks piled into the wagon and went along out to the farm. Even though the house wasn't large, Grandma was equal to the situation and managed to provide plenty of food as well as a place for everyone to sleep – beds on the floor and everywhere.

They had a good time – just plain old-fashioned fun, but as is often the case on such occasions there was more party than slumber. Three girls in one bed (Lucille was one of them) talked and giggled all night, not going to sleep at all. Some of the others were not grateful to the sleep-robbers, and by the time they went back to town Sunday evening some of the kids were not on speaking terms! But they had a lot of fun in spite of it all.

Mrs. Waller remembers that her first train ride when she went away to normal school (teacher-training institute) at seventeen was a thrill, but even that couldn't equal the thrill seeing a train for the first time. She was probably eleven or twelve the first time she saw a train. Uncle Arcy and some other men were going to South Dakota for harvest and went to Terry to catch the train. A man took them to Terry, and she was allowed to ride along so she could see a train.

Just about the time the Great Depression was getting a firm grip on the country, Lucille married a neighbor's son, Harold Waller. As children she and her sister had often walked to the neighbor's to play, but they seldom saw Harold. He was so bashful that as soon as a girl would appear on the place, he'd disappear. But that changed.

Except for nearly a year when they were first married, Lucille and Harold have lived on her grandmother's homestead all their married lives. And she lived there all her life before that, too, except the first five years. Sometimes she feels a bit cheated that she has lived all her Montana years within a mile of the place she 'landed' in 1910.

As it is, she well remembers the growth of the house from the original homestead shack, the addition Grandpa built on when three little orphans came to live there, on through the changes, additions and remodeling up to the present.

In 1939 they moved the house onto a new foundation. In the earlier years when the DeLapps were on the homestead the cellar was tight and cool enough that milk, butter, and other food would keep very well, but in time the dirt foundation wore away and it was either move the house or let it fall into the cellar. Earlier there was also a sod shed against the back side of the house, providing a cool place to spend warm summer hours.

In spite of the depression prevailing when the young couple married, they managed to make a living. The second year after they were married, Mrs. Waller worked in a restaurant in Terry a few months, and Harold hauled coal to schools, making an extra dollar wherever he could. Between them they made about a hundred dollars and got through the winter on it.

The next year was another crop failure so Harold worked out near Helena with a brother. The $150 he brought home put them through another winter. After he returned on the first of September they tried to mow some short thistles to feed a few cows for the winter.

In 1932, they finally had some crop. Cutting it with a binder, he had a runaway (he was breaking some broncs). It broke up the binder, but he patched it up and harvested some grain that year. One fall they had a little wheat to sell but no license on the Model T truck so they had a neighbor freight some into town. Instead of selling it for them, he brought it back; wheat was twenty-two cents a bushel! He figured they could store it, but the children had to have shoes and overshoes as the weather was getting cold so they had no choice. They sold the wheat.

Many farmers yet today look back to that painful period when they sold two-year-old steers for $20 to the government – ewes for $1. Many who had bought land when the railroad came to Circle now pulled up and left along with homesteaders who decided there was no use trying any longer.

In the late thirties Wallers found themselves in the sheep business along with their cattle raising and farming interests. They started out with some bum lambs*, then bought a few sheep, making just a small band. Small band or large, they had to be herded and, except on weekends, the job fell to Mrs. Waller. A couple years they took in about 600 lambs to run for two months in the fall, and they really kept her traveling.

Most of the time she had to do the washing, ironing, and housework in the evening. In 1942, while World War II was in progress, they bought a bottled gas range. During the war you didn't just walk into a store and order what you wanted. For many, many items priorities had to be established and so it was with the stove.

When the man selling the stove came looking for Mrs. Waller, he had to drive out into the hills where she was herding sheep to find her. In filling out the forms for ordering, he put down that Mrs. Waller was herding sheep and needed the stove for faster cooking. She got the stove and it was marvelous.

The new gas stove was not only faster; it spared the kitchen much heat build-up during the summer months. When using the coal stove she usually, in hot weather, got up at four o'clock in the morning to get her washing done early. Then while there was a good fire in the range she'd probably bake bread, cook whole wheat pudding or perhaps a kettle of beans. The new gas stove started a whole new set of habits.

One winter — about 1937-38, they had a man staying with them helping with the chores around the farm for his room and board. The neighbors had a similar arrangement with another man, and between the two of them there was always something 'cooking', what with breaking horses, fixing cars — what have you.

One morning the neighbor's hired man was thrown from the horse he was riding. No one saw the incident, but a little later Waller's man saw the riderless horse on the hillside and didn't need a blueprint to figure out what happened. He jumped on the horse he was breaking, intending to go to the rescue, but he, too, promptly returned to the good earth. After that they really had a rodeo as both men reclaimed their horses and rode them until they had them broken.

Another time Waller's man provided excitement while they were all putting up ice together. The temperature was twenty degrees below zero, and he fell into the water. They fished him out, got him into the house and into dry clothes as quickly as possible, and he suffered no ill effects — didn't even catch cold. You didn't need much money for entertainment when you had diversions like that to keep life interesting!

The Rural Electrification Association and the telephone have brought some welcome changes to the farm and have made life much easier. The electric refrigerator, for example, is quite an improvement over the old icebox . Before the REA brought electricity, Wallers were already enjoying the benefits of 110-volt current with their Jacobs Wind Electric Plant. Even their first six-volt windcharger, which provided electricity for one light bulb when the wind was blowing, was something in its day.

Now modern improvements and inventions are making farm life easier. Mr. Waller winters 200 cattle, traveling to and from feeding grounds every day with a four-wheeled drive pickup over a road he has had elevated for that purpose. Just about the time he has roads, corrals, and other facilities fixed the way he has always wanted them, he laments, it's time to retire.

In 1949 it wasn't so easy to commute to the place where he was wintering the cattle. It was about eight miles from home, and during the time the snow was so deep he had to stay in the house on this place. One morning, there all alone, he poured kerosene on coals in the stove to hurry up the fire, and it blew up in his face. He rolled in the snow (in his pajamas) to put out the fire on himself then shoveled snow into the house to put out the fire in there. The fire extinguished, he rode his saddle horse home while the thermometer was registering twenty degrees below zero.

His face was so blackened Mrs. Waller couldn't be sure how deeply it was burned so she just applied Ungentine to all the affected areas. Later in the day she rode horseback to a neighbor's to have them find out if any roads were open. In places the horse had to lunge to get through the belly-deep snow.

After two days a plane was sent out to get Mr. Waller, but by that time he was better. They feared it might be worse for him to get outside so he didn't go in to the doctor. However, the county plowed the road and a brother-in-law brought medicine from the doctor. Mr. Waller recovered satisfactorily and eventually spring came, but it was a long, hard winter.

Branding time is always a busy time and has become something of an attraction for city relatives from east and west, mostly Chicago and Portland. They enjoy seeing ranch life first hand, and they also enjoy the fresh air and country quiet. One family (six people) has come twice in their own plane – landed on the scorio road* two miles from the ranch.

Even with modern conveniences it is still hard to get away from the farm, but in recent years the Wallers have managed to do some traveling, visiting places as widely separated as Washington State and Washington D.C.; Canada and Florida; and even Hawaii.

Mrs. Waller has become interested in many hobbies over the years. She has collected over 500 salt and pepper sets as well as spoons, agates, rock tables, and lamps. She also enjoys crocheting, knitting, and reading. She is a regular blood donor (just received her four gallon pin) and has been an active member of the V.F.W. Auxiliary for nearly twenty years.

Mr. and Mrs. Waller have two sons and seven grandchildren. Both sons are farmers in the Circle area, close enough so the families can get together often. Mrs. Waller's sister lives in Circle, while her brother, Vincent Strecker resides in Washington.

Her uncle, Arcy DeLapp wrote from Eureka, Montana this summer to describe some of his early experiences, particularly as he was freighting with horses and wagons. Mrs. Waller remembers how, as a girl, she used to help get the grub box ready for those long freighting trips, but she decided it would be easier to let Uncle Arcy tell about the actual trips.

Harry Green

October – November 1973

From a mansion in Iowa to a one-room shack on the bank of a creek in Montana – forty miles from the nearest town. What would motivate anyone to make such a move? Perhaps Mrs. Harry Green in the days – weeks – months – years that followed their immigration to Montana may have wondered. Yet hundreds and thousands left the comfort and comparative security of their homes in established communities of the Midwest and the East to 'rough it' on the Montana prairies during the homestead era.

Harry Green, from Early, Iowa, came to Montana in 1909 and homesteaded in the Union country. This summer his six children, with their children and children's children, met at the old home place for a reunion. They were joined by an aunt and fifteen cousins from Iowa and Minnesota whom some of the Montana Greens had never met. The July reunion marked the first time all six Green children have been together since 1943 when their father passed away. Mrs. Green passed away in 1931.

In the early 1900s people all over the country and in Europe were hearing about the opening of homestead lands in Montana's eastern counties and the opportunities offered. Iowans were no exception, and in the fall of 1909, Harry Green, his father, and his brother made an exploratory trip to Dawson County. They arrived just when Roy Kimball was ready to relinquish his homestead.

Kimball had planned to have a horse ranch and had selected his 160 acres in a rather unique fashion. Instead of taking his acreage in a rectangular block as was customarily done, he had picked forty-acre plots strung out along the creek. The southeast corner of the first plot joined the northwest corner of the second plot and so on for the four plots. In this way he was able to satisfy homestead specifications, yet have the benefit of a much longer portion of the creek – a creek that actually had running water in it.

The plan seemed like a good one but other homesteaders soon surrounded him. He got disgusted over the prospects for his horse ranch and was ready to throw out the whole deal when young Green came along.

This creek has a big spring in it and, unlike many creeks in Eastern Montana, runs the year around. The setup looked good to Harry so he bought Kimball's rights to the homestead – eight miles southwest of Lindsay on upper Clear Creek in the Union community.

In the early days people came from miles around to get their drinking water from that spring. Paths leading to the spring can still be seen to this day. Neighbors not so blessed with a plentiful water supply even built a lane to the spring so they could water their cattle in dry years.

Henry Green (no relation) also homesteaded and the next spring they moved to Montana. They brought their horses, machinery, and furniture in an immigrant car*. Harry brought the first grain binder to that part of the country.

Consequently he did a lot of cutting the first few harvests while his was the only binder.

In 1905 Harry had married Mabel Alice Needham in Iowa. In March 1910 she, with their three children, came by passenger train to join him on the homestead. Their youngest child was only two weeks old at the time. Delbert, the oldest, was four years old, Mary was two. What courage pioneer women had to have!

Mabel was born in Chicago to a banker and his wife. As a very small child she wanted a violin and was thrilled to receive one on her fifth birthday. She thought of it only as a plaything but soon discovered that was not what her father had in mind in granting her wish. He firmly told her, "You're taking lessons," and take lessons she did. In time she graduated from the Chicago Conservatory of Music.

Years later when she was a Montana farm wife living miles from even a small town, a fellow from the Twin Cities visited the Herschel Purdums, Green's nearest neighbors. They lived in a tent just across the creek from Greens. (Compared to living in a tent perhaps the shack wasn't so bad after all — especially with a two-week-old baby.) The visitor played the piano so the neighbors urged Mrs. Green to bring her violin for an evening of music. The city slicker thought the least he could do was humor them and play while she 'fiddled' a little. She hadn't played long before he stopped and demanded, "What are you doing out here? You are a concert violinist!" The pioneers on Montana's frontier indeed represented a wide spectrum of humanity. Visitors from the East were often surprised to find hidden away on the ranches and farms men and women with college degrees.

While Harry Green was a native of Iowa, Mabel Needham Green had lived her early years in Chicago. Every year the Needham family took a trip, usually to the Great Lakes, during hay fever season to escape the pollen to which they were allergic. When she was about sixteen Mabel had her first introduction to Montana. She, with her family, toured Yellowstone National Park. They traveled by train to the park, then hired a guide with a team and covered wagon to take them through the park. Little did she dream then that she would one day make her home on the prairies of eastern Montana!

Within a few years of that trip her father bought a bank in Early, Iowa and moved his family to the small town. There he built a luxurious home, the largest in town, for his family. This house was recently purchased by a Chicago couple and restored to its old-time elegance. It is sometimes opened to the public for tours.

In Iowa Mabel met a young farmer by the name of Harry Green. His father was an auctioneer, 'Colonel Green', known all over the state. The first time she saw Harry was through a window of the family home as he drove by — a young man with black curly hair, driving a fancy team, hitched to a fancy rig. She immediately decided she had to meet him and she did. The interest proved mutual and in 1905 they were married. Her parents were less than enthusiastic

155

about her marrying a farmer and probably would have been even less so had they been able to see ahead to the years on a Montana homestead.

The first few years following their marriage they lived on a farm in Iowa. Their home was not so luxurious as her parents' home, of course, but they were comfortable. Their first three children, Delbert, Mary, and Charlotte, were born in Iowa.

One day, in preparation for going into town, Mrs. Green dressed little Delbert in a white sailor suit with a little white hat on his head, then turned her attention to other matters. When all was ready, she looked for Delbert but no little lad was to be found. A railroad track ran through their farm and their search brought the information from a neighbor that Delbert had been seen strolling down the track – solo. They lost no time pursuing him, and when they caught up with him he was nonchalantly meandering along, his white hat on his foot!

That was not the last unauthorized stroll he took. After they moved to Montana he found himself in trouble more than once for that very thing. Much of the country was still open range when the Greens settled on Clear Creek and Delbert had been strictly forbidden to venture away from 'home base'. Delbert, however, was of a venturesome spirit and had to go exploring. The neighbor boy who lived on the 120 acres just north of the Greens was a kindred spirit, and he was with Delbert in forbidden territory when they suddenly found themselves surrounded by a bunch of longhorn cattle.

There was no time to run for shelter, no place to hide. Long horns clanked against long horns as the cattle encircled the boys. What could two small boys do? Not much of anything so they just stood back to back, looked at the longhorns and the longhorns looked at them. The encounter couldn't have continued for the eternity it seemed to the boys. Finally, with no movement from them, the cattle wearied of the confrontation, broke ranks and went on about their business. Two frightened boys scurried on home. Later the owner of the cattle told them they had done the only thing they could have done to survive. If they had tried to run, the cattle would have chased them and, no doubt, trampled them.

When Roy Kimball homesteaded on Clear Creek, he had chosen a site on the creek bank to build his homestead shack. Harry Green preferred another location, however, about half-a-mile east and back a quarter of a mile from the creek on a little knoll. This knoll was on the slope of the only hill on the farm. Harry thought this slope would give a little protection from the wind so he moved the house onto it. With the big spring at the creek to provide water, the Greens hadn't been faced with any particular urgency to dig a well as most settlers were. But now that they were farther from the creek, this was one of the projects. Also at the first site they had managed with just corrals for the livestock, but now that they had selected a permanent location they built barns using sod.

The first year he was on the homestead Green broke up about twenty acres using a walking plow. He planted this acreage with oats and wheat. 1910 was a

156

dry year and his first harvest consisted of twenty shocks* of oats and ten shocks of wheat. As it turned out, he didn't even have to thresh those. Jack Thompson had had a bunch of longhorn cattle fetched up from Texas – that same bunch of longhorns that had surrounded Alfred Colby and Delbert. They didn't have much respect for homesteaders' property rights, and one night they broke through the fence, demolishing the entire crop.

One of the advantages of buying a relinquished homestead was that some of the improvements had already been made. For one thing, the acreage was already fenced. Delbert speculates that Kimball had selected the longest cedar posts so that in years ahead, when a post rotted off, he could just cut off the bottom and reset it. That way he wouldn't have to go get another post. As it turned out, he didn't stay around long enough to benefit from this strategy but it was a good idea.

The first settlers in eastern Montana found the grass tall and thick on the prairies – wonderful for pasture but a hazard where prairie fires were concerned. Delbert recalls one fire that almost took their new home. Glasspool was breaking sod with a steam engine when a spark set fire to the grass. Delbert and his mother could see the fire coming toward them from the southeast a mile wide. No place to go to escape it, what could stop it? Some thrill that was!

His dad and a neighbor by the name of Bartell saw the fire from where they were working. They quickly unhitched their team and each jumped on a horse, raced to the buildings, their horses on a dead run. The only hope for saving the little house was getting a fireguard plowed to turn the advancing flames and this they set about doing in a hurry. They quickly hitched the horses to the walking plow, then Bartell held the handles while Dad drove the team keeping them on the run. There was no time to spare but they did get the sod turned under in time to stop the fire before it reached the house.

Meanwhile, with the sparks flying, Delbert and this mother joined forces to throw water on the house to keep stray sparks from igniting it. Delbert exercised the pump handle (the pump handle wasn't all that was exercised!) while his mother ran from the pump to the house throwing on water. The little house wasn't very elaborate, but it was the only home they had and must be saved. Poor Mother! Running in those long skirts, carrying those buckets of water! As for Delbert, he declares he pumped 'til his eyes bulged out and he's never liked a pump handle since.

Furnishings in the little house on the homestead were far from elaborate. 'Bare necessities' probably meant something quite different to them from what that term would mean to most young couples setting up housekeeping today. But in a one-room house, perhaps 12'x18', there would hardly be room for much extra furniture.

The three children, after Charlotte was big enough, slept in a bed suspended from the ceiling by a chain at the foot while the head of the bed rested on the head of their parents' bed. It was made of slats and could be rolled up like a snow fence, although the children can't recall that it ever was.

After the little shack was moved to the new location on the hill, additions were built on – first an 'entry', then a larger room with a loft. Later a front room was added also. This house still stands and was used this summer during the family reunion.

Building a life on the prairie wasn't easy, but was taming a frontier ever easy? Mysterious things sometimes happened – take for instance, the time Mrs. Green couldn't find the rice she planned to cook for dinner. The mystery was solved when Mr. Green found the rice in his boots in the closet – evidently the work of a pack rat.

Trips 'to town' (Glendive) were infrequent except during grain hauling season. The trip, forty-five miles each way, required two days when they were freighting. They'd go in one day with a load of grain, spend the night at Almy's Roadhouse, then make the return trip the next day. On the return trip they would bring supplies for the winter.

Often when Mr. Green was freighting, Mrs. Green would sit with the children in the kitchen around the stove and tell stories. To economize she would open the front of the kitchen range and let the light from the fire brighten the kitchen, thus saving kerosene. One night as they were sitting so, an electrical storm came up – with plenty of fireworks. Suddenly one of the bolts of lightning invaded the kitchen. It struck the stovepipe, causing the lids to fly off the stove, and scattering ashes all over the kitchen, while a ball of fire streaked along the mopboard. They might not remember the story for that particular night, but they'll never forget the hour.

Now even rural areas in Dawson County have daily mail service, but when the Greens arrived such was not the case. At first they picked up their mail at Billy Wood's 2E Ranch, then later at Skillestad's, another homesteader in the Union community. Either place, they had about six miles to go to pick up their mail so during the winter months two or three weeks might elapse between 'pick ups'. Then Olsons established a post office so from then on they only had to go five miles to get their mail.

School attendance from the first grade through the twelfth presented problems to many of the pioneers. (School attendance still is not without problems for many rural residents even in 1973, but methods for coping with the problems are perhaps more sophisticated.) For the first eight years of schooling the Green children attended the Pierce School, two-and-a-half miles away. When weather permitted, they walked and in cold weather Mr. Green took them with team and sleigh.

As they grew older Delbert was able to take over the driving. One night as they started for home they found the storm was so severe they could not see where they were going. The girls sat in the rear of the sleigh with their backs to the wind but Delbert sat on the seat to drive. He soon found that he couldn't do much driving because he couldn't see facing into that wind. One thing about a good horse – he'll take you home if he has a chance. Delbert gave him that chance. He tied the lines together and draped them around his neck, giving old Gyp his head. Unhampered by direction from his 'driver', Gyp headed into the wind and took them home. Mother, anxiously watching from the window, saw the little sleigh come down the lane and hurried out to open the gate and let them into the yard. Safe, thanks to good horse sense!

Several times when the weather became too severe during the day while they were at school, they weren't able to get home at all. One time when Effie Bryan was teaching they had to stay at the school house all night.

Pierces lived about a mile from school but even the Pierce girls couldn't go home. Their brother, George, who had graduated from the eighth grade, followed the section* fence to bring some food to the trapped scholars – all of them, not just his sisters. One of the items he brought that Mary Starr particularly remembers was the loaf of bread, a knife sticking in it. What a welcome sight! The children slept on the benches that night.

Lehmans lived about half-a-mile from the school so sometimes they and Pierces were able to pick up the neighborhood children and divide them between them for overnight accommodations when parents farther away weren't able to get to them. Several years ago no school was held for two months during the winter because of the difficulties snow and cold presented.

As transportation improved and the children grew older, Mrs. Green sometimes went to Glendive with her husband and left the children home alone. One summer day while their parents were gone a hailstorm struck. (Those hail storms seemed to follow the creek so, since the Green's land followed the creek too, they frequently had hail.) This particular storm was severe and as hailstorms pounded at the windows, shattering glass, Delbert grabbed a mattress and backed up against the window to keep the hail out.

Often during their parents' trips to town the children at home would try to do something 'special' –perhaps some extra cleaning – scrubbing – baking cookies. But sometimes their projects didn't turn out as anticipated. There was the time they made a batch of taffy, for instance. That taffy just wouldn't 'pull'. Rather than exhibit their fiasco, they carefully washed up all the dishes and threw the taffy down the well so there would be no evidence when the folks came home.

A neighbor family, inspired by the Greens' example (of successes, not the taffy failure), decided to surprise their folks, too, so they tried making bread. But that bread would not rise. They too, preferred to dispose of the evidence before their parents came home so they pulled the dough into little pieces to make it inconspicuous and scattered the bits over the hillside. However, they hadn't reckoned with the perversity of that yeast.

After their folks were home, Dad happened to look toward the hill and with puzzled wonder wanted to know, "What's going on up there?" With a sinking sensation they looked in that direction, too. After the bread was thrown out, it did rise. Each little portion had swelled to a conspicuous size and little white nodules dotted the landscape.

As they were growing up the Green children didn't have the variety of toys available now and it wasn't easy to go places, but they had good times anyway. Some of their diversions were picnics with Mother; playing in the creek;

swimming in the horse tank (one dry year a muskrat built a den right under the tank and in the evening he'd come up and swim); or just lying in the yard watching the clouds and letting their imaginations run loose as they 'identified' various forms and shapes in the clouds. One of their favorite pastimes required laboriously pulling the buggy up the hill so they could have the fun of riding in it as it rolled back down.

Visiting with neighbors was high on the list of pleasures. For years the Union community held a Children's Day picnic in June. Contests of many kinds were held and races were run. These would be followed by a ballgame and then a dance in the evening. Of course, there was always the Fourth of July picnic and dance. These picnics and community affairs were held at the Hill's granary until the community hall was built; then they were (and are) held at the hall.

When the time came for them to enter high school, they worked for their room and board to enable them to attend. Delbert and Mary entered together in the fall of 1924. To pay for his high school education, Delbert worked at the high school, helping Mr. Fleischman with the janitorial work. Part of the time he had sleeping quarters at the high school, and one year he stayed near the present fairgrounds, walking to high school from there.

The girls worked in homes, assisting with housework and childcare to pay their way through high school. Was an education acquired in this way perhaps appreciated just a bit more than when the 'right' to attend high school is taken for granted?

One year while Mary and Charlotte were in high school the winter was particularly severe and prospects were dim for getting home for Christmas because their folks couldn't get to them. The day before Christmas two homesick girls walked down town, and they happened to meet the Union mail hauler. He was driving a 'converted Model A' – a car equipped with sled runners – so he was able to navigate the roads when others couldn't. There was no oil road connecting Glendive and Lindsay then. If the road had been oiled, what difference would that have made when the snow was so deep it covered the fences?

The mailman told the girls they could ride out to Lindsay with him so they lost no time getting ready. They spent Christmas Eve with the Henry Greens in Lindsay and telephoned home. Next morning their father came to take them home for Christmas.

Another time when road conditions discouraged automobile travel, their parents arranged for them to travel by train to Lindsay. Other parents in the area did the same for their high schoolers so when the train arrived in Lindsay, sleighs and teams were waiting. Again snow was so deep it covered the fences so Dad disregarded trails and headed for home 'as the crow flies'.

One winter while they were in high school Mary and Charlotte both contracted scarlet fever so they spent seven weeks in 'the pest house' – a little cottage on the ground of the General Hospital. The doctor would check on them once a day, and the handy man from the hospital brought their meals.

It was a long seven weeks. Charlotte dropped out for that year after her prolonged 'vacation', but Mary went on to graduate that spring. By this time their mother was quite ill with asthma and hay fever and needed help at home. Charlotte helped that year, then, after Mary graduated, she helped while Charlotte finished. The younger children, in turn, also went through high school.

By the time Donald and Duane reached adolescence 4-H Clubs were being formed throughout the county, and they were active in club work under the leadership of Don Gibson and Jim Glasscock. One of their projects was the growing of potatoes. These were displayed at the County Fair, of course, as were other 4-H projects. The boys won many blue ribbons at the fairs during their 4-H years.

Mr. and Mrs. Green were both active in community affairs. They donated two acres of land for a community hall, which was then used for church services, picnics, and many other community events. Mr. Green was the neighborhood barber – veterinarian – butcher.

Mrs. Green contributed much to the community with her musical talents. She played the violin for various activities and also gave violin lessons. Gretchen Utterback gave piano lessons so the two women exchanged lessons for their children.

Mary (Green) Starr points out that not only did she take piano lessons from Gretchen Utterback; so did her daughter Norma Jean and Norma's daughter Peggy. With a laugh she quotes Mrs. Utterback, "Your great-grandmother Green would be so proud of you, Peggy." Then, turning to Mrs. Starr she added, "She has a natural rhythm – which you didn't have!"

Sundays were carefully observed in the Green home and were not to be used for idle pleasure. They faithfully attended Sunday School and church services, first in the school house, later in the community hall. When there was no other way to get there, they walked. Sunday afternoons Mother would play the piano while the family sang.

In the Green home Christian living was not limited to Sunday, however. Christian principles were taught by word and example. Each morning at breakfast, devotions, with Scripture reading and prayer, were conducted, and each evening Mother listened to the children's prayers.

Strict Sunday observance did not preclude inviting company home for dinner. Company was always welcome, invited or uninvited, and the older girls particularly remember one Sunday when unexpected company came – one Sunday when only two chickens had been prepared.

Just so many people could sit around the table and the others had to wait. Mary and Charlotte, old enough to help with the cooking, naturally waited. Doris's main contribution was helping wash dishes. Since she was younger and didn't get to go places with the older girls she was told, with special magnanimity, she could sit at the table if she would PROMISE TO TAKE ONLY ONE PIECE OF CHICKEN.

Doris sat at the table. Demurely she ate her piece of chicken. Then, with a roguish look at her sisters, she deliberately speared another piece of chicken. Desperately, Mary and Charlotte tried to signal to her reminding her of her promise, but she just sat serenely eating her second piece of chicken. And then, with another wicked glance at her horrified sisters, she speared yet a third piece. The older girls didn't feel they could say anything then but they've said plenty since. To this day, when the sisters get together, Doris is reminded of her treachery.

But her treachery doesn't make them cringe as does the memory of Donnie's brutal frankness on another occasion. This time they were the guests. Pie was served for the dessert. As Donnie, just old enough to talk clearly, struggled with his pie, he announced to his mother, in a voice that carried around the table, "This is the toughest crust I've ever eaten."

These, and many other incidents, were recalled as the brothers and sisters met together this summer for their reunion at the old family home. Along with the six children came grandchildren and great-grandchildren as well as a sister-in-law, nieces and nephews – about sixty-five in all. They met at noon for food and fellowship, spent the afternoon visiting and playing games. Saturday evening a few neighbors joined them at Union hall for a dance.

Saturday night the 'six' and their spouses slept at the farm and had breakfast together in the morning. Sunday noon all but two of the neighbors who had lived in the community while the Greens lived there were represented at a potluck dinner at the old homestead. Many of them also attended Sunday forenoon services in the Union hall. Sunday afternoon the dispersion began until that night only the 'six', again with their spouses, remained. Again they spent the night at 'home', then Monday they had their family picture taken in Glendive.

Delbert's wife (the former Laila Davidson) had fixed up the old house for the reunion. On one wall family pictures were arranged and picture albums were conveniently placed for perusal. The old telephone, redone, was back on the wall. During the two-day reunion there was much picture taking and visiting; there was horseshoe playing and races and baseball. The little children fished in the creek for pollywogs and frogs or anything they could bring up. There was even a frog jump with each sponsor prodding his frog along trying to get him to go.

There were nostalgic memories of winter evenings with corn meal mush for supper and popcorn later on. Many who experienced some material deprivations during this frontier's 'growing pains', determined to give their children 'the things we didn't have' – and fail to recognize the value of the things they did have. As the Green children met together they were reminded again of values money can't buy. After thirty-nine years, it was a great get-together.

From an Iowa Mansion to a Shack on a Montana Homestead

The Green Homestead in later years – shed, sod barn, home

Sunday gathering in Union, Montana

Four-horse team pulling the binder cutting grain

Rev. A.E. Plummer

February 1966

Several months ago the Wheat Ridge Methodist Church in Colorado decided they wanted to learn about the circuit-riding preachers of an earlier day and were discussing sending for films on the subject when someone asked, "Why send for films when we have one of those riders in our congregation?"

Yes, the Reverend A.E. Plummer, visitation minister for the congregation, had been a Montana Methodist circuit rider. Although Reverend Plummer has been in Colorado since 1938, Dawson County still holds strong ties for him. It was here he met and married his wife, Cordia Chaney, and here he buried her in June, 1965. Their two daughters also are buried in the Glendive cemetery.

The newly developed Bloomfield area had no resident minister, but Deaconess Laura Jones had been there several months when the new preacher arrived. She was in Bloomfield with a horse and buggy (borrowed from Lester Brown) to meet him when he stepped off the stage that brought him from Glendive.

When the newcomer had folded himself into the buggy seat and had time to survey the accommodations, particularly the diminutive horse, he asked of the deaconess, "Do we have to ride this way all around the parish? Seems to me we need something bigger between the shafts. I keep feeling as though he should be up here, and I should be down there!"

Brown had a bigger horse, all right, and when they started out next morning, Plummer was gratified to note that the quadruped between the shafts looked big enough for his job. Miss Jones made no comment on the change, but when they reached the first hill, before they started down into the draw, she told him, "You can let me get out." He couldn't see the necessity for that and protested, "If that thing can't hold us both back, we'll run over him!" But Laura was adamant so he stopped and let her get out.

As Arch started down the hill, he began to suspect a previous acquaintance between Laura and that steed for as soon as the buggy got close to the horse's heels, he began kicking and kicked all the way down the hill while Laura followed afoot and laughed. She only stayed a couple weeks after the preacher arrived on the scene, but day after day, as they continued their rounds, before every coulee* she would get out, and down every hill that horse would kick.

The deaconess and the new parson were invited to one of the homes in the parish for dinner on a certain day, but when they heard that the district superintendent, the Rev. Edward Smith, was coming for their quarterly conference, Plummer suggested that Miss Jones go ahead and keep the dinner appointment while he stayed with the superintendent, then he and the visiting prelate would come down that afternoon for the conference.

Accordingly, the day of the dinner appointment Rev. Plummer and Miss Jones, in the buggy behind 'Old Faithful' ('faithfully kicked on every downgrade') started for Zellers. To get there they had to go down the Table

165

Hill, a long steep slope, so Miss Jones suggested, "You take me to the top of the Table Hill, and I'll walk on down." Then, confident that he would stop as usual, she chatted serenely as Old Faithful jogged along. The Reverend was serene too, because he knew that this was once he was not going to stop.

As he started over the brow of the hill, she rather sharply reminded him that he was supposed to let her out, but he kept right on going and waited for the fireworks. Nothing happened. Not a thing! That perverse equine carefully minced down that hill, not one misstep the whole way!

Plummer went back to Brown's and that afternoon he and the superintendent headed for Bloomfield. No sooner had they started down the Table Hill than up came the heels, pounding against the front of the buggy. The farther they went the worse the kicking got. Plummer, leaning as far as he could over the edge of the buggy on his side, pulling with all his might on the reins, was shouting, "Whoa! Whoa!" while the superintendent leaning as far as he could over the edge of the buggy on his side was pleading, "Hold the road! Hold the road!" They did reach the bottom of the hill safely, but not until Old Faithful had kicked the dashboard right out of the front of the buggy. And Laura Jones could still laugh when she left the country.

After another of Reverend Smith's visits, Rev. Plummer took him to Glendive, but not with Old Faithful. They used a team belonging to Roy Reed for the trip. This team was well-mannered enough but barefoot so before they reached their journey's end, both horses had sore feet.

As they neared Bamber Hill* Plummer noticed a team of mules rapidly approaching from behind and recognized the teamster, who had a reputation for driving like the Biblical Jehu. He declared to his passenger that he was not going to turn his sore-footed team to the rocky roadside to let anyone pass. At the foot of Bamber Hill they stopped at the schoolhouse for a drink of water, and the mule team whirled past in a cloud of dust to be seen no more that day by the clergymen.

Soon after that incident some of the members started telling him about a rumor going the rounds and identified the teamster's wife, a notorious gossip, as the instigator. "Fine preacher we've got," the story began. He gave little heed to the tale at first, classing it as too absurd for serious attention, but finally one of his good parishioners warned him that it was time to put a stop to the story. Those who knew him recognized it as the fabrication of an over-worked imagination, but to others it might begin to sound convincing.

According to the gossip, instead of letting those mules pass he had accepted a challenge from the teamster to race for a pint of whiskey (the day he had the superintendent with him). Not only had the parson accepted the challenge, chattered the scandalmonger; he had won the race, had gone into the saloon, bought the whiskey, and had treated the crowd!

A crowd customarily gathered at the Bloomfield store to await the arrival of the stage bringing the mail from Glendive so the next time the mail came in, Brother Plummer called Mrs. Gossip outside and told her, "You've had your

166

fun, but now this has gone far enough. You go in and tell the folks that it was all just a joke." She refused.

Reverend Plummer next wrote a letter to a Sidney lawyer with whom he was well acquainted, describing the situation and explaining, "I don't want to make an issue of this, but just give her a scare." Not many days later the postmistress confidentially informed him, "She got a letter from an attorney in Sidney," then added significantly, "You got one from the same attorney." The letter he received explained that the other letter carried notice of a $7500 slander suit.

Next stage day as he was standing in the door of the post office he noticed Mrs. Gossip across the street at Crockett's store. He had a hunch she might have something to say to him, but he was in no hurry to let her say it. When she started across the street, he slipped out the back door of the post office, and when she reached the post office, he was at the store. Again she started across the street, but again by the time she had crossed, he turned up on the other side.

He let the cat and mouse game continue until the mail had been distributed. Then as she hurried through the door and began calling, "Mr. Plummer!" he gave her his attention. Profuse apologies began tumbling from her lips, but those words deserved a larger audience. Calling to the crowd, he got their attention and let them listen to those apologies.

Then, reminding her of some of the damage to other characters caused by her loose tongue, he concluded with, "You got hold of the wrong character this time. If you spread any more stories about me or anyone else while I'm in this community, we'll go ahead with that suit." There was an immediate decline in malicious rumors in the area.

The young preacher had plenty to keep him busy during his Bloomfield residence, with preaching points at the Morgan Creek School (ten miles south of Bloomfield), Independence School (ten miles north), Bradbury (or Wold) School (twelve miles west), and the Bush School (between Bradbury and Bloomfield). Occasionally he also preached at the Red Top School (five miles east), but not regularly. Sometimes he rode horseback to keep a preaching appointment, but more often he went with horse and buggy, in cold weather or hot, wet or dry, stormy or calm.

Services among the pioneers were not weighted down with formality, and Rev. Plummer chuckled as he recalled once when Mr. Gregg, father of the late Virgil Gregg, spoke up in the middle of his sermon and drawled, "Well, Brother Plummer, we know that already." Unperturbed, Brother Plummer replied, "My mother used to tell me, 'We don't need to be told as much as we need to be reminded,'" and went on with his message.

During the first months of his sojourn in Bloomfield he stayed in the homes of some of the faithful, first at Joe Reeds. Reed lived in a little two-room house with a loft, reached by a ladder. In spite of their limited facilities, the first evening the new preacher was there they entertained quite a group for supper. Besides Mr. and Mrs. Reed, Reed's brother was there plus Miss Jones, Scotty Kuhns, Arvid Erickson and the preacher.

After the evening meal they gathered around the organ and all joined in singing (that Scotty had a wonderful voice!). But the group wasn't there just for the evening; they were all staying overnight! As they sang, the newcomer couldn't help wondering where all these people were going to sleep.

After the singing session the other bachelors in the group picked up their hats, one reached for a lantern, and they started for the door, so Plummer picked up his hat and started for the door, too. Their destination, he discovered, was the oats bin.

They found blankets waiting for them and soon were retired for the night with Arch next to the partition, Scotty against the outside wall, and the other two fellows between them. Before long it occurred to Arch that this would be a good time to have a little fun and get better acquainted. He found Scotty willing to cooperate so they made a 'sandwich'; they each pressed their hands and knees against the wall and pushed, squeezing the hapless fellows who were in the middle. If the other young men had been feeling any stiffness or awe at having a preacher in their midst, the feeling was certainly dispelled by the time the 'squeeze play' was finished.

After he had stayed in various homes for a time, the parish supplied a parsonage by purchasing a little two-story house from somewhere east of Bloomfield and moving it into town. Plummer lived in the upstairs while the N.B. Sacketts lived on the main floor.

Sackett was a farmer, and in common with most farmers of that day, hired an outfit to come in and thresh his grain. The threshing crew pulled into Sackett's yard late one Saturday evening, and as they bustled about getting everything lined up, they explained to Sackett that they wanted to get an early start in the morning. Sackett reminded them that the next day was Sunday, but they insisted that they couldn't stop for Sunday. Sackett stood firm. "You don't thresh at my place on Sunday," he maintained, so the foreman warned him they would move on, and he would have to wait his turn some other time. They moved, and he waited. It was six weeks before they came back, yet not a kernel of grain was lost because of the delay.

Little wonder then, in view of his convictions regarding Sunday labor, that one of his neighbors was amazed to find him in his cornfield on the Lord's Day. He had moved up onto Morgan Table by this time, and one Sunday as Mrs. Lunsford was on her way to church over in the Morgan Creek Schoolhouse, she was surprised to find that same N.B. Sackett at work in his field. She stopped to inquire the reason for this breach of his custom, and a chagrined Sackett confessed that he hadn't realized what day it was!

A.E. Plummer was born and reared in England, coming to the United States in 1910. Growing up in England hadn't given him opportunity to learn about the wonderful sport of baseball, but after coming to the States he had seen one game during his brief stay in Michigan.

The first summer he was in Bloomfield that metropolis planned a big Fourth of July celebration with a baseball game as the main feature. But before the Fourth it rained. And rained. The great day dawned beautiful and clear, but

168

Montana gumbo* doesn't forget quickly, and the visiting team from Intake couldn't make it to Bloomfield, ball game or no ball game.

The Bloomfield regulars, all set to play ball, weren't about to be cheated out of a game so they began scouting through the crowd to 'pick up' a team to oppose them. When they approached the new parson, they didn't ask about his experience; they just asked him what position he wanted to play. He didn't volunteer any information about experience, he just told them; "Put me as far away from that bat as you can!" So they put him in center field.

As he looked the situation over from that vantage point, he figured he'd have plenty of time to see that ball coming if it came his way, and he did. He had to run a little, he says, but when he got close, he stuck up his glove, and the ball landed in the middle of it. He hung onto it, and everyone cheered.

When it came his turn to bat, it seemed to him that pitcher looked awfully close, throwing those balls at him, so he took that old bat and swung as hard as he could. Most of the time (as he tells it) he missed, but one time he connected and made a home run. The crowd went wild. When the game was over, the regulars crowded around, wanting him to join their team. He modestly demurred (he didn't tell them he'd seen only one other baseball game besides that day's), but they insisted. He pointed out to them, "I can't join the team; I work the day you play." (The team regularly played on Sunday.) Not to be discouraged, they told him, "We'll play on Saturday if you'll play with us." So he agreed, "Sure, I'll play." He joined the team, "And," according to Reverend Plummer, "I never made another hit, never made another catch!"

Soon after he began holding services in Bloomfield the new minister took several new members into the church. Among those received were two sisters, Ora and Cordia Chaney, living about a mile east of 'town'. A year later Ora married Menno Mullet, and two years later Cordia married the preacher.

Edward Smith performed the marriage ceremony for Arch Plummer and Cordia Chaney on August 24, 1914. The newlyweds attended the Methodist District Conference at Forsyth for their honeymoon. At the conference Reverend Plummer was assigned to the Joliet circuit. Five years later, August 24, the Plummers were back in Glendive. This time Rev. Plummer was ordained elder in the Glendive Methodist Church.

Although they were assigned to different parts of the state through the years, they managed to get back to Bloomfield for occasional visits. When they came back on their first vacation, he was promptly put to work, and one of his preaching appointments was at the Bradbury School. They borrowed a horse and buggy from Mose Mullet to drive over to the school on Sunday morning, and late that afternoon Cordia's sister and her husband drove over in their automobile for the evening preaching service.

Before the evening meeting Arch brought the borrowed horse out to give him a drink. To his consternation, Menno slipped the horse's halter off, slapped him on the rump, and started him down the creek toward home. Arch protested, "Wait! I've got to get home!" For answer Menno tied the buggy behind the car, and after the service they all started home in the automobile. It's

169

been fifty years since that ride, but Reverend Plummer's memory of it hasn't dimmed.

There wasn't much resemblance between that new Overland car and a '66 model. As for roads – they just weren't – so Menno struck out across country through coulees and over bumps that today's low-slung cars wouldn't dare attempt. The car wasn't equipped with seal beam headlights for night driving, either. It was a wild ride, and when his sister-in-law recently reminisced, "Cordia was scared to death that night," Reverend Plummer fervently declared, "She wasn't the only one!" But they arrived home safely and well ahead of the horse, who reached his home corral about midnight.

Cordia related another frightening experience she had before she married Arch. She was spending the night with her friend Ruth Lunsford (Christie) when Ruth's brother Charlie came by to see 'the folks'. As he walked past the window he saw that only the two girls were there. He didn't want to alarm them by knocking on the door so he slipped quietly away. But Cordia had seen the FACE at the window.

Terrified, she spent a sleepless night watching and listening for any sign of an intruder. There was no sign, and in the morning's bright sunshine she was able to tell Ruth what she had seen. Ruth declared that if she had known, she would have died! But Cordia contradicted her. "No, you wouldn't have. I prayed all night I could die, and I didn't!"

Next day innocent Charlie came back to see if the girls might need anything. Cordia was relieved to learn the identity of the visitor, and Charlie was stricken to learn that his good intentions had caused such distress.

The Plummers served in various parishes throughout the state of Montana, beginning with his first assignment at Birney and concluding at Shelby, before transferring to Colorado in 1938.

When Plummer had received word of that first assignment to Birney, he started looking on the map to get an idea of where to go, but there was no Birney on the map so he went to the public library. There he found that to get to Birney he'd take the train to Forsyth, from Forsyth he'd go by stage seventy-five miles to Ashland, and from Ashland, he could only guess how he would go the last fifty miles to Birney.

As it turned out, a man with a team and buggy met him in Ashland to take him those last fifty miles. Rev. Plummer observed that when he settled in Birney, he made a big increase in the population, percentage wise. Where there had been two residents, now there were three. This was ranch country, with the ranches big and far apart. His preaching points were far apart, too – fifty miles apart.

Many of those miles could be traversed only on horseback so the young Englishman, who had never ridden or saddled a horse in all his life had to make quite an adjustment. The first time he tried to straddle a horse he landed behind the cantle, but he climbed over into the saddle and was on his way. By the time he left Birney for Bloomfield, two and one half years and 16,000 horseback miles later, he'd made the adjustment.

170

He'd made some other adjustments, too. Often in his visitation work, night coming on would find him far from any ranch so he'd sleep out all night, his saddle blanket for a bed, his saddle for a pillow, one end of his lariat looped around his own foot and the other end tied to his horse's front fetlock. All the night long his horse never tightened that rope.

The effect of these 'adjustments' on his health? He's still hale and hearty after fifty years of active ministry and five years of semi-retirement. Most of his other assignments were a little less rigorous than the Birney stint (Birney was the only place he preached a funeral with a gun in his back to make sure he didn't say the wrong thing), but the years were by no means always easy. "When God directs a life, He doesn't promise all will be easy, but He does promise 'strength for the day.' Glory be to God!"

Arch and Cordia Plummer

Mrs. Bert Crockett

September 1965

The Twentieth Century was just getting a good start when Bert Crockett left his Nebraska home to view homestead prospects in Montana. He had spent some time in Minnesota but wasn't satisfied there so had come on to the Treasure State. He must have been satisfied with what he found here because he sent for his family as soon as possible — maybe sooner — and he spent practically all the rest of his life here.

The various 'revolutions' — electrical, mechanical — hadn't made much impact on the West when the Crocketts began their search for a new home. They left Nebraska for Montana in a covered wagon, cooking over campfires, camping nights on the open prairie as they traveled. Mrs. Crockett reflected that it wasn't much of a problem to get food along the way because they'd pass through towns often enough to keep their supplies stocked. It was after they settled on the homestead in Montana that getting food became a problem!

Mr. Crockett first came to Montana alone. After looking at some of the available land, he chose for his homestead a site a half-mile northeast of Bloomfield, only then there was nothing but the waving prairie grass where Bloomfield now stands. He was the first of a number of immigrants from Bloomfield, Nebraska, who settled in the area and later gave the name of their former home to the little town that grew up some thirty miles northwest of Glendive.

When his wife and small son joined him, the sole 'improvements' on the homestead were a well and a tent. Mrs. Crockett recalls that one afternoon that first summer she had put young Charles to bed for a nap, then she herself dropped off to sleep. Suddenly she was awakened by a frightening rubbing and scraping against the tent. Hurrying to the door, she found a bunch of longhorn cattle milling about the tent and rubbing against it. Her shouting 'spooked' them and quickly put them on the run, but if it hadn't, she declares she'd have used the shotgun! The sight of the longhorns soon became commonplace, and many times she pounded on the bottom of the dishpan to scare them away.

Prairie wolves, too, were still common when the Crocketts first came to Montana, and the stillness of the wide open spaces was often shattered by their 'serenades' in the vicinity of the tent. The first summer the Crocketts were in Montana a group of Indians camped just on the other side of the range of hills back of their homestead.

Mr. Crockett plowed a garden soon after he arrived so they had a fairly good garden that first year. He didn't have much other breaking done to demand his attention so he had time to help with the garden. All field work, of course, was done with horses. Trips to town were infrequent so when he did go to Glendive, he would fetch a load of flour, sugar, and other staples. It was important to have the grocery list complete; if anything was overlooked they just got along without it so she was careful not to forget. Mrs. Crockett herself

172

didn't get back to Glendive for about four years after her arrival here. Later they ordered their groceries by mail from Montgomery Ward – after there was mail service to Bloomfield.

By fall they had replaced the tent with a dugout in the side of the hill. It wasn't fancy, but it was good and warm. The dirt roof, however, developed leaks after a time. Their second son, Jim, was born while they were living in the dugout, and during one 'spell' of particularly hard rains, Mrs. Crockett had to make a bed for him on top of the flour barrel, and even then propped an umbrella over him to keep him dry.

Lack of facilities didn't keep the Crocketts from being hospitable. As they wrote letters to friends in Nebraska, some of their old neighbors became interested in homesteading, too, and after a few years many more Nebraskans joined the trek to Montana. Since the Crocketts' roof was the only one around, it was under that roof that the different settlers slept as they came to look and build. Mrs. Crockett would make beds on the floor for the guests. Sometimes there would hardly be room for her to walk between 'beds' when she would have to get up during the night to take care of the baby, but pioneers willingly shared what they had with those who came.

Life wasn't easy for those who came first and smoothed the way for those of us who came later. Seven children were born to the Crocketts after they came to the Thirteen Mile Valley, none of them in a hospital. Rather, a midwife from the community (the community extended over many miles) would be summoned to assist. When one of the little girls was born, Mr. Crockett went to get help but the baby came before the help did so Mrs. Crockett was all alone when the baby arrived.

It was the Crocketts who donated land for a school to be built in Bloomfield. Mr. Crockett's parents also moved to the area a few years after their son came and it was 'Grandpa' Crockett who built the first store in Bloomfield.

Mr. Crockett died in 1936, but Mrs. Crockett still lives in the area where she pioneered. No longer able to live alone (she will be eighty-four in November) she makes her home with her children. She has five sons and two daughters living.

Mr. & Mrs. Henry (Mary Bush) Zimdars

September 1966

With all the North Dakota jokes that have made the rounds in recent months Hank Zimdars might be able to contribute a few of his own, but one thing that was not a joke sixty years ago was the North Dakota prairie dog.

Zimdars was a native of Wisconsin, but as a young man he had come to North Dakota to work. There was homestead land available in North Dakota around Bowman so he thought of filing there, but when he looked over the land available he found so many prairie dogs that he decided that he wasn't interested in competing with them. Instead he, with two or three other fellows, came on to Montana, and here he found miles of unclaimed — even by prairie dogs — prairie. The homestead site he chose was five miles west and one mile north of Bloomfield.

His nearest neighbors were the Wienkes, one-and-one-half miles to the east of him. He stayed with them a few nights until he could get a shack put up. Putting up a 'shack' then didn't involve quite what building a house today does, so it wasn't long until he was ready to move in.

He arrived in Dawson County April 1, 1908, to homestead and decided to take the full seven years allowed to prove up* on his new claim. He could have fulfilled the requirements in as little as three years, but why be in such a hurry to start paying taxes? In 1915 he got the deed signed by Woodrow Wilson for his land, and he still has that deed today. When he filed in 1908, they were allowed a quarter section, but later the law was amended to permit a half section so he then took another quarter in the same section.

When he first built his shack, he was about half-a-mile from a spring so he hauled his water from there. After he got his other quarter he moved his buildings closer. He only had to dig twenty feet for water when he dug his well.

That first year he was on his claim he broke up fifteen or twenty acres, then each year added more acres for tillage. He brought three horses with him, while a plow and disc made up his line of machinery when he started. He borrowed a drill from neighbor Wienke to seed his first crop. Brody, one of his neighbors who had come about the same time as Zimdars, had shipped out a binder so Hank used that to cut his first couple crops until he got a binder of his own. A fellow east of Bloomfield threshed it for him with a big wood-fired steamer outfit (fired with wood). The same outfit threshed for other homesteaders, and each farmer joined the threshing crew, making the rounds of the neighborhood with the 'rig'.

Even though Zimdars came in the spring of the year, he found that he hadn't missed all the 'winter'. In May, they had a big snowstorm with vicious winds that piled snow banks ten feet high. The storm caught Hank at home, but Adolph Hidle, across the divide*, was not so fortunate. He had gone to Glendive for supplies and was there when the blizzard struck. He managed to get back as far as Holleckers but had to change to a sled to go on from there. By

174

the time he reached Zimdars' place his team was so played out they could go no farther so Zimdars let him use one of his saddle horses to get on home. He came back later to get his team and load.

They didn't do much running to Glendive in those early years when they had to go horseback or with team and wagon. Twice a year to get supplies was about all the commuting they did. Zimdars bought his first Model T in 1912, and after that he could get around much more readily.

During his bachelor days on the homestead he didn't fuss much about elaborate foods, but he managed to keep well fed. Potatoes were his main standby, but baking powder biscuits were an important item in his fare, and he learned to make them right good. And of course there were plenty of wild cattle running loose, so when you wanted fresh meat you could always go out and kill a CK steer! Sometimes he bought bread from Mrs. Wienke. She also did his washing for him, as she did for some of the other bachelors around. By 1920 he decided he had been bachelor long enough and married Mary Bush, daughter of homesteaders. The Bush family had come to Montana from Nebraska in 1907.

Early in the twentieth century much talk was circulating in Nebraska about homestead land available in eastern Montana. As a result, a large number of families around Bloomfield (Nebraska) immigrated to the frontier, and many of them settled northwest of Glendive, forming a community in the vicinity of the Adams Post Office. The name of the post office was later changed to Bloomfield, Montana.

Among those coming from Nebraska was the Bush family. The oldest son, Charlie, was very much interested in filing on a homestead so the entire family came, and Mr. Bush filed on a homestead, too. The youngest member of the family was eight-year-old Mary, now Mrs. Henry Zimdars. Although almost sixty years have passed since that March day in 1907 when they drove to their new home (to be), Mrs. Zimdars vividly recalls the ride on a four-horse wagonload of lumber. The lumber was to become their house.

Mr. Bush had filed on the quarter four miles west of Bloomfield where the Lutheran Church now stands. Son Charlie filed on the quarter joining it on the southwest. It was on Charlie's claim that they built their first home. While the home was being built, the family lived in a tent, thrown over a bank. Old timers still talk about the hard winter of 1906-07, and even though the Bushes had waited until March to come, they still found much snow and cold, as spring was late in coming.

Today's Dawson County resident, living in an insulated, centrally heated modern house, might have difficulty appreciating the Herculean problems confronting the pioneers only a generation ago — unless you happen to be one of those pioneers. One of the immediate problems facing Mrs. Bush was that of keeping her family warm in the tent until they could get the house ready. Some nights she sat up all night keeping the fire going as she battled the elements. Although they built a house first on Charlie's quarter, after a few years they built on the family's land, just about where the Lutheran Church was later erected.

The newcomers soon found that they had chosen a homesite closer to neighbors than they had realized. Some Indians regularly camped in Bull Camp Coulee, a couple miles to the west. It was the task of Mary and other of the Bush children to go after the cows in the evening, but Mrs. Zimdars admitted (after all these years she could chuckle about it, but it was no joke then) that if they saw Indians they came home without the cows! Sometimes the whole tribe of Indians would start for Glendive and as they trailed past the little homestead shack the Bush children 'made themselves scarce'.

Many rattlesnakes infested the area and called for caution on the part of the new settlers. Mrs. Zimdars noted that on one occasion she would have stepped on a rattler had not her brother pulled her back.

Schools were scarce, not because they had been consolidated into larger schools, but because they had not yet been built. Certainly there were no buses to transport the pupils when there was no school close by. At first the Bush children had to walk the four miles (one way) to the Bloomfield school. Later on they went with a team and buggy, other times horseback. Whichever way they went the going was rough in the winter. In the severest weather it was sometimes necessary to miss school.

High school now is taken for granted by most young people, but not so when Mrs. Zimdars was a girl. She wanted desperately to go to high school, but her oldest brother 'set his foot down'. Girls, he declared, didn't need an education so she wasn't even allowed to go to Bloomfield to take her eighth grade exams.

In 1920 Mary Bush married Henry Zimdars, a neighboring homesteader. The Zimdars have seven children. Before the fifth child was born Mrs. Zimdars suffered considerably with arthritis. Until then all the family clothes had been washed on a scrub board, but then a salesman came around with a 'new-fangled' machine that was just being introduced, a gasoline-powered washing machine! They bought one, probably the first one in the community, and what a blessing it proved to be!

Even though the early settlers had to work hard and had few conveniences, they found time to visit. They visited much more then, Mrs. Zimdars reflected, than they do now, even though then they had to go with team and buggy or sled. Neighbors were neighbors! Young and old together had good times. No leaving children home with a baby sitter then. Who would be the baby sitter when the whole neighborhood went to the same parties? Mrs. Zimdars feels that if parents would spend more time with their children, there would be fewer juvenile delinquents.

In 1957 Mr. and Mrs. Zimdars moved into Glendive. Two of their boys were in Dawson County High School and finding a place for them to room and board presented a problem. It would have cost $75 a month for each of them so they decided it would be better to buy a home in town and live here. Their son who was doing the farming was about to get married, and they didn't feel they were especially needed on the farm so they decided that was a good time to retire. They have lived in Glendive since.

Joseph Holling

May 1969

Although Joe Holling lives in Miles City, not very many of Glendive's current residents have spent as many years here as he has. He started out in Glendive in 1888 and, with the exception of a few years, lived here until 1949.

Joe's parents both came from Norway, but they didn't come together. They were from different parts of the country and had never met until both had come to Glendive. Mr. Holling couldn't say just when his father came except that he came to work on the railroad when Glendive was the end of the Northern Pacific tracks. The railroad reached Glendive in 1881.

He doesn't know whether his mother came before or after his father did, but they were married in Glendive, and Joe's oldest brother was born in 1884. Although the exact date of her arrival is uncertain, it's safe to conclude that the 1880's had not advanced very far when she arrived in Glendive.

Mr. Holling described his family as the 'bell sheep' of Norwegians in this area. Seemed like all who came later – and there were many – would come to the Holling home. He recalls how the youngsters used to laugh at the trouser style of the newcomers. That many did follow was evidenced by the fact that once during a performance at the Opera House when a Norwegian singer was performing, he counted twenty-two of his cousins in the audience – none of them born here.

Karl Holling (Joe's father) had come first to Baldwin, Wisconsin, when he emigrated from Norway. Joe remembers yet his father's trunk with the name and destination, Karl A. Holling, Baldwin, Wisconsin, still stamped on it. From Baldwin he had 'shipped' with a bunch of men to work on the railroad. They went as far as the tracks went at that time, which landed them in Glendive.

Joe's mother came with her brother, Mike Kalberg. At first he ran a boarding house and she cooked there. Did Karl Holling perhaps stay at this boarding house, meet and marry the cook? That boarding house is still in Glendive, although it's been many a year since anyone boarded in it. It was on Merrill Avenue, across the street from the city hall, when Mike Kalberg operated it, but later Frank Kinney moved it to the back of the lot now occupied by Guelff's Lumber on Clough and Power.

After their marriage Karl Holling and his bride took up ranching. There was plenty of space for new ranchers in Dawson County in the 1880's, and Karl chose a location around Colgate. The hard winter of '86-'87 nearly cleaned them out, just as it did scores of others in Montana and North Dakota. All he had left was a few crop-eared horses and bobtailed cows, but he didn't give up the idea of ranching. He just changed locations and started over again. He had learned one lesson, though; he determined never again to keep more cattle than he could feed and keep in sheds.

When they started over again they located along the river several miles north of Glendive. They built a log house there, a log house that was later moved to the McGaughey farm on Seven Mile. To move the house, Mr. McGaughey dismantled it, piece by piece, numbering each log. On his chosen site he reconstructed it according to number.

The Hollings started raising cattle again and as a side industry, Mrs. Holling sold homemade butter and eggs. Every Saturday she went to town with many pounds of butter and sold it to the townspeople, along with the eggs.

When little Joe was just three years old – his first time in pants – the Hollings and the Kalbergs went chokecherry picking on the Halvorsen ranch, five miles up Deer Creek. The men ate first, then departed for the berry patch.

Joe saw them leave and followed, but he didn't follow quite soon enough. He didn't see which ravine they took so he followed the wrong one and landed on top of the plateau in what is now Johnny Horst's pasture, just west of the new golf course. From that plateau the road led toward the town – and the river.

He was lost from noon Sunday until noon Monday. The whole town turned out to try to find him, with the ferryboat giving free rides and the people of Glendive donating free eats.

Monday, just about noon, Mr. Jerry Fall, bringing a load of hay into town, found the little three-year-old at a spring near the Bamber Ranch about two miles north of Glendive. Needless to say, a greatly distraught mother was much relieved to have her boy back again, apparently none the worse for wear.

Karl Holling seemed to have the cattle business figured out and was doing all right when disaster struck. In 1893 he died of pneumonia, leaving Mrs. Holling with five small children (Joe was the third child). Mrs. Holling decided it would be best to move her family to town. In those days ranchers didn't own the land they used so there was no land to sell, but she sold the cattle and brand to her brother. This enabled her to buy property in Glendive.

She bought two houses in Glendive, one of which she rented out while the family lived in the other. Even though they were now city dwellers, they kept four or five cows and sold milk for five cents a quart. The children carried the milk to their customers. Prairie hay was six and seven dollars a ton. Cows were always a source of income for the Hollings, and they required morning and evening attention.

A few years later Mrs. Holling married again, married a cousin of Karl's so she was still Mrs. Holling, now Mrs. Ole Holling. Then, in 1898, Mrs. Holling also passed away. Had it not been for their stepfather the five children, the oldest only fourteen, would have been thrown upon their own resources, but thanks to him they had someone to care for them.

Ole Holling was in no way the ogre of fiction (and, too often, real life). Joe attests that he was marvelous – the best man in the world. And a stepson ought to know. They could never repay him, he reflects, but they tried. Ole himself was a stepchild from Norway so perhaps that gave him added understanding and compassion for the orphaned children left to his care.

Ole Holling worked for $1.25 a day, riprapping* the Yellowstone River under the bridge. That was during Cleveland's administration. Of course, while wages were lower, prices were lower, too. Joe remembers, for example, going to the store and buying three pounds of steak for twenty-five cents. Even so, there was no money to spare. Ole was a wonderful manager, Joe noted, and his credit was always good. When he went to the store he always took a little book along in which he would write down all that he bought.

There were no luxuries and no extra nickels and dimes. But the children didn't expect extras. They were, in Joe's words, "tickled to have a place to stay. We appreciated it!"

Ole never married again – though he had plenty of chances, Joe was quick to add. Instead he devoted himself to taking care of his stepchildren. Little wonder they were devoted to him.

Joe had started at the Kinney School on Deer Creek while the family was still in the country. Nora Johnson, Cy Johnson's daughter, was his first teacher. Since there were two children in the family older than he, there were three of them attending school when he started. All three rode one old mare. One day she unloaded her entire cargo, and the children had to walk the rest of the way to school. That made them late so they had to go back to school on Saturday to make up for it.

After the family moved into Glendive they went to the Washington School – not to the Washington School building where today's school children go, but in the building that was later used by the Bismarck Grocery* and eventually razed to make way for the First National Bank building*.

Miss Grace Skinner (Mrs. Chet Murphy) was his first teacher in town. The Holling children prided themselves on never being tardy. If they had a perfect record all week they didn't have to go to school on Friday. A sister was the only one of the family who ever missed and had to go to school on Friday afternoon. Brothers and sisters teased her, Joe remembers, until she cried.

After elementary school Joe went on to high school (in the same building) graduating with the class of 1907. There were six graduates that year with, as far as he knows, Everett Brown in Minneapolis the only other member still living.

One of Joe's sisters (the one who broke the family record by being tardy) went to night school because she had to keep house during the day. Each of the evening teachers, Daisy Kimball and Lora Kelly (Mrs. Harry Stubbs), gave her her assignments so she could keep up with her class. She graduated with the class of 1909.

With their mother gone the children had to pitch in and help with the housework. Joe recalls that one of his jobs was to turn the wheel on the side of the wooden washing machine. He was supposed to turn it fifteen minutes per load, and "Those girls," he declares, "saw to it that it was fifteen minutes!" But though they were all expected to help with the work, they never suffered for lack of clothes or food.

To make a little money on their own, the Holling boys hunted beer or whiskey bottles – gunnysacks – anything they could sell to earn a nickel. When the circus came to town, they'd lead the dogs or the ponies, ride (dressed like jockeys) in the parade, carry water to the animals — anything to get in to watch the circus.

With Joe Widmeyer's opera house, too, they used to work to earn admittance. Traveling shows and orchestras would come through, perhaps once a week, perhaps not that often, and make one-night stands. The boys would carry the scenery on stage, set it up, then after the show dismantle it and put it away for a free ticket to the show.

It was in this connection that Joe first saw an example of the duplicity of human nature. The show for the evening featured a woman comedian who laughed and joked on stage as the jolliest of women. But when she came back stage after the performance, she displayed an entirely different temperament. All jollity had vanished, and she "chewed them out" in most unjovial fashion.

During the summer Joe would work on one of the surrounding ranches. His first such job was on the Adams ranch, helping with the garden, raking hay, what have you. He was only ten or eleven years old that summer so his legs were a bit short to reach the lever to trip the rake. He had to slide down the seat each time to trip it so he'd wear out the seat of his trousers. Mrs. Adams would patch them for him.

Mrs. Adams sold vegetables around town so another of his jobs was to help load the vegetables into the wagon. When they reached town, he'd drive from place to place and also would hold the horses at the various 'stops'. Other ranchers for whom he worked included Charlie Krug, George McCone, Ed and George Haskell, and Joel Gleason.

He was taking care of Hans Halvorsen's sheep, just below Hollecker's Ranch on Deer Creek when the freak May 21 snowstorm of 1907 hit. The trees were all leafed out, the weather had been warm for weeks, and snow was about the last thing expected. No sheepskin coat for him when he started out with the sheep that morning at four o'clock; slicker and hat seemed entirely appropriate.

He hadn't been out long, however, when the snow started falling — wet, heavy snow. As the morning wore on and the snow fell faster and covered the ground deeper, herding the sheep became more hectic. One band went one way, the other band another, and his efforts to get them back together were futile. Then he ran his horse back and forth between them a few times, making a trail, and was able to get them bunched again.

He was herding about 270 sheep and older lambs. As the storm increased in intensity he kept walking around the sheep and kept them milling so they would not get snowed under. The sheep themselves found a big, narrow coulee with high banks — stumbled onto it in the storm — and it was a good place for them. This afforded them considerably more protection than they'd have had on the open prairie and helped to keep down losses — although if they hadn't been kept moving they probably all would have suffocated. Halvorsen came out of the storm with 80% of his sheep and lambs while at a neighboring ranch the ground was white with sheep after the snow melted (which it did in a hurry). After lambing was over Joe and his cousin put up hay for Halvorsen up near the HS Ranch.

180

In the fall of 1907 Joe started to college in Bozeman. He hadn't expected to be able to go – government grants and loans weren't handed out so freely in those days – but Mr. Flemming approached him and offered to advance him the money for college so he enrolled. He was able to attend only until April, however, when he had to quit on account of his health.

Mr. Gleason, who had a ranch in southern California, wrote the next fall and offered him a job so he spent that winter in the sunny south. While in California he saw the first Los Angeles to Phoenix auto race.

Joe Holling spent his first night in California in Palm Springs at an empty T.B. sanitarium. The next morning the auto racers, who had also spent the night there, started out for Indio in their cars. Mr. Gleason started out in the same direction with his horse and buggy, while Mr. Gleason's son Dade and Joe started walking. They all arrived at the Harvey House Restaurant in Indio about the same time. Mr. Gleason's horses had all they could do to pull the buggy with its one passenger through the sand; the autos kept getting stuck in the sand, the radiators got hot – all kinds of trouble; and the boys plodded on, making almost as good time as the wheeled vehicles.

After the winter in California, Joe's health improved so much that he returned to Glendive. Again Mr. Flemming helped him, reporting to him, "Arnold Griffin wants to see you." Griffin ran a feed barn, and Joe went to work for him – $75 a month. He worked in the feed barn seven years.

When he started that job, he already knew practically everybody in Glendive, and during the years in the feed barn he learned to know about everyone in the surrounding country, too. ('Surrounding country' took in everything north to the Missouri River and south halfway to Miles City; from beyond Jordan on the west into North Dakota on the east.)

Joe Holling served in France with the 91st Division during World War I. During the time he was overseas his stepfather passed away, and Joe feels that he never did get a chance to really show Ole how much he appreciated him.

After he returned from the war, he bought the ice business from Charlie Hilliard. People didn't have electric refrigerators to plug into an outlet and make their own ice, at the same time keeping their perishables cold, so Joe's business was to put up ice in the winter and store it to sell to people for their ice boxes. The first two years in the ice business he didn't make much money because he wasn't experienced, but once he 'learned the ropes' he found he could make money at it. He worked every day just like a laborer, right with his men.

In 1930 he bought the bottling works. He paid a little too much, he figures, but it turned out to be a good investment. Again he found that he had to learn the business before he could make it go, but by the second year he had learned enough that he made more money than the first year, even though his volume was smaller.

Joe Holling ran the bottling works for nineteen years before he sold it and moved to Colorado in 1949. He had a heart attack and wasn't expected to live. He thought it wise to move to Colorado where his wife had some relatives so she wouldn't be so alone.

When he got down there he was so weak that when he tried to walk the three blocks to church, he would have to stop and rest three or four times each block. Going from a lower altitude to a higher was against all the rules for a heart patient, but his health improved. In time he could even endure the elevation of 14,000 foot Mt. Evans. He didn't get out of the car, but he nevertheless could manage in the thin air at that high altitude. He improved so much that now he 'guesses' he "doesn't have a heart."

1963 found the Hollings back in Montana. They bought a house in Miles City, a duplex, with the idea that they would live in one end, their daughter and her husband in the other. Ironically, within a short time the son-in-law died of a heart attack. Mr. and Mrs. Holling still live in Miles City. Although Mr. Holling just spent some time in the Holy Rosary Hospital, he's back in his home again, and his heart is still strong.

Mrs. Pius (Monica Kuntz) Geiger

January 1966

Pioneering was nothing new to Monica Geiger when she came to Montana in 1909 as the bride of Pius Geiger. She had been brought up on the frontier. She was only two years old when her parents brought her from 'the Old Country' to Richardton, North Dakota where they homesteaded.

Memories of those early years are understandably vague, but she does remember the little sod house where they first lived. She can also recall seeing her mother, Mrs. Kuntz, driving a team of oxen, guiding them by calling 'gee' and 'haw' while she broke sod. Mr. Kuntz, also preparing farmland, used horses to pull his plow.

There's nothing vague, though, in her recollection of the time she met the antelope. She was just a little girl and was taking a drink of water to her father in the field. Topping the brow of a little hill she found herself face to face with a bunch of antelope. She turned and ran as fast as she could toward the house without taking time to look back. If she had, she'd have seen that the antelope, as scared as she was, were running in the opposite direction. Her father told her afterwards that he saw her coming, then all of a sudden she wasn't there, but he saw the antelope running and guessed what had happened.

When Monica Kuntz was twenty years old, she married Pius Geiger from Dawson County. Pius, too, had come from 'the Old Country'. His widowed mother, coming when her father immigrated to the United States, had brought her family to the New World in the spring of 1904, settling first in Richardton, North Dakota. After about two years she married Charlie Houser and they moved to Glendive. Soon Houser and the boys of the family old enough to qualify filed on homesteads on Seven Mile Creek, twenty five miles northwest of Glendive. Pius was one of those old enough to file.

There wasn't much in Glendive and certainly not much on the Creek when the newlyweds set up housekeeping in the little two-room shack on the homestead. That little house was the only improvement on the claim; not even a well had been dug. They soon took care of that, however, digging a well sixteen feet deep, shoveling out all the dirt by hand. Then they rocked up the sides. They must have done a good job because the well is still in use after sixty years.

In spite of the primitive condition of their new home site she thought from the start that this was a great country. Folks have sometimes expressed surprise that she hadn't seen her home-to-be until after she was married, but, she logically points out, she wasn't marrying the homestead; she was marrying Pius. Maybe she did walk in 'blind', but she always thought she got a good bargain.

As spring approached she began planning for her garden. Pius told her to choose the spot she wanted, and he'd plow it for her. All that virgin soil from which to choose! They decided on a garden spot, and she sent off an order for seeds to Oscar H. Will and Co. She remembers that with that first order for seeds was an order for six stalks of horseradish and six stalks of rhubarb, as well as potato eyes. How they grew! They didn't have to irrigate that first year in the freshly turned sod. In her mind's eye she can see yet those nice, big potatoes.

As they worked, the little quarter section on the vast prairie began to take on a home-like appearance. From North Dakota they brought chickens, ducks, geese, and a pig that had young ones in the spring. One thing that especially pleased her was the abundance of wood – plenty of wood along the creek for building fires. No electric or gas ranges for the housekeeper of 1909!

Mrs. Geiger didn't know there was such a thing as a roundup so she was both surprised and puzzled one morning to see covered wagons and cattle coming around a hill to the north. Pius had gone out to milk the cow so when he came back to the house, she asked him what could be going on. He explained to her that the XIT was having their spring roundup, gathering all their cattle from the range and branding them.

The wagons camped at the spring about a quarter of a mile from Geiger's house while they branded the cattle they had gathered in that area. One afternoon one of the cowboys came to the little house and invited them to eat supper that evening with the roundup crew. Young Mrs. Geiger felt rather timid about eating with a bunch of cowboys and declared she was not going. But when Grandma Houser announced that she would go, Mrs. Geiger changed her mind and joined the party. It was a wonderful meal that they were served, and she was glad she went. Certainly it was an experience never duplicated for her. The next morning one of the men came, bringing a front quarter of beef. He explained that they were moving on and didn't want to take it with them, so Mrs. Geiger had meat to can.

Neighbors were scarce, but there were plenty of long horned cattle around. Mrs. Geiger says that she always looked carefully before she started to walk up the creek to Grandma Houser's but even so sometimes she would see a trail of dust start, meaning that a steer had seen her, and she'd have to run.

The first woman that she met in this new country was Mrs. Jim Seeds. There weren't many other women! There were a few, though, and a little later she learned to know Mrs. Kalberg (mother of Martin and Gust). Later as other settlers moved in they became acquainted quickly. Neighbors were neighborly.

Geiger decided he would go into the sheep business so George McCone started him out, but it was only two years until little homestead shacks began appearing all around them. The open range with its sections of free pasture was gone so they sold their sheep.

He bought a team of horses, also from McCone, and Houser had two horses, so by combining their teams they had four horses for breaking sod. It was hard work. Mrs. Geiger observed with a laugh that, "lots of people say they should have left this country to the Indians," and confessed that sometimes she wondered, too, but her husband liked it, and he was making the living so she was content.

The first year that they had a little crop to harvest they found they had a problem: how to get it cut and threshed. A farmer over on Thirteen Mile Creek had a binder and promised to cut it for them, but he was so busy that he was slow in coming. Finally Pius rode over (horseback) to find out what the delay was. The lady who came to the door evidently still found thinking in German easier than thinking in English, and in response to his inquiry for her husband told him, "Oh, he went to the Fiddlers."

Pius was puzzled at this information, but then he realized that the German word for 'fiddle' is 'geige'. Instead of going to the 'fiddlers' the binder was on its way to the Geigers. He had missed them as he rode over so he hurriedly started home again and overtook the slow-moving outfit before they reached his place.

With the arrival of children the little two-room house proved to be rather close quarters. Population throughout the school district was increasing, too, so District 68 decided they'd have to have a larger school. When they built the new school, Pius Geiger bought the original building and moved it to their place, joining it to their little two-room house. The additional space was much appreciated, but somehow, even when they had had to crowd their family of six children into the limited space in their first little house, there was always room for one more if some visitor needed a night's lodging.

After the big, new schoolhouse was built it was used for many community activities – church, socials, dances, or even a potluck dinner on Thanksgiving.

Geiger preferred stock-raising to farming and began to build up a herd of Black Angus cattle. But then tragedy struck. As Geiger, with his brother, was returning home from Glendive, driving in a snowstorm, they failed to see the train coming as they approached the crossing at Bamber Hill*. The train struck them, and Mr. Geiger's chest was crushed, injuring his heart. Now medical science has the answer for such cases, but then, even though he went to Rochester, the damage could not be repaired. He lived another five years, part of the time a semi-invalid, part of the time bed-fast, but in 1926 he passed away, leaving his widow with seven children to rear, the oldest just sixteen.

Before long the Great Depression began, increasing the burden. The Black Angus had to be sold for $20 a head. Many people moved out during that period, but Mrs. Geiger explains that she didn't know where they could go that would make it any easier. At least they had their home here so they struggled on. As her boys grew older they helped to carry the responsibility for the farm work. At long last crops and farm prices improved, and the struggle eased.

After the many years of burning wood and coal, carrying water, lighting with kerosene and gasoline lamps, electricity finally became available a few years before she moved to town. At first they provided their own current with a 32-volt wind charger. Their use of appliances was somewhat restricted, but the day the REA current was hooked up they came to town and bought all those appliances she'd been wanting.

Sixteen years ago she had an opportunity to buy a house in Glendive, conveniently located near the downtown area. It was early in the summer, and the crops were good so she made the investment. A few years later she moved into town, leaving her oldest son and his wife on the homeplace. Now she can take it a little easier than during those years when she helped to transform the frontier into a settled farm and ranch community.

E. A. Wolff

November 1966 – January 1967

"Wonderful country for farming! Just hitch onto a plow and start plowing. No trees to cut down, no stumps to obstruct. See from one end of the furrow to the other. All the coal you want in the cut banks; just pry it out and haul it home. Grass so rich you can work horses all day, then pull their harnesses off and let them go. Free grass everywhere. The only way people can keep track of their cattle is to brand them. They graze wherever they want to, then in the fall you collect them and ship what you want to sell. Horses can winter on the range, but cattle need some feed. No 'Heavy' horses in Montana – the feed out there will cure them."

No wonder, back in Wisconsin, farmers and businessmen were trying to sell out so they could move to this much-publicized Utopia. Of course, there were a few details the land promoters failed to mention – details such as drought, hail, grasshoppers. How could you go wrong when the land was free?

Edwin Wolff had served three years apprenticeship in his father's Wisconsin wagon factory and machine shop, then had worked two years in carriage shops and garages in Minneapolis. When he heard about the homestead opportunities in Montana, he decided that was the place for him.

In the fall of 1908 he made a trip to Montana to view for himself the Promised Land. He already had a pretty good idea of what he wanted in a location. It must have a creek and plenty of level land.

Charles E. Miller, land agent for the Spring Valley Land Company, took him out to view a large tract of land that had been a part of the Lindsay sheep ranch. Practically the entire country was open for homesteading, and Wolff, one of the first home seekers in the region, found just what he was looking for several miles northwest of the Lindsay home ranch headquarters. His brother, Ira Wolff, and Bernard Rusch had homesteaded nearby a little earlier and had told Ed about this area.

At that time they were allowed only 160 acres, but instead of taking his quarter section in a square block, he selected four forties, making his claim one fourth mile wide and a mile long. The following year a law was passed granting half-a-section so he took another quarter of the same description joining his original claim.

After filing on his claim Wolff returned to Wisconsin and made preparations to move to Montana in the spring of 1909. Besides getting ready to move he was also busy telling others about the wonderful country where he had homesteaded.

In March he loaded an immigrant car and about the middle of the month his wife and five-month-old baby joined him on the wide-open prairies. It was too wide open on the homestead for a family so Mrs. Wolff and baby Gerald stayed at the Green Road Ranch until he could get organized. The Green Road Ranch, started a short time before, was located about a mile west of Lindsay's.

186

Jim Corsan was the foreman on the Lindsay Ranch, and from him Wolff hired a team to haul out his lumber from Glendive. With all his wagon and carriage making, that was the first time Wolff had ever hitched a team to pull anything!

He hired a fellow who was supposed to be a carpenter to help him build a shack, and in three days they erected a 12'x18' house with a gabled roof. Mr. Wolff added that his dad claimed they took too long at that for what they turned out. He didn't know much about building, and the so-called carpenter he hired knew less, but at least they had something they could move into.

When he went to pick up Annie (Mrs. Wolff) and Gerald, Mr. Green suggested he'd better take some dry coal along so they did. That dry coal was a big help until they learned about lignite.

Mr. Miller, waving his arm toward the cut banks when Ed was claim hunting, had told him they could get coal anywhere so when he found some on the creek bottom, he dug out a load – just as easy as the land promoters said. Ed's brother Ira had come out a little earlier that spring so Ed offered him half the load if he'd haul it. Ira looked rather dubiously at the pile of slack and told Ed it didn't look like what they had been getting at Deer Creek, but he hauled it home.

Next morning Ira came over and asked how they got along with the coal. They admitted they hadn't fared very well, and Ed declared, "It's absolutely fireproof!"

When they hauled out the first load of their belongings from the immigrant car*, they tried to get everything they would need to start out, but in the shuffle they somehow overlooked the stove lids. They had brought along a little laundry stove for cooking, but it wasn't much good without lids. Where there's a will there's a way so they set kettles and kettle lids over the holes – and thus directly over the fire – and got by, but they were poor stove lids. Next morning they saw a team and buggy coming across the prairie. The visitor turned out to be Dr. Blackstone, their neighbor up on the Divide*. Dr. Blackstone also had moved to Montana in the spring of 1909.

Dr. Blackstone was on his way to Lindsay and assured the newcomers he would be glad to bring them anything he could. Wolff had noticed some old stoves at the ranch so he explained about their lid problem and told the doctor they'd surely appreciate it if he would ask Corsan if they could borrow some lids. When Dr. Blackstone came back through he had the lids, and Mrs. Wolff was 'so tickled' she couldn't thank him enough. Lids may seem a small thing, but they surely make a difference on a stove! Wolff told Blackstone that if he ever had a chance to return the favor he would gladly do so, but the doctor replied, "If you don't get a chance to do something for me, do it for someone else. That will be just as good." Dr. Blackstone, Mr. Wolff reflected, was a wonderful man.

A nice creek ran through the homestead, but when Wolff built he chose a site up on a hill in the corner of his claim, about half-a-mile from the creek. Once the house was livable, digging a well was next on the agenda. Back in

Wisconsin Ed had anticipated some of his needs in the new country so he had made a windlass* in the shop before he moved out. Now that he was ready to dig a well, the windlass was put to work. A good old shovel, a bucket, and the windlass completed the line of machinery he used to dig down the fifty feet to water.

They fixed a box on the back of the shack to store meat and other perishables, but they soon found that wasn't adequate so they dug a root cellar, and that did the job fine. That entire spring was a busy one for the newcomers, trying to make livable the home on the homestead. When you start with just the prairie, and your old home is hundreds of miles away, you have to do a lot of planning and hustling.

The homesteaders had been warned before they left Wisconsin to be careful of the ranchers as they did not like to see the farmers coming in, but Mr. Wolff says that in his case the warning was unnecessary. Some of the ranchers in the area around his homestead were among the best friends he ever had. Jim Corsan, foreman on the Lindsay Ranch, was especially helpful. Some of the other ranchers were Garfield to the southwest; Harvey to the northeast; and Billy Rust near the Divide*. Farther north was the Libby Ranch, and over on Clear Creek was Billy Wood – the only one of the old ranchers left and "still a top friend."

The spring wore on quickly as is always the case when a person is busy. As soon as they had a little slack time, the Wolffs began exploring their creek and had a great time figuring out just where their homestead boundaries were. Mr. Wolff made a little wagon to haul the baby in, and Mrs. Wolff would take little Gerald all over the country in that. The running gears to the little wagon are gone now, but they still have the box.

On the west end of their place they found a water hole and buffalo heads were scattered all around it. They gathered twenty-five of the best heads and made a pile of them. When Ed went back to Wisconsin that summer, he "sure told the folks back East about that." Next fall when he returned, however, the pile was gone. Corsan told him that every homeseeker coming through had a buffalo head tied to his rig. In spite of that plunder the Wolffs still have a few good buffalo heads as souvenirs of a bygone day.

By the early summer of 1909 the homesteaders were really coming in. Land was being taken up rapidly, and Harry Sample was kept busy making out the filing papers. Back in Wisconsin the senior Wolff's business was not sold, and he was anxious for Ed to come help in the shop. Ed began to realize that it was going to take money to homestead so about the middle of May he returned to their former home, leaving Mrs. Wolff and Gerald to hold down the homestead for the summer (and fulfill residence requirements).

Mrs. Wolff was an Easterner, but she was becoming westernized fast and showed her courage and grit as she 'stuck it out' on wide, lonesome prairies that summer. Her nearest neighbor was Ed's brother, Ira, who had homesteaded a mile-and-a-half north. No telephone, no radio, no TV, no transportation except her own two feet – an isolated little shack in the middle of the wide, uninhabited prairies – just Annie and Gerald – and Bob. Without Bob that summer would have presented a different proposition. Bob was the family's bulldog, and with him around, Mrs. Wolff felt no qualms about possible intruders. No stranger dared even make a gesture toward her with Bob around so she felt secure even without her man on the place.

Glendive didn't have much in the line of a shop so Mr. Corsan urged Wolff to start one. While in Wisconsin he was able to buy a top-notch set of tools and a good supply of wagon repairs – spokes, rims, axles and poles, as well as horseshoes and other equipment. Some of that equipment is still in the shop.

In the fall he came back to Montana to get his family, and they all spent the winter in the East. Ed made good use of his time that winter. He worked in the shops all the while he was in Wisconsin but still managed to find time to build a light spring wagon, a lumber wagon, and a sleigh for use on the homestead. He must have built well, for he has all of them to this day.

The next spring, 1910, when they returned to the homestead, Wolff again shipped an immigrant car of equipment. He still couldn't get everything he wanted into that car so he shipped another car of tools and equipment that fall. Annie's brother Bill had come with them in the spring. He was only sixteen years old, but he was good help that summer.

When Wolff built his first shack, he had a nice, level place on the hill and thought he had chosen a fine site, but the ranchers, Corsan particularly, told him his buildings should be down along the creek. He didn't abandon the first house, however. He moved it down to the new site and included it in the larger house. It now serves as kitchen. They put a basement under the new house and were well satisfied with their living accommodations. The house has been remodeled in recent years, but it's still the same house, and Mr. and Mrs. Wolff still live in it.

The creek has good springs in it, but they wanted water at the buildings so they dug a twenty-foot well at the house and a fifty-foot stock well. The stock well has never been pumped dry. Mr. Wolff says they've always been thankful they moved near the creek.

In the fall of 1910 he started work on a shop, building it into the bank. Even before he was through building it, customers started coming. He found great demand for his services and supplies. Word spread fast that a shop was operating on the Wolff homestead, and many came long distances for his services. One thing that concerned those who traveled a long way – from up on Redwater, for example – was that they might reach the shop and find no one there. Wolff assured them that they needn't worry about that; he would be at the shop. He was accustomed to shop routine where they didn't leave except for a funeral, and he stayed on the job.

There never was a dull moment around the homestead. Not only was he kept busy, so was Mrs. Wolff. He was always there to take care of shop needs, and she was always there to cook for the men who came. There was never a day but what she had extra men at the table.

That was the year the big steamers started coming in to break up sod. Some of the local outfits were owned by Long and Seamen; Johnson Brothers (Theodore and Jonah); Thompson at Lindsay; and Hans Thompson (no relation); and Reinhart and Voss.

Those steamers were tremendous outfits pulling eight or ten plows and all the machinery they could behind them, but Mr. Wolff feels they were ahead of their time. All of the equipment at that time except the plows was built for horses and simply wasn't strong enough for the huge tractors.

The trouble wasn't only with the machinery to be pulled; the engines themselves required much repair. The alkali water was hard on the boiler flues, and most of the time there were steamers in front of his shop, getting the flues replaced. Fortunately he had 'put in a hitch' at a boiler works and understood retipping and replacing flues so he could keep the outfits repaired. These steamers were just too expensive to operate and gradually they disappeared from the scene.

Then in 1913 a new wave of homesteaders came, bringing with them a new type tractor – gasoline or oil-powered engines. Brogheimers and Stortzes came from Iowa, while Wisconsin gave up Parishes, Kreimans, Al Wyse, Gust Nelson, and Lenz. About this time Dick Mold got a big tractor and so did Hoffmans. One day as Mr. Wolff talked with Lenz, the former observed, "This country must be all right because new people are coming in every day." Mr. Lenz replied, "We thought it must be pretty good because all these homesteaders are staying."

These new tractors they brought, which seemed so much better than the steamers, wouldn't make a very good showing now. For the most part they had open, cast-iron gears. A little later the semi-dustproof tractors were introduced. That, Mr. Wolff explains, meant that now the dust could get in but it couldn't get out. He should know. They all made a lot of work for him in the shop. Along with the tractors he still had plenty of work with horse-drawn vehicles and with shoeing horses. All year long there were horses to be shod, but in the fall of the year horses would be booked two or three days ahead.

Busy though he was with the shop, he had expanded his farming operation and kept two hired men, one of whom was busy most of the time freighting from Glendive. Wolff by then handled two carloads of farm machinery every year, and that had to be freighted to the farm with team and wagon.

Wolff had never had any experience caring for horses before he came to Montana so those first years he just didn't know how to handle or feed them. In spite of the glowing claims of the land promoters regarding what horses could do on Montana grass, his horses were failing under the strain put upon them. One day Corsan, who knew horses as Dr. Spock knows children, asked him how he was getting along, and Wolff admitted, "My horses are playing out hauling those heavy loads from Glendive."

Wolff was concerned because even then he had much equipment and supplies to haul out, and his horses were in no condition to haul. Great was his relief when Corsan (the rancher who was, categorically, the foe of the homesteader) offered, "I'll send Emmett over to help you. Get your good wagon and we'll put the wool rack on it. Emmett can put four good horses on that wagon, and you can put two of yours on the other wagon. Let your team haul a light load, and put all you can on Emmett's."

Wolff quickly responded, "You don't have to tell me that more than once." They made up their wagons and headed for Glendive, but when they started piling the contents of that boxcar onto the wagons, they began to realize just how much there was to pile. They were careful not to load Wolff's team too heavily, but when it came to the other wagon, they followed Corsan's instructions to "put on all you can." They were doing right well and had almost everything loaded, including a binder, but there were still twelve or fifteen poles to go.

Wolff hated to leave those behind when they had all the rest of the stuff on so he suggested tying them on with baling wire. "Do you realize," Emmet asked him, "just how much weight there is on there?" "Jim told me to put on all I could!" Ed reminded him. "Well, all right," Emmet agreed dubiously, "we'll try it." They tried it, and they made it safely to the homestead with the whole load. "To have friends like that," Mr. Wolff declared, "is worth more than any money."

Even though his shop 'sideline' kept his nose to the grindstone, Wolff was interested in cattle, and Corsan knew that so whenever he had a critter he didn't want at the ranch, he'd send it up to Wolff. That may have been an inauspicious beginning for a herd of cattle, but there's nothing inauspicious about Wolff's prize Angus herds now.

Wolff did all of Corsan's blacksmith and wagon work, such as making thirteen wagons and rebuilding a buckboard*, but they never exchanged a dollar. When it came time to settle up at the end of the year, they usually found themselves pretty nearly even. As a sample of their settlements, one year Corsan owed him a little when everything had been balanced, so he told Wolff, "I have some fence posts down here that I don't need; pick them up." Such was the spirit between that rancher and homesteader.

Jim Corsan talked much about the winter of '86-87 and emphasized the importance of always being prepared for another like it. "We could get another winter like that any time," he used to warn, "and if you aren't prepared it will wipe you out."

The team Corsan always chose to drive on the buckboard – Jimmy and Eddie were their names – were a wild pair and would have been the undoing of a horseman less skilled. As Jim made the rounds of his sheep camps he would come as far as Wolff's homestead with one wheel of the buckboard tied until the horses calmed down a bit. As he made his rounds, Corsan would stop and talk with the homesteaders along the way. He was always ready to help where help was needed and did much to assist newcomers in adjusting to a new land and a new way of living. He was a great morale booster and encouraged many a homesteader with his assurance that if they stayed here long enough they would see times when they would wish it would quit raining! He assured them that they could grow crops here nine years out of ten, and they couldn't do better any place. Mr. Wolff remarked that he often pictured in his own mind these men going home and telling their women folk what the old rancher had said about their prospects and feeling better for it.

Mr. Wolff remembers much advice Corsan gave him, one bit especially. Jim always encouraged him to keep cattle, pointing out to him, "Cattle and a little savvy sure do fine here. No better grass anywhere." Mr. Wolff observed, "In the years since then I've found that he was 100 percent right, especially on the savvy part!"

He has always thought of a cow he got from Corsan as "the mother of my herd." When they 'settled up' the last time, Ed had $45 coming so Jim told him about a cow and her calf that got away while they were delivering cattle in Glendive. She was a good cow, the rancher told him, but wild as they come, and she knew all the tricks there were for getting into hay stacks. She had even, Mr. Wolff declares, learned to back into a haystack so folks would think she was coming out!

He agreed to take the pair in settlement and Corsan offered to help get them home. They found her on Timber Fork over south of Lindsay and had no trouble getting her back to the ranch that evening. Now that he had an opportunity to size her up he saw that he had a real nice cow and calf, but Corsan was right – she could not have been wilder. She had just one horn, a long, twisted, wicked looking one, sharp as a needle.

Ed was frankly apprehensive where it was concerned. He was willing to take her home the next day, sans that horn, but hardly otherwise. Jim, always accommodating, agreed to cut it off and rounded up a saw and a couple lariats preparatory to performing the operation. When Roanie saw Jim approaching the corral, she lowered her head and charged toward him. Fortunately there was a corral post in between, and she connected with it instead of him. When she hit the post, that one remaining horn went spinning into the air like a top, and Jim's part of the deal was done. Probably the simplest dehorning he ever witnessed.

There was a little snow on the ground so next morning Ed and his brother Ira went down with the sleigh and hauled his livestock home. Mr. Wolff reckons that his experiences with old Roanie would fill a big book. They kept her until she was a real old cow, and she never did forget about crawling fences. Even now hanging down in the barn is the yoke he finally made out of ash poles and hung around her neck to keep her on her own side of the fence.

Corsans moved to Bridger in the fall of 1912. Before they left he had Ed repair all his equipment, including putting new axles, tires, and pole on the buckboard. The buckboard was as important to the rancher then, Mr. Wolff reflected, as the pickup is now. It was a sad time for the community of homesteaders when the old rancher moved away. Perhaps not many folks make in a lifetime as great an impression as Jim Corsan made in those few years upon the farmers who moved in on his range.

About this time Mr. Lindsay told his son Roy to gather up all their horses that he could and try to sell them. After gathering them Roy came and told Ed that Jim would like to have him look them over and take his pick of the bunch. Wolff selected three mares, each with a colt, and Roy helped him halter break them before he took them home. The next spring his hired man, Ted Perry, had all the mares working. They kept all those horses, including the colts, until they died.

When E.A. Wolff first opened his wagon and blacksmith shop on his homestead northwest of Lindsay, most of the farmers used a walking plow for breaking sod, but by 1912 the sulky* (one-furrow) or gang* (two or more furrows) riding plows had pretty well taken over, mostly pulled by horses. As tractors became more common, horses were used less and less, and were finally pushed out altogether. The first tractors left much to be desired, but improvements were constantly being made. The old steamer men were positive gasoline would never replace steamers for threshing because gas power, they insisted, was not steady enough, but that, Mr. Wolff succinctly pointed out, is history.

Ed's father, Fred Wolff, visited them in 1912. Ed told him they needed another wagon and had plenty of material on hand to build it so Mr. Wolff, Sr. took the hint and helped build a complete freighting wagon with grain box and all. Ed did the iron work and his father did the wood work. That wagon is still in use but has graduated to rubber-tired wheels. The original wheels decorate the gate of son Clarence's yard. There are wheels at the gate of Ed Wolff's yard, too; those wheels, sixty years ago, kept Corsan's oldest sheep wagon rolling.

That winter Ed built a snowplow for Art Goff. He warned Art that it would be expensive as he would have to send for special parts, but Mr. Goff retorted that ten-dollar hay is expensive, too, so the plow was built and used for many years.

It was about that time that he built the 'Stork Sleigh'. Although a homesteader, Dr. Blackstone actively practiced the medical profession (how fortunate the residents of that area to have a doctor so close at hand!) and he sometimes needed a sleigh in the bitterest of weather. Wolff built him a sleigh with high back and sides to protect him from the weather, and many were the errands of mercy on which the sleigh transported the doctor.

Practically all the freighting in those early years was done with horses. Almost everyone hauled heavy loads so horses had to be well shod. Breakdowns were frequent. The power plant in Glendive was burning coal from the numerous mines in the surrounding area, and during the winter months the ice company was putting up many tons of ice, all of which meant hauling jobs for local men. They had to have their outfits in good shape to do the job, and that, in turn, meant work for the shop.

Ira Thompson of Lindsay tried something new when he started freighting with his tractor, but the tractors were not intended for such work, and he soon went back to horses. It was Ed Haskell who really came up with an innovation. He had a field of flax near Lindsay, and after threshing he had the flax all sacked. He had just shipped in two flat-bottomed trucks for his garage in Glendive so he had those sacks of flax piled onto the trucks and hauled into town. The road to Glendive was only a rough trail at that time, but the trucks made it all right. Hauling with trucks was quite an event, and as the trucks crossed the old wooden bridge over the Yellowstone, camera men were on hand to record the history-making performance.

Crops were good during this time and everyone was full of hopes and ambitions as they determinedly carved new farms and homes from the virgin land, but the main events of life – deaths, births, and marriages – did not pause, waiting for those goals to be reached.

The first death among the homesteaders was that of Mrs. August Koepke. She was just a young woman – in her early twenties – but she was taken suddenly ill and went very quickly. She was taken back to Falls Creek, Wisconsin, for burial. Next was the young son – in his early teens – of John Harrison, one of Wolff's nearest neighbors. Funeral services for the young lad were held in the Lindsay Hall, and he was buried in Glendive. Next to go was the oldest child and only daughter of Dr. Blackstone.

If death seemed to single out the young, it was because the young had dared to challenge the frontier, and there were no older people to strike in this new land. A new homesteader whose claim was just above Dr. Blackstone's was the next to go, the first to be buried in the churchyard of the new Lutheran Church north of Slagsvolds. Then Mrs. Elmer Ramberg died, leaving several nice little ones – all of whom, Mr. Wolff notes, grew up to be useful citizens.

During a siege of severe winter weather a small baby of Robert Thompsons died and was buried on their homestead. Dr. Blackstone was to conduct the service for the little one, but he was called to Bloomfield, where another youngster was wanting to come into the world so Bob Strong, one of the ranchers of the area, took over and did very well. Another new baby, that of Price Powers, was also buried on the parental homestead, two miles north of Wolffs. During this time the Rust family lost two nice boys and a fine girl. So that was the other side of life.

Anything could happen on the homesteads, and often did. One night the Wolffs were awakened by a pounding on their door, and Ed, answering, found their neighbor, Billy Rust from up on the Divide. Billy explained that he was taking his wife to the hospital, but the brake rod on his car broke, and he couldn't go on. Could he borrow Wolff's car? He was welcome to the car, but Ed questioned the advisability of Mrs. Rust's attempting to go on to Glendive.

There were no oiled highways connecting Lindsay and Glendive in those days, and what road there was was in terrible condition. Ed held a hasty consultation with Annie – herself still in bed after the arrival of their newest baby. Then they urged Mrs. Rust to come in and stay there while someone went for a doctor. They got her comfortably settled and Billy went to Lindsay to telephone Dr. Strowd to come. He hadn't been gone fifteen minutes until they had a new girl. After calling, Rust hurried back to find his new daughter using a clothesbasket as substitute for a bassinet. They named the baby Annie in honor of Mrs. Wolff.

Next morning when Dr. Strowd arrived on the scene, he looked everything over, then assured them, "I can't see how you could do anything better. Just keep on doing the way you are." Another episode in pioneer life.

Their grocery list of that day might read something like 100 pounds of sugar, 1,000 pounds flour, sixty pounds honey (don't forget the honey!) and so on. They bought groceries only once a year so they would lay in a supply in the fall to last until the next fall. Ready to make out your grocery list for the next year?

Every morning while Ed had the shop, Annie would take the light buggy and go pick up plow lays at Lindsay. As long as she made the trip anyway, she picked up the mail and soon was picking it up for all the neighbors, too. Corsan had the old mail sack that had been used for carrying mail to Paxton so he gave them that to use. Then all the neighbors would come to Wolff's to get their mail. Later a mail route was established from Lindsay to Mink, a post office just below the Divide. Then there were thirty-six mail sacks; now there would be five or six.

The first school in the Lindsay area was held in the bunkhouse of the Lindsay Ranch with Ruth Rusch as teacher. Later a 'proper' schoolhouse was built in Lindsay, and in 1913 a school was built on Spring Creek, just across the creek from Wolffs. At its peak the Spring Creek School had nineteen pupils. The first teacher was Miss Pearl Murphy. Miss Murphy boarded at the Harrisons, but all the later teachers except two boarded in the Wolff home.

E.A. Wolff was on the Spring Creek school board for many years, and he also served several terms as clerk. Their first four boys attended the Spring Creek School, but it closed in 1927. So many people had moved out there were no longer enough pupils to maintain a school, and the last Wolff, Bill, had to attend at Lindsay.

The community wasn't very old when some of these enterprising homesteaders hooked up a telephone system among themselves. The first line connected Ed Wolff, Ira Wolff, and Price Powers, one mile north of Ira. Those phones worked pretty well unless a cow jumped a fence or something. In time that system graduated into the Lindsay Phone Company with Dr. Blackstone president and Ed Wolff secretary-treasurer. Later the lines were extended from the Divide to Union. They used those phones a good long time until settlers started pulling out, and too many miles of lines were left with no one to keep them up. Range horses would rub against the lines, and the remaining subscribers just couldn't maintain all of them so finally it was dropped.

Among the settlers leaving their homesteads standing empty was Ed's brother Ira, the one responsible for getting Ed to Montana in the first place. Ira had worked in a paint shop, but he developed painter's colic and had to quit. He wanted to find something outside, and a Montana homestead seemed like just the thing.

As for Ed, as a youngster he had always dreamed of being on the wide-open prairie and riding a saddle horse. Even after he was grown, working in machine shops and garages, he couldn't get that dream out of his system so when Ira came back from a preliminary trip to Montana with such glowing report of the prospects there, Ed decided it was a chance to make his dreams come true. He still thinks so. It's been fifty-eight years since he filed on his homestead, and he's still living on it. Ira, however, left Montana in 1922. He had married a schoolteacher, and she wanted their boys to be educated so they returned to the East where schooling was more attainable.

At first there were no church services in the community, but later a priest would come out once a month and hold services in one of the homes. After the schoolhouse was built they used it for church services. Occasionally a Protestant minister would also hold services in the school building. In 1917 the Lutheran Church north of Lindsay was built. They had been holding services in the homes since 1910.

Mr. Wolff recalled the picnics the neighbors used to have together and the wonderful times they had. He especially mentioned picking chokecherries and June berries together. After the Lindsay Hall was built they used it for their get-togethers. Often Mrs. Hoover played the piano, and they'd all sing. In those days Mrs. Wolff sang a lot.

The years slipped by in a hurry until finally one nice bright morning when two of Long-Seamen's men were at the shop to refuel their steamer, Seamen came out from Glendive with news – big news. The United States had entered the Big War – the war to end all wars.

Not long after that Wolff received word that the two men he had working for him were up for draft. He thought everything over carefully, then decided there was only one thing to do: he locked up the shop. Although he continued to use the shop for his own work (his sons use it yet) he never opened for business again. He had just shelved a load of new repairs, and much of it is shelved to this day. He finished up the work he had in the shop at the time, and if anyone came in with new work, not having heard the shop was closed, he didn't charge for it, and they 'got weaned away' quickly.

When he told his wife of his decision to close the shop, it was, she declares, the happiest day of her life. By this time they had four little boys, and with the shop open there were always men hanging around. They didn't feel that was a good environment for the little fellows and besides that, there were always two or three extra men at meals.

Not only had the shop bound him to the homestead as effectively as though he had been chained; the day 'Pop' opened the shop, 'Mom' had, in effect, opened a restaurant. None of today's modern conveniences lightened her workload to offset the burden of always cooking for extra men. The children had to be cared for just the same, the clothes had to be washed (without benefit of an automatic washer; she'd have been thrilled with a gas-powered wringer-washer!); the ironing had to be done with the old sad irons* (now items for antique collectors) heated on top of the range.

No freezer stored quantities of food with which to lade the table. All the meat and vegetables had to be canned, or with the meat, perhaps cured, much of it in the heat of August, with the coal range supplying the heat for that operation. The bread, too, came from the oven of that same range, and all of it spelled long, hot hours. Little wonder, then, that she rejoiced when he announced he was closing shop. Now she would have more time to take care of her boys. As for Ed – after he closed the shop, he went to Glendive and stayed two days, the first time he had been away from the homestead since he opened the shop.

Not long after he received notice that his hired men had been drafted, Dr. Blackstone came into the shop one day and informed them that he, too, had been drafted – for an army doctor. Rancher Bob Strong was going to run his place. Annie and the doctor's wife had become great friends, and the boys of the two families were about the same age, so this news was a great setback for them, but they were happy that if Dr. Blackstone had to go, that Bob was going to be on the place.

When World War I was over, the farmers in E.A. Wolff's area were not among the businesses benefiting from the high prices of that period. They had not learned to summer fallow*, nor did they have the equipment then to do it so they just were not raising the crops they could have with modern 'know-how' and machinery. Wolff bought his first tractor, a little Fordson, in the spring of 1927. It had a plowing gear, and its top speed was three miles an hour, but the boys had a lot of fun with it, running it day and night to show how much it could do.

They traded it off for a larger one the next fall, bought their first combine in the fall of 1928. Goodbye threshing crew! Their first combine was a twelve-foot Minneapolis pull-type (the self-propelled didn't come until much later) that cost $1,400. Since those 'firsts' for the Wolff farm, all the machinery has certainly improved but none, Mr. Wolff dryly observed, as fast as the price tag. During the time they were first using mechanical power, horses were still used somewhat, but they gradually left the picture. For many years the only horses left on the ranch are the saddle horses.

From the early 'semi-dustproof' tractors (that let the dust in but not out) with the cast iron gear, tractors were improved until dust is kept out quite well and gears are all steel. Mr. Wolff was in a good position to watch the machine age ushered in.

Soon came the Big Depression, and all prices skidded. Mr. Wolff tells of shipping one carload of three-year-old steers to Chicago for three cents a pound and a carload of three-year-olds to Hedegaard of Savage for six cents and Hedegaard lost money on them. Now the Wolffs have their own feed yard and finish out their own cattle. Hogs were two-and-one-half to three cents, and wheat was twenty-five cents a bushel. He had a lot of hogs and slaughtered about thirty-five a week, selling the cured meat for twenty-five cents a pound.

During this time the oiled highway from Glendive to Circle was under construction (one of the last big dirt-moving jobs done with horses), and Wolff furnished the crew with 400 pounds of cured meat every Monday morning while they were building to Lindsay.

In the fall of 1935 he shipped cattle to Chicago. By this time conditions were improving a little so he made a deal for a new '35 four-door Chevrolet while he was there. The '36's were coming out the next day, and the dealer wanted to get rid of the '35 model so he got the new sedan, equipped with two sun visors, two windshield wipers, filled with prestone, for $812 and drove it home.

A few more years and World War II was on. As in World War I, the draft was closing in so in fall of 1940 sons Addis and Neil decided to enlist leaving Gerald, Clarence, and Bill to carry on with their dad. By this time their operations had expanded considerably, and they had their hands full. Addis and Neil each spent four years in the army, and both came back all right, for which they were all thankful. They were both discharged with rank of lieutenant.

Mr. Wolff saw the big oil boom come and was happy that for several years he was able to lease the oil rights on his land. He had accumulated considerably more land than that original half-section and gladly accepted the oil lease money.

Four of Mr. and Mrs. Wolff's five sons farm in the home community. One, Neil, is in Billings. Asthma drove him from the farm so for many years he has been parts man for Ryan Motors in Billings. Gerald, their oldest son, has the 'Harrison place' while Addis has the 'Dunlap place' near the old Rimroad site. Addis got his start in cattle in 4-H and built up his herd from there. Clarence, who bought 'Uncle Ira's place', is a member of the Wolff Corporation with brother Bill and 'Pop', but all the family works pretty much together.

The boys are all married now and have families of their own. "We are thankful," Mr. Wolff expressed himself, "that we can live amongst them. Annie and I are two of the very few that are still on their original homestead and in the same house. When we think of our place as it looked when I filed on it and the way it looks now, we are really proud of it. It was a great experience, all but when I had to leave Annie here alone with a five-month old baby."

"The shop as well as the house was rebuilt and modernized some years ago. We have equipment in the shop that would have been useful in the early days, but the boys make good use of it now. The old wagon and buggy-making equipment and the horse shoeing material, as well as the steam boiler repairing tools, are stored away, but the old forge is used quite often."

"The places they tied their horses are still in the shop, and that is about all the average person would notice, but fortunately some things can't be stored away. The memories of building up a ranch and raising five boys are among the best anyone ever had, and they are too precious to store away."

The First 29 Stories – 1964

In 1964 Montana celebrated her Territorial Centennial. It was during this time that Mrs. Kauffman began interviewing the pioneers who had settled Eastern Montana.

Those first articles, published in Glendive's Ranger-Review, were all introduced with the same paragraph, with only the number of the interview changing, as follows:

(Editor's note: Following is the first of a series of articles to be carried by the Ranger-Review during this, Montana's Territorial Centennial year. The observations are being compiled by Mrs. Morris Kauffman, 417 Grant, Glendive.)

Here are those first stories, printed in the order of their original appearance in the Ranger-Review. Throughout the "As I Remember" series, the logo with the pioneer wagon introduced each article.

Mrs. C.A. (Mary Kelly) Banker

Thursday, May 28, 1964 – First in the Series

There wasn't much to the town when the covered wagon driven by Mrs. William Kelly, bearing the family's household effects and six-year-old daughter Mary, arrived in Glendive in October of 1885. There was the Yellowstone Hotel, a little frame building on the site of the present Jordan Hotel. M.M. Coleman's General Store had been in a tent the year before, but then his brother Alfonzo took over and built a brick building where Anderson's Department Store* now stands. The railroad had come through Glendive so the old depot was here. A few little frame houses and some tarpaper shacks and shanties across the railroad tracks gave promise of more permanent dwellings later. A Mr. Norton had built a little four-room cottage where the Auble house stands at 611 S. Sargent. Later William Lindsay, the sheepman for whom Lindsay, Montana was named, bought it and built on the two-story part of the house. And there was one block of board sidewalk.

A day or so before the Kellys reached Glendive one of the big red oxen pulling the covered wagon had gone lame so a little strawberry roan from the horse herd had to be hitched in his place. Mrs. Kelly, who had driven the wagon all the way from Sleepy Eye, Minnesota, insisted upon camping on Glendive Creek until nightfall, then coming through Glendive under cover of darkness so her oddly matched team would not be so conspicuous! The family camped at the old fairgrounds site south of town until they could get a little log house built. They chose a site well out of town in the area across the creek from the present Zion Lutheran Church* for this modest little structure.

Mr. Kelly, with the help of two cowboys, had trailed their herd of cattle from Minnesota to Ekalaka, Montana where they had turned them loose in the lush grass country. He had previously helped with three or four cattle drives through the area, and it was the good range that had been responsible for his decision to move to Montana. He intended to go into the cattle business, but when the hard winter of 1886-87 wiped out his herd, he switched to sheep and horses.

Mrs. Banker's formal schooling was begun in a summer session near Ekalaka under a teacher from Miles City. Then the family moved back to Glendive, and she started attending the red brick school formerly located in the lot bounded by Kendrick Avenue, Valentine, and Douglas Streets.

In their early Glendive days they bought water for twenty-five cents a barrel. When they wanted water, they put up a red flag. This proved to be a source of consternation to the many book agents who came through. (Yes, even then!) Did those red flags mean small pox, typhoid fever, or what?

Although the Indians gave no trouble after the Kellys arrived, there were some reports of Indian threats. The citizenry agreed that in case of danger the roundhouse whistle would be blown and everyone would go to the roundhouse, the women and children for protection, the men to defend the stronghold. They were glad it was never necessary.

Mrs. Banker made her first real estate purchase with money earned by giving music lessons. Although she could have bought the lot on which the EUB Church* stands for $50 less, she chose frontage on Main Street and purchased the lots on the corner of the 500 block of North Merrill from Tom Hagan. This she deeded to her mother, and her father built the house at 521 North Merrill.

She met her husband-to-be in the Methodist Church Choir where she played the organ, and he played the clarinet. Mr. Banker had worked in a store in Wibaux before coming to Glendive with Mr. Cannon to start the Exchange State Bank. In November of 1906 Mary Kelly and Charles Banker were married and made their home in Glendive together until 1955 when Mr. Banker passed away. Mrs. Banker still lives in her home on North Merrill.

Mrs. Charles Johnson

Thursday, June 4, 1964 – Second in the Series

Seventy-four years ago this week, on June 2, 1890, Mrs. Charles Johnson arrived in Glendive from Sweden. Of all the places on the map, Glendive was chosen by the twenty-one-year-old immigrant simply because that was the town designated on her ticket. And it was a tough-looking town.

A Swedish friend from Glendive had sent her the ticket that brought her here, but such was her homesickness in the months that followed that if she had had the money, she'd have gone right back! A stranger in a strange land, her problems were multiplied because she couldn't speak any English. She soon found employment doing housework for a family with four children (and five cousins next door), but how do you take care of children when you can't understand them and they can't understand you?

Neither could she communicate her problems to her mistress, even when, as she was eating her dinner after the family had been served, the children came and snatched her dessert! No wonder she was relieved when, after a couple months, she began working at the McIntyre Hotel. (The hotel was located on the site of the present city hall and was moved later to make way for that structure.)

In the mean time she diligently applied herself to the study of the new language and in a few months had mastered enough for basic communication. She had the help of another young Swedish girl, fluent in both Swedish and English, who worked for Mrs. Mead in the apartments above the Douglas-Mead store. A local professor also coached her.

In the years that followed she worked in various places, including a combination hat and dressmaking shop. In 1895 she married Charles Johnson, who passed away in 1947. They had eight sons and two daughters, all of whom are still living.

Although the town first impressed her as a desolate place to live, she feels that over the years it has grown to be a good town and clean, as good a place to live as any. The old, broken boardwalk has given way to cement sidewalks, the dusty (or muddy) streets to pavement, the dry yards to green lawns and trees, the log stores and shacks to brick and frame buildings.

Even the milkman with his horse-drawn cart who, when asked which was his best cow, pointed to the well, has given way to the modern milkman with the latest in trucks and sanitary equipment. Mrs. Johnson, a resident of the General Nursing Home, still presents in conversation a vivid and interesting picture of the Glendive of yesteryear.

C. A. (Chris) Buller

Sunday, June 7, 1964 – Third in the Series

When Andrew H. Buller read a letter from Rev. Joe Borntrager in a German language newspaper telling of homestead land available near Glendive, with railroad land for sale at a low price, he suggested to son Chris that he come to Glendive and investigate.

Chris came, found thousands of acres available, and filed on a homestead before returning with the good news. He filed in June but waited until after harvest to begin moving preparations so it was Christmas morning, 1906, before Chris and two companions arrived in Glendive with their immigrant car.

With ten inches of loose snow on the ground and no road or fence to follow, they headed north. They loaded their wagons, one pulled by a four-horse team, the other by a two-horse team, with the most necessary items from the immigrant car and left town about eleven o'clock in the forenoon. Darkness overtook them by the time they had gone twenty-five miles.

Hardly prepared to bunk in the open, they parked the big wagon, hitched two more horses to the light wagon, tied the other two behind, and plodded on, Chris leading the way with a lantern. The skies cleared so they were able to get their general directions from the stars.

It was with great thanksgiving that they finally reached the Joe Mullet homestead on Thirteen Mile Creek where they were told, "You're going no farther tonight!" The next day, in spite of snow and wind, they were able to reach the shack they had rented for the winter. They didn't have things exactly handy – half-a-mile to the stable and a mile to the nearest watering place – but they managed.

They had planned to put up their shacks that winter, but the weather was so severe they couldn't do a thing until spring. His parents joined him in the spring and lived with them until they had a house built on their own homestead. Andrew Buller and his wife had left Russia thirty-two years before in search of a home they could call their own. Now, thirty-five 'moves' later, they had their home, and here they planned to stay (and did) until called to their heavenly home.

Now Chris had to do his own housekeeping, but in time he solved that problem, too. On October 3, 1911, he married Miss Lena Schmidt. They didn't send out engraved invitations to a select number – in South Dakota, where he had been reared, the custom in case of wedding or funeral was to tell the nearest neighbor, he would tell the next neighbor, and he the next until all had been notified. Chris, however, loaned his team and buggy to a friend and had him drive around the neighborhood, inviting everyone to the wedding.

In the spring of 1912 Chris and two other men were selected as a building committee to make preparations for building a church house. A Sunday School had been organized earlier, and services were held in a stable. The church house was completed in November at a cost of $1,500 and named Bethlehem Mennonite Church because of its beginnings in a stable.

In 1946, forty years after he had homesteaded, the Bullers sold out and moved to the home they had purchased at 208 Gibson, Glendive. In 1948 he began working at the Glendive Greenhouses and continues, at eighty-one years of age, to work an eight-hour shift, six days a week. Mrs. Buller passed away in 1957, but Mr. Buller, with his daughter Adeline, still lives at 208 Gibson. He still has a vital concern for the Lord's work and also takes a keen interest in the Gateway Museum.

Mrs. W. B. Pomeroy

Thursday, June 11, 1964 – Fourth in the Series

Mrs. W.B. Pomeroy, who came to Glendive in 1917, does not consider herself an 'old timer' in this area, but she was able to introduce us to a real 'old timer', one with an infallible memory – an issue of the Glendive Times, dated June 27, 1886.

A full column advertisement, sponsored in part by G.R. Tingle of Glendive, proclaimed:

Town lots   Town Lots
in Glendive the
Gate City!   Gate City!
At the junction of the Northern Pacific Railroad with the Steam Boat Traffic of the Yellowstone and Upper Missouri Rivers. Glendive was laid out in October, 1880 and the first permanent buildings erected on completion of the railroad to this point in July, 1881, since which it has grown to be a thriving, bustling business place of 1500 inhabitants.

Glendive has the largest and finest machine shops on the great trans-continental railroad - the Northern Pacific. These shops and their connection employ about 300 men.

Choice Business Lots from $250 to $1500. Title is secure.

The advertisement contained much more, lauding the beauty of the country, the excellent hunting, the possibilities for livestock and agriculture, and many other attractions to home-seekers. Co-sponsors of the ad had offices in Bismarck, Fargo, and Chicago.

A glance at other ads gives us a survey of some of the earlier business establishments. For instance:

Douglas-Mead
Groceries and Dry Goods, General Merchandise
Lumber, Lime & Building Material.

E. W. B. Harvey
Headquarters for General Supplies
Staple and Fancy Groceries in any quantities desired,
at the lowest possible rates for the best goods in the market.

New Livery and Feed Stable
W. W. Casey, Proprietor.
Stable Near Court House.

Glendive, M. T.

The Gem Restaurant & Short Order House

Blacksmithing Of All Kinds by Morris Cain
Shop opposite Court House

John Trumbull Attorney at Law
Collections a specialty
Office near Court House

Dr. A. R. Duncan Physician & Surgeon
Office - On Bell Street, near Henry Dion's Store

Dr. J. G. Benjamin Dentist
All work carefully attended to. Nitrous Oxide administered for painless extraction of teeth. Office in rear of Prescott's drug store.

A news item announced that "work will begin on the stone work of Douglas & Mead's store next Monday. The stones are now being hauled.

"There has been no such building activity in the town since the spring and summer of 1882. While it was as active then, the class of buildings was no comparison to those at present underway."

An editorial comment might have been plucked from a partisan paper today:

"It does not require a prophetic vision to foresee the introduction of an enormous urgent deficiency bill during the early days of next December, after the Democrats have run the congressional campaigns on the economy dodge" – Washington National Republican.

And finally an invitation to a Celebration:

"John L. Burns will have a Fourth of July celebration at his ranch, which will also be the 9th anniversary of civilization in the Yellowstone. There will be a bowery dance, horse racing, foot racing, and other sports appropriate to the national holiday. John L. invites every one who can, to attend and promises 'a rattling good time.'"

When the Pomeroys remodeled and put new fronts on their three buildings in the 100 block of South Merrill, about 1950, a workman found the old paper, rolled tightly, where it had been dropped into the wall. With great care they unrolled the brittle paper and mounted it between sheets of glass, thoughtfully preserving it.

Mrs. Pomeroy's father-in-law, Adrian D. Pomeroy, was Conductor of Construction when the railroad came to Glendive in 1881.

Mrs. Moore (Adda Miller) Eyer

Thursday, June 18, 1964 – Fifth in the Series

"Oh, my goodness, the world is empty!" was the reaction of Mrs. Adda Eyer when she stepped off the train in Glendive and saw how much there was with nothing in it.

Coming from Eyersgrove, Pennsylvania, in 1907, the only attraction for Mrs. Eyer in Montana was her husband. Adda Miller and Moore Eyer had grown up together, and even as little children when they played house and 'dressed up', he was always her 'beau'. As a young man he spent some time in Iowa, then came to Glendive to visit his two brothers, Clark and Wilson.

When he went back to Pennsylvania to marry his childhood sweetheart, she had declared, "We're not going West!" But here she was. The West had cast its spell upon him, and he had come back to Glendive in 1906, then returned to Pennsylvania to bring his family. Now Mrs. Eyer, with five-year-old Claude and three-year-old Alton, was here with him, but she shared none of his enthusiasm.

Their first home in Glendive was on the corner of what is now Anderson and Hughes. The next, most vivid in Mrs. Eyer's memory, was a little log hut on Barry Street. Exclaimed Mrs. Eyer, "We spent seven months in that purgatory place!" Following this, they made two moves on the north side. While they lived in the alley back of what is now the Chevron Station, the Indians, who often camped on the present Buttreys* Store site, would come up town right through this alley. If the milkman had brought the milk, they'd take the bottle right from the porch, even if you stood and watched them!

Claude's interest in the city's engineering department goes back a long way. When the boat which brought Glendive's first sewer pipe about 1909 or 1910 was docked here, Claude decided to investigate and played on the boat. His interest at that time was not encouraged, however, and he recalls that he got a licking for it!

Mr. Eyer never did like to rent so when they found a house that suited them at 200 S. Sargent (where the Claude Eyers now live), they bought it. When the last payment on the house was made, he came home, called her over to where he stood in front of the coal range and told her, "Now, Mother, we're going to burn the mortgage!" "Really?" she asked. Then they stood together as they watched the mortgage burn.

Mr. Eyer was a railroad man, and Mrs. Eyer, who had been a dressmaker back in her hometown, continued her practice after she came to Glendive. One hot summer night as she was sewing past the midnight hour, suddenly there came a tap, tap on the door. "I was scared stiff," she recalls, "but it was Mr. Eyer himself. He thought he would try to scare me and he surely did!"

Montana just didn't bear much resemblance to Pennsylvania with all her relatives and friends. Mrs. Eyer was homesick after they came, and so was Claude. He wanted to go back to Grandma's house and 'go upstairs' so the year after they came to Glendive his aunt took him back for a visit. While he was there he contracted typhoid fever. Mrs. Eyer hurried to be with him, and they were able to nurse him back to health, but when Montana was mentioned, he just wasn't interested in going back – that is, until he saw his daddy. When Mr. Eyer came to get them, Claude ran to put his arms around him and told him, "Yes, Daddy, I'll go back with you."

When they returned from Pennsylvania, Claude entered school in the red brick school on West Valentine Street. Mrs. Dennis Kelly was his first teacher. When he was in high school, just two of the students – both from the country – came in cars. At present Claude is Glendive's city engineer, and son Alton is a doctor in Belleview, Washington.

In spite of her reluctance to come to the West, Mrs. Eyer found herself becoming attached to Glendive, and when death claimed her husband in 1922, she withstood the pressures of her family back in Pennsylvania to 'come home' and stayed on in the town that had so won him. Mrs. Eyer clerked for twenty-nine years in the Douglas-Mead store and is widely known throughout the Glendive area.

Mrs. William (Florence Ellis) McGaughy

Sunday, June 28, 1964 – Sixth in the Series

Have you ever been annoyed because your mail was half an hour late? What would it be like to wait three months for your mail? Mrs. William McGaughy can tell you. In 1905 Florence Ellis married William McGaughy and joined him on his homestead on Seven Mile Creek, northwest of Stipek. In those pre-automobile days she came to town perhaps twice a year, once in the spring and again in the fall. Most of her shopping was done via the Montgomery Ward catalog. Montgomery Ward sold groceries then, too, so they ordered many staples, including a good supply of dried fruit, etc., to last through the winter. Mr. McGaughy's policy was, "Anything that will keep, get plenty of it because we can't get to town in the winter." Their mail came to Glendive, twenty team-and-wagon miles away, so whenever anyone in the neighborhood went to town, he'd bring the mail for all his neighbors.

Mrs. Jim Seeds, several miles 'down the creek', was about the only other woman in that vicinity. Mrs. A. Kent lived a few miles farther on, and in 1909 Mrs. Isaac Evans came with her husband to their newly acquired ranch 'up the creek' a couple miles. But even though she had little opportunity to visit and fewer opportunities to get to town, Mrs. McGaughy says she did not consider isolation a hardship.

She had come over from England in 1903. Her mother was no longer living, and her father wasn't well. He was concerned for her in case something should happen to him so when her oldest brother made plans to come to the United States, her father arranged for her to come, too. Before their departure date the brother changed his mind and went instead on a ship that was going around the world, but she came anyway. Her sister and an aunt were living in Billings so she went first to Billings.

She had been in the States about a year when a relative of her brother-in-law, Mrs. Ben Johnson of Glendive, needed help with housework. Florence came to Glendive to supply that help. During this time she met William McGaughy, a cousin of Mrs. Johnson's who had come to the United States from Ireland in 1888. He worked as a fireman on the railroad for a time, but his heart was in farming so in 1900 he filed on a homestead. From Joe Holling he bought a house that stood down by the river. The house was built of old railroad ties so Mr. McGaughy carefully numbered each piece, dismantled the house, moved it to his homestead, then reassembled it according to number. He paid $100 for the house and they lived in it until his death in 1950. Around them was open range with XIT cattle roaming the entire valley. About the only fence was around their yard.

In those first years on the homestead they raised mostly oats, which they cut for hay for their cattle and horses. They raised just enough wheat for feed for their chickens. This wheat he threshed on the barn floor during the winter months with a flail, which he himself made. After the first threshing machines

209

were brought into the country they increased their wheat acreage, and the threshing machine was moved from farm to farm to do the threshing. In addition to his farming, Mr. McGaughy helped with lambing and shearing on the various sheep ranches throughout the area.

The McGaughys had six children, five of whom are still living. The day after Mrs. McGaughy came home from the hospital with their only boy was one of those never-to-be-forgotten. When she came home everything seemed normal, but the August night stretched out unnaturally long. Mr. McGaughy remarked, "It must be time to get up; I'm tired lying in bed," but she pointed out that it was still completely dark. Finally they got up anyway and found that it was eight o'clock! They didn't know what to do. They lighted the kerosene lamp (they had no electricity all the time they were on the farm); presently neighbor Seeds came up. A little later Mr. and Mrs. Evans came, and then Mr. and Mrs. Mace, Evans's sheepherder, came. Communication then wasn't what it is now so they didn't know whether the world was coming to an end or what might be happening. Later in the day the sun shone through a little, blood red. Not until much later did they find out that huge forest fires in the western part of the state and Canada had caused such heavy smoke as to darken even this area.

Mrs. McGaughy, since the death of her husband, has lived in Glendive.

James Osborne, Sr.

Thursday, July 2, 1964 – Seventh in the Series

James Osborne Sr., Glendive's ex-mayor, ex-fire chief (he had to resign as fire chief when he became mayor because the mayor might buy the fire chief some new hose, he explains), was interested in the fire department long before he became chief. His father had bought him a little wagon, a replica of the farm wagons of the day, through Davis & Farnum. One day he and some of his chums decided to use the wagon as a fire cart so they filled a tub with water on the wagon and hitched Jim's little dog to it. To provide the 'house' for a fire they built a little shack of lath, then draped it with gunnysacks. Tommy Cullin, with his head sticking out a hole which served as a window, was the resident of the 'house', and he was to be 'rescued' from the burning building by the courageous firemen. However, the overzealous firemen, concerned that the sack might not burn fast enough, soaked it with kerosene. It burned fast enough then all right, and the firemen were hard pressed to rescue the victim in time. Miraculously, they did.

Jim had attained the age of one year when he came to Glendive in 1880. His mother was from Scotland, his father was from England. They met while they were both working in the shipyards in Edinburgh, Scotland. Several years after they were married they migrated to Canada where Jim was born. After a period in Canada, Mr. Osborne found work as a boilermaker with the Northern Pacific Railway, and they moved to Glendive. He was boilerhouse foreman for many years.

Glendive didn't boast a band in those early days so Jim's father was the 'band'. Anybody could play a bass drum so when music was needed for a political rally or such, he'd round up someone to play the drum, then the drum-player and Mr. Osborne with his concertina (a small octagonal-shaped instrument of the accordion class) would make the rounds with the politicians. One night it might be for Republicans, a few days later for the Democrats, but Mr. Osborne (a staunch Republican) was impartial music-wise and played for either because there was no other band. Jim never did master the concertina, but he did play other instruments (he took his violin lessons from Mrs. C.A. Banker) and has been active with the city's band and orchestra.

When Jimmy was about ten, he had a job hauling cameras and lunches for the local Camera Club on their outings. He hitched his white bird dog to his little wagon (J.J. Stipek had made a harness for the dog, complete with shiny brass buttons) and 'freighted' supplies for them. Finding something to do wasn't the problem for Jim that it seems to be for some youngsters today. The family lived for a number of years on the South Side in the area that is now the 200 block of South Taylor. They had fourteen cows, and by the time the barn was cleaned, the milk delivered, and the other chores done, spare time wasn't much of a problem.

For a time they also had chickens — 3,000 of them. Peddling eggs was quite a task, but the biggest task was providing chickens for the Sunday dinner at the Jordan Hotel. Every Sunday the 'big shots' went to the hotel for chicken dinner, and the Osbornes provided the chickens. Saturday evening meant early supper while two boilers full of water heated on the stove. Then fifty chickens had to be cleaned, dressed, and delivered to the Hotel. To this day Jim can hardly eat chicken and has very little appetite for eggs!

Mr. Osborne had bought his land on Taylor from the local school district. The State owned five acres of land on the south side but wouldn't sell to individuals. However, when the district needed a site for a school, they bought the entire plot from the State, kept the block where the Lincoln School is located, and sold the remainder. Mr. Osborne bought the 200 block between Taylor and Rosser. Bob Perham was the contractor who built the Lincoln School.

In 1909 Jim paid a dollar to join the Fire Department. The hose cart was kept in a tin-covered wooden building where the Glendive Transfer is now located. If the fire alarm sounded during the day one of the two draymen, George Muxlow with his mules or Jack Whittum with a good team of horses, would rush to the fire house, hitch to the cart, and race to the fire. (They were paid five dollars for it.) But if the alarm sounded during the night, the firemen themselves had to pull the cart to the scene of the fire. Rather a drain on their energies, to say the least!

Jim was round house foreman with Northern Pacific from 1926 until his retirement in 1955. He and his wife, the former Maylo Murphy (the Murphys for whom Murphy Table is named), also of pioneer stock, reside at 720 N. Kendrick in Glendive.

Mrs. Desmond J. (Esther Cavanaugh) O'Neil

Thursday, July 9, 1964 – Eighth in the Series

Mrs. Desmond J. O'Neil, daughter of a sheriff and wife of a lawyer, lives in what is perhaps the oldest residence (in good livable condition) in Glendive. The house at 214 W. Bell was built by Dr. A.R. Duncan, one of Glendive's first doctors (the June 27, 1886, Glendive Times carried his advertisement). Mrs. O'Neil's mother, Mrs. Dominic Cavanaugh, bought the house in 1898.

The Cavanaughs lived on one of the earliest ranches of the area, the OU Ranch on lower Thirteen Mile Creek. When daughter Esther was due to arrive, Mrs. Cavanaugh chose to stay with her mother, Mrs. Wamsley, at her ranch on Morgan Creek rather than come to Glendive to the doctor. Mrs. Wamsley had helped deliver many babies so the doctor agreed that that would be all right if there were no complications. But there were complications. On that stormy March day, Mr. Cavanaugh set out for Glendive to get the doctor.

Because the Yellowstone Bridge had washed out previously a ferry had been put into service to cross the river when the channel was open; during the winter the crossing was made on the ice. Now, however, the ice was breaking up. Crossing on the ice was not safe, yet the ferry could not operate, so when Mr. Cavanaugh asked Dr. Hunt to accompany him, the doctor refused because of the condition of the river.

With his wife's life at stake, Dominic Cavanaugh was in no mood to take 'no' for an answer. So, at the point of a gun, Dr. Hunt did cross the ice, and both reached the other side safely. In spite of the blizzard they arrived at the ranch in time to save Mrs. Cavanaugh (she lived until 1963) and the baby. Mrs. O'Neil whimsically remarked that it's of no use trying to keep her age secret from the townspeople, because too many recall the date of her birth as "the day of the big storm when the bridge was out."

About this time Mr. Cavanaugh ran for sheriff, was elected, and they moved to Glendive. The county jail at that time was located in the courthouse, and the sheriff's residence was behind the courthouse. The stables were located in the general area of the present El Centro Motel*. Trustees, in for six months or so, took care of the horses and did other chores. Mrs. O'Neil recalls a standing joke between two of the trustees, one in for stealing a watch, the other for stealing a saddle. The first would ask, "What time is it?" and the other would reply, "Time to take the saddle off!"

In the elections of 1898 the sheriff's deputy ran against Mr. Cavanaugh and was defeated. Mr. Cavanaugh had urged the deputy to wait another term before running because he was too young. The sheriff had promised his support in the next election when Cavanaughs would go back to the ranch. But the deputy couldn't wait and so lost the election. He nursed his bitterness until Christmas Eve when Sheriff Cavanaugh returned from the last of the Christmas shopping. The deputy followed Cavanaugh into the barn and hit him over the head with an iron rod, fatally injuring him. Instead of running for sheriff next election, the deputy was hanged.

Mrs. Cavanaugh with her three small children – Esther, Ray, and Dominic, Jr. – did not go back to the ranch. She sold her share to Dominic's brother, Jim, and bought the house in Glendive from Dr. Duncan. She also bought Miss Eleanor's Millinery Shop – now Water's Style Shop. Although the shop has changed location under Mrs. Water's management, it has been continuously operated as a millinery shop for over sixty years.

Mrs. Cavanaugh's shop was the only millinery store in the area. Each spring and fall she would take a display of hats to Terry and to Wibaux. One night after they had gone to bed in their headquarters at the Graham Hotel in Wibaux they heard a lot of shooting and yelling in the street. Miss Graham came in and calmly – almost casually – instructed them to lie down on the floor close to the windows. Thirty or forty cowpunchers had come into town, imbibed too freely, and were 'shooting up the town'. The commotion did not last long, and Esther and her mother were soon able to go back to bed.

Mrs. Alice LeMoyne, Jim's sister and Dawson's first County Superintendent of Schools, homesteaded near the ranch, now operated by 'Uncle Jim'. Though the Cavanaughs lived in town, Esther and her two brothers, Ray and Dominic, spent their summers on the ranch. From the time he was thirteen Ray worked on the ranch as a cowhand. Ray later moved to California. Dominic, Jr. died in 1926 when son Tommy was eleven months old. Esther and her husband, Glendive attorney Desmond J. O'Neil, reared her brother's two sons, Tommy and his older brother Dan. Mr. O'Neil passed away in 1958.

Desmond J. O'Neil's father, Edward F. O'Neil, was engineer for the Northern Pacific's first passenger train through Glendive. He was also one of the founders of Glendive's First National Bank. Mrs. O'Neil continues active in many phases of Glendive's business, social, and political life.

Mrs. H. V. (Nettie Almy) Robinson

Sunday, July 12, 1964 – Ninth in the Series

Mrs. Hedley Robinson didn't have much choice in coming to Montana – she was only a year old – but she has chosen to stay here eighty years. Her father, James Almy, a civil war veteran, came to Montana in 1883 looking for a ranch site because he liked to be off by himself. Coming from the New England States, he had homesteaded in Minnesota, but that became too populated so he looked for wider spaces.

He found plenty of space at the head of the Redwater River so his family came from Minnesota to join him the next spring. The area was primitive enough that they saw dead buffalo in the tall grass along Clear Creek when Mr. Almy first took them to the ranch. On one occasion buffalo had gone through their pasture and torn the fence down!

Living 'way off' presented school problems, however, and as the children reached school age they bought a house in Glendive on Sargent Avenue (it wasn't an avenue then; it was just a road). During the winter the family lived in town to permit the children to go to school, then during the summer they went out to the ranch. When that didn't work out satisfactorily, they sold the ranch and moved to Glendive.

Mr. Almy worked for the Northern Pacific in the bridge department, then as a bookkeeper in the storeroom that stood where the new Safeway store is being built on South Merrill Avenue near the underpass. Thus the children were able to attend school, and Nettie went from the primary grades through high school in the red brick school that later became the Bismarck Grocery Building*. The school had two rooms downstairs and two rooms upstairs in addition to the room that was fixed over for a high school.

The Glendive of those days had many saloons but few churches. When the Almys moved to town, the Congregational Church was located on the corner of Power and Sargent. Later the building was sold to the Catholic Church and used for their worship services. In the early 1900's a new Congregational Church was built on South Pearson Avenue (Pearson was a road then, too), and about once a month an Episcopal minister would come from Miles City and hold services in a rented hall.

Even in town the neighbors weren't very close. Mrs. Robinson recalls that the Nortons lived where the Auble home is now, and the Days were next to them. The Johnsons lived a little farther toward the river on the edge of Caines Coulee, where their back yard sloped down to their cow pasture. The Johnsons had a dairy herd and delivered milk around town. Nettie often went with them as they went from customer to customer, dipping milk with a quart measure from the can. She testifies, as have others, that milk delivery then didn't have the sanitary regulations it has now!

Then, of course, there were the Osbornes, way out on the edge of town on 'Sagebrush Flat' (the 200 block between Taylor and Rosser, according to Jim

Osborne). Mrs. Robinson noted that two families homesteaded right in Glendive — the Keenes on the south side of the tracks, the Allens in the area back of the First National Bank. Later they had a good time selling lots!

After the Sargent Avenue sojourn the family bought another ranch about fifteen miles southwest of Glendive in the Pleasantview area, and moved out of town again. When Nettie was twenty-four, she married Hedley Robinson. Hedley, son of an Episcopal minister, came to the States from Ireland. He was born in New Zealand and lived for a time in Australia before reaching Ireland. His father was then assigned to Miles City so he brought the family to Montana.

Hedley, whose father died when Hedley was in his teens, turned cowboy and worked on the H S Ranch on the Redwater before starting his own ranch northwest of Glendive. No town marred the landscape when he took his bride to her new home. In those days buying and leasing land weren't necessary; all the range around was free. The coming of the railroad changed that, however, and where their hay meadow had been, the little town of Richey sprouted. Homesteaders, too, began coming in and fencing their claims so ranch boundaries had to be more definite. Gradually the ranching changed to farming as the area became more settled.

Although Mrs. Robinson now lives in Glendive, she still owns the farm just south of Richey (her husband passed away in 1956). Recently she sold twenty-eight acres to the State to make an airport where only a little more than half-a-century ago the cattle roamed at will and the team and wagon provided the standard transportation.

Harry and Fred Dion

Sunday, July 19, 1964 – Tenth in the Series

Dion roots go deep in Glendive – about as deep as Glendive itself. Mr. Henry Dion (father of Harry and Fred Dion) freighted with his wagon train ahead of the Northern Pacific Railroad as it progressed westward. This region then had a string of forts to protect settlers from Indians. As Mr. Dion freighted from Fort Lincoln at Bismarck to the fort at Miles City, his route took him through the Glendive area, and in 1879 or 1880 he settled in Glendive.

He came from a family of eleven boys and two girls in the old, settled community of Quebec, Canada. Their farm was small, and the boys had to go to work at an early age. In 1860 when he was about fourteen, Henry came to the United States and hired out to a Dutch farmer in Pennsylvania for fifty dollars a year. Just before the end of the year he was fired so he received no pay. His brother Jerry was a wheelwright and had a blacksmith and wagon shop in North Bend, Nebraska, on the Oregon Trail. Henry joined him there, but business was poor in the '70s so he worked at other jobs as he had opportunity. He was a construction worker on the Union Pacific Railroad as it stretched westward, a carpenter in Chicago after the Great Fire, and also a construction worker on the Northern Pacific Railroad.

He contracted to build the barracks at Fort Lincoln in Bismarck before beginning his freighting business. By this time gold had been discovered in the Black Hills so he made regular trips to Deadwood, South Dakota, as well as to Miles City. To protect the prospectors and settlers rushing to the Black Hills, the government arranged for them to gather at Bismarck until there was a large group, then take them to Deadwood by wagon train.

On one occasion some stragglers arrived in Bismarck after the wagon train had departed so, too impatient to wait for the next group, they started on, hoping to catch up with the train. Before they caught up with the train, Indians caught up with them and attacked. The Bismarck paper carried the story of how they were rescued by Henry Dion's wagon train returning from Deadwood. Mr. Dion himself never had any trouble with the Indians although he was constantly in Indian territory. He was in Fort Lincoln when General Custer left for his famous last battle.

Glendive's original site was on the old golf course. Mr. Dion had put up two buildings there before the railroad reached Glendive in 1881. Then the depot was built at its present location, and the town moved down to the depot. In 1882 he was appointed first sheriff of Dawson County by territorial Governor Potts. In 1886 he built the Exchange State Bank building on the corner of Merrill and Bell, using brick from his own brickyard across Caines Coulee. In 1931 the Dions remodeled and resurfaced the original structure, added the annex on Bell Street where Kolstad's Jewelry is, and built the Penney store.

Mrs. Dion was born Margaret O'Connor in Virginia. Her older sister and husband, the Snyders, had moved to Deadwood, South Dakota, where he was a buffalo hunter, and Margaret joined them there. She came as far as Sidney, Nebraska, on the Union Pacific, then took the stage to Deadwood. There she met and married Lou Elliot, a mine operator. Elliot became ill and died three weeks before their only child was born. Mrs. Elliot (Margaret) returned to Virginia until after the baby was born but then rejoined the Snyders in Deadwood. When the Snyders moved to Glendive, the widowed Mrs. Elliot and small son, Louie, came also. Mr. Snyder started the butcher shop (he still hunted buffalo) where later Meissner's Meat Market* was located.

In 1882 Mrs. Elliot married Henry Dion. Her wedding dress was made by Charley Krug's sister, Emma. The Dions then lived on the corner of Bell and Douglas, but the house has since been moved to Towne Street, next to the river. Originally the house had two bedrooms, but as the family grew, they built more rooms until it reached its present size. There were five children, Louie (Elliot), Harry, Fred, Bill, and Marie. All are living except Bill.

The Dion home was the first in Glendive with waterworks. Pressure was supplied by an elevated tank in the yard, and water was pumped by windmill from their own well. At that time there were many windmills around town. Also in the back yard the Dions had a large washhouse, corral, and barn. In the barn they kept a fringed-top surrey used for Sunday afternoon drives. Marie noted that her usually modern father would not buy a car until her mother told him she would not go on any more horse rides (in the surrey) on Sunday unless she got a car. He bought her a Cadillac.

Marie observed, "Life was very formal in the early years of Glendive. My mother never left the house without putting on her hat and gloves, even if it was just to go downtown shopping."

The children, all except Marie, received their schooling in the old red brick school on West Valentine. Their father was instrumental in getting the current Washington School built on Meade Avenue, and Marie attended there for junior high. Harry graduated from Glendive High School in 1898, went on to North Dakota Agricultural College at Fargo, then to Missoula, and later to business college in Chicago. Fred received his higher education at Missoula, as did Marie.

The day Marie left on the Northern Pacific train for Missoula in the fall of 1920, her father left on the train in the opposite direction bound for Rochester, Minnesota, to be treated for throat cancer. In November she was called home because of her father's death. She returned to Missoula the following quarter, and on June 15, 1925, was awarded a Bachelor of Arts degree.

Mr. Dion had great respect for education. He always told Marie, "Any girl can get married, but not every girl can be a teacher."

After Mr. Dion's death Mrs. Dion had moved to Los Angeles. Marie joined her there where she first taught in elementary schools, then in junior high before being assigned to counseling. In time, the principal asked her to be the head counselor, a position she held for twenty years. Because of arthritis Marie had to retire in 1962 and she returned to Glendive. She was given a certificate of service from the L.A. City School Districts for her long and faithful years in Los Angeles. Marie always maintained, "There never is a problem child, but there are problem parents and problem teachers."

Harry, for many years president of the Exchange State Bank, lives at his home at 603 North Kendrick, and Fred, proprietor of Dion's Men's Store, lives at 817 North Kendrick.

From the papers of Marie Dion, courtesy of Fred Dion, Jr., comes this first-person account of the Yellowstone flood of April 7, 1899, in which Margaret (Mrs. Henry) Dion's older sister, Mrs. R.W. (Nellie) Snyder, and her younger brother, Eugene O'Connor, perished.

Joseph Myers had gone to the Snyder home on the Marsh road when the ice in the Yellowstone River broke up. Mrs. R.W. Snyder, Mr. Eugene O'Connor, Miss Nellie Regan, and Miss Rose Wybrecht perished in the icy water, with Joseph the only survivor.

Their first intimation of the break-up was the noise of pressing ice in the main channel of the river. They were not overly concerned when they observed water backing up in the old creek bottom. Joseph noted that the party, standing outside, observed in a joshing way that if the water came up, they could get on the roof of the house.

Eugene suggested that they all go to the railroad track, but when they noticed considerable water in the ditch, Eugene asked Joseph to go in first to see how deep it was. The water was over three feet deep, and the rest of the party laughingly remarked that they didn't care to take a bath and started to return to the house.

Before they reached the house the first mad rush of water came. The water was waist deep, but there was no large floating ice. Mrs. Snyder became faint so Eugene and Joseph carried her almost thirty feet toward the house while Nellie and Rose held onto the men.

They then realized they could not reach the house so decided to try for the shelter of the first large tree. One was close by so the men attempted to raise Mrs. Snyder on their shoulders to one of the lower branches, about eight feet from the ground. She was unable to retain her hold because her hands were so numbed by the water. They next tried to get Nellie and Rose up the tree, but they could not retain their holds either. By this time the water had reached their shoulders.

Eugene first attempted to climb into the tree but did not have the strength to raise himself out of the water. Joseph succeeded in climbing onto the branch and threw his leg over the limb so that he could get hold of Mrs. Snyder, but she could not hold on. They next tried Nellie and Rose, but with no success. Eugene became excited at not being able to help the ladies. All they could do was hold them to the tree. From Joseph's position on the tree he could reach them so he took off his suspenders and tied one wrist each of Nellie and Rose on each end of the suspenders and hung the center over the broken branch below the one he was on. That compelled Nellie and Rose to stand with the tied arm raised above their heads.

Mrs. Snyder and Eugene were in the meantime holding onto the trunk of the tree with one hand and the other alternately holding onto Joseph's left hand and arm. By this time the water had risen to the heads of the four that were standing. Eugene said that he would change his position to the other side of the tree. As he attempted to do so he was forced away from the tree by the water, without a sound, and that was the last seen of him.

Joseph had twisted a piece of his suspenders around Mrs. Snyder's wrist and held onto it. After Eugene was swept away Mrs. Snyder missed him and kept asking where he was. Joseph told her he was behind Nellie, and that satisfied her because she could not see Nellie on the opposite side of the tree. Mrs. Snyder attempted to work her way around the tree, but the piece of suspender broke, and she was gone.

Nellie, Rose, and Joseph were talking to each other when they noticed lanterns on the railroad track. This encouraged them with the hope of rescue, and Joseph tried to cheer them and keep up their drooping spirits. It seemed to Joseph all of an hour after Mrs. Snyder was swept away that Rose became terribly excited, moving around in a half frantic condition and incessantly inquiring for Mrs. Snyder and Eugene until her end of the suspender broke, and she disappeared without an outcry of any kind. Joseph related, "I made a grab for her, missed her, but fortunately caught the end of the suspender to which she had been tied, with which I then tied Nellie more securely to the tree, and finally raised her onto the branch where I was so that her knees were out of the water. In this position she rested comfortably, and from that time until she fainted, never lost hope of being rescued.

"She fainted a second time and when the men hollered to me from the railroad tracks asking how I was, I answered that I was all right but that Nellie had just died, as I could not hear her breath. She finally regained consciousness and talked to me, but gradually ceased as she fell into a half unconscious condition, in which she remained until about two o'clock, when the ice began coming down in large pieces. I took off my coat and shoes, tying the shoes to the branch of the tree, to stand on. Just then a large block of heavy ice struck the tree, breaking it off near the ground, when I lost sight of Nellie, who I am satisfied died before the ice struck the tree.

"I was thrown into the water and probably swam three or four feet when I crawled onto the large piece of ice that broke the tree. I was on this piece of floating ice for two hundred yards when I caught the branches of a tree, the trunk of which I judged was a foot through, and climbed three or four feet above the water. A few minutes later another large piece of ice came floating down, snapped the tree in two and I had barely straightened up on another piece of ice before I caught the branches of a third tree and climbed four feet above the water.

"I remained in this tree until daylight when Sam Eakers, Andrew Larson and a stranger, by using 2x12 planks, reached the tree I was on from the railroad track, the ice being gorged. As they reached the tree the gorge broke and Eakers and the stranger were compelled to climb the tree I was on, while Larson started for the railroad track, got on a large piece of ice and was pulled out to the track by men on the end of the rope which he tied to himself when he started to assist my rescue. About ten minutes later the ice, which did not break all the way up, passed me. Mike Lacey and my brother Lawrence came out on a boat and the three of us reached the tracks safely. I was chilled through and through and could not walk, but willing friends hurried me home where I received all the kind attention that was needed for my speedy recovery."

The Glendive Independent relates that in the same flood, April 7, 1899, on the west side of the river at Glendive, the entire Sullivan family drowned: James Sullivan, age sixty-five; Mrs. (Mary) Sullivan, forty-one; Margaret, eleven; Edward, nine; John, seven; Barney, five; Thomas, three; and Mary, five months.

"Their remains, and Miss Rose Wybrecht's, whose body was found Monday afternoon at four o'clock, were laid out in the courtroom of the County Courthouse by the ladies of Glendive. It was a sight never to be forgotten by those who viewed the eight caskets, Mrs. Sullivan's youngest child being laid in her arms, to see an entire family thus prepared for burial. Although there were no mourners (family) at this funeral Thursday, many sympathizing friends joined the cortege to St. Julian's church, as did the children of the public schools, three of the Sullivans attending the school. When the Cortege reached the church the caskets were arranged with four before the sanctuary and two in each aisle. The impressive requiem service of the day before was repeated during which the pastor eulogized all who risked their life to recover the bodies of the unfortunates to give them Christian burial, and to all who assisted in any way in the perfect conduct of the funeral. The scene at the cemetery was affecting, as the Sullivan family were laid in one grave."

There was much devastation and destruction to livestock and property throughout the Lower Yellowstone Valley, but no other loss of human life.

Lenus Schloss

When Lenus Schloss came to Glendive in 1902, he was just a young fellow looking for work. He had been working with the extra gang on the railroad out of Richardton, North Dakota, (Joe Wester was running the crew) but when his brother quit and moved to Glendive, Lenus came to Glendive, too. He worked first for teamster Harry Tripe, but then he decided to try ranch work. He'd been brought up on the farm and liked horses so in 1904 he went to work on the Bob McNealy ranch, now owned by Russell Evans. Their range extended for miles, and they cut their hay in the Bloomfield area. When a young fellow came along in midwinter and offered to work for twenty dollars a month, five less than Lenus was getting, Lenus wasn't interested in the pay cut and quit.

The next year he worked for Jim Seeds, but then he got the idea of homesteading. He didn't intend to farm, but he thought it would be good to have his own place, then get a team and haul coal (coal mines all around). The location he chose was on Deer Creek, near the river, not too far from town. The country was open range so he bought a few cattle, planning to expand to ranching. In 1906, however, the homestead rush began, and he soon found himself fenced in on 160 acres. By 1915 the range was gone so he had to settle for another half section three miles up Deer Creek for his pasture.

Those first years on his homestead he concentrated on necessary improvements, and by 1911 he had his house built, fences made, and the machinery he needed on a little farm. By then he was tired of batching, too, but girls were scarce. They were so scarce that the Beanery* had to send back East to get waitresses. In three or four months the waitresses would all be married, and they'd have to send for a new batch! Lenus had been so busy with his homestead he'd had no time for social activities, but now he decided to get out a bit. That first Saturday night when he went to town, he met Mary Nichols. In three months they were married. The Homestead Act had brought Mary's parents to Montana from Colorado's coal mines, and they homesteaded near Circle. Mary was working for Mrs. Jordan when she met Lenus.

Lenus, youngest of five children, was born near Odessa, Russia, and had been orphaned at an early age. When his oldest sister and husband decided to come to America to homestead (some of his aunts were already in North Dakota), they wanted to bring Lenus along for help, but Lenus didn't want to come with them so his older brother, Jack, came instead. When they reached Richardton, North Dakota, they found they would need some capital before they could homestead so the brother-in-law went to work in a brickyard, and Jack started working for the extra gang on the railroad.

Jack kept urging Lenus to come to America so he finally came. When the necessary papers were in order, his older brother took him to Odessa to begin his journey. The brother was dismayed to find that no one else from that area was scheduled to sail from Bremen, Germany, on the same ship. Let a fifteen-year-old boy cross the ocean to a strange continent by himself? But Lenus wasn't about to turn back so he came – alone. They assumed that Richardton would be a large city like Odessa so his brother's instructions were to go to the streetcar, give them his aunt's name and address, and they'd take him where he wanted to go.

Simple. But when he reached Richardton he found a very small town. The conductor pushed him, with his satchel and coat, out onto the platform, and the train went on. Not a soul was in sight – and no streetcar, either. He could speak both Russian and German, but not a word of English. How could he ask instructions? Even as he stood, wondering, a Russian-German who had a store just across the street saw him standing there and knew by his clothes and boots that he was from Russia. The storekeeper hurried over and began speaking to him in German. It was easy then to explain his predicament, but he soon learned that his aunt lived ten miles out in the country. It was nearing dark on a February night so the storekeeper urged Lenus to spend the night with him. Lenus was determined to go on, however, so his new friend told him that from the top of a distant hill his aunt's light could be seen (there were no neighboring lights to confuse him!). He walked toward that light, and reached their home about nine o'clock that night.

When he applied for work on the extra gang, the boss was a little afraid to hire him because he was only fifteen, but he finally decided to just "mark him down as a little bit older."

Mr. and Mrs. Schloss reared their five children on their homestead, living there until 1959 when they retired and moved to Glendive.

Mrs. Adolphus (Margaret Henry) Kent

Sunday, August 2, 1964 – Twelfth in the Series

Mrs. Adolphus Kent vividly recalls the fall of 1893 when, as a twelve-year-old girl, she came in a covered wagon from Wisconsin with the William Henry family. Her father and younger sister were also in the party. Her mother had died when she, the oldest of four children, was nine so she and one sister lived with their aunt, Mrs. Henry. They enjoyed beautiful weather as they traveled slowly over the prairie with their two covered wagons, plus a one-horse sulky*. They bought milk from farmers along the way, but sometimes they encountered a problem getting water because of the severe shortage in some areas. Some of the territory through which they passed had been ravaged by prairie fires, presenting a desolate sight.

When they reached New Salem, North Dakota their Indian summer suddenly came to an end in a blizzard with severe cold, but they were able to find shelter from the storm for the night with a farm family. The farm buildings were all in one unit, with an alley connecting the house to the barn. Straw was piled deep on the floor of the room where they were to sleep. Even though the hinges on the door were broken and the pigs kept trying to come in, they were grateful for the accommodations. The farmer's wife couldn't speak English, but the man could communicate fairly well. The next morning a railroad man from Bismarck came to buy a couple pigs. When he offered a check in payment, the lady angrily threw the piece of paper on the floor. She sought the opinion of Mrs. Henry, who tried to explain that if the man was of good reputation, the check should be acceptable payment. Reluctantly, the farmer's wife finally accepted the check. That day the women and children boarded the train and were soon in Glendive. The men arrived a week later with the wagons.

Two uncles, Bill and John Henderson, were already in the Glendive vicinity. When John had become very ill, the Henrys had decided to come to Montana, too. Mrs. Kent's other sister, Tina (Fred Schepens' mother), and her brother Bob were living with John. John's home was on Three Mile Creek, near the present Clapp coal mine, and Henrys settled just across the creek from them.

Rural schools were almost non-existent, but by this time there were a number of school-age children between Deer Creek and Three Mile so Mr. Kinny, a rather gruff but good-hearted Civil War veteran, told them they could use one of the rooms in his two-room shack for a school. They bought some outdated books from a school where Savage is now, and with Miss Nora Johnson from Glendive as teacher, school began. It was located near the site of the present Deer Creek School.

One winter morning as they prepared school lunches snow began falling. There was some doubt about the wisdom of sending the children, but when they saw Bob and Tina starting from across the creek, they decided Mattie and Polly (Mrs. Kent's name is Margaret, but everyone called her Polly) should be able to go, too. There was no fence to follow, only a trail, and in the storm they couldn't follow that. They missed the schoolhouse entirely and wandered almost to the river. They were dressed warmly but had no idea which way to go so they kept walking.

Suddenly they came to an unfamiliar building, which confused them even more until they saw Mr. Kinny emptying ashes. Accustomed to approaching the schoolhouse from the front, they hadn't recognized the rear in the storm. Tina and Bob had not reached school at all so Mr. Kinny hurriedly bundled up and started for the Hendersons. Tina and Bob were there, safe and sound. During a lull in the storm the folks had seen that the children were circling instead of going toward the school so they had brought them home.

Adolphus Kent had heard there was plenty of work in the West so in 1888 he came looking for some of it. He had come from England and spent some time working in the iron mines of Minnesota before heading west. He went first to the Townsend-Helena area, then back to Miles City where he worked on the Tongue River irrigation ditch being constructed. He didn't stay long because of lousy (literally) working conditions.

When he reached Glendive, he found work herding sheep on the Merrill ranch out Burns Creek way. The life of a sheepherder was a lonely one. Sometimes he would see no one for six weeks at a time. The larder usually wasn't very well stocked so he lived mostly on bullberries and sheep milk. He worked for a number of ranchers in the area before he went into the sheep business with Jim Seed, an early rancher on Seven Mile Creek. Mr. Seeds had been an interpreter for the Indians at Poplar and was well known by the Indians.

In the fall the Indians often camped in the region of the present home of Ike McGaughey while they hunted their winter meat. One fall an Indian borrowed a gun (a 45-70, now in the Gateway Museum) from Adolphus and promised him a hind quarter of every deer he got. He also borrowed seven shells, and for every shell he brought in a quarter of deer. The last grizzly bear in the area was killed after Adolphus had come, and he slept on the hide at night after it was skinned out.

Those first years in Montana Polly's father, Mr. Frankenberg, worked for various ranchers, including Bob McNealy on Seven Mile, Wamsley on Morgan Creek, and Jim Brooks on Thirteen Mile. He was working for Dominic Cavanaugh at the jail when Mr. Cavanaugh was murdered. When Polly was fifteen, her father bought railroad land near the river (Mrs. Balback Smith's place now), and Polly went to keep house for him. Through their ranch work Adolphus had become acquainted with Mr. Frankenberg's daughter. He was quite a bit older than Polly, and she didn't guess then that he might some day be her husband, but on April 18, 1900, they were married.

They lived for a time on her father's place, then homesteaded on Seven Mile Creek about fifteen miles northwest of Glendive. They lived for about thirty years in a house of hewed logs (son George says he still remembers the tubs sitting all around the house to catch the water when it rained) before they built the present frame dwelling. The Kents had seven children, one of whom died in infancy. Of the other six, all but one are living in the Glendive area.

Mr. and Mrs. Kent had lived together sixty-three years before Mr. Kent passed away in March 1963, a short time before his ninety-fourth birthday. Mrs. Kent still lives on the old homestead with her youngest son, George, and his wife. She can make the hours pass quickly as she tells stories of "what used to be."

Eivend Kalberg

Sunday, August 9, 1964 – Thirteenth in the Series

"Remember, this land is not in August like it is in May," were the words of the Bozeman professor who, with some of his students, had come in 1908 to classify and survey land in Dawson County and had camped on the Eivend Kalberg ranch.

In the year 1901 when Eivend came to Montana, they wouldn't have needed the admonition. That year it was in May like it is in August. When he arrived on May 16 the temperature was 110 degrees and not a green spear in sight. He had just emigrated from Norway, coming through England, and in both countries everything was a lush green, making the contrast more marked.

Eivend's uncle, Michael Kalberg, and Mike's two sisters had come to Montana in 1882. (One of the sisters had married Jonas Halvorsen, the other had married Karl Holling.) Eivend had decided to try Montana too. He could speak no English so when he got off the train in Glendive and noticed a group of men standing nearby he asked, "Can anyone speak Norwegian?" Immediately Louie Kolberg stepped forward with the assurance that he could.

Although they were not related, were not even acquainted, they had come from the same farm in Norway, hence the same name (though Louie Kolberg's spelling had been changed since coming to America). In Norway the farmers, according to custom dating back to earlier times, all lived in a village in the center of the 'farm' as protection against raiders; each individual's land extended out from this village somewhat as wheel spokes from the hub. Each farmer then took his last name from the name of the farm as Kalberg. Louie knew Mike because their wives were sisters, so Eivend had no problem finding his relatives.

Eivend's first job in Montana was sacking wool at the shearing pen run by Sheriff George Williams and located on what is now the Tom Hagan ranch. He was paid three dollars a day and was well satisfied with his wages. When this job was finished, he went with Henry Nelson and William Henry to put up hay for Tom Carter at his ranch on Redwater. A snowfall on September 2nd put a stop to the haying so Eivend went to work for Carter, building a twenty-mile fence across the Big Sheep Mountain. Carter had about 40,000 sheep, 10,000 to a band, two men with each band, always on the move for more grass.

Lars Stangeland had come from Norway with him but had gone on to Washington so Eivend went to Washington to visit him after the fall work was done and spent the winter in the woods. In the spring he thought he'd go to Ashland, Oregon, but at Ellensburg, Washington he met a man looking for someone to shear his daughter's small bunch of sheep. Eivend took the job and before he was through, bankers, saloonkeepers, farmers – everyone, it seemed – were contacting him to shear their sheep. He was paid twenty-five cents a sheep in these small bunches compared to seven cents a sheep for the big flocks in eastern Montana! When this shearing was done he headed back toward

Glendive, paying his way by taking care of sheep on the freight train. He got off the train at Glendive – and went to work shearing sheep!

He worked on various ranches and a little later ran sheep on shares with his brother, L.L. Kalberg who had come over in 1902, and Hans Halvorsen on the latter's ranch. Halvorsen didn't own a foot of land but in those days that was a small matter. He had been there since 1882 and used the range without the formality of buying or renting. Eivend's brother quit here after the land was surveyed because he didn't want to buy land as was then necessary, so he moved to Harlowton and started a store.

Over on Morgan Creek, John Davison operated on somewhat the same principle as Halvorsen (and the other ranchers). He squatted* on a quarter section of railroad land, a practice sanctioned by the railroad, and had about a section fenced for his horse pasture. The land had not been surveyed so there were no section lines to follow. When he decided to sell out in the fall of 1907 Eivend bought his quarter section, complete with house and furniture. The Kalbergs still have, among other things that came with the house, the organ (bought from Sears-Roebuck in the 1800s), writing desk and chair, a wall clock, and a dresser.

Thursday, August 13, 1964

In 1918 they dug a basement, moved the house onto it, and built an addition to it, but the main portion of the house is the one he bought from Davison. They also installed running water at that time, a rare thing for a rural dwelling in 1918.

The same fall that he bought the Davison place; Kalberg homesteaded a few miles up the creek. His original log shack is still standing, as is the house they built in 1910. On the homestead he had to do quite a bit of farming which gave him hay fever so in 1918 he sold to Mr. and Mrs. Jake Karlen.

The Karlens had bought a ranch near Allard and trailed 300 head of cattle from the Sweetgrass country to their new ranch. When they arrived, they found that the pasture had been grazed off by horses, leaving them without feed for their cattle so they refused to take the ranch and instead bought Kalberg's homestead.

In 1908, Eivend's sister Grete and Gurine Stangeland, a sister of his friend Lars Stangeland, had come to the States. Gurine went on to Washington to join her brother while Grete stayed in Montana. She later married Svend Assland and they homesteaded on Clear Creek. Gurine found work cooking in a hotel. Eivend had continued to correspond with Stangeland in Washington. When Andrew Helland, who ran a hotel on Bell Street in the Dion Block*, needed a cook for the hotel, Eivend wrote to the Stangelands and told them. Gurine came and the hotel had a good cook for awhile but it wasn't long until Eivend had the cook and Helland had to find another. Gurine and Eivend were married in January of 1910. They had four children; Lars and Dorothy at home with their father; Einar of Corvallis, Montana; and Goodrun (Mrs. Sig Undem) of Pleasantview.

Before the Bell Street Bridge was completed in 1925, a watchman was stationed at the old wooden bridge to make sure too much livestock didn't cross at one time. Fifteen on the bridge at a time was the limit for sheep. Much experience had taught Kalberg that the bridge shook less if he'd string the sheep out than if he tried to take them across in a bunch so that was the method he used.

In April of 1907, he shipped in 3,000 sheep from Bridger and unloaded them in Glendive to trail them to the range on Morgan Creek. The sheep were crazy for green grass after the trip and even five men found it hard to control them. When they reached the bridge, the watchman insisted the sheep had to be bunched to take them across. Kalberg was convinced that the only way to get those sheep across was to string them out and told the watchman, "I've had more experience than you have." The watchman was obdurate.

Finally, in desperation, Kalberg told the watchman, "If you don't let those sheep, I'll throw you in the river!" The watchman replied, "If you do, I'll make you pay a fine!" Mr. Kalberg didn't throw the watchman in the river (just moved him off the bridge) but he did string the sheep out and he did pay a fine. The sheep were strung from Glendive to Stipek before they got them all rounded up. In retrospect, Mr. Kalberg added that the watchman was a real nice man even though they couldn't agree on the best way to take sheep across the bridge.

As Kalberg reminisced, he recalled the mules be bought from a Utah outfit that had come in with horses for sale. They were fine horses so Mr. Kalberg bought some. Then the horse dealer asked him if he wanted a good team of mules. Mr. Kalberg didn't know what he'd want with mules, but they were offered for just sixty dollars so he decided to take them. He soon began learning what those mules could do. The first time he went to Glendive with them, the liveryman asked what he'd take for them and Kalberg priced them at $100. He didn't sell them. The liveryman was still interested but the next time he inquired, the price was $150. He wasn't ready to pay that much and by the time he was ready, Mr. Kalberg was quoting $200, only the mules weren't for sale.

The mules weren't averse to running away and when they did, the only way he could stop them was to throw the lines and jump from the rig. Before long, the mules would stop and turn around to see what had happened to him.

Once as he was going to town in the spring wagon, taking some plow lays to get them sharpened, the bolt connecting the wagon tongue to the axle came out as he was going downhill. He threw the lines and went back to get it but as he started back to the wagon, the mules took off. Plow lays rattled in the bottom of the wagon and the bird dog he had with him added to the confusion, but presently the mules stopped to see what had happened to him. He replaced the bolt and they went to town in a hurry.

Those mules would never founder themselves even though they always had access to oats on the back of the sheep wagon. Unlike cattle or horses they knew when to quit eating. One fellow who was riding the jenny mule hit her on the head, and after that he couldn't get into the barn. The mules were in the stall next to the door and if he tried to come in, she kicked him back out.

Mr. Kalberg feels that a review of those early days wouldn't be complete without mention of the winter of 1904. It had been a hard winter and it was climaxed with a spring storm, the worst, on March 24th. Eivend had been to a birthday dance out on Crackerbox. When his knee, injured in the army in Norway, began to hurt, he knew a storm was coming and headed for home.

Barometers in Glendive confirmed his prediction so he hurried on out to warn the herders to get the sheep to the home corrals. They got them in just ahead of the blizzard so, even though they couldn't feed them because of the wind and snow, their loss was small. Most of the other ranchers were not so fortunate, however, and many sustained heavy losses. The D.T. Ranch on Redwater lost 5,000 sheep in that storm and some ranchers were wiped out by the winter.

Mr. Kalberg will soon be eighty-seven but he still appears hale and hearty and looks many years younger. He has sold most of his sheep because of the difficulty of getting herders but he is still active at his ranch on Morgan Creek.

Mr. & Mrs. Glen (Cora Chupp) Borntrager

Sunday, August 16, 1964 – Fourteenth in the Series

"Let's turn around and go back!" Nineteen-year-old Glen Borntrager, with his father Joe Borntrager, stood on the edge of Morgan Table, looking down over Thirteen Mile Valley, viewing their home-to-be.

It was September, 1905. Mr. Borntrager had come out earlier in the summer and filed on a homestead; now he was bringing the family. The rest of the family had come by train, but Glen had come with the immigrant car* to care for the livestock.

When they reached Glendive, they decided it would be best for the family to stay in town that first night. Only Glen and his father would go to the homestead that day. The roads were just wagon trails so they didn't try to take much that first trip out. They loaded the chickens and some provisions into the wagon, tied the cow behind the wagon, and started out about three o'clock in the afternoon for the homestead, thirty miles to the northwest.

Progress was slow over the rough trails. The cow, like most cows, didn't like to be led. Sometimes she needed encouragement so Glen was obliged to encourage her. It was dark by the time they reached the badlands, but with the aid of their kerosene lantern they were able to find their way and started up Morgan Creek. When they came to a gate, his father thought they had reached the Joe Mullet place (two miles from their destination).

They continued on a little farther, but instead of coming to Mullet's, they came to a sheep wagon. They had gone too far west and were lost. The herder was a foreigner, and they couldn't understand each other very well. When Glen asked him, "Where are we?" the only enlightenment the herder could give was, "I don't know where we are, but I know we're here!"

They went back out through the gate, then camped for the night – what was left of it. They fixed their beds on the ground, and when they lay down, Glen asked his father, "What about the coyotes?" Mr. Borntrager didn't think the coyotes would bother them, and they didn't.

Next morning they started back and in the daylight they were able to see where they had missed the trail that took them up over Morgan Table. From the north edge of Morgan Table they were able to see Thirteen Mile Valley spread out before them so it was no problem to find their way from there. Mr. Borntrager had hired Isaiah Kauffman to build their house during the summer so their home was ready for occupancy when they arrived. This was no 'shack'. It was two stories, well designed and built; one of the few 'real houses' on the homesteads. No staying in tents. Other homesteaders came to Glendive with wagons and teams to help the new arrivals move to their new home.

Back in Fayette County, Illinois, Mr. Borntrager had heard there was homestead land available in Montana so he decided to move West where there would be land for his boys. He homesteaded on the quarter section where the

Red Top Church is located, and within two years Glen was eligible to file and settled on the quarter just north of his father's place.

A few other homesteaders had already located in the Thirteen Mile Valley, among them the Eli Chupp family. They had come in 1904. Mrs. Chupp and the boys had come with the covered wagon, driving their herd of cattle, but daughter Cora had come on the train with Mrs. Joe Mullet. The Joe Mullet family (including sons Bert and Lou, who still live in the Glendive area) had come in the spring of 1903, but Mrs. Mullet had been back East to visit her sick mother so Cora came with her and missed the covered wagon trip.

Mr. Chupp had homesteaded in North Dakota so he couldn't homestead here, but he was able to buy railroad land for three dollars an acre. He had settled where the Art Dietz place is now (Mrs. Dietz is the youngest daughter of the Eli Chupps).

In 1907 Glen and Cora were married and have spent fifty-seven years together on the old homestead. Although it was Glen who said, "Let's go back," he is the only one out of the family of five boys and one girl who stayed with Montana through all the droughts, hard winters, depressions, and grasshopper plagues. His seven children also are still living in Montana; all in this area, except for one in the western part of the state.

During those first years Glen ran an experiment station as an extension of the Bozeman Agricultural Department. They raised small grains such as wheat, oats, barley, and rye. Glen farmed some strips every year and let some strips lie fallow* every other year and compared results. The land was fertile enough that they could grow crops every year, but even then he found that in a dry year the strips that had been farmed every year might produce about five bushels to the acre, while the summer fallow would produce about fifteen. His highest winter wheat yield on summer fallow was forty-four bushels. The oats yield was eighty-eight bushels.

In spite of these experiments summer fallow did not come into general use throughout the area until the 1930's, and winter wheat was hardly used until the 1950's, even by Glen himself.

Mrs. Borntrager recalls the excitement of watching the cattle roundups conducted by the big ranches those first years she was here. They brought herds and herds of cattle to the big flat on Thirteen Mile just below the Chupp place. There they sorted and branded their stock. While they were camped there, they got water from the Chupps.

They'd kill a steer to feed the outfits, then bring the left-over meat to the Chupps after the roundup. There were cattle all over the country when they came – wild cattle with long horns! Sometimes when the wild cattle were close by, the children were afraid to go bring in their own cattle.

Now the longhorns have given way to the registered stock, and the ranches have been replaced by carefully managed farms. Mr. and Mrs. Borntrager, with son Floyd, still live in their home in Thirteen Mile Valley.

232

Mr. and Mrs. William (Ruth Blades) Muir

Sunday, August 23, 1964 – Fifteenth in the Series

Two of Montana's old timers moved from the Big Sky Country last Thursday when Mr. and Mrs. William Muir left for Illinois. Both had come to the Treasure State before the turn of the century.

Bill Muir was born in Scotland April 27, 1890. His father had planned for the family to emigrate to South America and had gone ahead to make arrangements. He disappeared, however, and they were able to find no trace of him. Perhaps he had been killed. With her husband gone, Mrs. Muir decided, instead of going to South America, to come to the United States. She had some relatives in Pennsylvania who had written, urging her to come, so she stayed there briefly. Then, the Jim Wings, distant relatives of hers living on Morgan Creek northwest of Glendive, encouraged her to come there so she decided to try the West. After spending some time on the Wing ranch, Mrs. Muir accepted the job of cooking for the jail 'residents' for Dominic Cavanaugh.

One of her chief concerns was to get Bill into school and now that they were in Glendive, this desire could be realized. Although Bill was only six, he had already been introduced to education. In Scotland school was compulsory when a child reached the age of four years. Bill recalls that Sheriff Cavanaugh bought his first set of school books for him in America. Bill didn't quite share his mother's enthusiasm for school so he and some of his friends tried 'playing hooky'. However, Mr. Cavanaugh had the solution, and he escorted them to school with the buggy whip. If their enthusiasm for school was dim, their enthusiasm for 'playing hooky' was a bit dimmer thereafter.

As a youngster, Bill picked up odd jobs whenever he could. One of them was to clean out some abandoned lodge rooms. E.P. Baldwin had hired him and one of his chums for the job, and he told them to throw out everything unless there was something the boys wanted to keep. Bill saw an old Montana history book which he thought was worth saving and took it home. In the sixty-some years that followed, the book became a treasure which he prized considerably, and only when they moved this past week did he part with it, leaving it with a family friend.

When he was about fifteen, Bill landed his first job. It was with the railroad as caller for the engine crews at fifty dollars a month. After the death of his mother, he left Glendive and traveled around the country a good bit but finally wound up in the Gate City* again. He had a chance to go firing on the Northern Pacific so Bill took it and stayed with the railroad, working up to the position of conductor before his retirement.

Although his wife, Ruth Blades Muir, didn't come to Glendive until 1913, she traveled to Montana about 1898 from Oklahoma in a covered wagon. Her father had come on ahead to find a place for the family. Then the family and her uncle came to join him. Her mother became very ill on the trip and died just out of Lewistown, the day before they met her father. They lived for a time on

Warm Springs Creek near Lewistown, before the children were taken to Helena and placed in a school. There were no roads and no way to get to Helena in the winter except by a dog team, so the children rode in a sled pulled by dogs, while the driver stood on the back or followed.

Later on they went back to Oklahoma, and Ruth married while there. When they returned to Montana, they had to cross Logan Pass, a formidable undertaking in those days. That first night in Montana they had no money for a hotel so they slept outside. Her husband was a miner and made the rounds of the gold-mining towns. While they were in Kendall, Montana (her uncle helped sink the shaft for the mines there), her husband died. She went to Billings, then in 1913 came to Glendive to work in the NP Lunchroom. Here she met William Muir and in 1915 they were married.

The couple wanted to keep their marriage secret so they went to Miles City to have the ceremony performed and asked them not to put it in the paper. The Miles City newspaper didn't print it, but the Glendive paper did!

Mrs. Muir mentioned that when she came to Glendive in 1913, she spent her first night in the Jordan Hotel. Now, fifty-one years later, she was spending her last night in Glendive in the Jordan Hotel.

As the Muirs prepared to leave for their new home in Elgin, Illinois, they expressed earnest appreciation for their many friends in Glendive and extend sincere thanks.

Mrs. Peter Quilling

Sunday, August 30, 1964 – Sixteenth in the Series

"When I came, I thought this was the most desolate place in the world!" exclaimed Mrs. Peter Quilling as she recalled her introduction to the Treasure State in 1907. Then she hastened to add, "But I'm all for Montana now!" Coming from the wooded, rolling hills of Wisconsin, and arriving in a snowstorm, is it a wonder she thought the prairies and badlands were barren?

Mr. Quilling had come in 1906 and homesteaded, then sent for his family the following spring. Mrs. Quilling had never been away from her Wisconsin home so coming alone on the train with her four-month-old baby and little girls aged two and three years was quite an ordeal for the shy, timid woman.

When she had to leave the Great Northern at Mondak (rail stop on the Montana-North Dakota border) on the banks of the flooding Missouri, the ordeal became frightening indeed. There was no bridge across the river, and the ferry which ordinarily operated could not be used because of the spring breakup, the only way to cross was by rowboat. Large trees had been uprooted and were tossing amid great ice chunks on the raging river so the prospect of a rowboat crossing would have struck a far bolder soul with apprehension.

The boats with their owners were on the opposite side of the river, and the owners refused to cross over until the wind subsided, which would probably be after sundown. The depot was so close to the river that Mr. Quilling, on the opposite bank, could see his little girls in their red coats trotting around in the mud and slush and snow on the depot platform. He felt he couldn't leave his family there alone. The boat owners steadfastly refused to attempt a crossing under the conditions but agreed to let him take one of the boats if he wanted to cross by himself. While his wife anxiously watched, he made the dangerous crossing and was soon reunited with his family.

When the wind quieted that evening, the other boat was brought across, and the whole family was transported over the river to begin their wagon journey to the homestead on Mt. Pleasant Table, about seven miles west of Sidney. They spent the night at the roadhouse, and the next day made their way through a blizzard up the valley to their new home.

Neighbors were watching and hurried to greet them, intending to take the newcomers home with them for the night, but Mrs. Quilling refused to go any farther. This was their first home (they had lived with her folks in Wisconsin), and here she intended to stay.

Mr. Quilling's brother Walter (father of Sidney's present Walter Quilling) and Garfield Tubbs, Wisconsin neighbors, had homesteaded earlier, and it was they who influenced Pete Quilling to try a homestead in Montana. He promised his wife faithfully that if she'd stay five years so he could prove up* on his homestead, he'd sell out and go back east to live, figuring that should give him something to start on. At the end of the five years she couldn't get away fast enough. Since her husband was working down along the river and couldn't be home with family anyway, they decided she and the children might as well go back to Wisconsin for a visit until he could get the homestead sold. After a few months in the East, she couldn't get back to Montana fast enough!

Her husband soon wrote that he had a buyer for the homestead, but by then she was so homesick for the prairies that just the thought of selling made her panicky. She was greatly relieved when her husband wrote that the buyer backed out, and they could return. She came back satisfied and has been satisfied here ever since. Reflecting on those early days, Mrs. Quilling commented, "We had some rough times, but I'd do it again!"

She recalled that the cattlemen predicted that the homesteaders wouldn't last two years, but they weathered the adversities and, she feels, it was they who built up the country. Homesteaders who pulled up and left didn't amount to much elsewhere either, she observed.

Thursday, September 3, 1964

When Mrs. Quilling arrived in the spring of 1907, her husband had their house framed up, but it wasn't finished on the inside. He had dug the basement the preceding fall, then went away to work, leaving it uncovered all winter. The basement filled with snow, the snow thawed and then froze, resulting in a cellar full of ice.

When spring came, he just built over the ice so it took a long time for the ice to melt. The unfinished house was so cold that for about a month, when the little girls woke up in the morning, she would dress them in their coats and bonnets and set the two older girls on chairs, one on each side of the open oven door, with the baby in the rocking chair in front of the stove.

If a basement full of ice didn't make heating the house easier, it did provide some recreation for the neighborhood. One of the neighbors remarked that if they just had some ice, they would make some ice cream. Pete assured them that there was plenty of ice in his basement so they chopped some loose and had an ice cream party.

Mr. Quilling had bought a team of broncs, and they still ran away just about every time he hitched them up. One evening he suggested she wrap up the children, and they'd go over to his brother Walter's place. The wagon had a high box with the seat in the bottom, so when he brought the team around to the hitching post (the post had been set into the ground but not yet tamped in), he put the two older girls into the wagon, then took the baby so Mrs. Quilling could climb in.

Just as she started to step up, one of the horses saw her. She dropped back as the horses sprang. She called to her husband to drop the baby and grab the horses, but it was too late. The horses had knocked over the hitching post and were gone! The last thing the anxious mother saw as the horses disappeared with the wagon was Bess, the older child, holding tightly to the edge of the wagon box and screaming at the top of her lungs.

Mr. Quilling managed to stay within range long enough to shout, "Bess, go back and sit down on the seat, hold onto Blanche, and shut up." She obeyed, and when Walter caught the horses as they plunged into his yard, he thought the wagon was empty because he could not see or hear anyone. When he looked into the box and saw the two little girls, he became much alarmed, thinking the rest of the family must have been thrown out. Pete soon arrived, however, and allayed his fears.

When the horses took off, they had headed straight for Walter's, going through two barbed wire fences (hard to find in those days!) on the way. Walter had been out in the yard watering his own horses and had seen them coming so was able to stop them.

They examined the horses for cuts, intending then to go back for Mrs. Quilling, but before they started, she was there, carrying the baby. She doesn't know how she got there, but she does know that when she got inside the door and saw the two little girls, quietly sitting on chairs, she herself dropped into a chair and became hysterical, laughing and crying at the same time. She was ready to go back to Wisconsin right then!

Homestead provisions required that they break up five acres that first year so they planted four acres of wheat and one of oats. When harvest time came, they had no machinery, so her husband arranged to borrow the neighbor's. He told them he would get up at two o'clock and work until they came to the field. He was able to get his all cut and made a few rounds in the neighbor's grain, but the wind began to blow, and soon after the other men had come out, the wind reached such velocity they were compelled to quit cutting. The heat also became very intense. When the wind had subsided and they went out to look at the grain, they found every horse track, every wheel track, every furrow full of wheat. The wind had threshed out all the grain, and there was no way to get it.

During those first five years on the homestead, Mrs. Quilling went to Sidney just once, and that was for a Fourth of July celebration. Such a storm came up that the celebration was abruptly concluded. Rain fell in torrents, the wind blew down tents, and to add to the confusion, horses broke loose from the wagons. She gathered her little girls and hurried inside the Valley Hotel to wait out the storm.

All the while they were on the homestead, and even after they had sold the homestead and moved to their ranch near Lambert, she was always content to stay home with her family. When a group of neighbor women were discussing their families and when they would enjoy them most, some thought it would be when their children were grown, some thought when they were teenagers, but when one of the ladies finally asked her, she replied, "I couldn't enjoy them more than I do right now!"

The children's first Christmas tree was a Russian thistle decorated with paper flowers, but they enjoyed it just as much as if it had been the fanciest.

The homesteaders soon started a Sunday School, and Pastor Blake, from the Sidney Methodist Church, came out to preach for them. In order to start a school, the community had to hold school 'on their own' for three months;

then they were eligible to organize a district. A young lady from the homestead community, Miss Mabel Young, taught during their 'probation' period, then the district was organized and school started in earnest.

When the Quillings retired, they moved to Lambert, but after her husband's death in 1941, Mrs. Quilling moved into Sidney where she now lives with her daughter, Mrs. Mae McMorris. Many years have passed since her husband bought the first article sold in the new Valley Hardware, but Mrs. Quilling's enthusiasm for Montana is undiminished. This is where she loves to be.

W. W. (Billy) Woods

Sunday, September 13, 1964 – Seventeenth in the Series

Billy Woods had to borrow the train fare that brought him to Montana. By the time he had ridden eighteen miles into a Chinook wind to reach the ranch where he was to be employed, he'd have been glad to borrow another fifty dollars to take him back to California! He couldn't, so he stayed. He says he's been trying to get hold of that fifty dollars ever since so he could quit the country, but he's still here.

Sixteen-year-old Billy was working for twenty dollars a month on a farm near his California home. At Christmas he had a week off so he went to Los Angeles, where his folks then lived, and found his uncle, Andy McLain, visiting from Montana. His uncle offered him work in Montana, but Billy went back to his job. However, when his employer told him help was plentiful and he could hire all he wanted for fifteen dollars a month, Billy decided to let him hire it, saddled up, and went back home. His uncle was still there so Billy asked him about wages, how long the job would last, and what else he might expect. The job would be permanent and starting wages would be twenty-five dollars a month the first year, then thirty-five to forty a month after that. Billy said he'd come as soon as he earned the fare (he planned to go back to the job as messenger boy which he had held previously), but Mr. McLain told him he'd loan him the money, and they could come together. So it was that on the evening of March 22, 1891, W.W. Woods arrived in Glendive.

That same evening George Williams (later undersheriff when Aiken was sheriff) came to see Mr. McLain, and he asked Billy when he was going out to the ranch. Billy replied, "As soon as I get a chance." Mr. Williams then announced that he was going out that way the next day and had an extra horse across the river (there was no bridge at that time), so if Billy had a saddle, he could go along. Billy's saddle was in his trunk so Mr. Williams left with the understanding they were to meet at the pump house next morning at nine. Billy was there, and when they got to the river, he found there were two young fellows taking people across in a rowboat at one dollar per head. One of the boys was Billy Allen, about the wildest kid in town, and the other was Joe Hurst, the most exemplary. These three young men, whose ways crossed so briefly on their first meeting, were to take widely divergent courses. Within a few years, Allen was murdered in Culbertson; a little later Hurst was hanged in Glendive for the murder of Sheriff Cavanaugh, and Woods, years later, became sheriff.

The river had started breaking up so the ice had risen in the middle with a channel of water on each side. They would row across the first channel; drag the boat over the ice in the middle, then cross the other channel. When they reached the ice, Woods was the last to get out of the boat. As he did so, one of the boys started to warn, "Be careful – there's an air hole around here some place!" but the warning came too late; Billy was already going down. However, he managed to get his arm over the side of the boat and only got wet up to his waist. The remainder of the crossing was made without incident. Then Billy and Mr. Wilson saddled their horses and started for the ranch, eighteen miles to the west. It was thawing, but that Chinook wind was cold.

Thursday, September 17, 1964

The Fourth of July that first summer Billy Woods was in Montana was a day to be remembered – by Billy, anyway. He and his uncle got up at three o'clock that morning to get to town for the celebration. They had loaded up the night before so they could get an early start, and before ten o'clock they drove their wagons onto the ferryboat to cross the Yellowstone.

They were planning to feed their horses and get some breakfast before unloading. That would still give them plenty of time to get to the fairgrounds before the races started. They crossed the river all right, but when they landed on the town side, Whoop Up Brown let out too much slack on one of the ropes connecting the ferry to the overhead cable and the ferry started to capsize.

Quick action averted that catastrophe, but the boat sprang a leak so Frank Kinney (he was running the boat for Mr. Mead) told Brown and Billy to keep the pump going while he went for help. Brown was so badly scared he couldn't stand up so Billy had to man that pump until four o'clock that afternoon. Mr. Mead gave him a dollar for it, but by that time he'd almost made up his mind he'd about as soon drown as run that pump any longer. He didn't get any breakfast, and he didn't see any races that Fourth of July.

When sheep shearing time came the second year he was in Montana he started shearing sheep for the McLain boys for eight cents per sheep. He had done a little shearing the year before, and after a few days, he was able to shear about seventy-five sheep a day. The next seven springs he ran a shearing crew and was able to double that rate.

The second year he ran a crew they sheared at the McLain ranch first, then planned to go to the William Lindsay ranch next, but Lindsay sent word that he wasn't ready so Billy went over to the Kernick ranch to tell them the crew would be there for dinner. Mr. Kernick, a widower, and his housekeeper were eating breakfast when Billy arrived. When he announced that the boys would be there for dinner, the housekeeper jumped up with the cry, "And me with no bread in the house!" She dumped a bunch of freshly hatched goslings out of a dishpan into a paper carton, took her gunny sack apron and wiped out the dishpan, put flour in it, and started the bread. He didn't eat any bread while they were there, but he didn't tell any of the crew about the bread deal until they were away from there.

After working a year for the McLain brothers, the brothers split up and Billy went into partnership with the older brother, June. Then in 1893 they sent for Billy's parents to come work for them. They hadn't been here more than two months until his father traded a section of land in Kansas to June McLain for his interest in the business, and Billy was in partnership with his father.

Because Billy's younger brother and sister were with his parents in 1894 they built a two-room shack in town so his mother could bring the youngsters in for school. They looked around for a lot to buy, but when they talked with E.P. Baldwin and Bill Kelly, who lived along Caines Coulee, they told them buying wasn't necessary; there had been no survey so they could build any place. They built their shack near where these two men lived, but the next year the city decided to survey the land and found that they were in an alley one way and in a street the other way so they sold that shack and built a better house closer to town.

Billy and his father continued in partnership until 1898, when his father sold his sheep and went to Missoula for school for the children. Billy also sold his sheep and went into the cattle and horse business.

In the spring of 1896, Grant Gibson and Billy were on a horse roundup and stayed all night in Glendive. His mother wanted him to go with her and his two sisters to a church social at the home of William Lowe. There he met a Miss Mabel Fleming. His oldest sister became very well acquainted with Miss Fleming, and just before New Year's the next winter, invited her out to the ranch. It began to storm after their arrival, and the roads got so bad she didn't get back to town until the first week of March. By that time Billy and Miss Fleming had decided to spend the rest of their lives together, and they were married March 25 that same year. They lived together a little more than fifty-eight years, until she had a stroke and passed away.

Their daughter, Helen Leslie, was born in February 1898, and they were very proud parents. They lived on the ranch on Clear Creek until 1916; then they leased the ranch and moved to Glendive so their daughter could go to school.

Twible was sheriff when Billy was appointed undersheriff January 1, 1917. In 1922 he was elected sheriff for a two-year term. During their Glendive sojourn he worked at various jobs. Among others, he worked for Ed Haskell in his garage. According to Mr. Wood, Ed was quite a nice looking young fellow then – he had almost as much hair then as Mr. Wood has now, and the wrinkles didn't show up much. Billy also worked a couple years for the Reid Motor Company, and spent a few years in Florida.

They went back to the ranch in 1927 and stayed until 1944, but then, because he wasn't able to do all the work and couldn't hire anyone, he sold out and moved to Glendive, where he built up a little place on Dry Creek. In 1946 he went to work as field man for the Agricultural Stabilization Committee, and worked there for fifteen years.

Then a new auditor noticed that Mr. Wood was past seventy years of age (he was only eighty-six) and explained he would have to retire, as the Government didn't hire anyone over seventy. Mr. Wood insisted that didn't apply to him because he was seventy-one when they begged him to take the job fifteen years before, but he was retired anyway February 1, 1962. And, he quipped, "has been tired ever since."

Since his retirement, he spends considerable time working with agates. He has an outstanding collection which he has cut, polished, and mounted at his Dry Creek home where he lives with his second wife. In the fall of 1955 he started for California, but just before he got to Pompey's Pillar, he skidded on some glare ice, struck a Northern Pacific transport, and was hospitalized in Billings. A get-well card from Cornelia Harpster, widow of John Harpster, started a correspondence which lasted through the winter while Mrs. Harpster was in Maryland and Mr. Wood was in California. After their respective returns to Glendive they saw quite a bit of each other, and on June 26 they were married.

Reminiscing further, Mr. Woods volunteered that he decided to become a Republican instead of a Democrat because the Democrats put sheep and wool on the free trade list, dropping wool prices from thirty or thirty-five cents a pound to about ten cents a pound. Lamb prices, too, dropped more than half, so the young rancher aligned himself with the Republicans. He's been a Republican ever since, and, he declares, is proud of it.

Mrs. Percy Baldwin

I was born on the banks of the Yellowstone River near Glendive just a stone's throw from my aunt and uncle Fred Bean's home. Fredda, my cousin, was born a few days before me. When I was two years old my mother and father, along with my grandparents with their cattle, decided to emigrate to Wyoming. It was a bad drought year so with their cattle and horses, they left Glendive. The Bean family emigrated to Williston, North Dakota, at the same time.

It took us from early May to September to reach our destination in Wyoming. I was always sorry I wasn't older to enjoy that trip. They didn't encounter any hardships, only they always had to be alert for stray Indians. They were being put on the reservations at that time. Only once a few bucks acted hostile and put out our fire. Papa decided we had better move on so we traveled all that night and could just see their smoke in the morning. We would stop sometimes in lovely places where the grass was up to the cattle's knees for several weeks at a time to rest them. Elk, deer, and antelope were always visible and fish in the streams so there was always wild game.

As we journeyed along, fresh morning's milk put in the churn had butter in it by noon. My family consisted of brother Willie, 4 1/2 years; I was 2 and sister Carrie, a baby of 6 weeks, Papa, Mama, and a hired girl, Lottie. She did a lot of the driving. My family located on a homestead at Elk Mountain, Wyoming. Our ranch was just in front of this lovely mountain, 11,500 feet high. It was always an inspiration to me. When things went wrong, I would go outside to look up to it.

As we reached an age where my parents thought my brother Willie and I should start school, we moved for the winter to Carbon, a little coal-mining town. When we went back to the ranch in the spring we walked 4 miles over the hills to a country school. We did this several years. Going back to town for the winter we were put in a higher grade.

I worked my way through high school in Rawlins and at the University of Wyoming in Laramie. During summer vacations I worked one year on a ranch; taught country school, and was in a telephone office one year. When I was 21 I went to teach school in Buffalo, Wyoming. At Christmas time I went to Glendive, Montana, to spend the holidays. That was the first time I had seen my cousin, Fredda, since we were two years old. After teaching in Buffalo for several years I went to California, where I did private teaching. One summer I decided to take a trip to Wyoming to visit relatives, then go to Glendive, Montana, to visit more relatives. While there I went out to visit my cousin, Fredda. She had taken up a homestead at Lane, Montana.

The town of Richey was just being built at the end of the Great Northern Railroad at this time, so we attended the first dance. It was in a rough building built by Fred Luchsinger. Well, it started to rain and it rained all that night. With no place or no hotel to stay, they decided to go to the Baldwin ranch after the dance was over. With this steady downpour we were there a day and night. Fredda then invited them, that is Percy and his niece Dora, to come over to dinner the following Saturday night. After dinner we would all go back to Richey for a dance that night. I left the following week and Fredda said, "Let's stop at the Baldwin ranch to say goodbye to them."

Mr. Baldwin said he planned to go to Minneapolis the next day on business, but that night he came to Glendive and came to my aunt's where I was visiting and asked me to go for a ride. Percy Baldwin, being a very busy rancher, didn't know much about love affairs. In the middle of a conversation he said, "If I come to California this winter, will you come back with me?" Confronted with such a quick proposal, I was silent. He said, "Will you?" That was the first of September. We were married the following January 14, 1917, in Los Angeles, California.

That was a terrible time to get married. We arrived in Glendive February 2. We took the train to Sidney, then the Goose* to Richey. The train that left the next morning going to Sidney never came back for two weeks. It was 40° below and under all that time.

Percy was getting nervous; he expected to be shivareed*. He had brought several cases of wine from Los Angeles along with us. One evening I had gone to bed, but he was pacing around, then came and said, "Did you hear that?" I said, "Coyotes!" He replied, "No, a shot. They are coming. You better get up quickly." There were twelve men who came to shivaree us; I was introduced to all of these men. Later Percy asked the hired man, who had said he was familiar in serving liquors, to treat these men. First light wines, then the heavier wines were served. As they went to leave he gave them a quart of brandy to keep them warm going back to Richey. They had quite a time. The sled tipped over several times before they finally reached town, where "feeling good" they decided to have a meeting. They gave us a lovely dining table and chairs as a gift. Later we had a wedding dance.

Our first baby, Janet, was born December 2 that year. There were twin girls born but one died at birth. Several years later George Thomas came to us; this completed our family.

Percy Baldwin was a very busy man when Richey was getting started. He had an interest in the Hub, the first store; he helped build the Farmer's Elevator; he built three or four small houses to rent; he was a vice president of the First National Bank; he was a charter member of Tyre Lodge AM & FM where he was later a worshipful master for one year. He organized the first baseball club in Richey. He was elected to the school board when it was deeply in debt and was there for twelve years; after that was all in the clear, he was instrumental in building a large gymnasium building. During the bad years of the Depression when men stood around on street corners, he organized them to form volleyball teams, in which all became very interested.

On his passing December 1, 1940, Richey lost a good citizen.

Ernest Temple

Sunday, October 4, 1964 – Nineteenth in the Series

One of Dawson County's early pioneers, Charles Temple, has a number of descendants living in the Glendive area. Another old timer, Ira Alling, at the age of eighty-two, wrote a letter to the Temples on October 14, 1942, to establish the date of the Temples' arrival. Mr. Alling's account of his own arrival, his meeting Charles Temple, and subsequent events, follows:

"I arrived in Glendive, Montana, March 5, 1882, on the Northern Pacific R.R. and made acquaintance with a man by name (I have forgotten). We called him the old sailor. After a few days in Glendive, the old sailor and I hired Newman, the livery man, to take us down on this Harpster bottom with all our personal belongings where we pitched a tent and to talk over our future plans.

"While there a fellow by the name of Skippy came along. We was flat broke, and we took him in, and being a smooth, interesting talker, he talked us into having the sailor build us a boat – as he was a good carpenter; and Skippy and I would put it in the Yellowstone River, sail down to the Missouri River, and down as far as Sioux City, Iowa, and from there across to Pleasantville, Iowa, Skippy's home. But the plan was abandoned for we felt if we could get to Bismarck alive, we would take the train, for we came near drowning several times by the rapids we encountered.

"Skippy didn't have a sou*, so I had to dig up for him as well as for myself, and being only twenty years old and never away from home 'til I left it for Glendive, Montana, Skippy's voice and talk was music in my ears. He was to pay me his share when we got to Pleasantville, but as yet I am still waiting for a sou. Now, to go back to Bismarck, we took the train and when we got to the Twin Cities, we ran across Charles Temple and George Turner, and they were on their way to Montana looking also for the pot of gold, and they also were taken by the music of Skippy's talk and threw in with us to go down to Pleasantville, Iowa, buy a little bunch of cattle, drive them out to Glendive, Montana, and start in the cattle business.

"When we got to Pleasantville, Iowa, I soon found out Skippy's finances were 'no good', and there was only one thing to do with him and that was to drop him, which we did – Charles, George, and I. After a few days, we found a little bunch of cattle, also two saddle horses, and a team and covered wagon, and started overland back to Glendive, Montana, which was about 1,000 miles by the way of Pierre, where we crossed the Missouri and took the trail to the Black Hills and around by Spearfish and Fort Mead and across No Man's Land of the Little Missouri, finally striking O'Fallon Creek, which we followed across the Yellowstone and down the Yellowstone to Glendive and Belle Prairie.

"I had gotten acquainted with the Brown family at Belle Prairie and hunted buffalo with them as well as George Turner, but Charles Temple went back East and came out the next spring, which was the spring of 1883."

Charles Temple, merchant, was born in Lowell, Massachusetts in 1848. In 1882, having caught the western fever, he decided to go West to become a stockman. He and his brother-in-law, George Turner, stopped in St. Paul on the way out, and there they met Ira Alling. The three went to Iowa to buy cattle and trailed a small herd of Durham stock from Iowa to Belle Prairie and put them on the range. In the fall they built a log house, and Charles Temple returned by railroad to Massachusetts.

Turner and Alling were joined by Jim Brown and his father. They spent the winter hunting buffalo for their hides and hind quarters. The remainder of the carcasses was left on the ground. Once when Jim and Ira hauled hides and meat to Glendive, they were caught in the grip of a severe snow storm which lasted for several days. They were unable to get back to camp for some time, so the two who had stayed out ran out of food except for coffee. The storm had driven all the game away, and there was no food except the front quarters of the buffalo which had been left lying on the ground. The wolves and coyotes had been feasting on these, but Turner and Brown were forced to salvage some of the meat for their own use until their partners returned with provisions.

Charles Temple sold his Lowell business, and in the spring of 1883 he arrived with his wife and five children. The two youngest children were born after they came to Montana. That same year a school district, No. 2, was organized on Belle Prairie, the second school in Dawson County. Fourteen children attended the first three-month term, taught by Mrs. Laura Crawford, resident of the district.

In 1884 Temple bought cattle on the St. Paul market and shipped them by train to Glendive. That winter was ideal for stockmen, and in the fall of 1886 Temple sold his beef steers, although beef prices had dropped considerably that year. During the summer and fall of 1886 very little rain fell and it was said the grass was in the worst condition since the country had been known to the white man. All hoped for a mild winter, but in November it unleashed its savage worst. Snow fell almost without abating: the mercury dropped down into the bulb of the thermometer and stayed there. Cattlemen were marooned in isolated cabins, sometimes with insufficient supplies, for months. Cattle tried to rustle at first, but as the snow grew deeper and the crust hardened and the cold continued intensely, many gave up and huddled together under cut banks or in the shelter of thickets. The result was a heavy loss of livestock. In the spring of 1887 Temple rounded up the few cattle he had left and sold to Pierre Wibaux. Wibaux had confidence in the range and bought remnants of other outfits also at about twenty dollars per head.

In 1888 the Temple family moved west of Billings, but in 1902 they returned to Glendive with cattle and purchased the railroad land located on Joe's Island, across the river from where Intake now stands. That same year Mr. Temple filed on a homestead on the mainland opposite the island and established his residence there. Three years later Charles Temple died, but his family continued to live on Belle Prairie.

246

Ernest Temple, oldest son of Charles Temple, was eight years old when the family came from Massachusetts to Montana in 1883. The hard winter of 1886-87 had wrought havoc with the family fortune so Ernest early joined the battle line on the economic front. When he was about eighteen, he went to work for the Weaver brothers, who had a horse ranch out by Harts Mountain in Wyoming. First he was to ride all the horses they had 'broke' the year before to make sure they were gentle enough to sell. Next he helped round up their horses, which ranged all the way from Harts Mountain to Pryor Mountain, a distance of about fifty miles. Two riders worked together. When they went outside the limit of the range, each selected three horses. The first two they left in the corral at camp; next they picketed one horse for each about twenty miles from the starting point; then they rode on to their farthest point on their third horse and began rounding up horses. When they had them gathered, they started toward the corral at Harts Mountain with them.

The range bunch was wild and fresh and traveled fast so at first it was hard for the riders to keep them in sight. The horses they were riding had traveled perhaps forty miles and were tired. When they reached the picketed horses, each saddled a fresh mount and turned their tired horses loose on the range. The horses stationed at the corral were used in case the wild horses ran past the corral. As a general rule they were quieted down by the time they reached the camp, and the horses tied in the corral were not needed. This was one day's work and, according to Mr. Temple, the hardest riding he ever did. "This kind of work," he added, "was what made me bowlegged."

In 1898 gold was discovered in the Klondike, and Ernest joined the stampede north, one of the ten thousand that reached Dawson City that year. During his six years in the Klondike his experiences were many and varied and sometimes rough. Just crossing Chilkoot Pass to get into the area was in itself a formidable obstacle. Steps had been cut into the side of the mountain to make it accessible, but carrying a year's provisions (the minimum amount to take in) up the steep trail was a Herculean task. Temple and his partner surmounted this first hurdle by hoisting their stuff over the hump with a block and tackle.

Another man joined them later, making three. They traveled on foot, dragging their provisions (about 4,000 pounds) on sleds. In about two weeks they reached a river so they camped long enough to build a boat. For the boat they cut down pine trees and sawed them into lumber. They had brought tools and caulking with them. When the boat was finished they started down the river to Lake Linderman. The lake was frozen over so they put the boat on four sleds and dragged it across. By the time they had crossed two more lakes, the boat had to be repitched before entering the second river, which took them to Dawson City.

Their only means of transportation was by dog team or their own two feet. Many had teams of six or more dogs, but Temple just had two dogs which he used to haul provisions the forty miles from Dawson City to his claim. Once, while out on his claim, he got a throbbing toothache that sent him to Dawson City on the trot. By the time he reached the dentist the tooth (as is the way of teeth) had quit aching, but he was taking no chances. The tooth came out.

Hardship and tragedy were the lot for many who battled the elements of the North in their quest for gold. Mr. Temple related the experience of a young man who had stopped at their cabin. This young fellow and his father had been on their way into the Klondike but had realized they couldn't make it before the severe weather caught them (temperatures dropped to seventy degrees below zero while Temple was there) so they built a cabin of logs and prepared to spend the winter. They had food with them but not the vital vitamins. The father contracted scurvy and died. Cut off from all the world outside, the son had to spend the rest of the winter in the cabin with the dead body of his father until spring brought release, and he could come on in.

The gold was mined by the placer method. Some of the veins were as much as seventy feet under ground. During the winter the ore was hoisted to the surface with a windlass* and piled in heaps; then when the creeks thawed in the spring, the gold was washed.

In 1904 Ernest came back to Montana and bought a homestead on lower Belle Prairie. He went into the cattle business, and as time went on he bought and leased other land also. About this time his father had built a two-story house on the mainland and moved over there, but the log house was still on the island so Ernest and his brother Charlie wintered there, caring for the cattle.

During the spring breakup, the ice jammed in the bayou* and the thousand-acre island was flooded. Huge ice cakes were tossed onto the island, and the brothers hurried to get the cattle into the corral. As the water continued to rise and an ice chunk struck the house, the men decided they'd better let the cattle go, and took to the big cottonwood trees. They grabbed 'bachelor's biscuits'* (no telling how long their tree sojourn might last), and Charlie, already up a tree, shouted to Ernest, "Hurry up or you'll never make it!" He did make it, though, and for the next six hours they watched the flood from the vantage of the treetops; then the jam broke and the water began to recede. During the crest of the flood, water was belly-deep to the cattle, but all survived except one cow and her calf that refused to be corralled.

In 1909 Ernest married the district school teacher, Bessie Shong. They have one daughter, Irma, who is married to Bill Adams and lives in Glendive. The Temples lived on Belle Prairie until their retirement in 1944, when they sold their ranch and moved to Glendive. They have made their home here since.

Anna (Caldwell) Stiefvater

Sunday, October 18, 1964 – Twentieth in the Series

Many of Montana's early settlers, from many parts of the globe, chose Montana for their future home after careful consideration of the opportunities offered – not the least of which was free land. Others were brought by circumstances and stayed for the same reason: free land. Andy Caldwell was one of the latter.

Andy, from Salina, Kansas, planned to go see his aunt in California but decided to visit his Montana uncle, A.F. Kelly, first. He went no farther. His uncle, who owned forty-five sections of land that he had bought at seventy-five cents per acre, persuaded Caldwell to stay and take up a homestead. Caldwell built a little log shack and batched for eleven years. When his shack burned down (he was heating oil for his tractor on the stove when the oil boiled over and set fire to his cabin) he put up a two-story, eight room house. This was just about the time he went to Chicago with a shipment of cattle.

Some of his neighbors in Montana asked him to look up some Chicago friends while he was there. The friends were an old couple so they, in turn, asked a young friend of theirs to show him around Chicago. She did and that's how he met his bride-to-be. When he told her he was building an eight-room house and owned 320 acres of land, she thought he owned half the world.

Anna was born and reared in Chicago where she had never had so much as a back yard in which to play. Her only contact with farm life came when she was twelve years old. Their church sent her and her sister to a farm in Decatur, Illinois for a two-week vacation. It was then and there that she decided that some day she would like to live on a farm where she could have all the fresh milk, cream and eggs she wanted.

She worked in the sweatshops of Chicago: forty-eight hours for $1.16 – two-and-a-half cents per hour. After five months, when she asked for a raise, she was paid $1.25. Then the child labor law came into effect and all this was abolished. She worked on the twenty-first floor of the building with 500 employees on every floor. She figures that after she came to Montana she didn't see 500 people in the twenty-one years she lived on the ranch.

After walking seven miles a day to and from work for ten years, walking after a breaking plow* was a pleasure to her. Just to be out in the fresh air and sunshine was heavenly. And to have an eight-room house just for herself and her husband after living in a tenement building that housed twenty-three families was more than she ever hoped to have. Little wonder, she says, that she was known as the singing farmer from Chicago. Through the years she has done considerable singing at weddings, funerals, public functions, and in the church choir.

Mrs. Stiefvater feels, as she recalls her introduction to Montana, that the experiences of the 'green' farmers when they come to a large city are dwarfed by the misadventures of the city green horn that comes to the farm. When she came, she knew nothing about cooking or about building a fire in a cook stove. She couldn't even keep a fire going after her husband started it for her. She surmises that if he hadn't known how to cook, they'd have both starved to death. But cooking for as many as twenty-four men at a time when he ran the cook car for a threshing crew had given him plenty of experience so they didn't starve.

Since they lived forty-five miles from Glendive and had to make the trip in a lumber wagon, they came in only two or three times a year. Buying 1,000 pounds of flour, 200 pounds of sugar, twenty pounds of coffee, and a barrel of kerosene at one time was quite different from her Chicago shopping habits where she bought perhaps five cents worth of butter (at thirty-five cents a pound), three cents worth of sweet cream, two eggs, one bar of laundry soap, one pound of sugar, and ten cents worth of soup meat.

She had never made nor even seen a garden and didn't know radishes from cucumbers. When her neighbor was having threshers and asked Anna to dig some potatoes, she couldn't find any. She looked high and low, pulled up a beet and a turnip, looked in the plum trees and in the gooseberry bushes but still no potatoes. She went back to the house and told the neighbor there were no potatoes left. "Why," exclaimed the neighbor, "we have a whole acre of potatoes." Back to the garden they went together and the neighbor, seizing a hoe, began chopping off the tops (Anna thought she was angry with her for not bringing the potatoes so she was chopping down the pretty flowers). Then she took a spade, dug down, turned the ground over and lo and behold, there were the potatoes. Anna told her, "No wonder I couldn't find them way down deep in the ground like that!"

When her husband took a load of grain to town after her garden was growing, he told her that if she got lonesome while he was gone, she could go down to the garden and do a little hoeing. After he was gone, she went down to hoe. She'd raise the hoe high over her head, then come down with all her might and main, chopping and whacking at everything. A neighbor happened by and stopped to watch. Finally he asked what she was doing and when she told him she was hoeing, he burst out laughing. He said he thought she was killing gophers. He then showed her how to hoe and also pointed out that she was chopping out the cucumbers that were coming up. She demanded that he show her a cucumber and when he pointed to a little plant she told him she thought he was crazy. She thought the cucumbers came up out of the ground and were ready to slice and eat right away. He explained that they had to vine first and then blossom before the cucumbers started to form. By then she was sure he was crazy and he thought she was.

The first time she tried to wash clothes, the water would not suds and she was dismayed to see how yellow the clothes were. When she related her woes to a neighbor, Mrs. Hubing pointed out that she had to break the hard water. Anna had never heard of breaking water so she concluded this neighbor was crazy too, and let it go at that.

While out riding in July, she saw some fields of shocked grain and asked a man what farmers raised that grew in bunches like that. When he replied, "Lady, that's what you make your bread with," she thought, "Another crazy man!"

Her husband had only a few hens so she decided to raise a lot of chickens and have fried chicken every day. Another neighbor asked her if she had ever set a hen and when she answered that all she knew about chickens was that you bought them at the butchers, he decided to have some fun at her expense. He told her that she had to have a cluck to set. She didn't know what that was so he explained that it's a hen that wants to set: "She makes a clucking noise; you give her a batch of eggs, put a rock on her back, and that was all there was to it."

Hardly had he got the gate closed when she started for the Schmidt boys' place to get all the eggs they could spare – fifteen dozen. She waited impatiently for dark so the hens would go to roost and she could get those clucks to set them.

When the hens were finally on the roosts, she hurried to the chicken house and gave each hen a poke. If she made a noise, she was a cluck. Of course, they all made a noise so she got busy gathering boxes and baskets, set all fifteen dozen eggs, put a rock on each hen's back (their place had a lot of shale rock), and eagerly waited for morning. She thought those eggs would hatch overnight so at four o'clock in the morning she was out of bed and down to the chicken house. As soon as she opened the door, out came all the hens. The rocks had slipped off and mashed all the eggs so all she could do was stand and cry. When her neighbor came over later in the day, she would hardly speak to him. Finally she told him what she thought of him and showed him the mashed eggs, but he thought it was a joke. He told her the hens had to cover the eggs and keep them warm for twenty-one days before they'd hatch, then went off to tell the other neighbors what a joke he had played on her.

An old bachelor heard about her experience setting hens and felt sorry for her so he brought her a hen with thirteen little chicks. She recalls that she was tickled with the present but not for long. She walked after that old hen and her chicks all day in the hot sun. When a chick would get caught in a weed or something, she'd try to pick it up to free it and the old hen would fly at her and she'd throw a stick at the hen and so it went all day. She explains that she didn't have enough sense to give them water. The poor things were so hungry they yipped and made such a racket that she gathered them up in the evening and gave them back, explaining that she couldn't walk after them all day in the hot sun. She chuckles that "he couldn't believe anyone could be so dumb." He advised her to take the chicks home, put them in the hen house overnight, next morning give them a pan of water and some wheat, then go in the house and stay there! So began the chicken raising. But she was willing to learn and bound to show that 'where there's a will, there's a way'.

Learn she did until she was able to plow with a sulky plow* with three horses, stack hay, shock grain, mow grass, milk cows, raise chickens, and make gardens along with the hundred and one other things that went with farming in those days. She even helped her husband break broncs – she held on to the trip rope. She also learned how to break hard water with lye and wait for rainwater, although if you waited for rain you were out of luck because it only rained twice a year.

In 1938, they left the farm and moved into Glendive. When you get hailed out three years in succession, dried out, stripped by armyworms two years and by grasshoppers two years, what else, she asks, can you do? Mr. Caldwell died in 1957, but the children (six) are all living and all have a good education. She has a lovely home – a piano, something she'd wanted all her life – a modern car, so she can look back and wonder how she stood all the hard work. In spite of it all, she learned to like the wide open spaces and asserts that she would not go back to live in Chicago if they gave her the entire city with a fence around it.

J.F. (Frank) Miskimen

Sunday, October 25, 1964 – Twenty-first in the Series

Glendive's first mayor, J.H. Miskimen, arrived in Glendive thirteen years before the Gate City's incorporation. He came as a brakeman on the railroad, but his uncle C.F. Little, had a jewelry store and in a few years, Mr. Miskimen took over the store and quit the railroad. He was an optometrist too, and over the years he also sold real estate and insurance besides being a photographer and merchant.

In addition to his many and varied personal interests, he found time to be very active in civic affairs. He was appointed postmaster in 1898 and dispensed the mail from his jewelry store, located where Woolworth's* now stands. His son Frank still has the deeds showing the purchase that same year, of those two lots at $200 each from the railroad.

In 1902, Glendivians decided they were ready to be recognized as a city. In order to incorporate, they had to show a certain minimum population and Frank recalls the story his father used to tell that even the dogs and cats were listed as residents to make the required number! However, the number was met and Glendive was incorporated that year, and J.H. Miskimen was elected the first mayor for a two-year term. During this first term, city government was organized and a plan of financing put into effect.

Files of Dawson County Review of April 5, 1907:

A large majority chose J.H. Miskimen, independent candidate for mayor, running on a ticket by his lonesome in last Monday's election, mayor of Glendive. Considering the circumstances it was certainly a victory in every sense of the word. It was the first ward that stood by Miskimen. In fact, it was admitted by his supporters that they let the 'bloody second' entirely alone having conceded to Foster from the start. The effect of their work was seen however, in the first, which gave the gentleman with the feminine prefix to his name, a majority of fifty-one over his opponent. Foster carried the second by only twenty-nine, which made Miskimen's majority in the city twenty-two.

E.C. Leonard made no canvass for office of police magistrate. He did not want the office and freely said so. This being generally understood, it is not surprising that Burdick's majority was eighty-nine. There was no contest for the office of city treasurer, which was handed to C.A. Banker on a silver platter. W.F. Jordan and J.C. Taylor were likewise elected to succeed themselves as aldermen of the first and second district wards, respectively. Taken all in all, it was rather a warm little election with a large percentage of the registration realized in votes.

During this period a good deal of sidewalk building was done and the waterworks plant was installed. Mr. Miskimen was one of the organizers of the First National Bank and was captain of the 'Militia Company I' stationed here.

In 1898 J.H. Miskimen married Miss Nellie Miller who was born in Detroit, Michigan. She made the trip to Montana as an infant in 1876. Her mother brought her and her two small sisters by stagecoach to the Yellowstone River, then up the river by steamer to join her father in Miles City. Daughter Lillian was born there. Nellie's father, who worked as a civilian in Fort Keogh, deserted the family, leaving Mrs. Miller alone with four small children. In 1887 W.F. Jordan brought Mrs. Miller to Glendive to be cook and manager at the Yellowstone Hotel, and the following year he married her. Mr. Jordan had come to Montana in 1884 via the Chisholm Trail. Frank greatly admired him and recalls that as a boy he liked to hide in the back of the buggy when Jordan was going hunting (chickens were plentiful just out of town along Dry Creek in those days) so that he could go along and 'play dog' – retrieve birds.

Following is a reprint from Aug. 27, 1954, Daily Ranger, describing Mr. Jordan's immigration to Montana. Mr. Jordan has passed away since this interview.

Files of Dawson County Review of Aug. 27, 1964:

Making a trek from Texas to Montana over the old Chisholm Trail was right considerable of a chore even in those days but William F. (Billy) Jordan, 93, who, with Mrs. Jordan, is living this summer in a cabin on Lakewood Drive, Kenilworth, chuckles as he recalls incidents of that trip.

Jordan says he was just a plain cowboy in Texas and furthermore he was a little depressed by all the poverty he saw around him. While he had no trouble holding down a cow-punching job, he was determined to seek greener fields.

"I was brought up in northeast Texas but when I was grown I went out to West Texas to work with cattle," he says. "It was rugged work in those days and I could not see much future in that life. So, when a man from Montana bought 3,000 head of cattle to be delivered to him in Montana and I was offered a job to join in the trail party, I took it."

He explained that the so-called Chisholm Trail was really not a trail but a name given to the operation of driving cattle north from Texas to Dodge City, Kansas.

"The route that each herd took had to be different because settlers were pouring into the country and a good watering place one year might not be accessible the next year," he says. "The only practical way to operate was to keep a scout out about twenty-four hours ahead of the herd and in that way know exactly where the next stop would be and how far it was from the last watering place."

It was the water, of course, that was the guiding factor in moving the cattle north and no move that would take the cattle away from water was made until the next watering place was spotted and found usable.

"The usual pace was about ten to fifteen miles a day for the herd, depending on the distances between watering spots, but in some cases a trek of forty miles was made simply because there was no water between those two points," he said.

This naturally was a terrible strain on the men in charge of the cattle and on the cattle themselves. They became spooky and hard to handle, being upset by as little a thing as the sudden appearance of a jackrabbit.

It was in 1884 that he joined the party of lean, hard-muscled idlers who were to take the 3,000 head of cattle north. That was on the Colorado River about sixty miles south of Abilene, Texas.

One of his jobs was riding ahead of the herd as the advance scout who spotted water and reported every night to the trail boss so that he would know how to keep cattle moving.

On the days when one of those fifty-mile hops was ahead, it was the custom to start the herd moving about noon, drive on during the afternoon and well into the night. The second start was made about three o'clock in the morning and the animals were moved on in this fashion until the water was reached.

These long jumps were avoided where it was at all possible but unfortunately, it was not always possible. The destination was Powder River, which runs into the Yellowstone. This was open range and the Texas cattle did well.

One of the men who had bought the herd took a fancy to Jordan and promised to help get him started on his own ranch. This was really what he was aiming for and so when the chance came, he had saved his money instead of blowing it and he took it and soon was heading his own outfit.

He became acquainted with the markets in Chicago and was a personal friend of Eddie Swift of Swift and Company. His interests also included banking and he served as director for some twenty-six years.

"I never worked in the bank," he said with a smile. "I stuck to cattle but I did serve on the board of directors."

Frank's aunt Lillian married Ira Bendon and it was on their Bar M Ranch that Frank, from the time he was six years old, spent all his vacations – even Christmas – and any other time he could. The Bendons also were early comers to Montana.

Ira's father, N.J. Bendon, built St. Matthews Episcopal Church in 1893 at a cost of $1,860. This building originally stood where the KXGN studios* are now located and was later moved to its present site. Members of the Church had started a building fund earlier and by the time it was completed, it was debt-free. An item in the history of the church noted that an entertainment, with proceeds to go to the building fund, was held in Miskimen Hall – the town's only entertainment hall, located where the Coast to Coast store* is.

The Bar M Ranch was located on Burns Creek, middle fork, and Mr. Miskimen is still having a hard time convincing his wife that when he was eight years old, he was allowed to ride his pony out to the ranch alone. On the way out he would stop at the Griff Ranch on Morgan Creek, next to Chet Murphy's, then on to Bendon's.

His Aunt Dott had given him his first pony. Her father, Mr. Jordan, had led the pony up to her room where, as a child, she lay sick in the Jordan Hotel. When she outgrew the pony, she gave him to Frank. This pony came to a sad ending when he was killed and eaten by wolves. His father then bought him another, an Indian pony called Shiwah.

At this time Bendon was running sheep and one of Frank's 'jobs' was to pick the wool off the winterkilled sheep in the spring. One spring when several wagonloads of Indians came through, they asked Mr. Bendon for some wool so he told them they could have the wool from the heads. After they had gone on, he sent Frank to see what they had taken. When Frank came back with the report that they had taken all the wool, Mr. Bendon grabbed his 30-30 rifle, jumped on his horse, and took after them at a gallop. Frank, of course, trailed after him and watched as his uncle repossessed the wool – from the heads and all.

Frank didn't need TV when he was a boy. The real, live cowboys and Indians were far more fascinating. One of his favorite riders, Mr. Miskimen mentioned, was 'Jimmy Hicks'. Frank's own greatest ambition was to be a cowboy so one day the ranch hands saddled a 'barnyard yearling' for him to break but the horse wouldn't even buck. Then 'Jimmy' saddled and mounted a 'Yakima' – one of a tough breed that horse traders would buy from the Yakima Indians, then peddle about the country. There was no problem getting this horse to buck, and Frank watched with admiration as Jimmy rode the Yakima, its nose bleeding, to a standstill. ('Jimmy Hicks' was the nickname Ira Bendon gave to Menno Mullet, this writer's father.)

Mr. Miskimen, Sr., took pictures of Frank, dressed in his 'cowboy outfit' on Shiwah, put them on post cards and sold them in his store. He also took pictures of the badland formations for the same purpose. Frank took a lot of razzing from his contemporaries about his cowboy pictures but the pictures sold!

J.H. Miskimen passed away in 1940; Frank and his wife still live in the Miskimen house on Towne Street. They have many old papers, clippings, deeds, and so forth, of interest to any who want to know about yesteryear.

A. O. Skillestad

Sunday, November 1, 1964 – Twenty-second in the Series

Union's first post office has been outlived by its first postmaster. A.O. Skillestad, appointed May 4, 1909 by President Taft, used his homestead shack for the post office.

Mail was delivered to the post office once a week by the carrier who had contracted to take the mail from Glendive to Circle. At the time the Union Post Office was initiated, Pete Rorvik had the Glendive-Circle contract, but he had another man hired to do the hauling for him. When Rorvik passed along the word to his driver that a stop must now be made at Union, the driver informed him that he'd have to do his driving himself.

Winter had shortened the days by the time the Circle carrier had received orders to deliver the mail to Union (prior to this the mail had been left at a point on the Circle road, north of Union), and Rorvik didn't know just where Union was so he spent most of the day driving around in the hills, trying to find it. Finally, after darkness had descended, he saw a light so he drove for the light (no fences to hinder in those days). When he reached the homesteader's shack, he asked for directions to the Union Post Office and was relieved to be informed by Mr. Skillestad that "this is it." Mr. Skillestad expressed regret that the mail carrier had had to spend so much time trying to find him, to which Rorvik retorted, "That didn't help much when I was driving around out in those hills!"

Later, when the Helland brothers contracted for the route, they kept one team of horses at Skillestad's place. They would drive to his place the first day, stay overnight, change teams, and go on to Circle the next day. That night they would stay in Circle, then reverse the procedure to get back to Glendive. Mr. Skillestad was authorized to sell money orders, and in 1912, the parcel post service was instigated. He got the scales, but before he had any actual business, the post office location was changed. A.A. Olson had started a store about five miles down the creek so, for the sake of convenience, the post office was moved to the store.

A.O. Skillestad was born near Kenyon, Minnesota. Both his parents had died by the time he was eighteen months old so he was raised in a foster home. This same family also provided a home for a girl who, of course, was like a sister to him. After they were both grown and she had located in Sisseton, South Dakota, he went to visit her. There he met 'the' girl, Grace Aldrich, so they married and settled down in Sisseton. Eastern South Dakota had been homestead country too, but dry years had come, and many of the homesteaders had given up. One fellow had traded his 160-acre homestead for a team and buggy so he could leave the country.

Mrs. Skillestad's aunt was married to Charles Stafford, inspector of the immigrant cars going through Fargo, North Dakota, on the Northern Pacific. As he inspected the cars of O.U. Cress and Andy Miller, homesteaders headed

257

for their claims in Eastern Montana, he became interested and decided to go take a look for himself. He not only took a look, he took a homestead, then wrote to the Skillestads back in Sisseton and suggested they come look it over, too. They didn't waste time or money coming out to look; they just moved to Glendive.

As soon as he had the opportunity, Mr. Skillestad caught a ride with a neighbor out to the Union country (the area where Stafford had filed and where Cress and Miller were located), stayed overnight with Miller, then walked (about thirty-four miles) back to Glendive the next day and filed on the quarter adjoining Stafford's. He bought the lumber for a 14'x16' shack, and Cress hauled it out for him. They got his shack built, then Stafford stayed with them while they built his shack.

Those first years they didn't do much farming because they had no machinery and no horses. He finally bought a couple saddle horses which he broke to work, also. A little later he and Stafford, working together, broke horses for surrounding ranchers in exchange for the use of those horses. This way they didn't have to buy any.

Skillestad didn't homestead until 1908. He was one of the first homesteaders to locate in the Union country, but there were a number of ranchers who had been there many years. Range horses, unhampered by fences, would often come up close to the house, seeking a little shelter from the elements. Not always of the best temper, they sometimes would get to kicking and kick the walls of the house.

In those early years when they had to freight to Glendive with the team and wagon, they took three days for the trip. Little wonder his wife didn't come to town for three years after they moved to the homestead! In May 1919 he bought a Ford truck (solid tires on the back) so then they could make the trip in one day.

The two oldest of the Skillestads' four boys were born in the homestead shack. The 14'x16' main building had a 10'x16' sod room on the backside, a coal shed on the front. The Skillestads lived on the homestead until 1934, when dry years and twenty-four-cents-per-bushel wheat drove them to Glendive. Mr. Skillestad soon went to work for contractor A.J. Rockne, then in 1937 he began work as janitor in the courthouse. Mrs. Skillestad passed away in 1961, but Mr. Skillestad still figures in the Glendive census.

Mrs. Billy (Retina Deaux) Rust

Sunday, November 8, 1964 – Twenty-third in the Series

As lively as Mrs. Rust is, one would hardly suppose her life had not always been one of ease. Perhaps she is evidence that people can thrive on adversity. Certainly life on a Montana ranch in the early 1900's was not easy!

Mrs. Rust came as a bride to Montana in March, 1904, and was welcomed with two feet of snow. That required some adjustment for a native of Tennessee. They had stopped in Chicago enroute to Montana, and she had done her summer shopping, but the new hat and its accompaniments, greeted by Montana's March, were subjected to the first of the adjustments.

Mr. Rust had first come to Montana in 1891. His parents died when he was just a boy, and his grandfather had raised him. One of his sisters and her husband were working on the Lindsay Ranch on East Redwater, and in response to their urging, when he was about nineteen, he came to visit.

The Great Northern Railroad brought him as far as Poplar, then he was to cross the river and contact some people, with whom his sister had made arrangements, to take him to the Lindsay Ranch. Crossing the river proved to be quite an obstacle. There was no bridge, and with the Missouri overflowing its banks during the June rise, it was hardly inviting for even an experienced boatman.

For a youngster who had never rowed a boat it was indeed formidable – especially when he was given a boat with just one oar for the crossing. He rowed first on one side of the boat, then on the other, but in spite of all his efforts he was carried downstream some distance by the strong current before he was able to get to the other side. Then he was faced with the task of dragging the boat, wading through the water among the willows, to get back opposite his starting point. There he tied the boat to a tree as he had been instructed, and started walking toward the ranch where he was supposed to find his transportation.

When he reached the place, dogs greeted him before anyone else did. Back in Tennessee, dogs were liable to be mean so he was taking no chances. He shinnied up a corral post and sat on the top rail, hoping the dogs would get bored and go away. After a considerable wait he braved the dogs, got to the house, and knocked. These folks then took him the fifteen miles to the Lindsay Ranch. In the years that followed he, too, worked on the Lindsay Ranch, also helping on the roundup.

He had never cooked in his life, but one day he decided to try and chose rice for a starter. He didn't let it get quite done, but he was so hungry he ate it anyway. He ate a generous portion, and before long he began to get such cramps he thought he was going to die!

After a few years, he decided to take up a claim on Sullivan Creek (about a mile from where the Paxton Post Office was later located) and run some sheep. In 1903, he sold his place to John Paxton and went back to Tennessee for the

259

winter to visit. While there he became acquainted with Miss Retina Deaux. They were married in February, 1904, and he brought his bride to Montana in the spring.

They came on the Great Northern to Buford, North Dakota, where a friend met them and took them to Fairview, crossing the frozen Yellowstone with a sled. They worked around Fairview until July, then went back to work for Lindsay, this time in the area where the present town of Lindsay stands.

They lived in a sheep wagon, moving around from place to place as they put up hay. She made her first visit to Glendive during Fair time, about September 22-24. They spent that winter at Lindsay's winter ranch on East Redwater, about twelve miles from the HS Ranch.

The following April Mrs. Rust came to Glendive to await the arrival of their first baby (a girl) in May, then back to the Lindsay ranch (near the town of Lindsay) again. The next spring they decided to locate on a claim for themselves and chose a site near a spring on Hay Creek where George Haggerty now lives.

In April they moved into a couple tents, planning to camp in them until they could arrange a more permanent dwelling. They were expecting their second baby in June, but the baby decided, instead, to come the day after they moved into the tents. Their nearest neighbors were the Gibsons, four miles across the divide*, so Mr. Rust decided their best course was to get Mrs. Gibson. When Mrs. Gibson arrived, she suggested taking Mrs. Rust over to the Garfields, about six team-and-buggy-miles away, but Mrs. Rust didn't think she could make it, so their first son was born in the tent with his father for the doctor and Mrs. Gibson giving directions.

They continued to live in the tent, and when the baby was three weeks old, Mr. Rust thought he could leave them long enough to come to town to get lumber for a house and a hired man to help build it. Rain poured down all the time he was gone (it wasn't just a few hours' trip to Glendive!) and after a day or two the tent started to leak; the wind blew the stove pipe off the cook stove so she couldn't have fire; and then the bed started getting wet. The downpour finally slowed to a drizzle, but Mrs. Rust realized she couldn't keep a three-week-old baby in a tent where everything was wet and she could have no fire. Yet she had no way to go any place except – walk. And the nearest neighbors were four miles away. So she walked.

She fashioned a kind of sling out of a wool blanket, put the baby in it, hung it around her neck with the baby on her back, picked up the little girl in her arms, and started for the Gibsons. She started at five o'clock in the morning and reached Gibsons at eleven. Mr. Gibson had gone out to picket his horse and saw something coming in the distance. At first he thought it was just a cow and started on back to the house. He didn't feel quite satisfied, though, so he went back for another look and began to comprehend the situation. He hurried to meet her, wading across the creek to take the children from her and carry them to the house. Then he came back and carried her across, too.

She protested that it wasn't necessary because she was already soaked to the skin and muddy all over, but he carried her across anyway. She was chilled, but

260

the Gibsons put her to bed, gave her some 'home remedies' to prevent complications, and she didn't even catch a cold. The little girl had begun to get a bit chilly, but the baby was snug and dry in his 'sling', and none of them suffered any ill effects from their experience. Mr. Rust wouldn't take her back to the tent, so they lived in Gibson's bunkhouse until the Fourth of July. The bunkhouse had a dirt roof and they had rain about every other day, so even there it was rather damp. They managed, though, and soon Mr. Rust had a dugout ready for them to move into. There it was dry!

They lived in the dugout for about two-and-one-half years. During this time Mr. Rust was getting lumber ready to build a log house. He'd go up to the divide and cut cedar logs, drag them over to a bank, park his wagon next to the bank, and roll the logs onto it to load them. He built a two-room house which they moved into about the middle of January, 1909. Just about the time they moved in a cold spell struck, and they thought they would freeze in the house after being accustomed to the dugout. They lived in the little house for several years, then built an addition to it.

They hadn't given any thought to homesteading, but one day in 1908 as they drove over to the Lindsay place they saw a new house going up. Inquiry revealed that Henry Green was the builder and that he had filed on a homestead. Green and John Harrison were the first homesteaders the Rusts knew about.

It wasn't until 1910 that the Rusts themselves decided to homestead. At that time they could only file on 160 acres. Since their buildings were on one quarter and all their farmland was on the other quarter, a choice would be hard to make. They took the matter to Leiper, Glendive lawyer, and he obtained a settlement in their favor, but it cost them $150. Later, they leased the other half of the section for pasture and fenced the whole section.

Mrs. Rust reflected that during the depression years the going was rough, and she sometimes felt it wouldn't take much of an inducement to get them to leave the farm. But they weathered the depression and stayed with the homestead until January of 1943 when they moved to Glendive because of her husband's poor health. Five weeks after they moved, Mr. Rust passed away. After he was gone her sister back in Kentucky thought Mrs. Rust might return to the South, but she concludes she's been in the West too long; she doesn't think she could like it back there now.

Felix Andorno

Sunday, November 15, 1964 – Twenty-fourth in the Series

Twenty-one year old Felix Andorno, recently emigrated from Italy, felt that life in a strange land with a strange language left much to be desired. He smiles now as he reports his resolve that when he got the money, he would go back to Italy, but then he adds that by the time he got his money, he didn't want to go back.

An uncle had preceded him to the United States, and it was as a result of his urging that Felix found himself in Montana in 1906. His uncle had told Bill Graves, Burns Creek rancher, that Felix was coming so a job with Graves was waiting for him when he arrived. In the years that followed he worked for various ranchers in the area – after Graves it was Ira Bendon, then Davison; when Davison sold to Kalberg, he worked for Kalberg, then Chet Murphy.

After about a year in Montana he filed on a homestead six miles northwest of Intake. He built a log shack in the coulee near the spring, and there he 'batched' when he wasn't working out. He recalls that in the spring of 1908 when he was working for one of the ranchers, a blizzard late in May caused a heavy loss of livestock. Many of the cattle huddled along a creek bank, and the snow drifted over them. When the storm cleared enough for him to get them, he found one of the cows had fallen in the creek. He uncovered her, then pushed and lifted her to her feet. In return she promptly charged him, but she had more spirit than strength, evidently, for she fell and died right there.

About 1910 he started farming. All his field work then, of course, was done with horses. On one occasion, when he had four horses hitched to a disc, the horses decided they were tired of the routine and took off on a run. There wouldn't be much left of the man who fell in front of those discs so while he still had a choice, Andorno jumped off behind the disc and let them run.

Late in 1912 he went back to Italy but not to stay. Instead he married the girl he'd left behind when he came to the New World and brought her back with him. He was married to Maria Delbene on February 1, 1913, and on March 19 of that year they left Italy together to make their new home in the western hemisphere.

Mrs. Andorno recalls her first stop at the little depot where they had coffee when they reached Glendive by way of the Northern Pacific Railroad. They transferred to the Sidney branch line and continued by train as far as Intake, where a neighbor, George Ladwig, met them to take them to their home.

In 1910 Mr. Andorno had replaced the little log shack in the coulee with a new house of sawed lumber on Murphy Table, and it was to this house he brought his new bride. By this time the English language was familiar to Mr. Andorno, but to Mrs. Andorno, as she listened to the chatter of a couple women on the train enroute to Intake, it sounded hopeless. She made up her mind, however, that she was going to learn the language of her adopted country.

Homesick though she found herself in the months that followed (no telephone, no women neighbors), she resolutely determined to read no Italian papers and concentrated on learning to read English. After they did get telephones, sometimes some of the women who had come from San Genuaria, Andorno's Italian hometown, would talk together on the party line, visiting in Italian. They decided, though, that this was not right. For emergency, yes, Italian should be used, but for just visiting they should use the English, even though it did not come so freely. In the course of time she learned to understand and make herself understood in her new tongue.

They had been in the Treasure State* a little more than a year when their only child, a daughter was born. Mrs. Maschera, who was there with Mrs. Andorno, felt they should have a doctor so Mr. Andorno rode horseback to Intake where there was a telephone and called for Dr. Danskin to come out. Dr. Danskin rented a car and was able to reach the homestead in a comparatively short time to deliver the baby.

Mrs. Andorno found life in the sparsely settled area much less lonely after the arrival of her little girl and learned to dearly love her new homeland. Then, too, the very day her baby was born she could see from her window the telephone pole being set in their yard, linking them to a neighborhood telephone line which helped her keep more in touch with other women in the area.

Life was by no means easy on the farm with years of drought and low grain prices. One year the stand of grain looked so promising that Mr. Andorno and a neighbor together bought a used combine to harvest their crops. The next day hordes of grasshoppers flew in, in clouds that covered the sun. When the hoppers left, the fields were stripped and there was no grain left to harvest.

During the depression, families left the area one by one. There had been as many as twenty-one families living on Murphy Table; now there are four. It was not until 1944 that a good crop and a good price combined to enable the Andornos to pay a sizable amount on the principal of their payment for land bought years before, although they had paid more than the amount of the principal in interest over the years. Another good crop the next year cleared the debts that had hung over them during the hard years. Surely many of our Montana homesteaders deserve tribute for waging and winning their own private 'war on poverty'. In 1952 Mr. and Mrs. Andorno went back to Italy but only for a visit; Montana is where they choose to be. They prefer the country, but as age creeps up, it seems unwise to be isolated to that extent, so in 1955 they bought a house in Glendive and moved to town.

Osmund Vashus

Thursday, November 26, 1964 – Twenty-fifth in the Series

"And it cost us each $8 a month to live." Before you start packing to head for this Utopia, we'll have to disillusion you. There are no tickets available to take you back to 1904.

Soon after Osmund Vashus arrived from Norway in May of 1903, he went to work for the Northern Pacific Railroad. However, the second winter work was scarce so the B. & B. gang* with which he worked was laid off until spring. He and Louie Thompson together bought a three-room shack, complete with beds, for the sum of $25, and there they spent the winter.

The shack was built right into the bank below the present Minot Sand and Gravel Cement Plant at the south end of Merrill Avenue – some distance from town. Most of the time there were at least two other fellows with them and sometimes more. At different times some of their friends would be laid off, and they would move in with them, too. They didn't have to buy wood or coal because they were close to the railroad track and could pick up all the coal they needed right along the track. They were snug and warm in their shack, but a little lonesome sometimes. And it cost them each $8 a month.

An uncle of Osmund Vashus had come to the United States so Osmund and two of his third cousins decided they'd try America too. Osmund had attended an English school in Norway, so language didn't pose quite the problem for him that it did for most immigrants. At least he could speak enough English to communicate his basic needs. Glendive was just getting a good beginning when he came. He recalls that the wooden sidewalk in front of the Jordan Hotel was rather tricky; if you got a little too far out toward the edge, the planks would come up and hit you.

Not too long after he came, a man by the name of Keene, who owned a rather large tract of land on the south side (the area is still known as the Keene addition), offered to sell the land to Vashus for about fifty dollars. Vashus didn't have that kind of money so Keene indicated his willingness to accept a small down payment and a little each month, but the practice of installment buying was not so firmly established in the American way of life early in the century as it had become by mid-century, and Vashus couldn't see it.

Another offer he declined was from one of the saloonkeepers to prove up* on a homestead. The liquor dispenser wanted a homestead on Belle Prairie, but didn't want to stay out there, so he offered to build a shack and furnish necessary supplies; then, at the end of the 'proving up' period, pay Vashus $2,000 for the homestead. The offer sounded good, but Osmund couldn't see himself staying out there alone that long so he passed up that opportunity, too.

His first job in Montana was with the section gang on the railroad. They were working on the tracks east of Glendive, but after two weeks he decided he'd had enough. There must be other work in this country, so he quit and walked the ten miles back to town. He says he never saw so many bull snakes in his life as he did on that walk to Glendive. He was soon able to get on with a Northern Pacific B. & B. gang and found that more to his liking.

His first winter here was a severe one, but he had warm clothes to dress for it. They didn't work for the three days when the mercury was down to fifty degrees below zero, though. At the time he was working with the gang that was putting up ice for the N.P. The ice was shipped in from Minnesota and other points, and their job was to store it in the ice houses here (no refrigeration in 1904, you know).

In 1908 he was working with Mike Lacey's gang building water tanks in Miles City when a tornado struck. Vashus jumped down into the stair well and was safe, but the foreman was killed.

After that the gang was laid off so when a Miles City banker offered him a job herding sheep for the winter, he decided to take it. The sheep were ten or fifteen miles out in the country, and he was to trail them to the ranch. Another fellow was to bring the wagon so they conferred, and Osmund pointed out a big hill about five miles distant where he planned to camp with the sheep that night. He started on right away, but the driver lingered to finish some jobs before following. He lingered a little too long.

Osmund, with the sheep, was able to get to the hill in spite of the snowstorm that descended upon them, but the driver was caught too far away. He couldn't find the place and wandered around all night in the blizzard. Vashus, however, got the sheep down into the creek where they were sheltered, and built a fire for himself and his dog. He found an old hollow log so he bedded down in that, close to the fire which he kept going all night. He stayed warm, but declares it was a long night! Once he reached the ranch, everything was fine. There were two or three of them working there, and they had a good time. He worked there about four months, and they lived mostly on antelope.

When spring came, he decided to go back to Norway for a visit. The panic of 1909 had struck, and when he got back to Miles City, he found that the law prohibited withdrawal of more than ten dollars a day from the bank – hardly enough to take him to Norway! However, he still had his last check from the railroad, uncashed, and the check the banker had given him for his winter's wages. He presented these to the bank and asked if the latter was any good. The banker assured him that it was, then finally permitted him to draw from his account so he was able to make the trip (roundtrip!) to Norway.

A visit to his native country was all right, but he no longer cared to live there. He was soon back in Montana, working for awhile for the Milwaukee Railroad out of Miles City, then back to Glendive, working for the N.P. again, this time in the carpenter shop. When their wages were cut, he took a pass and went to Seattle to visit an uncle. There was plenty of work in Seattle, but he wasn't interested in taking it. Then he received a telegram from the N.P., telling him to come back and that, he explains, is why he's here today.

In 1911 he was again laid off from the railroad. He worked on the Hollecker ranch during that interim. The Fourth of July celebration that year featured a special attraction: an airplane had been brought in by train and was to put on an exhibition flight. There was only one drawback – they couldn't get the plane into the air, despite the efforts of many to figure out the mysteries of its workings.

Another 'special feature' of the celebration that year was the beginning of his acquaintance with Miss Carrie Haageusen, recently arrived from Norway. He remarked that he thinks that at that first meeting she was more attracted to his saddle horse than to him! Miss Haageusen visited about a month with Mrs. Sam Berg (they had gone to school together in Norway), then went to Valley City, North Dakota, where she had a sister.

After a few years she came back and worked for Mrs. Berg, who was cooking for her husband's B. & B. gang. Perhaps this was her 'apprenticeship', for in 1917 she married Osmund Vashus. By then he had been promoted from second boss on Berg's gang to foreman, and she cooked for his gang. Mr. Vashus commented that she cooked for him and his gang until son Tollef was born, then he had to hire his cooks!

During this time his gang, which worked from Billings to Mandan, had spent a good deal of time on the Sidney branch. They did all the fencing and siphoning on that stretch of road. The size of his crew varied from thirteen to forty men, and their living quarters consisted of nineteen railroad cars – a cook car, a dining car, two tool cars, and bunk cars.

In 1919 Mr. Vashus quit the railroad and started carpentering, working for various contractors – among them Sterhan, Rockne, and Holmes.

When the flood of 1919 came, they were living on the west side of the river on the place they had bought from Charley Krug. An ice jam caused the water to back up and flood the entire flat. The ground where their house was built was a little higher than the rest of their land. The water came to about two inches below their floor level, but they didn't sit in the house, waiting to see how high the water would come.

A Mr. Pope, who lived on a dairy farm, came to warn them so they were sitting in their car on top of the hill, watching. They saw the huge ice chunks mow down thirty crabapple trees and the current sweep them downstream. They were glad the flood came in the middle of the day, and that the weather was warm. One of their neighbors, on lower ground, was sitting in his attic with the water just below him during the crest of the flood. Several days after the water had receded (it took part of the Sidney track before it did), he found big fish had been marooned on his potato patch. If he had only known! – but by that time they were beginning to smell.

Their only other child, a daughter, Marie, was born while they were living on 'the Krug place'. A year or so after the flood they sold that place and moved to North Dakota for a couple of years. They came back to Glendive in 1923, bought their present residence, and have lived there since. Son Tollef is well known at the First National Bank in Glendive, and daughter Marie (Mrs. Sokolich) lives in Helena.

266

Irvin Bawden

The West was raw and untamed in 1888, a place where a man might be shot for "speaking out of turn," when young John Bawden (father of Irvin Bawden) landed in Montana. A 'greenhorn' newly arrived from civilized Illinois had difficulty discerning just what might be his turn so generally the closed lip seemed most prudent. Even a funeral did not nullify the possibility of lead poisoning.

Soon after John's arrival a young fellow who had been with the Hudson's Bay Company in Canada died of T.B. in Nashua. It was up to the citizens of the town to bury him, but when time came for the funeral, those responsible for the task were all drunk. They stood at the edge of the grave, baffled by the problem of lowering the coffin. To John, a sober onlooker, the solution seemed simple, but to dare venture an opinion was another matter; they might decide he was being presumptuous and take offense. And offense might be fatal to him.

A four-mule government team was standing nearby, and the conclusion that the coffin would just have to be dropped into the grave emboldened him to risk suggesting, "Do you think we might be able to borrow a set of lines from that driver over there?" He breathed a little more freely when his suggestion was accepted with alacrity, and he was delegated to do the borrowing. The driver was willing so the coffin was lowered with the lines, then one of the inebriates jumped down into the grave to tighten the screws on the lid of the roughbox.

Again John watched in silence as a simple task presented seemingly insurmountable difficulty. The screwdriver would not connect with the screw head. Finally, gathering his courage to offer another suggestion, he respectfully asked, "Say, Old Timer, could I maybe help you down there?" Back came the reply, "Pistol," (a term applied to a young fellow) "I believe you could. I'm loaded for a hundred and ten and I can only pack ninety."

John tightened the screws, then the young widow, standing by the graveside, asked if someone would say a prayer. No one spoke. John, relating the incident later, observed that he could at least have repeated the Lord's Prayer, but no one had licensed him to speak so he remained silent, and the bizarre performance ended without even a prayer to comfort the heart of the bereaved. John was shocked by the seeming callousness, yet after the burial they passed the hat and collected enough money to buy the ticket home for the destitute widow. Such was the West.

John Bawden had been brought up in Illinois and married there. After his sister's husband, Dr. Atkinson, was appointed Agency doctor for the Poplar Indian Reservation and came to Montana, John and his young wife decided to try the West, too.

His first job was herding sheep on the Atkinson, Randall & Cowen Ranch near Nashua. There were no bridges across the Milk River (none across the Missouri either, for that matter) so to cross it was necessary to swim their horses. One day as they were crossing with the spring wagon behind the team, the buggy cramped and threw Mrs. Bawden into the river. He swam after her and brought her back to where they could cling to the buggy.

About that time the spring tooth harrow which he was hauling tipped out and a tooth went through his foot – in one side and out the other. He pulled it out, but not until he reached the opposite bank and the air hit the wound did he realize how badly he was hurt. It was the fellow who couldn't tighten the screws on the roughbox who came to his rescue, sober now, and carried him to the house. He had to stay in bed for six months, then walk on crutches.

Crutches didn't keep him from working. He cut the logs for their first house while he was on those crutches. They had located just south of the Missouri River, in a bend called Chelsea Point, living in a little two-room shack, but because this little peninsula flooded each spring, they decided to build on higher ground.

With the Reservation just across the river, contacts with Indians were frequent. One day as he was cutting logs in full view of the house, he noticed some Indians come into the yard and start sharpening their knives on his grindstone. After watching them a bit, it occurred to him that his wife might be frightened by their presence so he started for the house. When he tried the door, he found it locked, so he called her name, "Nora!" The door was promptly opened by his terrified wife. She had heard tales of Indian massacres so when she saw the Indians sharpening their knives, she thought they were after her scalp. She had been sitting on the bed with a forty-five-colt revolver pointed at the door; had her husband succeeded in opening the door before calling her name, she'd have been a widow.

Later, she became well acquainted with the Indians (John, getting around more, already knew many of them), and they both learned to speak Sioux fluently. The squaws often came to visit her. They would never sit on chairs, but instead would sit cross-legged on the floor, visiting with her. She learned to appreciate their visits as there were few white women in the area. There were just three, besides herself: Mrs. Scobey, the Indian agent's wife, Mrs. Walker, the agency clerk's wife, and Mrs. Atkinson, the doctor's wife. Whenever they planned a square dance, Dr. Atkinson would row across the river to tell the Bawdens because unless Mrs. Bawden was there, they didn't have enough women to form a quadrille!

Another Indian visit that Mrs. Bawden did not soon forget was the one by an old Indian named Yellowrobe. He appeared in his war paint, came in, then just sat in the middle of the floor, staring at her. He was sitting there when Mr. Bawden came in, his wife again "scared half to death." Mr. Bawden grabbed his rifle and ordered Yellowrobe off the place, but the Indian refused to be hurried, even with the business end of a rifle pointing at his stomach, as he backed several hundred yards to the brow of a nearby hill. He was a big, stately-looking Indian, and tough. Later when Scobey, the Indian Agent, wanted to arrest him for some offence, he sent thirteen Indian police, but they were afraid to take him. Yellowrobe told them to "Tell Scobey to go to ----; I'm going to Canada."

He went, too, and stayed for about two years. When he came back he evidently had reformed because he made no more trouble, and the Bawdens came to look upon him as a friend.

Irvin recalls Indian visits, too – one when he was about thirteen or fourteen stands out in particular. An old Sioux Indian and his wife were camped just across the creek from the Bawden home, and each day the buck would come over to visit. One day as he was reminiscing he described an encounter the Sioux had had with the Crows. The Crows had stolen some horses from the Sioux, so the Sioux retaliated by stealing about three times that many from the Crows. They had escaped with them almost to the Missouri River and had stopped to eat dinner (main and probably only course: the deer they had shot) when they looked up and saw the Crows coming. At this point the memory was so vivid that the buck jumped out into the middle of the floor, and let out a bloodcurdling warwhoop that just about shook the rafters. The whoop abruptly brought him back to the twentieth century and, at the realization of how he had let himself be carried away with his story, he sheepishly sneaked back and sat down in his corner again.

Dawson County, reaching to the Canadian border on the north and to the Musselshell River on the west, was very sparsely settled at the turn of the century. Holdings were generally large, though not necessarily owned. Mr. Bawden (Irvin) jokingly remarked that it took all the citizens of Dawson County to hold a court term, serving either as witness or jury – or defendant!

John Bawden's range included about twenty or thirty sections, and other ranchers regarded it as his, even though it did not actually belong to him. Range honor was strong and ranchers respected each other's rights, even though the 'rights' were not legal rights.

Stock roamed freely, and at roundup time cattle and horses that had strayed onto another's range were branded and thrown back onto their own range. With no fences to stop them stock sometimes ranged far. Mr. Bawden missed one of his teams, and when the Indians returned from their annual excursion to the Black Hills, they reported seeing the team in the Sheep Mountains near Miles City. It was in the dead of winter when Bawden started after them, and cold.

As night approached he came to a shack in the middle of nowhere so he stopped and asked if he could have shelter for the night. Five men occupied the shack and agreed to let him stay. He slept on his fur coat behind the stove, but during the night he began to get cold so he thought he'd add some wood to the fire. As he began to put wood in, a voice sharply demanded to know what he was doing. He explained his intention and was bluntly informed that it was colder outside.

He took the hint and lay down again but not to sleep. His guess was that they were probably rustlers, holed up there far from the outside world, who perhaps suspected him of representing the law. In the morning he lost no time clearing out, and he didn't pay them a return visit on his way home with his team.

The Bawdens, along with many other stockmen and ranchers, learned what a hard winter can do to the livestock census. They started the winter of 1896-97 with 5,000 head of sheep and lost 2,500 between the first of April, when they ran out of hay, and the fifteenth. He had ordered two carloads of hay, but it never reached him. A tracer later revealed that the hay had been sidetracked at Breckinridge, North Dakota, then finally sent on to Poplar. Before he found out about its arrival, it had been unloaded and appropriated by some of the settlers in the Scobey area. So his sheep died.

After the heavy loss, Bawden switched to cattle and horses, running as many as 750 horses. When the homesteaders began flocking into the Vida country about 1912, demand for horses rose sharply, and in three days Bawdens sold $3,000 worth of horses (unbroken) without leaving the place. The coming of the homesteaders marked the end of the era when 'range honor' dictated range boundaries. From then on land had to be bought or leased.

The Bawdens' first two boys were born in Poplar (the oldest is reported to be the first white boy born in Poplar). Irvin was born in the little log house, the logs for which his father cut while he was on crutches, on the ranch in 1901. They continued living in this house six more years, then built a rambling eleven-room house. The smallest room was 12'x14', and the pantry was 10'x16'.

Irvin's mother lived in the new house only about six months before she died at the birth of their youngest son. After Mrs. Bawden's death the Indian squaws no longer came to visit. About two years later they came back and chanted a weird dirge, then came no more. They explained that their 'hearts were bad', saddened at the death of their friend.

John Bawden, Sr., Irvin's father, built the first school in the Nickwall Community, sent to Illinois for a teacher (Grace Kimmell, later Mrs. Hank Cusker) and paid her out of his own pocket. When Richland County was carved out of Dawson, he was one of the first three commissioners, and when McCone County was organized, he was again one of the first commissioners.

Irvin and his wife live on Nickwall Creek, the same place where he was born. This creek, and consequently the community, was named after Captain Nickwall, pilot of the government boat that came up the Missouri River as far as Fort Benton to open it to navigation as early as possible in the spring. He returned at a time when the river was too low and stuck on a sandbar at the mouth of the creek. They couldn't get the boat off so they left it there, and the captain and crew stayed all winter. Hence the name Nickwall. The coming of the Great Northern Railroad in 1887 diminished the importance of navigation, and the boat was left to rot.

Irvin met his wife-to-be, Mabel Willoughby, when they were both attending high school in Poplar. Her parents came to Montana in 1905 and settled in Culbertson, then later homesteaded south of the river from Poplar. Irvin and Mabel were married in 1921. They had livestock, but their main emphasis was on farming, depending on horses for their 'horse power'.

He farmed as much as 550 acres with horses. When the depression and drought of the thirties hit and their soil blew away, they left farming for a time,

270

and he followed construction. In 1943 they came back to the farm, where they've been since. Their only daughter, Mrs. Russell Robertson, lives in Glendive. Their only son, Ralph "Dunk" Bawden, lived several years in Glendive but now lives in Salt Lake City. Mr. Bawden makes the old west live again as he relates stories his father told him and draws on memories of his own experiences as well.

Mrs. Menno (Ora Chaney) Mullet

Sunday, December 13, 1964 – Twenty-Seventh in the Series

Jacob B. Mullet had pioneer fever that kept him moving ahead of the settled community. Born in Ohio, he had moved on to Indiana, then with his family to Bisbee, North Dakota, where he was living at the turn of the century. Winters there were cold with a lot of snow and many blizzards which made stock-feeding difficult. He felt there must be a better place to live so early in the summer of 1902 he started west.

He was considering Bozeman, Montana, but when the train stopped in Glendive it was met by a real estate agent, E.C. Leonard. He offered to show Mullet a large plot of good land where they could either homestead or buy railroad land quite cheaply. They drove with team and buggy about thirty miles into the country, north to Thirteen Mile Valley. There indeed appeared to be good farm land and good grazing for cattle, with grass belly-deep to the horses and plenty of water. Fuel was easy to get as coal could be seen sticking out of the hills in places.

Grandpa bought a half section of railroad land at $2.50 an acre and went back to North Dakota to report his findings. Others, too, were eager to find land for new homes, and some came on over that fall to homestead. In the spring of 1903 his oldest son, Joe Mullet and wife, with bachelor John Kauffman and the Amos Millers, moved to their new homesteads in the West, shipping a carload of machinery and their household goods while they themselves traveled by covered wagon.

They found a lonely prairie with the nearest neighbor, rancher Adams, five miles away. They lived in tents until they had their houses built, hauling all their lumber and supplies by wagon from Glendive. Two of Joe's sons, Bert and Lou, still live in the Glendive area, but both their parents are dead.

The next spring, 1904, Grandpa brought his family to Thirteen Mile but left the cattle until fall when two other families came. Son Jacob J. went back then to Bisbee to help trail the cattle to their new range, a three-week drive, arriving here the last week in November, 1904.

In the spring of 1906, Grandpa made application for a post office. The request was granted, and he named the new office Adams. Later Adams post office was moved to the Bert Ennis home, then in 1909 to the new Bloomfield store and the name changed to Bloomfield.

Three more of the Mullet boys were old enough to file before the available homestead land was taken, but by the time the youngest son, Menno, was twenty-one, the desirable land was gone so he bought half a section of railroad land on Morgan Table, just south of the Thirteen Mile Valley.

Before settling down to farming, however, he worked at a number of other jobs. He was only fifteen when he started riding for Ira Bendon on his Burns Creek ranch. It was Bendon who gave him the nickname 'Jimmy Hicks', and to

272

this day Burns Creek old timers refer to him as Jimmy instead of using his given name.

He also worked on the Lower Yellowstone Irrigation ditch from Intake to Sidney. While he was 'flunky' for the cook, he learned enough about cooking so he didn't starve during his bachelor days the first few years that he farmed. Another job he found interesting was his work with the Geological Survey crew that surveyed the Ekalaka area for homestead land. Some of his associates suggested that he could easily pass for twenty-one and homestead, but he wasn't quite twenty-one so instead of homesteading there when the survey was complete, he came back to the Bloomfield area and started farming for E.C. Leonard, just a little over a mile south of the Adams (now Red Top) School. Ora Chaney taught the Adams School the winter of 1912 and 1913, and that fall, November 12, 1913, Menno Mullet and Ora Chaney were married. (Their sixth daughter, Gladys, is the author of these "As I Remember" stories, which explains why Jacob B. Mullet is referred to as Grandpa in this story.)

Ora Chaney, native of the 'Show Me' state, was introduced to Montana in 1907. Her father, E.B. Chaney, working in western Montana, heard about the homestead land available in Dawson County and came to investigate early in the spring of 1907. He liked what he saw and filed on a quarter section one and one-half miles east of Bloomfield. A rather steep bank offered a convenient location for a dugout so he began to prepare the dugout in anticipation of the family's arrival in the fall from Missouri. In the meantime he spent some time working on the "Ditch" between Intake and Sidney, and was on hand April Fool's morning when the cook served muffins for breakfast, light, fluffy muffins – filled with cotton.

In October the family came by train, the oldest son accompanying the livestock and household goods in an immigrant car. Upon reaching Glendive they stayed in town a couple nights until they could unload the immigrant car. They ate their first Montana breakfast in a local restaurant. One of the party found a hair in the food so at noon they chose a different eating place. The kitchen was in full view of the diners, and when they saw one of the dishwashers use her dishtowel for a handkerchief, they ruefully concluded they hadn't improved their lot!

The immigrant car was finally unloaded and the last lap of their journey to the homestead was begun. Two of the neighbors, Frank Coryell and Art Kitchen, had brought their teams and hayracks to help haul out their belongings. They packed lunch and started for Bloomfield, the two oldest girls with the Coryells (Vera Coryell and Nora Wienke had come in with Mr. Coryell), the others with the family wagon. The two cows were tied behind this wagon so progress was necessarily slow. The result was that even though the Coryell troupe stopped for an hour at noon to rest the horses, the wagon and lunch didn't catch up with them so they had no dinner. At suppertime there was still no sign of the lunch so when they reached a homesteader's place on Seven Mile, the four girls walked up to the house to see if they could get some food. The homesteaders were German and couldn't understand a word of English so

273

they weren't making much progress with their communications until Nora, who could speak German, stepped into the breach and explained their plight. When the lady of the house understood, she quickly sliced some ham, with a loaf of bread, for fifty cents. That tided them over until they reached Coryells where they ate supper and spent the night.

Their dugout was twelve feet wide (back into the bank), and forty-four feet across the front of the bank. That winter was very mild, and they worked until after Christmas, getting logs from the badlands of the Divide for their building and fencing needs.

The mild winter was climaxed with a May snowstorm that tried to spill enough snow for the whole winter in one dose. Snow drifted over the front of the dugout clear to the roof so, as the door opened outward, they had to remove a window and crawl through to shovel the snow from the door. With no fences to stop them, their team drifted with the storm until they were about five miles from home. One got into a coulee and perished so another horse had to be purchased to finish the spring work.

Over on the Williams ranch in the Union country where the oldest daughter, Ora, was cooking, three of the herders had been out with the sheep, unable to get in until after the blizzard. When the sun came out after the storm, the snow was such a dazzling white that the three were blinded by its brilliance by the time they could get to the home ranch. They stayed in the potato cellar, where it was completely dark, to ease the pain until their sight came back.

When the early settlers came, Thirteen Mile Valley abounded with rattlesnakes. Some unpleasant snake experiences in Missouri had left 'Sis' (Ora) with an almost irrational fear of snakes. Once when she was gathering eggs in a dimly lighted barn loft, she reached into a nest and found a big black snake coiled there. Another time during corn planting while they rested on the porch a bit after dinner before going back out into the heat, she felt something around her waist so she stood up to shake her skirts, and a snake fell to the ground. It was a harmless variety, but it contributed to the horror she felt at the sight of any snake. And now rattlers!

When she met her first rattlesnake, she had gone to the potato patch and was equipped with a hoe so she hit it with the hoe so hard she broke the handle. Her father dryly pointed out that she didn't have to hit that hard. He warned them never to leave the house without a stick, so when she met the next one while after the cows, she was prepared again. As she walked through the tall grass, her stockings and skirts filled with hay needles so she sat down on the ground to remove them. Even as she did so a rattlesnake buzzed, hardly more than a yard away. Forgetting the needles and seizing her stick, she made short work of the snake. Then, even though unnerved by the encounter, she severed the rattles and took them home as proof of her conquest.

Before the Chaney family had been in the Valley two years, sorrow overtook them. Mrs. Chaney, the wife and mother, contracted pleurisy and died in 1909. There were no churches in the new community and no ministers so the funeral was held in the Red Top schoolhouse with N.B. Sackett, one of the

274

homesteaders conducting the service. Burial was in the cemetery already established on the hill north of the schoolhouse. Besides her husband and daughter Ora, she left six other children: Clyde, Cordia, Sylvus, Gertrude, Bertha, and Robert.

Blizzards in the winter and prairie fires in the summer provided new, though not pleasant, experiences. One fire, driven by a strong wind for probably fifteen miles in spite of united efforts of homesteaders and ranchers to check it, was put out by rain just half-a-mile before it reached the Chaney dwelling.

Roundups, too, provided a new experience, but these were thoroughly enjoyed. Mother recalls seeing – and hearing – her first horse roundup while she was working on the Milan Brooks ranch. Horses from miles around were gathered, and they thundered down Thirteen Mile Valley to their first stop at the OU Ranch where Cavanaugh's horses were cut out, then on down the valley to Milan Brooks ranch where the horses belonging to Chet Murphy, to Jim Brooks, and to Milan Brooks were sorted. The pounding of the hooves could be heard long before the horses broke into view over the hill, and hundreds of horses galloped down to the flat below the ranch buildings where they were held for cutting*.

When the last longhorn roundup was held, the wagons camped on that flat, and several of the girls were invited to eat dinner at the camp. There were forty or fifty punchers. Everyone used tin cups and tin plates, and all was exciting to a southern newcomer.

In 1912 when the Miskimen's Jewelry, Lowe's Hardware, and The Dawson County Review jointly sponsored a contest to attract new business, Ora Chaney won a piano. Each dollar purchase counted so many points, with the customer designating the recipient among the contestants, and each new subscription secured for the Review was worth points. She was out in the country and hadn't been to town to turn in her points so she was trailing rather far behind. Just at the close of the contest she brought in her final Review subscriptions and placed third.

After her marriage in 1913 to Menno Mullet, they continued for a few years to live in the Valley, but in 1916 they moved to Morgan Table where they lived together for twenty-nine years (until his death in 1945; Mother still lives there). They raised nine children who provided an avid audience for the tales of 'way back when'. One of the stories we especially liked to hear our father tell was about the time he was threatened by longhorn cattle. He had gone to bring in his father's horse. He could never get close to that horse out in the open so had to drive it down to the barn. Suddenly some longhorn cattle came over the hill. Unused to seeing a human being on foot, they took after him – and their curiosity wasn't of a friendly sort. He scrambled to that horse that wouldn't be caught in the open, and this time she stood still and let him swing onto her back. Once he was on horseback, the cattle paid no more attention to him, and he rode safely to the barn.

Probably such stories are as responsible for this present series of articles as any one factor. Daughter Number Six was always fascinated with those tales and is convinced that interesting stories are being buried with each 'Old Timer' going 'the way of all flesh'. Surely someone should talk with the remaining pioneers and record some of these stories for posterity. So here we are with "As I Remember."

Ora Chaney (Mullet) pictured horseback in her riding skirt

Mrs. Linda Bryan

Sunday, December 20, 1964 – Twenty-eighth in the Series

In the 'good old days' when Mrs. Linda Bryan and her five children alighted from the train that brought them to Glendive the first time, they were met by a unique 'welcoming committee'. Sleeping hoboes covered the depot floor, and the depot agent had to chase them out to make room for the new arrivals.

The Bryans came from Salem, South Dakota. After one of their friends homesteaded in the Union country, they decided Dawson County might be worth a look so in the summer of 1909 Mr. Bryan came and looked and filed, and the family moved here the first week of November. Another family came at the same time, the women and children by train, and the men with the immigrant cars. The trip from Glendive to Union had to be made by team and wagon so they spent their first night in Montana at Almy's Halfway House. Tom Pierce, whom they had known in Sac City, Iowa, in their pre-South Dakota days, lived less than a mile from their homestead so they stayed there until they had their own four-room house built. They had nice weather until February (good thing they didn't come in '64) which was a great blessing because they had to freight everything by wagon from Glendive.

The winter was kind to them that year, but made up for it in later years. Many times a blizzard would last two or three days. In one such storm the snow drifted completely over their hog shed, which was built below a knoll, and the hogs all smothered.

But summers could produce storms, too. One day in August the first summer they were here, their neighbors with their four children and Bryans with their five children loaded up in a wagon and started out to see some more of the country. They saw a country parched from the summers drought, but the drought was broken abruptly when a rainstorm came up with such suddenness and violence that they had to stay at the Sheppard Ranch over night. That rain gave enough moisture so they did get a few bushels of potatoes from their sod plantings.

Prairie fires were common, especially during dry summers such as that one. Whenever they saw smoke, they dropped whatever they might be doing and went to fight fire. Standard procedure was to kill a beef and drag it behind a saddle horse along the fire line. Not only was much grass burned that dry summer of 1910, but many thousands of acres of forest were also destroyed by fire. That was the year that one August day remained dark the entire day because smoke from forest fires was so heavy the sun couldn't shine through.

Many range cattle and horses roamed the ranges freely and often gave them trouble. One encounter indelibly etched in the memory of daughter Veva (Mrs. J.W. Robson of Lindsay) was with a lone range steer. She and her brother Howard were playing house in the haymow of the barn when this steer came to visit, but they didn't consider it a social call. The steer ran around and around the barn, bellowing as he ran, until they were thoroughly scared. They finally managed to sneak out and dash for the house, but the steer discovered they were on the way and took after them. They won the race, but barely. They reached the house just ahead of him and slammed the door in his face. Then he kept circling the house but finally left.

With no fences to stop them, their own cattle would sometimes wander off, and someone would have to ride the range all day looking for them.

The big roundups were fascinating, and sometimes they would all pile into the wagon and go watch. Those roundup cooks knew how to prepare barbecued beef, and the guests found it really delicious!

There were no schools in the Union area when the Bryans came, but by 1910 so many homesteaders were coming in with families that something had to be done about a school. They had a month's school in Ralph Pierce's homestead shack, then built the Pierce School House in 1910. They had just short terms of school the first few years. After the school was built, it was the center of all the social activities of the community. Prior to that the I.H. Hill granary (now the Frank Eaton place) had been used for such functions. After the schoolhouse was built, it was also used for church and Sunday School.

In those early days there was no doctor within a half hour's drive so Mrs. Bryan often helped neighbors in sickness or at childbirth.

After threshing machines made their debut, big crews accompanied the machine from farm to farm to thresh the grain. While the men joined to thresh, the women of the neighborhood joined to cook. Sometimes there would be more women and children than men.

Mrs. Bryan, now past ninety, reflected that she has hauled many a load of grain with team and wagon to Glendive or Terry. She had to take two or three days for the trip that trucks make now in two hours or less. During her fifty-five years in Montana, she has seen it change from primitive pioneer frontier to modern farm and ranch country – modern, that is, until one of the 'old time' blizzards strikes and plunges them back into the pre-electricity era.

Bert Hilger

Thursday, December 31, 1964 – Twenty-ninth in the Series

Two years before the turn of the century Bert Hilger, son of Mr. and Mrs. Henry Hilger, was born in the Marias River country near Shelby, Montana. His father was from Minnesota, his mother from Toronto. They met and married in California, and spent most of their married life in Montana.

Two of Mr. Hilger's uncles, ranching in the Shelby area, lured them to the Treasure State, but in 1903 they changed ranges, moving to Redwater just below the junction with East Redwater. Henry Hilger knew many of the punchers who moved to Dawson County from Sun River with the C.K. outfit, and reports drifted back of good cattle country with plenty of grass and water so the Hilgers decided to make the move.

Even then most of the 'big' outfits were about done, but the CK and the XIT were among those still running roundup wagons. Bert recalls a visit, when he was just a little fellow, from one of the wagon bosses that made a vivid impression upon his memory. During the afternoon the CK wagons had pulled into camp close to the Hilgers' place, and that evening the wagon boss, Dave Clair, came riding up with a quarter of beef on the front of his saddle. He greeted Hilger with, "You bald-headed so-and-so, if you're too lazy to come and get this beef, I'll have to bring it up to you," typically covering a generous gesture or impulse with rough talk.

From the Hilgers comes another tale of heavy sheep loss from Montana's cold breath and white blankets. The winter of 1906-07 had made heavy demands on feed, and on March 27 they gave the last load of hay to the sheep. By April 10, when bare ground finally began to show, they had lost 500 of their 2,000 sheep.

Hilger salvaged the pelts of the dead sheep and became so practiced that he could skin a sheep in three minutes. Old timers referred to such a winter as an 'equalizer' – it brought the big man down to the small man and everyone was 'even' to start over again.

Bert's aunt had come from Liverpool, England the fall before, planning to stay a month. While she was visiting with them she contracted pneumonia and had to be in bed a month. On November 15 snow started falling (when did it start in '64?), and by the time she was able to leave, she was snowed in. It took them three days, stopping at ranches on the way, to get her to the train at Poplar. When the train left Poplar, it went only about ten miles before it was stuck in the snow. They were able to proceed again in a few hours, but during that winter there were periods as long as two weeks when the Great Northern could not get a train through to Poplar.

Snow fell until there were no little coulees left; they were all drifted full. Ranchers were accustomed to laying in groceries and other supplies for themselves to last the winter (and they didn't have to worry about their electricity going off) so they suffered no hardship in that respect, but cattle losses as well as sheep losses were heavy. Horses wintered all right because it had been a good grass year, and they were able to dig down through the snow.

In 1912 Hilgers sold their sheep because the influx of homesteaders had ended the era of the open range. From then on their emphasis was on cattle, horses, and farming.

In the early part of the century wild game abounded in the Redwater country and the ranchers felt they could get along with fewer grey wolves. These were big wolves, big enough to hamstring a two-year-old steer, as Hilger had occasion to know.

One night he heard a commotion among the cattle so he hastened to investigate and found that the wolves already had a steer down. Sheep, of course, were easy prey. The wolves also killed one of their colts, as well as stock for other ranchers. Finally five or six ranchers banded together and went out to get those wolves.

They found the den in a washout in the badlands. Bert was just a youngster, about fourteen, but he was allowed to crawl back into the bell-shaped washout, along with an old time puncher, Jim Montgomery, to get the four pups, about a third grown. Bert would reach back into the den where the wolves had an extension hole to get hold of a pup, then Monty would finish it with a broken pick handle. The two old wolves were captured the next winter by a fellow with some hounds, and that was the last of the big grey prairie wolves on the East Redwater.

In the years gone by, Indians had freely roamed the area and, although they now had to have a pass to leave the reservation, still frequented the region during the years of Hilger's sojourn there. Indians called Mr. Hilger, Sr. 'Henry Redwater'. Hilger recalls seeing the Indian caravan of seventy-five wagons from Fort Peck enroute to Glendive for the fair. They camped just across the creek from the Hilger home, and that first night when they began to beat the tom toms and dance, his mother (understandably) was somewhat apprehensive. They were entirely friendly, however, and when ready to move on, they stopped at Hilger's well to fill their demijohns and water kegs. The Indian police stood right by the well and kept them moving. While they traveled together on the way to the fair, on the return trip they'd scatter to hunt, and the wagons would come back one or two at a time.

An Indian had been buried in a tree near the Hilger place so Bert, his brother Clarence, and one of the herders poked it down and were rewarded for their efforts with the 'find' of a bunch of fancy beadwork and the like.

As usual in pioneer settlements, schooling was a problem. When Bert started to school in the summer of 1907, he and his brother rode horseback twelve miles on Monday morning to the nearest school, stayed at the Bawdens during the week, then rode back home Friday after school. The next year they moved to their winter ranch south of Brockton, where school was held in a deserted shack about five miles from their ranch house. Mrs. Hilger and her two boys lived in the kitchen of the shack, and school was held in the other room. Mr. Hilger would come over from the ranch whenever he could get away.

280

By the next year, 1908, more people had moved into the Redwater area so they decided they had to have a school. They started school in a log shack belonging to Mr. Nels Tolan near Hilgers and close to where the schoolhouse was built later. The plaster was so badly cracked they could roll up unwanted paper and poke it out through the cracks – providing the teacher didn't catch them at it.

When they built the schoolhouse, the money and labor were all donated. They hauled the logs from south of Wolf Point. A young fellow had had the logs all squared, ready to build his house, but then his girl wouldn't marry him so he sold the logs, and they used them for the school. Later they put on siding. When the schoolhouse was finished (it is still standing, but not used), each family provided their own homemade seats and desks. Miss Rena DeZell (later Mrs. Sig Custer) was hired to teach, and District 31 was ready for school.

In February of that year Bert was hired to build fires at the school. Each morning he would ride (horseback) down to start the fire in time to get the building warm before teacher and pupils arrived. He was paid $1.50 a month for this, his first remunerative job. No school buses came to pick up children. They either rode a saddle horse or drove a team with a buggy.

By the time he was eight years old, he was allowed to ride horseback to town (Poplar), twenty miles, to get the mail. Trips to town were infrequent, and women, especially, didn't get in often. Mr. Hilger (Bert) mentions that his mother was on the ranch and didn't go to Poplar for four years.

He recalls that when he made his first trip to Glendive with his father in 1908 on a four-horse load of wool, he was afraid to cross the old wooden bridge!

In 1927 Bert Hilger bought the ferry at Poplar and ran it for six years. Then he went to Omaha and got on the towboats coming to Fort Peck to help build the dam. He held a first class pilot's license but was working then as a diesel engineer. In 1936 he bought a garage in Glendive from Ed Haskell, and the garage became known as Hilger's Chevrolet. In 1944 he started the Glendive Flying Service and hired Martin Railey as instructor. Later Railey bought him out. Mr. Hilger, now retired, lives with his wife in Billings, and son Bob runs the garage in Glendive.

Early Homesteaders

A typical dugout home on the
Homestead

The famous 'Black Snowstorm'
Duststorm of May 28, 1937

Menno Mullet's threshing team at Chris Buller's

Early Missouri River Steamboat docked in Glendive

Glendive's Main Street in 1881

Glendive's Main Street (Merrill Avenue) in 1883

Above - Glendive in 1900   Below – Postcard of Glendive 1910

Sam Sampson

April 1965

Perhaps the difficulties Sam Sampson encountered on his first attempt to move his belongings to his homestead were portentous of the problems and obstacles that lay in the path of one striving to wrest a living from 160 acres of Montana's dry land – although dry land certainly was not his problem on that first trip.

When he and his party reached Glendive in the fall of 1908 they found rain and more rain. They headed out of Glendive with four wagons and four teams, proceeded as far as Steel Hill (just south of Ralph Newton's home), and there discovered what happens when Montana gumbo* gets wet. The hill was greasy, and the mud seemingly had no bottom. The horses couldn't get footing, and wagon wheels cut in so deeply that, even when two teams were hitched to one wagon, they couldn't get up that hill. So they came back to Glendive, put their cattle in the stockyards, and took the horses to the blacksmith shop to have them shod.

Sam Sampson, a native of Brookings, South Dakota, had first made the acquaintance of the Treasure State in the spring of 1908. A banker and a storekeeper from neighboring Arlington had bought railroad land in Dawson County and were interested in seeing the area settled so they were encouraging fellow South Dakotans to take up homesteads.

Sampson and his brother-in-law, Albert Limesand, with a couple neighbors, came to view the land. When they reached Glendive, they hired a livery team from Edward O'Neil and drove out toward the head of Deer Creek, about twenty-two miles from Glendive, where they contemplated settling.

Seth Hewit, a former neighbor in South Dakota, was already there and had his shack built so they stayed with him that night. As Seth started supper preparations he explained to them, "I'll have to get the potatoes," and disappeared around the north side of the shack. Presently he tossed the potatoes, frozen solid, onto the floor. They scrubbed them up anyway and cooked them, fried some bacon, and had a satisfying supper.

Hewit had only one bed and there were five men so three of them slept in the bed, while it fell to the lot of Sam and Albert to sleep on a grocery box in a big trunk. Next morning they decided on their homestead sites, then came back to town and filed, April 2, 1908.

They started back to South Dakota but had to change trains at Oakes, North Dakota. During the delay they walked the streets a bit to relieve the monotony. The monotony was relieved, all right. Three girls came driving down the street in a shiny rubber-tired buggy pulled by a high-stepping horse. Suddenly the back wheel came off and the buggy tipped over backward, spilling the girls. The horse promptly left the scene of the accident on a run and headed back for his barn. The barn had a divided door. The lower half was shut, but the upper part was open. With a leap the horse was over the bottom door and into the barn, leaving the buggy – or pieces of it – outside. That was about enough excitement for one stopover.

They remained in South Dakota that summer but made preparations to move in the fall. Sampson and Charley Weed shared an immigrant car* to ship their wagons, livestock, and household goods. Charley came with the car while Sampson accompanied the women and children as far as Jamestown where they stayed with some relatives until the men could get a place ready for them to live.

At Glendive Bill Moye and Ray Carpenter (two former South Dakotans who had preceded them to Montana), each with a team and wagon, met the newcomers to help them move out. Sampson and Weed each had a team and wagon in the immigrant car so they began transferring belongings from the car to the wagons for the trip to the homesteads, in the rain.

When their initial attempt proved unsuccessful, they tried again the next day, hoping for better results. Before they left town, though, Sampson pulled up in front of Stipek's Store for a last-minute purchase. He had brought hip boots and a rain hat with him, but he intended to have a slicker before he started out again, even though it wasn't raining just then. The others laughed at him, but when the rain started again just beyond Hollecker's, they weren't laughing any more. By the time they reached Carpenter's place, where they stayed until they could put up a shack, the others were soaking wet, but Sampson was snug and dry.

Three of them, Charley Weed, Albert Limesand, and Sam Sampson had homesteaded in the same section*. It was only a matter of a few days until they had Charley's shack built so they all moved into it until they could get the other dwellings ready. They didn't have a well at first, of course, but there was a good spring in the next section so they watered the cattle there and hauled drinking water from it. The first few days when they watered the cattle they drove them home again, but then they started just leaving them and letting them come home.

One night the cattle didn't show up so next morning Charley hooked up his team and they started out to look for them. One of the cows had just freshened, and at Hollecker's they found her (Holleckers had kept her and milked her), but the other five had gone on down the road toward Glendive. They were going back to South Dakota! They managed to get within five miles of town before the men caught up with them. They happened to be close to an old corral so they put the cattle into the corral while they went on to town, then the next morning took their stray livestock back home.

When the women came, the rain was again falling only now it was mixed with snow, and a cold, wet welcome it made. Charley had a covered Rawleigh wagon* for his family and Sam had a closed-in buggy so they were able to get their families in out of the rain when they met them at the train, but the women were frankly disgusted; come to a dry country and then have to ride all the way home in mud and rain!

Soon after the arrival of the women folk Sampson's house was ready for occupancy – just a little, one room shack – so they moved to their own place.

Later that same fall they added a small kitchen. The Sampsons had two children, Milford and Lyle, when they came to Montana, and Floyd was born in 1910. They moved into Glendive for a few months that summer. That same year Sam did quite a bit of freighting. He hauled lumber to Savage for the Goodrich Lumber Company, groceries, etc. to Paxton for Hopkins at the store, hay to Holleckers and for others as well. He also helped build a road from Steel Hill to the stage road that fall.

That was the summer of one of Deer Creek's worst prairie fires. Sam had gone to the homestead for a load of hay, intending to go back to Glendive the next day. He didn't feel good so he decided not to start back. He was lying in the shack when suddenly he heard such shouting outside that he ran out to see what was the matter. It was Chet Loudon that was doing the shouting. Chet had a big breaker plow* which he pulled with a steam engine. As he was moving the outfit, a spark had ignited the tinder-dry grass.

He had his water tank with him so he started putting on water, but just when he had the fire almost under control, his tank ran dry and the fire got away again. That's when he shouted for help. Sampson's buildings were protected by fire guards so his buildings were safe, but the fire swept around his guard and on across the prairie. Other settlers joined them, beating the fire with wet sacks. All at once a bunch of cattle appeared so they killed a steer, split it in two, and started to drag the fire line.

In case there wasn't enough excitement already, they had some more now. The horses objected to that kind of business and started bucking, throwing their riders. They just about had a rodeo for a while, but they soon managed to get their horses straightened out and back to the task of fighting fire. The fire spread across Three Mile Table, and in spite of their efforts to extinguish it, burned almost to the river.

Albert Limesand happened to be visiting at the Sampsons as Sam described his early experiences so he contributed a few stories of his own. The most vivid in his memory, even after fifty-five years, was the time Sam lured him into the path of a wild steer.

Sam, riding a little paint pony, had come to the house and told Albert and Charley he had something to show them. As they started for the door, Charley noticed the double-barreled shotgun hanging above the door and asked if he'd better take it along. Sam agreed that it might be a good idea so Charley shouldered the gun, and the three of them, Sam on his pony, headed for the point of interest. He led them to a draw about a quarter of a mile from the house, and then told them, "You guys just wait here and I'll chase him up." The sight that hove over that little ridge struck them with terror.

A big steer with the longest horns they had ever seen (so it seemed to them, anyway) was lying on the ground and jumped to his feet as Sam approached. Mr. Limesand's eyes widened yet at the recollection of that apparition! At the sight of the men on foot he charged toward them. Albert didn't wait for a second look. Shouting, "Shoot, Charley, shoot!" he bolted for the house as hard as he could run. Before that he never knew how fast he could run! Charley, at his heels, was so intent upon clearing out of there that he didn't take time to even try to shoot; he just made tracks.

He couldn't make them as fast as Albert was making them, though. When, about half-way to the house, Sam shot past them on his pony, the runners figured their seconds were numbered and redoubled their efforts. Not until they reached the safety of the porch did Albert, gasping for breath, turn to see just what his margin of safety was. To his amazement he saw that the steer was in practically the same spot as when they first beheld him. Only then did they discover how they had been tricked.

Sam, rocking with merriment at the unqualified success of his practical joke, explained that when a bunch of long-horned cattle had come past a little earlier, his milk cow had joined them so he, on the pony, had tried to cut her out. He couldn't get her so he started whooping and hollering and the longhorns stampeded. His cow couldn't keep pace with them so now getting her was no problem.

He noticed, however, that when the wild bunch took off, one steer dropped behind, evidently injured in the back, because he went down with his back quarters, then fell to his knees and finally, after dragging himself a short distance, fell clear to the ground. Sam, allowing him to proceed in this manner, had coaxed him to the water hole and left him there. Then, knowing well that the steer could manage only a few steps at a time, he had invited Albert and Charley for a look. Next morning the steer was dead.

To a man who had been reared in eastern South Dakota a storm cellar seemed of prime importance so Sam dug one that second year they were here. He dug a well, too, and though it was only eighteen feet deep, it was an extra good well, he recalls. As Sam was talking about his well, Albert started chuckling again, and then explained that he was just reminded of a tale of woe Smokey Secora had related to him. When Smokey was deputy sheriff of McCone County, Circle had no public water system but depended upon individual wells. The jail's well was just outside the door, and one evening Smokey sent one of his 'guests' to get a pail of water. "That," Secora lamented to Albert, "was ten years ago, and the fellow hasn't got back yet!"

There were no schools when Sampsons came because prior to that there were very few settlers, but by 1910 many sections had four families living on them with plenty of children for a school so they built the Twin Buttes School. Grace Burvee was the first teacher, while the first school board was comprised of Christ Rapp, Charley Carpenter, and Sam Sampson, with Joe Walbrink as clerk. By 1917 there were too many children so the Andrew Dahl School was built in the same district. Now the district doesn't even have a schoolhouse.

When they first came to Montana they'd go to the Adams Post Office about a mile east of the present Bloomfield office to get their mail. Then for a time their mail came to Glendive. All the mail for their community was put into a Twin Buttes box, and anyone who came to town picked up the mail for all of them. Then all the neighbors would come there to pick up their mail. Later on the Adams Post Office was moved to Albright's store in Bloomfield so they went back to getting their mail at Bloomfield. Sam and Albert often went to Bloomfield together. Albrights had a boy named Albert and according to Sam, every time Mrs. Albright would holler "Albert!" while they were there, Limesand would jump.

One day the little shed that was behind the store caught fire, and one of the fellows who happened to be in the store, fearing the store would go next, began a salvaging operation. He grabbed a bar of soap, tore out of the store and up the hill! As it turned out, his salvaging wasn't needed; the store didn't catch fire.

Cattle buyers from the east used to come to Twin Buttes for cattle, and one day when Sam was in Glendive, some fellows came in headed for Carpenters so Sam let them ride along out with him. The older buyer had a young fellow with him, perhaps to 'break him in' and as darkness began to fall, Junior began to be uneasy. Then the coyotes started to howl, and that did it. Junior wailed "Indians! We're going to be scalped!" Sam assured him it was just coyotes, but he refused to be assured. He kept insisting it was Indians and climbed behind the seat, then under it. Even after they reached Carpenters, he stayed right close to his senior partner.

When they had made their purchase, they brought them to Glendive for shipping, and the buyer warned Heck Neuman, at the stockyards, "Der vild! Der vild!" Neuman wasn't much impressed and replied, "I've seen more wild cattle than they've got dollars in Jerusalem." They happened to be loading sheep into a car just then. The lower deck was filled and the chute in place for loading the upper deck when one of the steers found it. Up the chute he dashed, over the top of the car, and headed for the Hungry Joe hills*. Even Neuman was a bit taken aback at that performance and exclaimed, "Look at that steer run!" About all the cattle merchant could do as his steer disappeared was squeal, "I told you dey vas vild!"

One day while Sam was in Glendive he chanced to meet Pete Rorvik who asked him how far he lived from Bloomfield. Sampson told him it was about eight miles so Rorvik asked if he could get him to haul a load from Bloomfield to Circle. Sam agreed to take the job and the next day loaded the Durham wheat, potatoes, and carrots – a four-horse load – for the Circle trip. Taking Louie Limesand with him, they managed to get across the divide their first day out and camped that night near Gust Voss's sod house. They picketed one horse, hobbled another and turned the rest loose. Then they rolled out their beds under the wagon and went to sleep. During the night he was awakened by the whinnying of the picketed horse, which meant the other horses were getting too far away, so he got up and rattled the feed pan. That brought the horses, but about then Louie woke up and started hollering at finding himself alone in the dark under that wagon.

Next morning they continued on their way to Circle. The roads were just trails and the trails didn't have any bridges, even across Cottonwood or Gip Creeks. He navigated Cottonwood without too much difficulty, but when they reached Gip Creek he didn't know if they were going to make it or not. The water was clear up to the hubs, but he whooped and hollered and put the horses to a run and they made it through. Once in Circle he found unloading his wagon a simple matter. He was hardly stopped before people started coming for the produce and wheat so in an hour-and-a-half his wagon was empty and he didn't have to lift a hand to unload it.

It was only a short time before that that Mrs. Sampson's folks (Louie was her brother) had moved to Montana, the spring of 1912. Mr. Limesand accompanied their immigrant car to Terry as they had shipped it on the Milwaukee, while Mrs. Limesand, the three girls, and Louie had come on the Northern Pacific passenger train. They sent word to Sampson to meet them so he started for town with the team and buggy. He had crossed the flat on top of Steel Hill and was just ready to start down into the draw when he saw some heads over to the side of the hill. When he heard one of the girls call, "Hurry up and get up here, sister, it might be Sam," he knew it was the party he had come to meet. They had decided to start walking to meet him and had almost missed him.

The town of Brookings stands on Limesand's South Dakota homestead. He had traded his rights for a bunch of horses. What became of the horses would be hard to guess, but the Brookings depot stands where he cut barley, and the Agricultural College is located on his flax field. He had broken the sod with oxen.

In 1913 disaster struck when fire destroyed Sampson's barn along with a big haystack and all of his year's grain except a three-box wagonload which he was able to salvage. Fortunately no livestock was destroyed. There were six horses in the barn, one belonging to a neighbor besides five of Sam's, but they were able to get them all out and save the harnesses, too.

The Sampsons' fourth son was born in 1913, just at the time of the spring breakup. Sam came to town to get lumber to build a bedroom, but about the time he reached the stage road he met Doolittle, who told him, "You can't get to Glendive because the road is all under water." In those days Stipek boasted considerably more in the way of businesses than it does now, so after he had eaten his lunch at Bamber Hill*, he went on to Stipek and picked up his lumber at the branch yard of Goodrich Lumber there. He had to stay over night in that fair metropolis, and then took his lumber home the next day. In two days they had the bedroom ready for use, and the next day son Raymond was born. Getting to Glendive was out of the question because of the mud and high water so Sam sent one of the neighbors to get Mrs. Houser, a midwife who lived on Seven Mile Creek several miles from Sampsons, to assist.

When Vyla was born at their home in 1916, complications developed and a doctor had to be summoned quickly. Sam hurried to neighbor Dave Johnston. His boys had a motorcycle so Irvin made a flying trip to Glendive with it and quickly hunted up Dr. Danskin. Dr. Danskin had a new Model T, which he asked Irvin to drive out for him. The trip to town (about twenty-five miles) had taken Irvin thirty-five minutes, and now the trip back in the car took fifty-five minutes – no record for today's cars on today's roads. It's rather doubtful that some of today's low cars would make much progress bouncing and jolting over the ruts and holes and through the mud of that day. The doctor arrived in time to save both mother and baby, and then Irvin brought him back to town. Later when Sam asked Irvin how much he owed him, Irvin suggested, "Oh, two dollars." And the doctor, for the call and delivery, charged only twenty-five dollars. Their youngest son, Lester, was born after they left the homestead.

The Sampson homestead seemed to be located right in the hail belt; they got more rain than some of the neighbors, but they got the hail, too, so in 1923, they let the homestead go and rented the Paquette place, three miles west. Mr. Paquette was a railroad man, and Mrs. Paquette was on the farm so she was glad to rent it and move to town. After three years there, they spent twelve years on the Dunham place five miles east of Lindsay. The water there was poor and not much of it. In the '30's they started looking for another place to buy, and were told by Mrs. Ralph Newton that her parents wanted to sell. They drove out to Gene Cummings, and Mrs. Cummings told them, "All you have to do is say you'll buy, and I'll put on my bonnet and wrapper and walk out." They did buy it and stayed there until 1951 when they quit farming. In the meantime the oil boom had increased the value of his land so he sold his oil rights and moved to town.

In 1952 he went to work for the city as janitor in the city hall. They bought a home in Glendive and are now retired. Sam still likes to make music on his mouth organ and auto harp. Back in the pioneer days music wasn't available at the flip of a radio switch or the electric hi fi, and Sam's mouth organ was much in demand. Even last fall at a reception in the church basement someone asked Sam if he had his mouth harp with him, but Sam figured that nowadays there's more appropriate music to play in a church basement. But he still enjoys making music at home.

Both Mr. and Mrs. Sampson will be eighty-two years old next month. They have been married almost sixty years, and, Mr. Sampson put in, "She hasn't thrown a spider at me yet!" (Note: a 'spider' is a type of frying pan).

Mrs. Mel (Jeanie) Johnson

September 1968

Mrs. Mel (Jeanie) Johnson met with many unexpected experiences when she came to live on a Montana homestead, but surely one of the most unexpected – and disconcerting – was coming home to find her larder depleted and some of her dishes missing.

The Johnsons had been to Glendive that day and came home rather late. She immediately started to get supper, then hastily summoned her husband. "Mel, somebody's been here!" she told him. Her bread was gone, the cookie jar was empty, dishes had disappeared.

Mel was unperturbed. "You'll find a note," he assured her. And sure enough, she did. Two or three plates were left in the cupboard, and under the bottom one she found the note from one of the neighbor's girls, explaining that unexpected company had come that afternoon from Wisconsin and had caught them unprepared.

When you lived twenty miles from town and traveled with horse and buggy, you didn't dash to the store if an emergency arose. Mrs. McCormick (the neighbor) considered this enough of an emergency to warrant action, however, so she sent Hazel to Johnsons to borrow.

"Go see what Jeanie has," she told her. Mrs. McCormick and Mrs. Johnson had become very good friends, and she knew Mrs. Johnson would gladly share what she might have. Hazel was familiar with the neighbor's kitchen so when she found no one home, she went ahead and helped herself.

She also knew that a trunk stored in the granary (there was no room in the little one-room house to store a trunk) contained extra bedding so she borrowed from there, too.

In a few days all the borrowed items came back. Mrs. Johnson explained, "Neighbors all neighbored in those days. We helped each other out and we managed to get by that way."

Mrs. Johnson came from pioneer stock so pioneering should have come natural for her. Her great grandfather was the first white man to settle in Lane County, Oregon, at Pleasant Hill, thirteen miles southeast of Eugene, Oregon, in the 1840's. Some of the furnishings he bought for his Oregon home are still in use in Mrs. Johnson's Montana home.

One of her souvenirs from her great grandfather is a clock. He went to Albany (the nearest trading center) sixty miles away, with a pack train, and the clock was one of the items he brought back. The clock is well over a hundred years old, but it still keeps good time.

Her rolling pin, too, is over one hundred years old, although it did not belong to her great grandfather. Her father gave it to her, explaining he was giving it, "not for what it is but for what it has been." His cousin had carved it by hand from hardwood when he was six years old. "It's still a mighty good rolling pin," she declares, "even though the end is burned." Their first cook

292

stove on the homestead was a laundry stove with the oven in the stovepipe. She stuck the rolling pin into the oven to dry it and forgot it until the end was scorched. It's the only one she's ever had so it's had plenty of use.

Anyone desiring to establish just what the fashions were one hundred years ago, consult Mrs. Johnson. She has old photograph albums with pictures, still sharp and clear, dating back to 1870. Another old book in her possession is her autograph album, bearing the date 1890 and filled with autographs of that date.

In 1906 Jeanie's folks moved to the state of Washington. Her cousin, Bill West, had also moved to Washington, and he and her father bought a farm together. The house on that farm, she informs us, was just like the Krug house on the east end of the Bell Street Bridge.

It was rather hard just then to find farm help, but the man from whom they bought the place told them that the young fellow who worked for him would probably stay and work for them also. The young fellow, Mel Johnson, did. And that's how Jeanie became acquainted with her future husband.

A year or so after Jeanie's family moved to Washington, Mel Johnson's father wrote from Wisconsin that Mel's brother had gone to Montana to homestead. (His claim was just across the road from where the 'big bone'* was discovered last summer.) Bill West was getting tired of farming, and Mel thought he'd like to look into the homestead proposition so in September of 1909 the two of them landed in Dawson County and both filed on sites in the Lindsay country. Bill returned to Washington after filing, but Mel went to North Dakota where there was still work in the harvest. After threshing was over he returned to Lindsay and spent the winter with his brother.

In the spring of 1910 Mel borrowed a team and wagon from Claude Christmas to haul lumber from Glendive to build his shack. A shack didn't have to be very pretentious to establish intent to live on the premises so Mel started out with one room 12'x16', right in front of a bank but not dug into it. Just down the creek from where he built, a sheepman of earlier days had fixed a watering hole over a spring for the sheep so at first he carried his water from there, but before long he dug a well. He only had to dig down twelve feet.

Mel worked that summer and the next for neighbors, especially Ed and Ira Wolff. He and Jeanie already were planning to get married, but they were going to wait until he had the homestead built up a little as he didn't have a thing when he started.

However, homestead sites were becoming hard to find, and family men coming in were contesting claims of young fellows who were working out and not spending much time on their own places. With this possibility threatening, the young couple decided to get married and settle down on a permanent basis. They were married in December, 1911, and stayed with her parents until February, then moved to the Montana homestead. The weather was comparatively mild when they arrived, but there was a lot of snow.

George West met them in Glendive and took them to the farm. The road (such as it was; they weren't following an oiled highway from Glendive to Lindsay) was blocked so they had to do quite a bit of winding around to get to where they wanted to go, but they made it. They met a 'cold reception' in the shack, but they soon had a fire going and warmed things up. They had brought a load of supplies when they came from town so they were ready to spend the rest of the winter.

Mel knew they had to be prepared because they had no way to go any place except by walking. As another example of how neighbors helped one another, Mrs. Johnson explained that when those who owned team and wagon started for Union or Lindsay, they would make a point of stopping at the homes of those whose only means of conveyance was 'shank's pony'. They'd either pick up a list or the homemaker and her list and take them along to the store. When the shopping was done, they'd leave them at their homes again.

That list, of course, was of considerable importance because if you forgot something you just went without – unless you borrowed. When you returned from one trip you started a list for the next and kept writing down the things you'd need. They expected to be snowed in for the winter so in the fall after the threshing was done the men folks would all go to town with a load of grain, then bring home the winter supplies.

Johnsons didn't have a team until 1912, but they had the running gears of a wagon, and Bill West had a team. His wife knew how to drive so they'd hitch West's team to Johnson's running gears and go berry picking. Mrs. West sat on the cross piece over the front wheels and drove while Mrs. Johnson sat on the cross piece over the back wheels and held Naomi, West's little girl. As for the berry buckets – they tied those to the reach*, and away they went to pick berries.

Mel's father, back in Wisconsin, was a leather man – made shoes, harnesses, and other leather goods – so when Johnsons bought a team of horses in 1912, Dad sent enough harnesses for four horses. Mrs. Johnson explained, "If one man had a team and another had a wagon, they could work together and get along fine."

The neighbors liked to get together when they could, but Johnsons found their house rather small for entertaining. There really wasn't room for company so when a bunch came one evening, they solved the problem simply by moving the furniture outside to make room for the guests to sit! To climax the evening the chair on which Mrs. Haggerty was sitting broke and sent her crashing to the floor.

Pioneers were resourceful and had to be. One time during threshing a severe storm struck. Usually the threshers went home at night, but this time the storm was so bad they couldn't go. Now they were faced with the problem of finding places for all those extras to sleep in a 12'x16' house. To make a table big enough to accommodate everyone they had put three or four planks across saw horses or other support, and now the table became a bed. Another bed was fixed on the floor under the table, and cousin Bill West shoveled the coal in the basement aside enough to rig another bed down there.

Johnsons' bed was on hinges and folded up against the wall during the day, then down to provide a bed at night – the only real bed in the house. The 'women folk' – Mrs. Johnson, Mrs. West, and little Naomi (two or three years old) slept there. So they all found shelter and a place to rest while the storm raged on.

In 1916 they enlarged their house a little when they built a ten-foot addition on the west end of it. Then 'the year the railroad went through' they built another room on the south and used that for the kitchen. They lived under the same roof for thirty-eight years before they moved to their present house north of Lindsay, just a few rods from the original homestead shack.

Mr. Johnson passed away in 1962. The couple's two sons, their only children, continue to live with their mother on the homestead where she has spent the last fifty-six years.

P. L. (Price) Vine

August – September 1967

If the train hadn't pulled out of the Poplar station while he stood on the platform talking with Charlie Hilger, chances are Price Vine never would have homesteaded in the Vida country. And if he had been left talking with anyone but Charlie Hilger, he probably would have caught the next train west instead of homesteading. But he missed his train, and he stood talking with Hilger.

Price Vine first came to Montana in 1908, looking for work. He had come in on the Milwaukee that time, stopping in both Glendive and Miles City, but he failed to find work in either town so he swung back through South Dakota and got a job as carpenter for the summer.

That fall he went back to his hometown of Greenwood, Wisconsin, and stayed a year-and-a-half before he and his pal, Ole Christopherson, got the idea of shipping from Seattle to Alaska with the fishing fleet. They made a deal with the Great Northern Railroad whereby they paid $2 each for their fare from Minneapolis to Havre. When they reached the latter they were to work out the remainder of the fare. But they didn't reach Havre.

By the time they reached Poplar time was hanging heavy on their hands so, for a little diversion, they decided to get off while the train stopped. Then it was that Charlie Hilger engaged them in conversation.

Hilger had settled on East Redwater, close to its junction with main Redwater, and was 'the watch' for other prospective squatters. He was on hand when the train from the east pulled into Poplar, and noting the two young men who didn't seem to be finding the diversion for which they were looking, he began promoting the prospects for developing the miles and miles of prairie south of the Missouri River.

Price and Ole became so absorbed they forgot to notice the rapid passage of time – until they heard the puff of the engine and saw their train pull away from the depot. If they had been undecided about interrupting their journey their decision was made now; they went with Charlie out to his ranch and 'viewed the land'. What they saw impressed them as good so they staked out claims on land as yet unsurveyed and ordered lumber to build their shacks.

While they waited for their lumber to arrive in Poplar, they and 'Gobbler' (Floyd) Davis made a deal. They would help him build his log house over on Long Grass (a tributary of East Redwater), then when their lumber came, he would haul it out to their claims for them. Gobbler gave them each a saddle horse to ride back and forth from Hilgers.

The horse he gave Price was Mrs. Davis's saddle mount and should have been a respectable horse, but he'd eaten loco weed and was – loco. Price was hardly in the saddle when the horse took off, straight for a pile of corral poles. They landed in the middle of the pile, but kept on going and cleared the other side, still together. Price was of a mind to head toward Hilgers, but the horse differed so they kept circling the flat at a hard gallop until he was 'run out'.

The sites they had chosen for their future homes were about six miles from Charlie Hilger's place where they stayed until they could put up some kind of shelter for themselves. When their lumber came, they walked those six miles every morning and every evening until Ole's shack was built; then they moved into his new dwelling and worked on Price's.

The two bachelors shared the household chores and took turns baking their bread supply. Once Ole decided to play a trick when it was Price's turn to bake. They generally set the yeast on the back of the stove where it was warm, but while Price was out doing chores, Ole slyly moved the yeast to the front of the stove where it cooked. Price, all unsuspecting, used the yeast to leaven the bread, but it didn't do any leavening. His bread didn't rise at all! They tried to eat the hard, soggy concoction but decided it demanded stronger stomachs than they could boast. To their surprise, a stronger stomach came along.

It was a rainy night when the visitor stopped at their shack. He was looking for a stray ox. Frontier hospitality assumed that a passer-by was invited to supper and overnight if the occasion warranted. At supper Passerby ate voraciously of the soggy bread (Mr. Vine declares they had to cut it with an ax!), insisting that it was fine, but before morning he began to feel the effects of his voracity. That soggy bread was resting pretty heavily, and his hosts awoke in the wee hours to find him standing under the unfinished part of the roof, gazing up at the stars and dolefully singing, "Just because she made them goo-oo-gly eyes."

Bread-eater always carried in his belt a big knife, which soon earned a nickname. When men drifted into a community, often they didn't bother to give their name, and nicknames were common. In this case Maggie Hilger had noticed this stranger outside and asked the natural question, "Who is that man out there?" Price didn't know his name either so told her, "Butcher-Knife-Mike," and that was his name from then on. Mrs. Vine recalled with amusement that one of the ladies in the neighborhood consistently called him 'Butcher-Mike-Knife', but never did notice that she was turning the words around.

Digging a well rated top priority so they started digging, but they didn't get water. While they dug, a water hole in the coulee served as their source of water – for drinking as well as all other uses. The cattle drank out of the same hole, and sometimes snakes had to be chased out, but in those days they weren't sending samples to the state's sanitation department for testing to see if it was fit for human consumption. They were just glad for water.

About the time that hole dried up the well-diggers over on the '14' Ranch struck water so they started hauling from there. Not only Price and Ole, but other 'squatters' who had come in also made regular trips to that same well. After the well had been in use for awhile the water began to have a decidedly offensive odor, and the taste was even worse. By this time the neighborhood had women folk and they – especially that schoolteacher who had come along with the bunch that had arrived in June – began insisting upon an investigation.

When they cleaned the well, the offensive odor wasn't hard to explain. They hauled out dead frogs, gophers, snakes – what-have-you. But, Mr. Price maintains, when there wasn't any other water around, you couldn't be particular. At least it was wet. A man figured that if his horse could drink it, he could too.

They dug other wells, dug with pick and shovel, sometimes going as deep as sixty-five feet, but with no success. Then on July 4 they hit water in the little well they dug near Price's shack. And it was good water! From then until 1930 when it suddenly went dry, as many as eight families hauled their water supply from that well.

As Price and Ole dug wells, they had a third fellow helping them – a fellow by the name of Lissack. One evening as supper time approached, Price went to the shack to prepare the meal, leaving Lissack down in the well to continue the digging and Ole up on top to haul out the dirt.

The hole by this time was deep enough that the fellow 'down in' had to have help to get out. After Price left the scene an idea popped into Ole's head. Quietly stepping back from the edge of the excavation, he lay down in the grass – and listened. He didn't have to listen long. Lissack soon noticed that no one else seemed to be around so he decided he might as well quit, too. But how to get out? Clawing at the sides of the hole, he tried desperately to gain altitude, only to fall back. Ole, listening in the grass, heard the 'plunk' when Lissack hit the bottom but played deaf to his call for "O-l-e-e-e-." Repeated attempts ended only in repeated failures, each accompanied by the call for "O-l-e-e-e" until Ole finally decided he'd had enough sport.

Appearing at the edge of the well, he casually announced, "It's about time to come to supper, Lissack," and managed to maintain a grave countenance as Lissack plaintively explained to him, "I couldn't get out. I thought I'd have to stay here all night!"

The first shack that Vine built on his claim wasn't very elaborate, but it provided at least a degree of shelter – though sometimes he wondered how much. During a rainy spell in 1912 when rain fell for a whole week without a break, Price's roof leaked so badly that rain soaked clear through his mattress. During the day he would go to the neighbors and get dried out and warmed up, then come back to his shack and crawl into his soaked bed.

But back to the shack's construction: it was 12'x12', its sloping roof covered with tarpaper and dirt. The stovepipe extended through the roof, and the area around the hole was covered with a piece of tin about the size of a card table so the roof wouldn't catch fire. Furniture inside was no more elaborate than the shack outside. It consisted of a little four-lid laundry stove, a bed, a table, and two or three benches. There wasn't room for anything else.

His bill of fare about matched the shack and furnishings. One fall he ordered 100 pounds of beans from the mail order house (Sears and Roebuck), but the beans were shipped in a coal car and were all black when they reached him. The company replaced the beans when he told them what had happened; then he discovered the black ones could be washed clean so his diet that winter was mostly beans – and bread. His parents had settled on a claim close by his so he was glad to be able to get his bread from mother – instead of having to bake his own.

298

Although the land was unsurveyed when Vine located in the spring of 1910 (the Northern Pacific had surveyed up to the south line of the section on which he built), the Rice Brothers' survey crew came through that fall and surveyed the rest of the land. Price was greatly surprised, when he met the crew members, to find Sam Johnson, one of his old school chums from back in Wisconsin, helping survey his land! Once the land was properly surveyed the various 'squatters' filed for homestead rights on their claims.

Since Price Vine and Ole Christopherson had not left Wisconsin with the intention of settling down on a farm where no one had ever farmed before, they didn't bring along an immigrant car full of machinery or tools or livestock or furniture. When they started, they started from 'scratch'. (Price had exactly $15 in his pocket to 'scratch' with!) When Ole had a chance to buy four oxen from a departing Russian couple (their baby had died, and they had no more heart for the frontier), he did so, and these oxen provided the 'horsepower' for their initial improvements. Two of the oxen were huge, yet so gentle that when two gals of the neighborhood were dared to ride them, they rode the lumbering beasts a mile just to prove they could.

But the oxen proved useful for far more than entertaining young ladies. The first sod broken on both Ole's and Price's claims was broken with those oxen in the yoke. Vine used one when he dug his barn into the bank of the coulee in which he had built his shack. Although the oxen broke the first sod, later he bought horses to pull his 'foot-warmer' – the breaking plow*, called a foot-warmer because there was no place for the operator to ride. 'Round and 'round the field he walked behind that plow.

But those plow horses weren't the ones that he drove 'to town' (Poplar). He bought a team of broncs from some Indians. The Indians were heavy drinkers, often trying to handle the team while 'under the influence' and had well-nigh ruined the horses instead of training them. Only one thing had they learned – that was to run.

Before attempting to hitch the broncs to his wagon, Vine snubbed them to a post for the duration of that operation. Once he had them hitched he would tie the lines inside the wagon, release the horses, and jump into the wagon box as it flashed past. For this preliminary run he was always careful to tie the wagon box to the running gears, and he also removed the wagon seat, seating himself on the floor with his feet braced against the front. He would keep them circling the flat on a hard run until they had covered ten or twelve miles, then they'd be 'run out' enough that he could bring them back to the barnyard, replace the seat, and load for the trip to Poplar.

Each year Vine would break up another twenty to forty acres of sod, whatever he could, just enough to eke out a grub steak on his homestead in the Vida country. He always sowed flax in the new breaking, then afterwards wheat. In a good year flax would probably run eighteen or twenty bushels.

Not much 'canned' entertainment was available on the frontier, but no one ever accused Price Vine and Ole Christopherson of needing the canned variety. They were quite adept at brewing up their own. To most folks an invasion of

299

lice would be a minor (perhaps even a major) crisis, but Price and Ole used it as an opportunity. It isn't clear which fertile brain conceived the idea, but no matter; the other embraced it as eagerly as if it had been his own.

Ole's brother Andrew was due to come for a visit the next week so together they schemed that they would just let their uninvited company stay around until he arrived, and then – but their unholy plot comes to light soon enough. Andy came as scheduled, and after he had been there a day or so one of his genial hosts abruptly asked him, "Were you lousy when you came here?" His answer was an emphatic, "No!" but they were undaunted. "I think you are;" one of them persisted, "take off your shirt."

They had been sleeping three in a bed so by this time their hapless victim did, indeed, have lice. Now that they had fixed the blame they boiled up their clothing – bedding – anything that might have been infected and rid themselves of the termites. But to this day Andrew has never discovered how he was exploited.

During his bachelor days Vine sometimes picked up a little extra income by working for the nearby '14' Ranch, owned by Butler at that time. The '14' had early made use of irrigation to help insure a good hay supply, and they had a ditch about six miles long from their dam on Wolf Creek to Redwater. The dam was only about a mile-and-a-half from Vine's claim, and every day, rain or shine, he rode the full length of the ditch to make sure the flumes were in order. His pay for this vigil was $20 a month – and he boarded himself. The Wolf Creek dam had washed out in 1909 but was rebuilt in 1910 to keep the alfalfa growing. Some years later it again washed out and never has been replaced.

One spring Vine and a neighbor rode together over to East Redwater to get a bunch of horses. They made it all right going over, but when they returned to main Redwater, it was running full of ice. Price was riding a fine-spirited, sure-footed horse so, since there was no way around, he started across, but under those conditions his mount could not keep his footing and fell, plunging both into the icy water. Vine was a good swimmer, but he was critically hampered by his riding boots and heavy winter clothing – not to mention the chunks of ice floating about. He realized that his only chance of survival was to hang onto his horse's tail and be pulled across the channel so he grabbed hold and hung on for dear life as his horse swam.

He survived the ice and water, but his ordeal was far from over – six miles from over. That was the distance still separating him from his shack in the subzero weather. By the time he reached home he was frozen fast to the saddle, and his clothes and boots were frozen on him, but he recovered without permanent disabilities.

The pioneers had to be a hardy lot because many times there were hardships to endure. Once when Vine went with a party of homesteaders to the Missouri River bottom to cut poles, the bottom dropped out of the thermometer, plunging the mercury to fifty-two degrees below zero while their party camped out. As they headed home they had to walk behind their sleighs to keep from freezing. But walking didn't keep fingers from freezing. As a result of

300

hat brush with nature's cold shoulder, some fingers swelled so badly they stuck traight out and wide apart.

P.L. Vine has long been a hunting enthusiast, and on one of his hunting rips in 1913 he learned what it is to be really hungry. He and three other ellows decided to hunt in the breaks now flooded by waters of Fort Peck Lake, and they even went beyond to Snow Creek, north of Jordan, when game failed o appear.

Price and one of the other fellows had each supplied a horse to make up a eam for pulling the wagon for the excursion. But though they hunted, they lidn't find. They kept going a little farther – and a little farther – but the game hey were expecting didn't show up. All they succeeded in getting was a few rabbits, and that didn't bolster their food supply very much.

Finally they were reduced to one can of hominy and a little flour. They carefully divided the hominy among them, but Andrew Christopherson (he had joined the community on a permanent basis by this time) simply could not eat hominy. Hungry though he was, all he could do was watch the others devour the contents of the can while his own hunger pangs continued to gnaw. Since they still had a little flour they tried stirring up flour and water for pancakes, then fried them in rabbit grease, but the concoction wasn't very tasty.

Somewhere along the way they came across a quarter-breed's teepee so they bought a loaf of bread, but it was worse, if possible, than the pancakes. They managed to eat the crust, but the rest of it tasted so strong of soap that, hungry though they were, they couldn't eat it. The moral is, be sure you take along plenty of grub when you go hunting.

That hunting trip is quite a contrast to those Vine made in later years. For about thirty years he went to the mountains hunting each fall in a camper of his own making. He started with a '28 Chevy truck; built gable ends and a ridge pole over the truck box, then stretched a tarp from one side to the other. The equipment was a homemade stove, table, and a bedroll.

Later they built more sophisticated models on larger trucks. One year they took eleven men to the mountains, but usually there were about six. One time as they drove through Libby they passed a grade school where the children were playing. Spying the travelers, they exclaimed, "Oh, look at the 'trucky house!'" and 'trucky house' it was from then on.

When Vine and Christopherson settled on their claims, they soon decided this was an opportunity that should be shared with others so they started writing letters home, telling about all the free land available. The letters caused quite a stir back in Greenwood, and within three months more than half-a-dozen Wisconsin families had come to settle on the prairies. Among those coming were Price Vine's parents and also a young schoolteacher, the future Mrs. P.L. Vine.

Miss Swenson had been teaching in the local school (the Christopherson School) back at Greenwood, and all winter long she had struggled to throw off a cold that wouldn't give up. The doctor had given her every medicine he could, and finally he told her that the best thing for her would be a change of climate.

301

When the Montana fever broke out in the community, enthusiasts urged her to join their migration; she might as well take a claim out there and teach school, too. It was just what the doctor ordered so she decided to try it.

No school district had been organized up to this time, simply because there had been very little need for a school. There had been a few children in ranch families here and there, but now with the homesteaders coming in, the school census increased rapidly so something had to be done about a school.

In the meantime Miss Swenson was able to get some books from a teacher in Poplar so she could study in preparation for taking teacher's examinations. While she studied she also taught. Three children came to her shack and she taught them gratis because there was no school available for them to attend.

In the spring of 1911 she had opportunity to take teacher's examination in Glasgow so she rode to Poplar with a neighbor who was going in with team and bobsled and planned to take the train from there. At that time there was no bridge across the Missouri River, and when they reached the river, they found the ice covered with water. They hesitated. Alida assured them they need not risk the crossing for her benefit (another year before she could take the examinations?) but men on the frontier did not give up easily.

They had started for Poplar and didn't plan to turn back unless they had to. They securely tied the sled box to the running gears so the swift current would not sweep the box away, then ventured into the river. The water was deep enough that it ran into the sled box as they crossed, but they made it across safely, and Alida went on to Glasgow for her tests.

She was successful in passing her examinations and was granted a certificate to teach in Montana. That fall she began her Montana teaching in the Hilger School, eight or ten miles east of her claim. Bert Hilger, president of Glendive's Hilger Chevrolet Company, was one of her pupils that year. During the winter months she stayed in his parents' home to be closer to school, but sometimes during the warm weather she rode back and forth from her little shack on a saddle horse she bought from Bert.

That winter of 1911-12, she says, was one of the hardest she's seen here. One morning she rode to school (the mile-and-a-half from Hilgers, not from her homestead) when the temperature was fifty-two degrees below zero. The next year she taught in a school farther west, closer to her home.

In 1915 her home location changed. That year she and Price Vine were married. They built a brand new house a short distance up the coulee from the little homestead shack, and there they lived until 1949 when they again built a new house, this time on the flat above the coulee. Water sometimes rose to a level in the coulee too high for comfort so they decided to move to higher ground.

Now the Vines have three branches: Floyd, their oldest son, lives in Houston; Blanch, their only daughter, lives in Plentywood; and John, their youngest, lives on the home place in his new house a few hundred yards from the house where he grew up.

302

They found that rearing children involved varying and sometimes harrowing experiences. Perhaps some people who complain that it's hard nowadays to get hold of a doctor have never shared an experience like the Vines had in taking little Floyd, fever raging, to the doctor. Floyd had become ill, but because of the distance to Poplar, where the nearest doctor was located, and unfavorable weather conditions they tried to doctor him at home. A trained nurse in the community gave all the assistance she could, but when his temperature soared to 105.8, she told them they must get him to the doctor, bad roads or no.

When they reached the Missouri River (still no bridge) they found the ice breaking away from shore on the Poplar side. Planks had been laid from the ice to the shore across the open channel so one man stood on the bank and carefully directed as the driver inched over the planks (they had gone in by car) across that span of water. They all breathed more freely when the back wheels were safe on solid ground once more. And the doctor, even without the modern wonder drugs, was able to save the little fellow.

Once before Blanche was two years old she and Floyd went for a ride with their dad in the back seat of 'Old Betsy', and soon after they returned home she was "limp as a dishrag, white as a sheet," then unconscious. Mrs. Vine was terribly frightened, but when she frantically summoned Dad, he took the whole affair quite calmly. He recalled that, as they were driving along, he had heard Blanche murmur, "Me chew 'baccie" so his diagnosis was that she had nibbled his plug of tobacco that had been lying on the seat. Sick though she was, he was confident that she would come out of it all right and, Mrs. Vine conceded, she did.

Outstanding in the memory of old timers were the range fires they fought when, for miles and miles, there was no plowed field to check them. Every man in the area would come to fight, fight until he was ready to drop and then fight some more. Women folk, too, shared the load by hauling water and preparing lunches for the firefighters. The old ranchers still talk about the conflagration when they killed seventeen steers to drag to bring it under control. That was before Vine's arrival, but the first year he was on his claim, a fire swept down from the north and just missed his place.

One of the outstanding fires he helped fight started on Sand Creek and burned across Wolf Creek. By working at the edge of the fire line they had been able to turn it enough to head it into the creek and bring it under control. It was two o'clock in the morning by the time they accomplished that, and they were just about famished for food and water. No one was home at the nearest cabin, but they went in to see what they could find to eat after their thirst was quenched. All they found was a loaf of bread, but that helped.

Two years ago the Vines celebrated their fiftieth wedding anniversary. They're still living on their farm, the site of the first little 'squatter's' shack and barn in full view from their house.

Peter Hangs, Sr.

February 1967

"What are the branches in our government?" Mrs. Perham, teacher in the night school, directed the question to a newly-arrived immigrant from the 'Old Country' eager to prepare for citizenship. He didn't know what she was talking about so Nick Scabad, seated behind him, leaned forward and helpfully whispered an answer: "The Sidney branch!" the innocent newcomer repeated.

Pete Hangs, not above practical jokes himself, chuckled as he recalled the incident from night school many years ago. Numerous foreign-born settlers had located in Glendive in the early years of the twentieth century, and the majority of them wanted to become citizens.

Mr. Hangs himself had come to the United States in 1906, to Glendive in 1908. He was hardly more than a youngster when he came and very much wanted to go to school, but school was out of the question; he had to work.

As he thought on his problem he began to wonder, "Why not a night school for those like him who had to work but yet wanted to learn?" He approached Judge Lieper with his idea, and the judge was 'tickled to death' to help.

He told Hangs, "You sign up thirty-five fellows interested in attending, and we'll get you a night school." In two days Hangs had enough signers for a school.

For three months that winter, and again the next two winters, classes met twice weekly with various teachers, even lawyers or other business men from the community to help them learn about citizenship, along with other fundamentals. A few times when no one else was available to teach, Mr. Hangs himself was appointed to fill in. That every class member 'made it' for citizenship bears testimony to the success of the school.

Pete had gone to school six years in his native Hungary, but one thing puzzled him when he came to the United States. Spelling. In Hungarian or German a word is spelled exactly as it sounds and there is no such thing as teaching spelling as a subject in school. Here the many silent letters baffled him. However, his learning in night school combined with what he could pick up through other avenues enabled him to communicate through writing, essential in the job he held on the railroad.

Although Mr. and Mrs. Hangs lived about five miles apart in their native land, they had to cross thousands of miles of ocean and land to meet each other. Pete's father had come to the United States in 1902. When he landed in New York, immigration officials asked him for the name of someone he knew in the United States. He did some rapid thinking and recalled the name of an acquaintance from Hungary who had settled in Richardton, North Dakota.

He gave that name so the officials called the Richardton man who confirmed the acquaintance, and the senior Hangs was allowed to enter. Then, because he didn't know another soul or any other place in this vast new country, he decided he might as well go to Richardton, too.

Two years later Pete's mother and sister also came to the United States, but another two years passed before Pete came. Even that was too soon to suit him. He had been staying with his grandparents, and he would have chosen to stay right there, but the choosing wasn't left to him. His father insisted he come to North Dakota so he reluctantly complied.

When he took his physical examination preparatory to coming he was turned down because of his eyes, but his grandfather told him to go ahead; he might be able to get through so he tried it and had no trouble.

By this time his parents were living in Dickinson so he joined them and hoped to go to school there. He was just fourteen, but he had attended only three days when his folks found him a job herding sheep. They figured they needed the money more than he needed the schooling. He hated herding sheep. He never wants to look another sheep in the eye even yet, he declares. He was glad when the chance came to work for a farmer and he could leave the sheep. He liked working on the farm and stayed with that farmer until he moved to Glendive in 1908.

In Glendive he got a job with the Northern Pacific Railroad in the car shops, building boxcars. He started working for the railroad July 23, 1908, and stayed with them until he retired in 1957, forty-nine years and seven months. He had learned the wagon trade while he was with his grandfather in Hungary and now found that training a great help. Within a month from the time he started working he received a promotion.

Pete Hangs recalls that when he came to Glendive, there were very few houses on the south side and not very many over town, but there were lots of saloons. The only sidewalks were gravel or board walks. The only sidewalk on the south side was in front of Keen's home on Benham. For the most part, the 'walks' were paths through the sagebrush.

When Pete, at sixteen, started with the railroad, he was paid twenty-three cents an hour. His parents had preceded him to Glendive, and his father also worked for the Northern Pacific, in the same department. He always turned his check over to his mother, but one month, when they had made pretty good – $115 each – his father told him he could keep some out. They went to the bank together, cashed their checks, and Pete kept $15, taking the rest home.

When he gave the hundred to his mother, she demanded to know where the rest of it was – she kept close track of the hours they worked. He explained that his father had told him he could have fifteen dollars for spending money, but she had other ideas. Very angry, she ordered him out of the house. He left and went on down the street a few houses to where his sister and her husband lived. A day or so later he had a chance to bid on a Miles City job for the railroad so he bid and got the job.

His father sought him out and tried to talk him out of going off up there by himself. "You can't live up there alone," he told him. "You don't know anything about cooking and you'll starve to death." Mr. Hangs admits that his father had a point there. He couldn't even cook water, but he was still determined to go. When his father saw that he was not to be dissuaded, he told Pete he'd try to get him some money (he had given even the fifteen dollars to his mother before he had left the house) and succeeded in slipping him twenty dollars. Twenty dollars to set up housekeeping and keep him going until next month's paycheck arrived!

Pete had only been in Miles City about a week when they began trying to get him to come home. (His father, of course, had been trying that all along.) They sent his brother to Miles City to look for him and try to get him to come back, but he happened to be working out of town just then. Brother didn't think to ask the dispatcher where Pete was so he didn't find him.

After two weeks Pete relented and came back to Glendive for over Sunday (he went to his sister's home), but he was back on his Miles City job Monday morning. His father, still concerned about his starving, had been doing some thinking during those two weeks, and now came up with what he figured was the best solution.

"You ought to get married," he told him. "How would I get married when I don't even have a girl?" his astonished son expostulated. But Dad had that figured out, too.

"I know the girl you should have," he assured him. "She's a good girl, and she'd make you a good wife." "And," conceded Mr. Hangs, nodding his head as he interrupted his story to momentarily come back to the present, "he picked me a good one."

The girl Mr. Hangs, Sr. had in mind was Anna Link, living across the street from them. Anna had come to Glendive from Hungary in 1910. When she was only five years old, her father died, so she went to live with her grandparents.

Some years later her mother married again, Peter Vogel, and in 1906 they came to America. She had a brother living near Stipek, Montana, so they came to Glendive. The oldest girl, Elizabeth, came along, but Anna stayed in Hungary with her grandparents.

After two years in Glendive the Vogels returned to Hungary, and another two years elapsed before they were ready to make their permanent move to the New World. Since the move was to be permanent, this time they insisted that Anna come, too. Anna was perfectly content living with her grandparents as she had for ten years, and she had no desire to go to a New World, but her mother would have it no other way.

There was a younger boy in the family who had broken his back and now was crippled who had also remained in Hungary when the family made their first trip across, but now they wanted the whole family to go. When they reached their port city, however, he could not get a passport because of his condition so he had to be sent back to the grandparents.

The family council recommended that Anna go back with him, then come later, but Anna emphatically made it known that if she went back with him she was going to stay there. Finally it was decided that Mrs. Vogel would go back with him while the rest of the family went on. Then several weeks later, she came with a cousin who was making the ocean crossing.

Again the Vogel family located in Glendive, and four years later several businessmen from the town, among them Lowe and Hollecker, arranged for the crippled boy to join his family. They signed a paper that they would assume responsibility to see that the lad went to school and that he would not become a ward of the state. After his arrival in Glendive, the boy sold newspapers at the Jordan Hotel to make a little money, but in 1916 he contracted pneumonia and died, just a little more than two years after his coming here.

Mrs. Hangs recalls it wasn't easy to adjust to a new land and new culture and new language. Her older sister, who had now been in the States four years, worked as a waitress in a restaurant, and Anna was able to get a job in the same restaurant, washing dishes. She couldn't speak a word of English but, she pointed out, she didn't have to talk to the dishes, so she got along fine.

So it was that Anna Link was living just across the street when Mr. Hangs decided Pete should have a wife. The idea was as much a surprise to her as it was to Pete. She had gone to a show with him once — she and her sister had, that is — but that was hardly grounds for expecting a proposal.

Besides that, she was only seventeen years old — "Seventeen years and three months," she hastened to add when Mr. Hangs mentioned that he was twenty years and six months when they married.

Be that as it may, two weeks after his father's recommendation Pete and Anna were married. Mr. Hangs explains that they had to rush things so she wouldn't have time to back out.

Their marriage ceremony was performed in the little Catholic Church on the corner of Power and Sargent. Fifty years later, 1962, they observed their golden wedding anniversary in the present Catholic Church on Meade and Benham.

Mr. Hangs recalls that when they were married he had exactly four pennies to his name — all that he had left of the twenty dollars. He still has those same four pennies in a glass in the cupboard. Their first eight months together they lived in an 'outfit car' — a railroad car outfitted for living quarters. They were so 'hard up' when they got married they didn't even have chairs in their boxcar. One thing, though, he would never do was borrow money, and he has never owed anybody a cent in his life. If he didn't have the money to pay for it, he didn't buy it.

At the time of their marriage he had been in Miles City about a month (so a pay check was soon coming), and they were there four months more before he was transferred to Beach. After three months he was moved back to Glendive where they have lived since.

The day they moved to Glendive a dozen eggs they had sitting on their stove froze. Fifty-two degrees below zero it was that day! They lived about thirty-five years on Towne Street before moving into their present home on Power.

In those early days of their marriage there wasn't much in the way of commercial entertainment so they arranged their own. They both loved to fish and hunt, and often when he would get home from work they would go down to the river and fish awhile. Sometimes they would get together with their friends in one of the homes and dance, perhaps in the basement or in one of the rooms from which they had removed the furniture.

One time they decided they wanted to celebrate so they got permission from Keene, the chief of police, then rounded up a hayrack and a team to pull it. They also rounded up Steve Meissner and his accordion, then up and down the streets — or trails — on the south side they drove, singing and having a great time.

The first few years after his retirement from the railroad in 1965, Mr. and Mrs. Hangs took advantage of his leisure to go back to fishing again, but the last few years he has developed arthritis so he can't drive the car to go. Perhaps if he hadn't teased Mrs. Hangs the first time she tried to drive a car, she could drive them to the fishing holes now.

In their early fishing days they had a Ford touring car. One time when he had to get out to open a gate, he suggested she drive through so she slid behind the wheel. It looked much more complicated now than when he was driving — all those pedals down on the floor! She grabbed the steering wheel in a vice-like grip, but with all those pedals to sort out she had to keep her eyes glued to the floor to make sure she hit the right one. Almost before she knew it she was through the gate and hadn't even had time to look where she was going. Even though she didn't hit anything, he kept laughing about it, and she would never try again. So now neither one can drive them fishing.

Even though they can't go fishing, they still do things together. Dr. Moe remarked of them, "You never see one alone unless it's at a meeting strictly for men or for women. Pete and Anna are always together." After almost fifty-five years of marriage, that's the way they prefer it.

Mr. Hangs has watched Glendive grow these fifty-nine years he has been here and has seen many changes take place. "Glendive surely isn't the same," he concluded.

Mrs. Ernest (Myrtle Tusler) Kirkpatrick & Sheldon Tusler

June 1966

Henry Tusler was one of those Montana 'visitors' whose brief vacation stay turned into a lifelong residence. Henry had come from Wisconsin to visit his uncle, a cattle rancher in eastern Montana. His two-week vacation over, eighteen-year-old Henry packed his suitcase, headed for the depot and Wisconsin. At the depot his uncle suddenly asked, "Why do you have to go back?" The question took young Henry by surprise. He had just taken for granted that, when his visit was over, he would go back to his Wisconsin job. He explained that he had hired out for the season so he just expected to go back.

His uncle, whose name also was Henry Tusler, jocularly observed, "Here we hire one day and fire the next, and our men have the same privilege." Back in Wisconsin Henry was getting two dollars more than the prevailing wage — $18 a month plus room and board. Uncle Henry offered him $40 plus room and board and suggested nephew contact his Wisconsin boss and ask if it was all right to stay. The Wisconsin reply granted him a release so he stayed. That was in 1889, and he was here until his death on August 10, 1941. Quite a vacation.

His uncle's cattle were in two main locations, one bunch near Terry and another bunch near Miles City. (The Tusler telegraph station, just out of Miles City, was named for the uncle, Henry Tusler.) Young Henry's job was to take care of the Terry cattle. If the winter of 1885-86 had taught cattlemen anything, it taught that a good supply of hay was a must for winters when cattle could not forage. The winter of 1892-93, another that stockmen remember with a groan, young Henry was feeding a bunch of his uncle's cattle at the home place just out of Terry, and an old fellow was feeding another bunch over on the Kempton Ranch. In spite of blizzards and cold, Tusler each day forced his cattle to water, driving them with a whip when necessary to make them face the wind. Losses from that bunch were very light, but the old fellow, who fed the cattle hay but let them decide for themselves whether they would drink, lost heavily from his bunch.

The closest Henry ever did get to going back to Wisconsin was Iowa. After he came to Montana he had gone to school some in Miles City, and he went to college in Iowa that one winter.

After six years in his adopted state, Henry Tusler married Clara Etta Braley. Clara was thirteen years old when she came with her parents to the frontier in 1892. The Braleys 'squatted' on Ash Creek, not far from Tusler's Terry headquarters. Uncle Henry Tusler also had just 'squatted' when he started ranching, years before any surveying crew mapped out the sections. Like many another rancher, he had selected a site near a good water supply and built, using the free range for miles around to run his livestock.

Ranchers as a general rule didn't go out of their way to encourage the homesteaders. When one of the homeseekers asked an old rancher, "How far is it to water?" he answered, "About two miles." "We mean down," they explained. "About the same," was the brusque reply.

Henry Tusler, Sr. died rather young, leaving his nephew on the ranch. When, after the turn of the century, the land opened up for homesteading and the homesteaders began flocking in, Henry filed on the quarter where the ranch buildings stood. The buildings were in a choice location, on a bank just above springs that provided abundant water. His son, Sheldon Tusler, remarked that he was raised on spring water and still can't get used to city water. He really doesn't have to because he is living on a ranch where springs are plentiful.

Clara Braley was only sixteen when she married Henry, but her twenty-four-year-old husband had been making his own way for a good many years. His parents had both died when he was still small, and he was accustomed to taking responsibility.

They had seven children, the oldest of whom was Myrtle (Mrs. Ernest Kirkpatrick). Mrs. Kirkpatrick recalls that as a little girl she spent much time with her father. Plowing, mowing hay, whatever his task might be, she was with him if she could arrange to be.

As he followed the horse-drawn plow, he'd tie the lines around his neck so she, trotting along behind him in the furrow, would play with the ends of the lines hanging down his back and pretend she was driving horses, too. When she was hardly more than six or seven she'd ride the mower (no power mower then), pulling the dump lever at the proper time. Grass was so abundant they could put up hay most any place on 'the bench' (Broadview Bench, southeast of Terry).

Mr. Tusler planted the first great northern beans in this part of the country. It was important in those early years of abundant grass and few plowed fields to plow fireguards around buildings. It was a good idea to have a guard around your haystacks, too, and even some of the pasture. It occurred to Mr. Tusler he might as well make use of the furrows so he planted some beans in them. During the busy summer he forgot all about the planting but that fall, scattered along the fireguard, he found the big white beans. The cattle had eaten the tops but the beans were still there.

When Myrtle was three years old, her parents left her with her grandparents for a few days while they made a trip to some hot springs to treat her father's rheumatism. One afternoon while Grandma was picking cucumbers, Myrtle stood nearby, breaking open the pods of radishes that had gone to seed. Suddenly a menacing buzz caused Grandma to whirl, grab Myrtle by the arm, and swing her to the side. A rattlesnake had reared its head right in front of the little girl. Grandma with her hoe made short work of the rattler, but for some days Myrtle's arm bore a black and blue mark where Grandma's hand had gripped.

A few years later Myrtle was awakened one night by her father, almost panicky, and told, "Run get Grandma!" Mama had some kind of spell and was unconscious. Dad thought she was dying. A few gray streaks were just beginning to lighten the sky as the frightened little six-year-old scampered over the trail to Grandma's house. She didn't actually see anything startling in the gray half-light (although some of those shadows took on fearsome and weird shapes), but she imagined coyotes or snakes or wildcats were lurking behind every bush and clump of grass, ready to jump at her.

She covered that half-mile in record time (safely) and burst into her grandparents' home with, "Come quick! Mama is sick!" In almost no time Grandpa had the team hitched up, and the three of them were hurrying back over the trail. They reached Mama's bedside to find her much better, and by the time a doctor arrived, she seemed to be all right. Dr. Andrews, summoned from Miles City, had caught a freight train to come see her. She never had an attack like that again, and they never did find out what was the matter with her that night.

Dr. Andrews was a good friend of Grandpa Braley, and one fall they planned a deer-hunting trip together. Dr. Andrews again came down on a freight train from Miles City, planning to join Grandpa at Terry and leave from there. Before he could get out of town, someone found out he was in and asked him to make a sick call. Then a baby decided it was a good time to arrive on the scene, and so it went. Dr. Andrews was in Terry three days and was kept so busy he didn't get to go hunting at all. He finally had to give it up and go back to Miles City.

The house on the homestead knew nothing of electricity when the Tusler children were growing up, but even so there were advantages most rural homes of the era didn't have. A carbide light plant was a great improvement over the kerosene lamps, and the little two-plate stove, so handy for cooking a hurry-up meal, was almost a luxury.

In the fall of 1916 Tuslers sold the homestead part of the ranch to Robert Empey, a nearby homesteader. Then in 1917 they built a new house and barn on railroad land a quarter of a mile down the creek and near a big spring. The Tuslers' son, Lester, now lives on this place.

Mother Tusler, after the death of her husband in 1941, lived in town with daughter Irene. When she passed away in 1964 at the age of eighty-six years, she had twenty-four grandchildren, thirty-six great grandchildren, and eight great, great grandchildren.

The seven Tusler children all made their homes in or around Terry. Miss Irene taught school many years and presently teaches first grade in the Terry school. Henrietta was the wife of a prominent Terry grocer, Archie Buckingham. She is the only one of the Tusler children no longer living. Sheldon lives on his ranch with its springs near Terry, as does Lester. The Tuslers (Henry) had one set of twins, Forest and Fern. Forest has worked for Prairie County with the road crew for years, and he also served with the U.S. Navy during World War II. Fern is a housewife and mother of six children, including one set of twin boys.

311

In 1916 Myrtle, the first of the Tusler children, married a homesteader who had come to Montana early enough to be classed with the old timers. Ernest Kirkpatrick came to Montana from Illinois for 'just a visit', too.

His sister and her husband, C.W. Grandy, were living in Terry so in the spring of 1908 Kirkpatrick came out to see them. During the visit he was persuaded that a homestead would be a good investment so he decided to file. Of course, he would stay just long enough to prove up* on it. But he also stayed the rest of his life.

At first he built a very 'temporary-looking' shack on his homestead and lived there in the summer. During the winter he stayed in Terry with the Grandys and drove out occasionally to his claim. He was handy with carpenter tools and did quite a bit of building throughout southeastern Montana – Baker, Ismay, and Ekalaka as well as around Terry. He also worked as a carpenter on the Milwaukee Railroad.

After a couple years of carpentering he bought some horses and turned his attention to farming. Mr. Kirkpatrick loved to raise corn (that Midwest background, perhaps) and usually had a bunch of pigs, too, as well as cattle. He wasn't one to "put all his eggs in one basket."

Mrs. Kirkpatrick observed that some years they raised bumper crops – and some years they didn't. In 1919 (many an old timer shakes his head over that year) they hardly harvested anything – their entire yield came from just a few low places. They did get their seed back, though, which was more than many farmers did that year.

She smiled as she thought of the philosophy with which her husband viewed a crop failure. He'd sum up the situation with, "Didn't do much this year, but we'll give it heck next year!" So next year they'd plant again with the hope that this would be 'the year'. And they did have some real good crops those last years he farmed.

After her husband's death in 1965 Mrs. Kirkpatrick moved into Terry. Now she and her sister, Irene, live there together. Mrs. Kirkpatrick, reflecting upon her childhood days, observed that they didn't have much of this world's goods, but they never went to bed hungry, and they had wonderful times together.

Bert Ekland

January 1965

Just a kid. Just a sixteen-year-old kid. Across an ocean, and across most of the continent, from home. A foreign land, a strange language. Just a sixteen-year-old kid.

But when sixteen-year-old Bert Ekland arrived in Glendive from Norway back in 1903, he didn't waste much time wondering what to do next. The very day of his arrival he met Joe Wester, foreman of a B&B Gang* for the N.P., who asked him what he planned to do. Upon receiving his reply that he was planning to do anything he could find, Mr. Wester told him, "I'll give you a job; you can go back out on the train with me in the morning."

So Bert went out the next morning, to where the crew was working near Mandan, and started on his first job in his new country. After about a year with the railroad he decided he'd like a change of scenery so he took a job herding sheep for the Rife Brothers in the Baker country. They had 15,000 sheep with about 2,500-3,000 to a band. He lived in a sheep wagon, and in the three years that he worked there, often for weeks at a time the only company he enjoyed was his own – and that of 3,000 sheep.

His employers were good about supplying provisions, but it was up to him to do the cooking. He had never done any cooking before, but now he learned the process – learned fast, because it was either cook or starve.

He recalls that while he was working there he drove the ninety miles from Ekalaka to Glendive and saw just one fence! Portraying a bit of 'life then', he remarked that if you stopped at someone's house and found no one home, it was perfectly in order to go ahead and cook yourself a meal. Nobody thought of objecting to that – provided you washed the dishes. In further contrast he added that if anyone borrowed money from you, you were sure to get it back; now if anyone borrows from you, you can be sure you won't get it back!

About five years after he had come to this country he decided to take a look at Canada and perhaps homestead there, but he didn't find anything he wanted. He did find, however, that he could get a ticket to Norway from there for thirty dollars so he went back home. Four weeks was long enough in Norway, though, and he was on his way back to Montana.

Through the years he made several trips from coast to coast, shearing sheep as he went, getting from seven to ten cents a head. It was hard work, but it paid his way.

Upon his return to the Treasure State after a trip to Norway, he filed on a homestead two miles below Intake on War Dance Creek. "All of Murphy Table to choose from and I picked the badlands!" he exclaimed in reminiscence. But of course he wasn't planning then on doing much farming.

He hauled logs up from the river for his house and plastered it with mud. What breaking he did was done with four horses pulling a walking plow. One

313

day George McCone came along and offered to buy his homestead rights so he sold to him.

Later, he bought Ray Salen's homestead on Deer Creek and started his operations in that community with just a half section. Other homesteaders in the area were interested only in moving out and warned him, "You'll starve if you stay here." He stayed and he didn't starve, either. As others became discouraged and moved away, searching for greener pastures, he bought their homesteads and other lands as well. He was located just two miles west of the Hollecker Ranch, and, after the death of Hollecker he bought that spread also.

His farming in those early days was done with horses – eight head to put in his crop. In addition to his farming he milked cows, raised chickens and turkeys, sheep and stock cattle – anything and everything to make a living. Coyotes were always after the turkeys and would get the sheep, too, if they got a chance. The government finally got rid of the coyotes, just about the time he got rid of his sheep.

He battled against dry years and low prices – recalls his vow that if calves "got up to eleven cents" he was going to sell, and sell them he did for that price. When a more prosperous era finally dawned he sold some calves for almost forty cents! In spite of all the adversities he observed that he has never been any place where he figures it would be any easier to make a living.

About fourteen years ago he retired and moved to Glendive, leaving son Ed in charge of the ranch. His other son lives in Shelby and his daughter in Glendive.

In 1960 Mr. Ekland made another visit to Norway, but things had changed so much there, even as here, that he didn't know his own home. He's been a lot of places and seen a lot of things in his day, but concludes that he'd still rather live in Glendive than any other place.

Mrs. Richard (Virginia Gosselin) Wing

March 1972

Virginia Wing – Virginia Gosselin then – came to Montana in 1910 from Mendota, Minnesota. All her life she had suffered with asthma, so much so that it was difficult for her even to attend school. After the third grade she was forced to drop out, and from then on, any schooling she had her mother taught her at home.

Her battle with asthma continued until she was twenty-one. Then, when the lure of free land brought some of her relatives to Montana to homestead, Virginia came with them in the hope that she would feel better in the dry climate. She did not hope in vain. Her asthma cleared up and she was able to enjoy good health for the first time that she could remember.

She had come to the Treasure State with Mr. and Mrs. Martin Rinehart, their two sons, Alfa and Ovid, and their daughter Olive. Irwin Babcock was also in the party. Olive later became Mrs. Babcock, mother of former governor Tim. Mr. Rinehart had made a trip to Montana earlier to see what was available in homestead land, and now the four men filed on claims in the Crackerbox area.

They arrived in October, and their first concern was to put up a shelter so they quickly built a little two-room shack. It was just a shell – that was long before the days of insulating houses – so it didn't take long to put it up.

Before long the two girls, Virginia and Olive, found jobs in Glendive, but they spent enough time on the homestead to learn what it was like to be twenty-five miles from the nearest town, with horses and wagon (or walking) providing the only transportation.

Mrs. Wing tells of riding horseback to dances and parties – to Fallon, to Terry, to Glendive. Once she and Olive rode to a dance while she was keeping house for an older man on a homestead. They returned later than he figured they should so he had locked them out, and they had to sleep in the haystack!

She also tells of an unfortunate experience baking bread for this same old man. She had been pastry cook in her parents' rooming house back in Minnesota, but perhaps she hadn't had too much experience baking bread. At any rate, she forgot to put in the yeast so the bread was a mess. The worst of it was she had used almost all the flour in the house so the 'old man' was understandably upset. On a homestead twenty-five to thirty miles from the nearest store with only horses and buggy to bridge the gap, you didn't run to town every day.

Virginia worked in several different homes in Glendive before she started keeping house for a photographer whose wife had died of cancer, leaving him with three young children. In the course of time she and Mr. Wing were married, and she was permanent housekeeper. She acquired a ready-made family of three children with the wedding ceremony, then added three more – a little more gradually.

Richard E. Wing had come to Glendive in 1907, from Elkader, Iowa. Back in his home state he had been a transient photographer, going from town to town with a horse-drawn (what else?) studio.

Mr. Wing had a photographer friend in Miles City who had a studio in Bowman, North Dakota. This friend encouraged him to move to Dickinson and set up business there. However, when he arrived in Dickinson, he found it was already supplied with two studios. He figured another would most certainly be a superfluity so he came on to Glendive. Here the field seemed wide open.

His first studio was a tarpaper shack across the alley from the Methodist Church. When he made the move from Iowa to Dickinson, he had shipped his photographic equipment and household goods (he brought a wife and family with him) to that location by immigrant car*.

In order to start up business in Glendive he had to have some of his equipment, but he didn't have the money to bring the car on to Glendive. He went back to Dickinson with team and wagon, and since he could figure out no other way to do it, removed (by night) the equipment he needed to start business and brought it back to Glendive. But he let the railroad company have his furniture.

Richard E. Wing began his photographic career in Glendive during the days of family and group pictures. He would go to some gathering – perhaps an auction sale, maybe a picnic – and take pictures. Then he'd sell the prints to those pictured.

For some years he had a circuit camera in conjunction with Mr. Booen of Miles City, and they specialized in large groups of people – the Elks convention, for example. They'd line up a long row of people, start photographing at one end, and swing on around to the other end until they had everyone pictured. Hurrying back to the studio, they'd develop their film, and in an hour they'd be back on the street selling the pictures.

Mr. Wing used to tell his family about a little incident when he went with some land promoters to photograph some land – sales promotion. As they bounced along in the horse-drawn buggy they came to a creek, and one of the fellows made the observation, "There's water in the creek!" Mr. Wing had been in Montana only a very short time, and this seemed to him a most peculiar observation. What else? After he had been around awhile, however, he realized that many of the creeks hereabouts are dry most of the time, and he understood why the native considered water worthy of comment.

From his first studio, the tarpaper shack across the alley from the Methodist Church, he moved into a new building Dave Leidahl erected across from the city hall. Leidahl built the studio, equipped with a skylight, on the second floor. The skylight (so essential at a time when they depended strictly upon day light for their photographing) always faced north. Depending upon daylight created problems, particularly during the pre-Christmas season – just when the days were shortest, business was heaviest.

Fire in a nearby building once threatened his studio while it was in these quarters. A log building, occupied by John Doebler, dry cleaner, and Bedor with agates, caught fire. Though it burned, firemen sprayed water on the building that stood between the fire and Wings and contained the blaze, but the heat cracked the glass in the studio skylight. The glass was replaced but was never satisfactory after that as it allowed dust to blow in.

In 1940 they moved to the studio's present site. Although it has changed hands (it is now Trier's Studio) it is still at the same location at 112 West Benham across the street from the Jordan Motor Inn.

In the early 1930's, Mr. Wing revived his Iowa practice of itinerant photography, only now his studio on wheels was motorized instead of horse drawn. He drove the unit, a huge thing, from town to town as he had done in early years.

This studio was equipped with skylight and darkroom. He'd develop his film, then send the film back to Glendive for printing. He had a couch in the van so he could sleep in it, and he also had it equipped so he could cook in it.

When the Northern Pacific Railroad reached Circle, Mr. Wing took his mobile studio to the little town on the Redwater for the celebration. The trip required two days so they stopped the first night at Rimroad, then went on into town the next day. On the trip to Circle he had his studio camera sitting on the couch, but as they bounced over the rough road (the railway reached Circle before an oiled road did, you realize) the camera fell off and broke the shutter in the lens.

The average photographer would have been stymied, but Mr. Wing was equal to the occasion. Instead of using the shutter, he put his hat over the lens. When he pulled the slide to expose the film, he'd reach around and jerk the hat away, then quickly replace it. He took a lot of pictures during that celebration!

In the early days of rodeo Mr. Wing worked with Doubleday, photographing cowboys and other activities. Mr. Wing was responsible also for the first movie camera in Glendive. Sometimes he would arrange beauty contests – for babies. Parents would bring their babies to the studio to be photographed with the moving picture camera, then he'd sell the pictures to local merchants for advertising. Each merchant would have a place to vote, and customers would cast their ballot for their favorite baby. At the end of the contest he would show all the contestants, featuring the winner, at the theater. You tried all kinds of angles to make a dollar in those days.

His specialty, however, was portraits. He didn't do much photographing of events – such as the ice going out, for example – unless he could sell postcards of it.

Another photographer about that time was Mr. Foster, former county commissioner. He ran a gift shop and made a hobby of photography. His specialty was 'events' – taking pictures of things happening locally. He'd make these pictures into postcards and sell them in his shop. In this way he acquired a good pictorial collection of 'happenings' in eastern Montana. Thus he and Wing's Studio complemented rather than competed with each other.

When Mr. Wing passed away in 1934, Mrs. Wing carried on with the studio. Perhaps now (she didn't mention) she did something about that trail of sludge

317

from the dark room to the studio! Mr. Wing coated his own film in the dark room, then took it directly to the studio. The quality of his negatives was superior to much produced today, but Mrs. Wing could never appreciate the mess on the floor as the sludge dripped.

In 1935 Paddy (son Ray; his aunt named him Paddy when he was born, and more people know him by that name than the name his parents picked for him) went to work in the studio with his mother, and they worked together until 1940 when Mrs. Wing retired.

She was hardly out of the business when World War II started, and Paddy enlisted in the Marine Corps so she came back and again ran the studio from 1942-45. This was probably the busiest period the studio ever had with everyone wanting pictures of departing soldiers or taking pictures to send to the soldiers.

When Paddy returned after the war to take over the studio once more, she retired again. Since then she has lived most of the time in Seattle, but the asthma which plagued her as a girl in Minnesota returned in the damp Seattle climate. A year ago last October she returned to Glendive. Since that time she has been living in the Grandview apartments – as soon as she was able to leave the hospital, that is.

She came back to Glendive a very sick woman, but has regained a surprising degree of health for a woman her age, considering her physical condition when she arrived a year-and-a-half ago.

Besides her son Paddy here in Glendive she has a son Dick in Seattle; another son, Gilbert, in Plentywood; and a stepdaughter, Marguerite in San Francisco.

A few years ago Paddy sold the studio to Gerald Trier. The business had been in the family almost sixty years – from 1907 until Paddy's retirement in July 1966, when he sold Wing's studio.

Gust Voss

January 1966

To Gust Voss "That Little Old Sod Shanty on My Claim" wasn't just an old folk song. It was bachelor days, hard work, drought, dust, wind, and cold as it identified with his early Montana days.

When Gust Voss came to Dawson County to look over the homestead proposition, he wasn't sure at first whether he wanted to file a claim or not. His brothers had come out in 1909 and had urged him to join them, so he came the following spring, but he looked around a couple months before he committed himself.

Plenty of homestead land was available when he filed, and he could have chosen a half-section with every foot tillable, but he didn't plan to go in for much farming. He chose rather to specialize in stock-raising so he selected a site near the breaks of the Divide*.

Law required that he make some improvements and spend a certain amount of time on his homestead so he built a little sod house on it and spent the required time there. 'Batching' wasn't his strong point, though, so when he wasn't working out (and he was, much of the time) he might be found at his sister's place, across the Divide, or a little later, after his parents came, at their home. They came in 1911 and settled two miles west of him.

The same year that the senior Vosses came Gust's older sister and her husband joined the trek to Montana. Gust, his brother, and his brother-in-law bought a plowing rig together, and the next two years they traveled from place to place breaking sod. On many an acre in Dawson County (and Dawson County was much bigger then) the first furrows turned were turned by their sodbreaker. Voss observed that those next two years he slept outdoors more than in the house.

Breaking sod with that rig was no one-man operation. One man had to fire the engine (their fuel was coal), one had to haul water, one had to steer the engine, and one man had to ride the plow to manipulate it. But they broke ground. Their plow turned eight furrows at a time, each furrow fourteen inches. That first year they had the rig they averaged forty acres a day from April 21 to June 28. That was plowing in those days!

With all that virgin soil broken for crops there was bound to be threshing needed so next they bought a threshing outfit. In this case, too, their services were in great demand. One fall they started threshing the latter part of August and kept at it until they pulled home Christmas Eve.

Those experiences took them into a great variety of homes. They always boarded at the farm where they were working, and the quality of the food served varied as much as the homes did. Sometimes the grub was very good, and sometimes it wasn't. Voss thought it best not to go into the details on that subject!

Most farmers starting out now find it necessary to go into debt, but Voss never had a mortgage against his place (which grew to considerably more than his original half section). He tried once to mortgage it, but at that time he couldn't borrow a dollar on it so he got by without it then and has ever since.

That doesn't mean that he always found smooth sailing. During the Great Depression the land didn't produce enough to pay the taxes. As one bad year followed another he found himself seven years behind with his payments. To one of the county commissioners he declared, "Don't think I'm going to work on W.P.A. to pay taxes on that land! If that land can't pay for itself you'll have to take it." But the commissioners told him they didn't want his land and finally the tide turned so he was able to pay up.

When he started out, an experienced farmer advised him, "If you have a hundred acres in flax, figure six bushels to the acre at a dollar a bushel: or for a hundred acres of wheat, ten to twelve bushels at sixty cents a bushel, and you'll come out." He found that gauge a pretty accurate one in his early farming days 'way back when'.

The plowing rig was good only for breaking sod so after his breaking was done he used horses and a gangplow* to do the backsetting and farmed with horses from then on for many years. After his brother Carl homesteaded in 1912 the two worked together a good deal. Voss explained that first one would be the farmer, the other flunky for awhile, then they would change off.

Transportation then was cheap and swift – with his bicycle he rode to Glendive and back, thirty-five miles, all in one day. True, he started out from the homestead at three in the morning, and it was nine o'clock in the evening before he returned, but it was all the same day! Usually, though, he did his going on horseback or even on foot. If there was hauling to be done it was done with team and wagon.

Homesteaders kept coming, and in 1913 the Volpp family from Nebraska settled about seven miles from Gust's homestead. Three years later Gust abdicated his bachelorhood and married the Volpps' eldest daughter, Minnie.

He brought his bride to his homestead, but now his sod shanty had been replaced by a frame house, and it was in a different place because he liked the new location better. Besides, he was hoping for better water. They dug six wells, trying to get satisfactory water!

The pioneers were sociable, and many were the neighborhood get-togethers. There was no segregation then; old people and young people alike mixed together for their good times. As for leaving the little ones home with a babysitter – unheard of! Anyway, who was there to get for a babysitter when everyone was at the party? Houses were not so fine that rugs or furniture had to be considered before children.

The first Christmas the Volpps were in the community there was no school as yet, much less a schoolhouse, but they had a program anyway – at the Volpp home. Their program had a variety of numbers with dialogues and singing of carols, and all shared in the potluck lunch. Such good times they had!

Trips to town were infrequent and most of their grocery shopping was done by mail from Sears-Roebuck the first two years. It was cheaper that way, even with the freight, and more convenient than buying locally. They bought groceries twice a year until they got their first car.

At first they picked up their mail at the Wold Post Office, then at Johnson's (Theodore). Next a post office was established at Mink so they went there for the mail for some time before a route was started. This route came out from Circle, through the Corral Creek community, and on across the Divide to Mink, then back to Circle past the Voss place. After the route was instigated they had very convenient mail service – closer for them than it is now that they are living in Circle.

Educating their three children was not always easy. When they were ready for high school, Mrs. Voss moved into Circle with them to enable them to attend. Two of their children, Gertrude (Mrs. Oscar Lokken) and Gene, on the home place, still live in the Sioux Creek community. Daughter Hazelle (Mrs. Kaul) teaches in the Lincoln School in Glendive.

Mr. and Mrs. Voss are now retired and living in Circle. It's a quiet life compared to the work-filled, activity-packed years they spent together on the ranch. 1966 marks the fiftieth year of their wedded union.

Mr. and Mrs. Conrad (Lydia Dickhoff) Hess

November 1968

Although Conrad Hess made his first trip to Glendive sixty-one years ago, 1907, the memory of that trip remains vivid and clear. He was only thirteen years old at the time, but it was nevertheless a man's assignment that brought him here. His father had just homesteaded near Richardton, North Dakota, and Conrad was sent to Glendive to help his older brother Joe move some machinery to the new farm. Joe was working for a rancher near Glendive. About the time his father settled in North Dakota, a farmer by the name of Grebeldinger sold his farm equipment, and Joe saw in this a good opportunity to get some necessities for the home farm.

He didn't buy any combines or tractors, but he did buy some horses, a wagon, a plow, and a mower. Conrad came to Glendive on the train, but for the return trip they loaded the plow and the mower onto the wagon and pulled it with the horses.

There were no roads then as we think of roads so they followed cow trails. When they reached the Little Missouri River at Medora, there was no bridge, but they had to cross so they swam the horses across and enlisted some help to push the wagonload of machinery across the railroad bridge. Before they were off the bridge they heard the train in the distance so, straining to the utmost, they put on a burst of speed that took them off and out of the way just before the train thundered on to it. That alone was thrill enough for the whole trip!

Conrad Hess was born in Hungary into a family of nine children. In 1904 his father, a widower, brought his family to the United States and settled in Virginia. His son Joe had preceded the family to America in 1903, but he had come directly to Richardton where they had relatives, then continued on to Glendive where he found work on a ranch.

When the family came to the New World the next year, John, the oldest son, didn't stop in Virginia with the rest of the family but came from New York to Glendive and joined brother Joe. John went to work for the Northern Pacific Railroad in the roundhouse.

The two youngest children, Conrad and Mary, had not completed their elementary schooling when the family left Hungary so after considering the matter, their father decided he should take them back to Hungary for school. They went back in 1905, but in 1907 they returned to the United States.

By this time all the other children had moved to the west so Mr. Hess headed for North Dakota, too. The area around Richardton was fairly well settled by this time so when it came to homesteads he had "to take what was left," but he found a quarter where he thought he could make a living. Back in Hungary he had had a small farm where they were largely self-sustaining. They raised their own grain, fruit, garden, and meat, and also milked cows. When their wheat was harvested they took it to the mill and had their flour ground. In

North Dakota they didn't have a mill to grind their flour, but their pattern of living – so far as producing their needs – was much the same.

John, the brother who had worked in Glendive at the roundhouse, had contracted a fever and died while Mr. Hess and the two youngest children were in Hungary so only Joe was in this area when the family located at Richardton.

Joe helped on the homestead that first summer, but in the fall of 1907 he married and started his own farming operations. He stayed in North Dakota a few years, but in 1910 he decided in favor of Montana again and homesteaded north of Fallon. His sons still own the farm he built up there.

Conrad was still too young to homestead, but he wasn't too young to be interested and looking forward to the time when he would be eligible. His next trip to the Treasure State came in 1915. Joe needed more horses on his expanding Montana farm while his brother-in-law, Frank Schultz, and Mr. Hess in North Dakota had some extras so it seemed reasonable to put the horses where they were needed. Frank and Conrad undertook to do just that.

They had seven horses to bring so they hitched one to a little two-wheeled cart loaded with groceries, saddled another – just in case they needed a saddle horse – and chased the others. Much of the time they could tie the saddle horse to the back of the cart and let him trail along, but when they needed him, they needed him. The trip from Richardton to Fallon took a full week.

As they entered the badlands around Medora they ran into a fog and took the wrong trail. They followed the trail to its end – a coal mine. Frank had a compass so they tried to get their bearings with that, but the compass didn't work very satisfactorily and didn't help much. Finally the fog began to lift so they could see, but which direction from the trail were they? Then they heard the whistle of a train. They went toward the sound, found the railroad, and knew which way to go again.

In Medora a fellow tried to talk them into trading the horses for a section* of land, but Joe was waiting for the horses so they turned a deaf ear to his proposition. Their groceries for the trip consisted chiefly of canned goods and dried foods. Not many opportunities along that stretch to go to a restaurant or grocery store, and even the ranch houses were few and far between so if they planned to eat they had to plan. Commercial canning then hadn't reached the standard we take for granted now, and a can of spoiled tomatoes just about ended the trip for both of them right there in the badlands. They both recovered, but they had to take a day's 'sick leave' before they could travel again.

They delivered the horses to Joe, and while they were out here Conrad, looked the land over and tentatively picked out a homestead, looking forward to the next year when he would be old enough to file. It was still available when he came back so he settled down, a bachelor, on his homestead north of Fallon. With the help of his brother Joe and Joe's brother-in-law, John Mayer, he built his shack that first summer. His shack was 14'x20', larger than many original homestead dwellings, and boasted two rooms. The second room, he explained, was for dirty dishes.

There was a spring about forty rods from his house so he carried his water from there – uphill, of course. Charley Holmberg, Mr. Hess recalled appreciatively, declared that he was going to move his house down to the well. Generally, it wasn't until quite a few years later that most farmers discovered that they could move the well to the house – if not the actual well, the water through pipes. Now, of course, in most farm homes the water bucket is a thing of the past, just as it is in the city homes. (In 1916 the water bucket was a part of the not-very-distant past even in Glendive.)

Conrad Hess remained a bachelor on his homestead for two years, then met Lydia Dickhoff. Lydia also had come to Montana in 1916. Her parents had immigrated to McIntosh County, North Dakota from Besarabi, South Russia, in the fall of 1893 and had homesteaded there. McIntosh County was still very primitive, and they could just about take their pick of the land. The original 160-acre homestead is still in the Dickhoff family, with Lydia's youngest sister and husband living on it.

Lydia had little opportunity to attend school as she was growing up on the frontier, but she used the opportunities she had. She and her brother spent many hours herding cows, and as they herded, they studied. She took along her ABC book and learned without a formal setting. Those hours gave opportunity, too, for studying her Sunday School lesson and reading from their German Bible. She learned a lot while she kept the cows out of the grain.

Back in Russia 'Grandma' had not only spun their thread from their own flax or wool but had woven the cloth as well. The spinning wheel came along to the New World, and though they no longer wove the cloth, they continued to spin yarn from the wool for knitting the family's socks and mittens. The wool had to be carefully washed before it was spun into yarn, so after a rain they would take the wool to the nearby dam and wash it, then dry it in the sun, dye it and knit. Knitting was more than a hobby in the Dickhoff home!

Instead of sleeping on innerspring mattresses they slept on mattresses of cornhusks. When the corn was husked in the fall, they'd save the softer, inner husks and fill the ticks. It was wonderful to bounce on the big, fluffy tick, but mother would warn that if they jumped on them, soon those husks would be all smashed down like the old filling. Their pillows, too, were home made from homegrown duck down.

When she was growing up near Ashley, North Dakota, Lydia considered 'going to town' a real treat. They'd spend the whole day, but instead of going to a restaurant for dinner, they'd take along a loaf of bread and buy a chunk of bologna. Cider barrels stood in the back of the store, and at noon they'd sit on those cider barrels, eat bread and bologna and drink apple cider.

Her home was near the Whitestone Battlefield, and one of the outstanding events of her childhood was a celebration when she heard an old Indian speak. Eagle Face, who was 108 years old when she heard him, had participated in the Whitestone Battle. The North Dakota state governor prevailed upon him to speak at the celebration so, although he was most reluctant, he began: "White people, as I look over you my heart breaks. You stole our land, but I'm glad you give us a living." With that his voice broke, and as the gallant old warrior sat down there was hardly a dry eye in the crowd.

Two other Indians, Holy Horse and Red Bow, who had been about eight years old at the time of the battle, gave their recollections of that historic event. They told how they had hidden two days in holes and caves while the battle raged. These speeches by the Indians made a lasting impression upon the young girl.

Lydia's older sister married and moved to Montana so in 1916 Lydia joined her here. She didn't spend all her time with her sister, however. She 'worked out' for various women in the community, including Mrs. Kempton on the well-known Kempton Ranch.

Her first meeting with Conrad Hess is described by their daughter, Clara, in an article written for the observance of her parents' golden wedding anniversary. She wrote: "Lydia Dickhoff met Conrad Hess at a dance. He was playing an accordion, and she was quite impressed at the lovely music he was squeezing from his box.

"He was playing a polka and she was dancing energetically trying to catch his eye. He pretended not to notice her, but finally he laid down his accordion and told one of his friends to play a slow one so he could dance with Lydia. Lydia, of course, was trying to pretend she was surprised that he would come and ask her to dance, but just five minutes before she had bet her sister Jackie that he would be around. So started the romance of Conrad and Lydia.

"A few weeks later Conrad took her for a buggy ride in the country, racing his buggy and horses up one hill and down another until she promised to marry him." Recalling that wild ride, Mrs. Hess noted that it was in a top buggy pulled by a pair of white horses, Jack and Prince. As she described that mad dash across country, how Conrad almost tipped her out of the buggy, son Bob drawled, "They talk about people driving fast now! They drove fast with horses in those days." Mrs. Hess could only laugh and concede.

They were married October 23, 1918, in Terry, Montana, with her sister Jackie and husband as witnesses. Then they settled down on his homestead ten miles north of Fallon. Mrs. Hess observed, "It didn't take long to look everything over," when he took her home to the 'little green shack', as they referred to the house on the homestead. Mr. Hess was careful to mention that he had things pretty well cleaned up when he brought his new bride home – even the second room that was for the dirty dishes.

With a touch of chagrin Mrs. Hess recalled the first batch of bread she made after she was married. She had never baked bread before and has no idea now how long she baked it – except that it was considerably longer than necessary. She was dismayed as she lifted the heavy loaves out of the oven, but she was even more dismayed when company came and she had to serve it to them.

Her new husband had loyally insisted, "It's good! It's good!" But the company departed and gossiped, "That Conrad! Got a city cook that can't even bake bread!" She learned, though. By the time she reared seven children and baked enough bread to feed them, she could be classed with the experts.

As Mrs. Hess thought of the early days of her marriage to Conrad she reflected, "It was interesting living in those days. You had to just think and get along with what you had."

"Interesting living in those days," she said. Perhaps Mrs. Hess is more of a philosopher than she realizes. Do our modern conveniences contribute to the boredom and discontent abroad today because everything is done for us, leaving no room to 'think and make do'? When the washer breaks down, the dryer won't work, the freezer quits, the TV blows a tube – all of it adds up to frustration and repair bills, but what does it call forth in resourcefulness? Maybe....

What a boon when she got her first sad iron* with a removable handle! Prior to that innovation they had heated one iron with attached handle, then removed it from the stove by grasping the handle with paper for that special purpose – because the handle, of course, heated too. The heavy iron retained heat much longer than its modern counterpart, but when it had cooled, it had to be set back on the stove and heated again before the ironing could continue, while coal had to be added to the fire at the right time. With a removable handle, two or three irons could be heated at the same time so when one cooled, another was ready to use. She smiled to recall how her oldest boy liked to have his shirtfront stiffly starched and would stroke it when he put on his freshly ironed shirt.

In her article written for celebration of her parents' golden wedding anniversary, daughter Clara further described the years on the homestead: "The years that passed were filled with hardships and a lot of hard work. There were pleasant and happy days, too – when the crops were good, stock feed laid up for the winter, and the family had flour and sugar, coffee stored in the attic with mom's canning in the old root house; potatoes, carrots, onions dug and stored; the long evenings playing checkers with Daddy who was the champ and just let the kids beat once in a while. Mom would make popcorn or candy if we behaved. We were happy and felt secure because Mom and Dad had worked and made it so."

There was no established church in the community, but they held Sunday School regularly in the schoolhouse and welcomed any minister who could come. The schoolhouse was always full when services were held. The Hess family had no car at that time to drive the one-and-one-half miles, but they were consistent in their attendance.

Two weeks of Bible School would be held during the summer, too, and the two oldest Hess children, Art and Clara, took first prize at the music festival singing, "I Love to Tell the Story," which they had learned in Bible School.

New clothes were hard to come by in the depression years, so when a new hat was bought for Clara, Mom carefully impressed upon her the importance of taking good care of it. Clara and Art rode horseback to school, and as they started out, Clara in her new hat, they saw with dismay overhanging clouds were threatening to unload at any moment. They knew what rain would do to a new hat so they prayed all the way to school that the rain would hold off until they were inside. And it did. Not a drop fell until the new hat was safely inside the schoolhouse.

For fuel they mined and hauled their own coal. The vein from which they hauled was close to the surface so they uncovered it with team and slip*, then used powder (dynamite) to blow it loose. Many tons of coal were hauled over the years with team and wagon to the coal bin.

From time to time they found Indian relics such as dolls, little dishes, and the more common arrowheads, in the area where they lived. But at the time everybody was busy with their families and didn't think to save the various items.

The children had some unusual pets along with the more conventional dogs, cats, and ponies. Perhaps one of the most unorthodox was Art's pet bull snake. The snake would lie by a certain corner post, and when Art would come along, he'd pick up the snake and drape it over his saddle. Sometimes he would ride for miles with his unique companion.

What farmer hasn't at one time or another brought home a bunny rabbit to his children? Mr. Hess was no exception, and the children derived much enjoyment from taking care of it. Even after the rabbit was fully grown and they turned him out, he would come back each evening at seven o'clock and scratch on the door to be let in. They'd give him some milk, and as soon as he was through eating he'd scratch on the door again, this time to be let out.

Conrad's original homestead had only about thirty acres of farmland. The remainder was grazing land so after a few years he sold it and bought the 'Frenchy place'. It was on the 'Frenchy place' they spent most of the years their children were growing up. Three years ago they moved from there to their present home closer to Glendive. While they formerly were thirty-five miles out, now they are about ten – close enough that they can drive in easily. Mrs. Hess explained that she could drive the team, and she drove the car some, but now he does the driving and she gives the instructions.

Last month Mr. and Mrs. Hess celebrated their fiftieth wedding anniversary. Their sons, daughters, and families hosted a reception in their honor at the Sacred Heart school dining room. All their children and grandchildren were able to be present for the occasion. Also present were six of Mrs. Hess's eight brothers and sisters (including Jacquelin, who was a witness at their wedding) and a sister of Mr. Hess.

Of the seven children born to Mr. and Mrs. Hess, six are still living; Arthur C. Hess, Glendive; Clara Denby, Hardin; John, Glendive; Frances, Glendive; Margaret Zabrocki, Glendive; and Robert, at home.

Closing her article written for their fiftieth anniversary celebration, Clara wrote: "The children and grandchildren of Conrad and Lydia Hess realize and appreciate the effort, the goodness, the love given to us by two wonderful people."

Mike Guelff

September 1966

"You mean you worked for fifteen cents an hour and walked sixteen miles a day to do it?" Mike Guelff affirmed that was just what he did. Obviously, he wasn't talking about yesterday.

Although Mike was only twelve years old when he came to Montana, he was the 'man of the family'. His widowed mother, Anna Guelff, had been left with nine children, several of whom were older than Mike, but they were working out. They were home very little so when his mother decided to homestead in Montana, the responsibility for helping with the moving rested upon the twelve-year-old.

The Guelffs lived in Minnesota. In the fall of 1905 Mrs. Guelff and a neighbor, Mr. Russ, had made the trip West to file on homesteads, then the next spring they loaded immigrant cars and made the move. Mr. Russ loaded two immigrant cars, Guelffs one, and 'the men' started for the new land. If the trip on the train was becoming monotonous by the time they reached Valley City, North Dakota, their stop there livened things up.

They were getting hungry so while the train was stopped, Mr. Russ and Mike hunted up a restaurant. In their absence the train had visitors. Mr. Russ had a couple stowaways hidden in his car, but there was no one in Guelff's car during that luncheon break. When they came back to the train after their meal they noticed some tubs and pans and boxes moving around in a peculiar fashion. Investigation revealed chickens under those vessels, and furthermore, those chickens had come from the crates in Mike's immigrant car.

Five or six youngsters had broken open one of his chicken crates while they were gone and had hidden chickens under any covering they could get their hands on. The travelers managed to retrieve perhaps two dozen fowl, but about a hundred escaped. When that train started up, chickens scattered in every direction.

The homestead was located in Montana, but they unloaded their cars at Beach, the nearest railroad station. They arrived there at night May 20, 1906, and when daylight came so they could look out, they saw about twenty immigrant cars unloading along the tracks.

There were no buildings where goods could be stored so each immigrant was allotted a 'spot' the length of his car to pile his goods. Mike's mother's sister was living near Beach. She had come to the Treasure State in 1904, and it was her influence that was responsible for Guelffs moving. After they unloaded the car they hauled their possessions out to her place until they could build a shack on their own homestead.

Getting the shack built turned out to be no overnight job. They were hardly in this dry country before they found that it can rain in Montana. It rained and kept on raining for almost six weeks. Mike's eighteen-year-old brother came to help them get a house built, but progress was slow with the weather so uncooperative.

During that interval when they were trying to get living quarters ready for occupancy Mrs. Guelff slept in her sister's house, but the house was small so the youngsters slept in a tent. They might have had a fairly comfortable existence, but what small fry can resist running a finger along a tent wall and watching the water start to dribble through the path they've made? The Guelff small fry couldn't, so by the time the shack was ready they were about like drowned rats.

After they had a chance to get settled a bit, Mike found himself a job. They lived close to Yates, about half-a-mile from the railroad tracks so he got a job with the section crew. Each morning he'd walk the eight miles to Beach to report for work, then each evening he'd walk eight miles home.

Soon after he started to work, the coal dock in Beach burned. The boss figured he needed his entire crew in Beach to get the dock rebuilt and since Mike lived near Yates, gave to him the responsibility of checking the tracks from Beach to Yates (seven-and-one-half miles) and maintaining the switch lights. In the evening he would light the kerosene switch lanterns, and in the morning he would blow them out. He also was to watch for broken rails or any problem along the track. The boss allowed him an hour in the morning and an hour in the evening to cover those seven-and-one-half miles, then he'd put in the intervening hours on the coal dock. And he received fifteen cents an hour.

When he, with his mother and siblings, came to their homestead site north of Yates in 1906, it was all site and no home. Building a shack had priority over all else, but after that there was a well to dig, fences to build, ground to break – and miles and miles of country to explore.

No well diggers with their efficient machinery were around to dig their well so they did it themselves with a shovel. After they dug down a few feet so the digger couldn't toss the dirt over the edge they used a windlass. There was room for only one to dig in the well so that one wielded the shovel, filling a bucket with dirt, while up on top two more operated a windlass and pulled the dirt to the surface.

Occasionally the windlass operators let the bucket slip, and the dirt dumped back down on the one who had sent it up, but they did get their well dug. Their finished product was four feet square and supplied them with all the water they needed. They had 'running water', too, but the youngsters did the running.

For their fencing needs they 'borrowed' ties from the railroad and split them for posts. Post by post, fences began stretching across a land where fences had never been before. Trails had to follow a more definite pattern, now, because the horseback rider or the teamster striking out in 'just any direction' was liable to come up against a newly built fence.

About the time Guelffs came to the homestead a horse trader in Beach acquired a skinny mule in one of his deals so he offered Mike the use of it to get the mule out on the lush grass of the homestead and surrounding area. What a blessing that mule proved to be! They hadn't brought any horses with them so the mule was used to haul the dirt away when they dug the basement for the shack, used to haul the railroad ties, used for transportation – everything!

Not the least of the 'everything' was exploring the new country. The skinny mule was sharp at first, and they had no saddle to use on him, but the Guelff youngsters didn't let that worry them. They used him anyway, and in time the lush grass did help.

The first summer on the homestead they didn't attempt to start farming, but the next spring they bought three horses and a 'heel burner' – a walking plow – and began breaking sod. They broke about forty acres that spring.

After Mike was a little older he ran a livery barn and dray in Yates, the first for the town. Chronologically he was still 'just a kid', but kids grow up fast when they have the kind of responsibility thrust upon them that Mike had.

Perhaps he was still a kid when he married Florence Russ in 1912, but he'd had plenty of experience providing for a family. Florence had come to Montana in 1906, too. Her father had homesteaded at the same time Mrs. Guelff did, and it was he who came with the immigrant cars when Mike came.

Mr. Russ had a store back in Eden Valley, Minnesota, and he built a store in Beach, too, about the third store in town. He had it built before they moved out so when he unloaded his immigrant cars, he had a place right in Beach to store his belongings.

When the family first came out, they lived above the store. The store was built with a slanting roof, as stores in those days were, but evidently the slant wasn't quite steep enough to cope with the rain those first six weeks in Montana. The tarpaper covering the roof was supposed to shed the water, but it didn't shed that much.

In an effort to protect at least the beds, they put boards above the bedsteads and laid tar paper over the boards. That helped the beds – some – but it didn't help at the stove. When Mrs. Russ tried to fry pancakes, water dripped down onto the stove and about every place else, it seemed. She was about ready to go back to Eden Valley (she surely wasn't finding this any Eden) but then the rain let up and she stayed.

Mr. and Mrs. Guelff laughed about the time the grocer offered his mother a 'good buy' on some 'old Lennox soap' that he'd had in stock a long time. What woman can resist a bargain? She bought the whole bunch for a quarter, but when she tried to scrub the floor with it, she decided even that was too much because it would not suds. A neighbor happened by and laughed at her troubles. "That" he told her, "isn't soap; that's maple sugar!" It wasn't much good for scrubbing floors, but the children had the time of their lives – while it lasted.

In spite of the problems and hardships of pioneering, Mike Guelff and Florence Russ homesteaded, too, out on Clear Creek.

The recent marriage of their granddaughter reminded Mrs. Guelff that weddings cost a little more now than in 1912. When she and Mike were married, their license cost $2.50 and they paid the priest $10.00 for a total expenditure of $12.50. They moved to their homestead in the spring of 1913. Mike had a fellow help him move to the shack on March 13, just in time to get

330

caught by a snowstorm. It was April 10 before he could get into the field. His wife had joined him before that, however, and since they couldn't get into the field, they decided to do some visiting in Brockway. Roads were one of the conveniences this new community didn't offer so they made their own trail.

The weather had warmed by the time they started on their excursion so, while it was pleasant overhead, all the creeks and coulees were full of water. They were young then and didn't know any better so they drove into the creeks and coulees anyway. Mrs. Guelff observes now that it's a wonder they didn't drown. When they reached Redwater, however, they didn't 'just drive in'. It was evident even to the boldness of youth that caution was demanded here. Evening was coming on by the time they reached the river, so they stayed overnight with a farmer on the east side of the flood.

Demonstrating the pioneer spirit, the farmer welcomed them even though high waters had prevented his crossing over to Watkins to get supplies, and they were just about out of everything. Breakfast that morning consisted of pancakes made with flour, water, and soda because they were out of everything else. The waters were taming, though, and after breakfast the young travelers were able to continue on their way with a pilot to ride into the river ahead of them and show them where to cross.

Settled in the little homestead shack back on Clear Creek, Mike had to be gone a good deal, working out for others. Other women of the community were amazed that the young Mrs. Guelff (she was only eighteen years old) seemed to have no fear of staying alone. When they told her there was a peeping Tom in the vicinity, she told them they could put curtains on their windows. They protested they couldn't afford curtains so she retorted, "You can hang your aprons or something else over the window. You don't have to let someone look in and see what you're doing."

When asked what she would do if she saw someone sneaking around her yard, she replied in no uncertain terms, "I'd take a pot shot at him." She always carried a gun with her and did a good bit of target practicing so there was no reason to doubt her assertion. She laughingly told how men coming to their place on business were careful to call out as they came into the yard, "Yoo hoo, Mrs. Guelff, it's me," just to make sure she didn't shoot first and ask questions afterwards.

They spent about twenty years out on the homestead, battling drought, grasshoppers, and hail. Mr. Guelff explained, "There was an old saying, 'Uncle Sam bet you a half section of land it could starve you out in five years,' but we decided we were going to stick it out, and we did."

When tough going grew tougher, he started trading horses. Through the hard years he bought thousands of horses, most of them for five dollars apiece, and shipped them everywhere – Wisconsin, North Dakota, to the canneries at Butte or Rockford, Illinois. He'd make about a dollar-and-a-half a head, but he was buying them by the hundreds. He figures he probably bought horses from ninety percent of the farmers in Dawson County.

Mr. Guelff remarked that he didn't put on the first horse roundup in Dawson County, but he put on the last big one. He made a deal with the Exchange State Bank to gather the horses that had been mortgaged to the bank, then just deserted by the farmers when they left the country. Between the horses Guelff bought and the horses belonging to the bank, the roundup lasted ten weeks. They went out with a model T Ford and a tent and scoured the country, bringing in horses by the hundreds.

Handling and breaking so many horses, runaways were common. Mr. Guelff says he can't even remember them all, but one of the runaways stands out very clearly in his memory. (It stands out vividly in his wife's memory, too!)

He had a couple broncs hitched to a wagon with a double box, and Mrs. Guelff with baby Marguerite was seated on the high seat beside him. They came upon neighbor Grant Sears who had been fixing fence so they stopped to visit awhile. As they talked, a pony stallion came up and started fighting with Grant's saddle horse so Grant hit him on the head with his shovel. It stopped the pony, but it spooked Guelff's team and they were off with a lunge.

As Mike braced himself and pulled with all his strength on the reins, one of the lines suddenly snapped, leaving him with one line to control a pair of runaway broncs. All the pulling on one line turned the team sharply and brought them up against a fence where they had to stop, but as they did so the wheels of the wagon cramped, and the wagon tipped over. Mrs. Guelff found her descent to the ground an unpleasant 'come down' as she unceremoniously slid from the high wagon seat, but she managed to hold the baby up, unhurt, while she herself absorbed the bumps and bruises.

Many of the winters they spent on the homestead were rough, but some were rougher. Their shack was close to the road so often they were called upon to help stalled motorists. One hill especially, about a quarter-of-a-mile down the road, would block with snow so Mike would go to help those who couldn't get through. During one siege it was blocked so long and so tightly that Mike kept the team in the barn, harnessed and ready to go, day and night. The team became so accustomed to the routine that when he'd take them from the barn, they'd head for that hill of their own accord and upon arriving there, start backing into position.

One Saturday night a fresh storm caught a good many of the community residents in Glendive. They were able to return as far as 'that hill', but there was no going any further so one by one or carload by carload, they came to Guelff's for shelter for the night.

As people kept coming the problem of where to put them all became acute. Their house wasn't large – a 12'x16' kitchen-dining room, two small bedrooms, and, off one end, a living room. In the present situation the living room was so cold no one could sleep in it so they moved the daveno (couch) from the living room into the kitchen. They made so many beds on the floor that next morning Mrs. Guelff had to climb over the daveno and over the table to get to the stove to start breakfast preparations.

One of the most devastating snowstorms they experienced came when snowstorms should have been past. One Friday in May, 1927 had been beautiful, and when the children came home from school, all the horses were turned out. That night snow started falling, rapidly increasing in intensity until visibility was almost zero. High winds blew the snow into drifts, and all but the most necessary activity came to a stand still.

As the weekend wore on, Marguerite (Guelff's oldest child) became increasingly concerned. She was in the seventh grade and had a perfect attendance record for all her years. Now, with the end of her seventh year in sight, was she going to have to miss a day?

Monday morning, still hoping, she figured that if the snow would only stop she could still get to school by noon and would just be counted tardy instead of absent. But the snow didn't stop. She couldn't get back to school until Tuesday morning, and by then her perfect attendance record was broken.

While to a seventh grader the broken attendance record may well have been the major catastrophe caused by the storm, it was by no means the only one. Guelffs lost 100 head of horses, and throughout the county loss of livestock was heavy. No up-to-the-minute weather reports had warned farmers and stockmen to take precautions so the storm, following mild weather that late in the season, had caught great numbers of cattle and horses out on the range and had buried them under high drifts, smothering them.

One of their most memorable hail storms struck about five o'clock one morning and was followed by another the same afternoon. Mike went to town that day so he was gone for the second installment. Some of his sisters were visiting with Mrs. Guelff and watched with her as the second downpour of hail and rain in less than twelve hours soaked the fiberboard ceiling to the saturation point.

Mrs. Guelff realized that, unless she took action, the ceiling would break at any moment and leave a jagged, gaping hole (not to mention the flood that would follow!) so she hurriedly fetched the wash tubs, then with a butcher knife poked a hole in the ceiling and let the water drain out while she admired her one neat little puncture instead of a ruptured ceiling.

They continued their battle with drought, hail, and grasshoppers (according to Mr. Guelff, they milked cows to buy bran to mix with the poison supplied by the government to feed the grasshoppers) even after they moved to Glendive in 1930. Other interests then helped them meet expenses, but they still retained ownership of the farm. By 1934 they had accumulated a good-sized bunch of cattle, but the severe drought that year forced them to sell to the government, the only market. They had held on as long as they could, hoping prices would go up, but finally they had to sell prime steers for $20 a head.

Crop returns were negligible during the dry 'thirties', but over the years they have learned summer fallow* and winter wheat can increase yields significantly in spite of lack of moisture, and they have had good returns.

When they moved into Glendive in 1930 Mr. Guelff bought an old truck and began hauling coal. He quipped that the only time he got back into school after he left in 1906 to come to Montana (twelve years old) was when he put coal into the basements. From hauling coal he expanded his business to hauling just about anything and everything. It was through his hauling that he broke into the lumber business. At first he handled his lumbering from his home on Prospect Heights, but about fifteen years ago he moved it down town.

As a youngster he used to dream of going back to Minnesota, when he had enough money, and buying back the old farm, but when he went back after he was grown, he found he didn't want it. He and Mrs. Guelff have retired (to some extent, anyway) but they still choose to live in Glendive.

Instead of finding time dragging as they grow older, they say it seems to go faster. Mrs. Guelff mentioned that the children tell her it isn't that time goes so much faster – it's just that she's getting slower that makes it seem that way.

Whatever it is, they can't seem to find time for all the things they'd like to do. They both have hobbies at which they could spend more time – Mr. Guelff with agates and plastic moldings, Mrs. Guelff with knitting and flower raising. She also collects pitchers and has a large assortment, including antiques, pitchers from foreign countries, from most of the states, pitchers with odd shapes, and – just pitchers. Included in her collection is a specimen from Mr. Guelff's agate collection. He made a small pitcher from an agate with a natural hole in it.

He cuts and polishes agates and makes a wide variety of decorative as well as useful items. In his hunting he found some pure black agate which he uses to frame pieces of the agate jewelry he makes. Perhaps one of his most unusual agates is the one with markings which make it resemble the familiar picture of Christ overlooking Jerusalem.

The Guelffs have three children plus eight grandchildren and two great-grandchildren. They have turned active management of their business interests over to their children – to daughter Marguerite the real estate, to son Bob the lumberyard, and to son Keith the farm, but still find plenty of activity to keep life interesting.

334

Dr. P. J. Moe

October 1965

Supposing cars were almost non-existent, and supposing roads were so primitive that much of the time the few existing cars couldn't negotiate them; and supposing you didn't have a horse and buggy; and that you bought a bicycle for transportation only to realize that you don't make much progress in the mud with bicycles, either; and supposing your girl lived fourteen miles away?

Trains ran but the schedules were all wrong so young P.J. Moe, recent graduate from the Chicago College of Dental Surgery, on the premise that "Necessity is the mother of invention," began looking around and found an attachment which enabled him to ride his bicycle on the railroad track; it was a third wheel which, while he rode in one track, followed in the other track. Now he could travel the fourteen miles in good time.

After his graduation from dental college in 1902, Dr. Moe located in Wonewoc, Wisconsin. There were plenty of girls in Wonewoc, and the new dentist didn't lack company, but there was one young lady he hadn't met. He had been in town about three months when one of the girls remarked to him, "You've heard so much about Ruby Lever, no doubt you're anxious to meet her. I'll take you over there."

Ruby had suffered a ruptured appendix shortly before his coming to town and had been very ill, but now that she was recovered enough to be up and around he was ready for an introduction. Appropriately enough she was sitting on a piano bench that first time he saw her, and that, according to Dr. Moe, "was the start of it."

After about three years in Wonewoc Dr. Moe moved to Kendall where he had bought his brother's share in a grocery store, and that was when his transportation problem began. The bicycle was a temporary solution, but he finally resolved the problem by marrying the girl and bringing her to Kendall.

The store had a balcony where he set up his dental equipment and continued his practice along with his store keeping. Such was his situation five years and two children later when R.P. Rainey started talking homestead in Montana. Prospects sounded so inviting that he decided it was worth taking a look. Rainey showed him the Lindsay area, and Dr. Moe selected 320 acres three miles south of the little town.

Before bringing his family to the new frontier he built a house (a two-story dwelling), dug a well (good drinking water), and made a cistern (so they could have soft water). He had their furniture, a cow, some chickens, and plenty of groceries from his Kendall grocery store shipped out by immigrant car, then rented an old barn in Glendive for furniture storage until the house on the homestead was ready.

Among the items stored in the cold, drafty barn was Mrs. Moe's Sohmer piano. After the trip west it was hauled to the homestead in a wagon, and after a few years hauled back to Glendive, again in a wagon. Mrs. Moe was giving lessons on that piano when she was still Ruby Lever, and continues to give lessons on it to this day, despite its years and sometimes less-than-ideal treatment.

Dr. Moe wanted to cultivate his entire 320 acres and figured horses were too slow so when a fellow with a smooth sales pitch lauded the 'Autoplow', he bought one – the poorest buy he ever made, he declares.

It was a gasoline-powered tractor with the plows attached underneath. It was shipped to Glendive where he picked it up and started to the farm with it. About three miles out of town toward Lindsay he reached a swampy area and his autoplow mired down. (There was no Lindsay highway to travel then, and if there had been he wouldn't have been allowed to drive on it with his steel-lugged tractor.)

He spent the better part of two days working to get his tractor out of the mud and on the way to the Lindsay country again. He started plowing with the new invention but found his troubles were just beginning. Every so often his outfit would break down, and he'd have to send for repairs, usually involving a long wait. His association with it was not a happy one so when one of his neighbors who had a tractor just like it – and was having similar luck with it – offered him $500 for his $1,800 investment, he sold it for use as repairs. Then he hired his plowing and seeding done by a neighbor who had a big, slow-moving tractor that could do both jobs in one operation.

When harvest time came, he did slow down to the horses' pace, cutting his grain with a binder, then later hiring the threshing done. While the threshing crew was at their place, the machine kept breaking down, and it took six weeks to finish. Besides the two men running the engine and the thresher there were about five bundle haulers, making a sizable crew to feed. Cooking for a bunch like that was a bit out of the line for a graduate from the Chicago College of Music who had lived in town all her life, but Mrs. Moe could cook so they enjoyed eating there.

When their own threshing was completed, one of their bachelor neighbors asked Mrs. Moe if she'd get dinner for them one more day while they threshed his grain. She obliged, then drew a long breath because it was finally over. But it wasn't over. The rig broke down again and the bachelor asked her to feed them another day!

Dr. Moe's brother lived with them much of the time they were on the homestead and helped with the farming. One day when he had hauled a load of grain to Glendive, he had started home with a partially empty whiskey bottle and arrived home with an empty one. At the homestead he tossed the bottle onto a haystack (they had put up sixty tons of hay) and forgot about it. But the bottle had a flaw in it and the sun beating down on it ignited the hay. The Lindsay community had a neighborhood telephone system so Mrs. Moe called for help, and the neighbors came flocking in.

Dr. Moe himself had hauled a load of grain to Glendive at that time and was gone when the fire started. On the way home he suddenly had a strange feeling that there was fire at his place. He tried to hustle the horses a little faster, but a tired team pulling a wagon is a little short on hustle.

About three miles from home he could see the smoke that confirmed his premonition. He reached home as quickly as he could, but by that time the hay was gone. Nothing could have saved it, but by diligent effort the neighbors had kept the fire from spreading to the other buildings, including a nearby granary with 3,000 bushels of oats.

Homesteading offered plenty of hardships, but they had many good times, too. Dr. Moe observed that their house was big enough for social get-togethers, and the people liked to come there. They'd come horseback, with a team and buggy, perhaps in a Model T – however they could get there. One of the neighbors could play while the others danced, often until daylight.

One of the other neighbors occasionally gave dances, too, so one evening the Moes loaded their children into their Model T (leaving children home with a baby-sitter was unheard of then) and headed for the dance. This time they decided not to stay until daylight so they piled into the Model T and headed down the trail when it was still dark. That trail proved to be an elusive thing. None too good at best, it was now covered with a generous layer of snow that laughed at their attempts to figure out which way to go. These neighbors owned an entire section with a fence around the whole thing, but there was a gate in that fence so they figured they should be able to find it if they kept driving. They drove around that whole section and still didn't find any gate and first thing they knew they were back where the dance was. They gave up and waited for daylight, too.

When the community decided they needed a place for their meetings and social activities, they worked together to build a hall in Lindsay and used that hall for many years.

After Moes homesteaded in Dawson County Mrs. Moe's parents decided to move West, too, and homesteaded about seventy-five miles from their daughter's home. They started a post office (White, Montana) and also built a store, beyond Brockway. Sometimes they gave dances in the store so one time when they had one scheduled, they sent word and the young Moes decided to go. Starting out early Saturday morning they didn't stay by the roads but just cut across country, no fences to interfere, taking the shortest route, and arrived in good time – extra good in fact; they found out they were a week early!

Now what! Dr. Moe suggested to his wife, "You just stick around here, and I'll go on back home to take care of the chores and come back next week." So Mrs. Moe and the children visited a week with the grandparents, and Dr. Moe drove 300 miles to go to that dance.

One thing about the old Model T, they didn't have to have an oiled highway in order to go places. Even buffalo trails could substitute for a road, and such was the 'road' from the homestead to Glendive. One night as Dr. Moe was coming home from town he was in that trail and dropped to sleep. When he woke up he was halfway through a barbed wire fence. He wasn't the only one half way through it. His brother and two other fellows were with him, and they figured that, even though they were asleep, it was his business to stay awake. His brother had such strong feelings about the matter that he declared he would rather walk than ride with a fellow who goes to sleep while he's driving. He suited his actions to his words and got out to walk. Dr. Moe and his other two passengers went on without the irate brother. About three miles down the road Dr. Moe started thinking that was quite a hike and decided he'd better go back. By the time he got back his brother had evidently done some thinking, too, and he was quite willing to get in the car and ride on home.

Thirty or thirty-five miles an hour was clipping along for the cars of those days, and Dr. Moe's Model T did right well. One day as he was driving into Glendive he was following one of his neighbors who was driving a Buick. That Buick just couldn't pull away from him. When they reached Glendive the neighbor asked him what he'd done to his automobile to make it go like that, and Dr. Moe confessed that he had put on oversized tires, making it go faster.

Cars of that day were not equipped with seal beam headlights, nor even the simplest electric beam. Instead carbide lamps were supposed to illuminate the way, but they didn't do much more than pinpoint the location of the car as it approached in the darkness.

In 1915 some of the local politicians did a little probing to find whether he was interested in politics and urged him to run for representative. He entered the race and was elected to the Fourteenth Legislative Assembly. All he has left of the record of that Assembly is the cover of the book. The first week he was in Helena he took the State Board dental examination and passed. By coincidence one of his classmates from the Chicago College of Dental Surgery was on the board, but the classmate later assured him his presence wasn't necessary. Dr. Moe had passed without any help from him.

Out on the homestead he had occasionally pulled a tooth for someone, but he hadn't been practicing because he didn't have a license. He took on only emergency cases and didn't ask a fee so he stayed within the law. Now that he had his license and had proved up* on his homestead he decided to start practicing in earnest so he bought out another dentist and moved to Glendive. His office was on the second floor of the building now owned by MDU*, but at that time the post office was on the main floor.

When Montana Dakota Utility Company bought the building, Dr. Moe moved his offices to the Main Motel where he has practiced since. But now that he has passed his eighty-eighth birthday, (some six months ago) he's decided he's old enough to retire and is even now in the process of moving out of his office. To many Glendivians Dr. Moe and his bicycle were a familiar sight on the Fourth of July. He has the distinction of participating in the parade every year for fourteen consecutive years.

About thirty years ago he spent about three months on business in a little Oklahoma town and had an interesting experience while there. Over in Joplin, Missouri two fellows had stolen a Cadillac from an Indian squaw and were reported headed west so the citizens of the little town where Dr. Moe was organized a posse to try to find the thieves. Dr. Moe was deputized to join the posse, and they spent most of the day driving and searching. About dusk they came to a little house on a side hill and asked the fellow sitting on the porch if he had seen a Cadillac. He said he hadn't, then asked if they'd take a passenger along back to town. They had room so they took him along. Later the car thieves were apprehended in Michigan, and one of them had a good laugh telling how he had ridden to town with the posse down in Oklahoma!

During that same period Dr. Moe got acquainted with five first cousins of the notorious Jesse and Frank James. Of these cousins one was a dentist, two were medical doctors, one was an FBI man, and one a motel man, brilliant men all, as were the criminals.

Dr. and Mrs. Moe had two children; Tony, now with the U.S. Immigration Service in El Paso, Texas, and Maxine (Mrs. Ray Jarding), who passed away nine years ago. They have three grandchildren and six great grandchildren.

Dr. Moe holds life membership in the Elks and all Masonic bodies and also belongs to the Moose. Mrs. Moe, who has been giving piano lessons in Glendive for about as long as Dr. Moe has been practicing dentistry, suffers crippling effects from a fall about seventeen years ago, but otherwise she is in good health, and Dr. Moe hasn't yet found any reason to feel 'old'.

His 'spryness' cannot be attributed to smooth sailing all his life because some of the time the sailing was anything but smooth. When they moved to Glendive, he let the farm out to renters, which proved unprofitable (to say the least), and during the depression he lost everything he had – his home, the homestead, two other sections of land, and had a $5,000 debt besides. But he seems to have weathered his adversities well.

In these later years he has seen no reason to change his schedule, still getting up at seven and going to the office at nine. As to what he plans to do after retirement – well, he'll wait and see.

Mrs. Ed (Mary Schumacker) Lamphier

October 1966

Perhaps most folks take for granted the city's garbage collection service, but when Glendive was organized as a city soon after the turn of the century, garbage collection wasn't included in the package. Not until 1928 was any such service offered in residential areas, and Mrs. Ed Lamphier, bookkeeper for the enterprising lads who instigated the service, remembers well some of the problems and surprises encountered by the boys in their new venture.

Times were hard and jobs were scarce in 1928 so Lamphiers' two younger sons, Don and Carl, created their own jobs. Previous to this, garbage was picked up for downtown businesses for six dollars a month, but throughout the residential area there was no such service and many yards were cluttered with piles of ashes, tin cans, and just plain rubbish.

With a team and wagon, the boys began making rounds, offering their services. For the original yard cleanup they charged one dollar. After that they picked up garbage twice a week for a charge of fifty cents per month.

Soon business places were asking for this more economical service, and before long someone reported them to Helena and the boys received a letter ordering them to quit because they did not have an M.R.C. license. The boys had received a permit from the city to carry on their business, and when investigations revealed that these 'haulers' were a couple of school boys with a team and wagon, charging only fifty cents per month per customer the demand for an M.R.C. license was dropped.

As they went from place to place on their route they never knew what they might find. Once they found a dead colt shoved down into the can to be picked up as garbage. Another time they cleaned out a chicken house, but when they asked for their one-dollar cleanup fee, the owner insisted that the refuse (and the cleaning) should be included in fifty-cents-per-month garbage pickup. He finally paid the dollar, but in another case a lady refused to pay until they dumped her ashes back into her yard. They hadn't picked up her ashes on the previous trip, she charged, so she wasn't going to pay for that month. The boys explained that they couldn't pick up the ashes the time before because there was still fire in the ashes, but she still refused to pay.

Mrs. Lamphier happened to be with the boys on that trip so she told them to dump the ashes they had just loaded back into the yard. They dumped them, and the lady promptly decided to pay after all – and caused them no more trouble. Such cases as these were the exception, however. Most people were cooperative, glad to have their garbage hauled away regularly. Many gave the boys tips in addition to the regular charge.

The boys advertised their services when they began their enterprise, and calls came in from all over town. Mrs. Lamphier took the calls for them and marked the names and addresses down in the ledger. Although they used a team and wagon when they started, business grew until they were able to buy an old

340

truck for hauling. After several years the boys sold their business for one hundred dollars, and Mrs. Lamphier agreed to continue keeping the books for the new owner for one year at five dollars a month. The cleaning up of Glendive streets and yards was well established.

When the Lamphiers first came to Montana, they had worked on the White Ranch on Cabin Creek, then homesteaded on a half section of land adjoining the ranch. Before coming to the Cabin Creek ranch they had worked for the same employer on his ranch in North Dakota. He transferred them to the Treasure State, and they've lived here ever since, except for one year in Canada.

They had horses to sell, and at that time (1925) horses were worth about $35 here. In Canada they would bring a good price so they took them to Canada, worked with them on a ranch for a year (they had to live in Canada a year before they could sell) then sold the horses for $125 each and returned to the States.

The first meeting of Mary Schumacker and Ed Lamphier was, literally, by accident. She was working in a Sioux City hospital; he was employed by the Novelty Iron Works. Ed and another fellow had been sent to the hospital to change the flue in a boiler, and as they worked his partner came in contact with a live wire. The wire caught him across the chest, knocking him down and out.

Ed found him and began rescue efforts while the young nurse aide assisted. One of her main contributions was fighting off the attempts of another worker to throw water on the unconscious accident victim, still not free from the hot wire. Their rescue efforts were successful, and after the patient was hospitalized he insisted that he wanted to marry the nurse aide in spite of the fact that he already had a wife and some children.

Again it was Ed to the rescue. He said he would take care of her, and the second night after the accident he walked home with her, carrying her bundle of laundry the seventeen blocks to her room. (In addition to helping the nurses on the floor, she also worked in the laundry and was given the privilege of using the laundry facilities for washing her own clothes.) That was the beginning of a romance which culminated in their marriage in 1906.

A few years after their marriage they decided to go to North Dakota for the harvest, he working in the fields and she cooking. After the harvest they stayed on at the White Ranch, and the next year the owner transferred them to his ranch on Cabin Creek twenty-six miles south of Glendive. Before long they began seriously considering the advantages offered by a homestead so in 1913 they filed on a half-section adjoining the White Ranch. For a time they continued to work on the ranch, driving back and forth to get their building program started, a well dug, and other essentials for a home.

Selling cedar posts was one of their main sources of income after they quit the ranch and moved over onto the homestead full time. Ed would camp up in the hills so he could put in full time cutting posts, and Mrs. Lamphier, using a wagon and four-horse team, hauled the posts out – and the food in. Posts were in great demand during this period with homesteaders all over eastern Montana fencing their claims so they found a ready market for all the posts they could supply. They used a goodly number of posts themselves. Although their original homestead was 320 acres, later the Grazing Act allowed them an additional 320 so they had an entire section* to fence – and it takes more than a few posts to put up four miles of fence.

Not long after the Lamphiers homesteaded, a large number of immigrants from Russia filed on nearby homestead lands. Though from Russia, they spoke German but no English so often Mrs. Lamphier, who had been reared in a German-speaking home, was called upon to be interpreter. After the outbreak of World War I these neighbors had to learn the English language. Often they would come to the Lamphier home to get her to help them with their language studies.

There was much exchange of help among neighbors, and Mrs. Lamphier especially recalled those who helped. Often the wives would come along, too. There was a lot of work involved in the scalding and skinning of a hog, cutting it up, stuffing the sausages, preparing the bacon and hams for curing, making head cheese, and rendering the lard, but visiting as they worked made the tasks seem lighter. Of course, it might be a beef instead of a hog, but the cooperation was the same.

In the evening, after the work was done, everything cleaned up and put away, they would have prayer meeting and a time of singing before they scattered to their various homes. There was no church in the community so sometimes the neighbors would come on Sunday evenings, and they would sing together.

The flu epidemic of 1918 took a heavy toll in the community where Lamphiers lived. During one period Mrs. Lamphier was cooking for three stricken families while her husband was doing the chores for those same families. Mrs. Lamphier would do all the cooking in her own home, then carefully pack the food and dishes into separate tubs and her oldest son, using a team and sled, would deliver the tubs to the homes, then bring them back and Mrs. Lamphier would sterilize the dishes to prevent the spreading of germs.

They managed to stay well while most of the community was sick, but they relaxed their caution in what might have seemed an insignificant area, and before they were through, the entire family had contracted the dread disease.

One of their neighbors had lost a wife and two children, buried all three in the same casket. He had been ill, also, but was recovered enough so that he could do some work again, and Mr. Lamphier took him to Terry to get some wheat ground into flour at the mill. The neighbor didn't want to go to the hotel that night to sleep lest he spread the virus so he just slept in the livery barn, and Mr. Lamphier slept in the livery barn, too. About a week later the flu struck him.

They had been helping all around, but now that the flu had overtaken them, no one knew – no telephone to summon help – so they had no way to even call the doctor. Finally a horseback rider happened to come through so they sent for the doctor. Although they were desperately ill, they all recovered, but it was a year before Mr. Lamphier recuperated enough to work again. Mrs. Lamphier and their oldest boy carried on with the farm work while he convalesced.

As homesteaders with their families moved in, schools became necessary so Lamphiers donated an acre of their land on which to build a schoolhouse. Twenty children attended the one-room school. But then hard times drove many of the settlers away again so after a time the school was closed.

Now the ranchers had their range back again (they had opposed the homesteaders coming), and the remaining farmers had to send their children to one of the little towns in the area to get to school — Mildred, Fallon, Terry, or Marsh.

Lamphiers moved into Marsh to get their boys to school (by this time they had three going), but they didn't stay long. It was during their Marsh sojourn that Mr. Lamphier decided to take his horses (he was always a lover of horses and took pride in his big teams) to Canada to sell them. He soon found work in the harvest and his family joined him there. While he worked his horses in the harvest, Mrs. Lamphier cooked for the harvest crew.

After the year's residency requirement had been met, he sold the horses and they returned to the States, this time locating in Glendive. It was at this time that the boys started their garbage collection route.

Their three boys are scattered now — one in Wisconsin, one in Chicago, and one in New Jersey. All three are married, and the Lamphiers now have seven grandchildren and eight great grandchildren. Mr. and Mrs. Lamphier still live in the home they bought on Pearson Avenue in 1929.

Carl Volpp

February 1966

My dad, like many others, came from Nebraska to file on a homestead in Montana. He came in October of 1912 and filed on a half section on Corral Creek, west of the Redwater-Yellowstone Divide, then returned to Nebraska to have an auction sale and get ready to move to our new home.

My mother, two sisters, and my only brother came by passenger train. They were met in Glendive by John G. Mahlstedt, a former Nebraska neighbor who was now located on Corral Creek. My dad and I came with two immigrant cars containing our cows, horses, one hog, some chickens, a plow, a wagon, and some household goods.

We got into Glendive on February 27, 1913, and found the weather beautiful. The winter had been an open one and remained that way until the forepart of March; then came lots of snow. We lived with the Jack Bicha family until our house was built and a well was dug (by hand).

Homesteaders came from various states and various walks of life: barbers, bankers, butchers, doctors, dentists, schoolteachers, and so forth. By the time we came, most of the claims were taken. Since every other section was homestead land, most sections had two settlers on them.

As new settlers came in, bachelors would look them up (bachelors were plentiful), to see if the new family had any marriageable girls. Homesteaders' daughters and schoolteachers usually did not remain single very long, and my sisters were no exception. Some bachelor would come along with a lovelorn (or hungry!) look in his eye; soon he would find a cook. Or perhaps a girl would come to visit a brother or a sister, and the visit would end in marriage and lifelong residence here.

Wedding trips in those days usually consisted of a trip out from Glendive on a lumber wagon, with a team traveling about four miles an hour, to the little shanty on the claim. What if the honeymooners became too absorbed in one another to pay attention? The horses generally knew the way home. Highway fatalities? They were unknown out here; so, almost, were highways!

By the time we came out here the CK cattle were a thing of the past. A number of bands of sheep and innumerable horses covered the range. A.M. Goff, Joe Storm, Joe Holtz, Nelson Brothers, John Butterfield, Betty Ross, and Art Sime were some of the ranchers still here. A lot of water has gone down the coulee since then!

There were many enjoyable times and some very sad ones. There were good years, with good crops and plenty of feed, and also dry years, with very little crop or feed. There were hail storms, floods, wind, and fires; weddings, births, deaths, and shootings.

In July 1916, Joe Holtz shot Jim Rider in self-defense. Fortunately, a livery stable attendant had overheard Jim declaring that he was going out and that he was going to 'get' Joe. Since Jim was drunk, the attendant, unknown to Jim, emptied his gun. Joe received word of Jim's coming, and was prepared when Jim reached the Holtz Ranch, just over the Redwater Divide. My brother Fritz now owns the Holtz place, and the Win Fritz family lives there.

On June 21, 1921, Walter Hagen, a young fellow farming with his brother Gunder (on the place where Jim Kirkegard now lives) drowned in a flash flood. In this same flood a home was washed away on Corral Creek. Ervin Root, his wife, and one child were in their house when it began to move downstream. It floated a few hundred feet, then grounded against a hill, but only long enough for them to get out the window and up the hill. Within minutes the floodwaters had moved the house back into the main stream where its former occupants watched it collapse.

On July 11, 1915, my dad was kicked in the abdomen by a horse. He died within eighteen hours. My mother was left with four children. In those days it was unthinkable to go on relief or to go to Washington, D.C. with hat in hand looking for a handout.

In July 1916, Mrs. John Arnett passed away, leaving six small children. Aunt Susie, John's sister, stepped in to 'mother' them. Eleven years later John passed away from an injury received while mining coal. This took place just prior to the big blizzard in May of 1927. The funeral was held on May 10. The body was taken to the grave on the farm with a team and bobsled. The preacher was unable to come out from Circle because of the deep snow so various neighbors read Scripture, prayed, and sang hymns at the grave.

In March 1929, Mrs. Sam (Annie) Kirkegard, a young mother of three, passed away after a long illness. Grandpa Gable, a widower neighbor, moved in with Sam and the children. He washed and mended clothes and helped out in general with the children, who ranged in age from two to nine years. Uncle Andrew Kirkegard helped with the cooking.

In February 1920, John A. Mahlstedt died of the Spanish influenza. Other old timers from the Corral Creek community, that I know of, who have passed away since then are: Mr. and Mrs. Harry Stone, Mr. and Mrs. Jack Bicha, Mrs. John A. Mahlstedt, Mr. and Mrs. M.C. Roberts, Mr. and Mrs. Walter Reinhardt, Mr. and Mrs. Albert Voss, Carl Etzel (Carl had come from Germany to New York, then on to Montana to homestead), Leo Knopp, Martha Surges, Mrs. Frank Knopp, Sam and Andrew Kirkegard, Mr. and Mrs. Pete Bicha, Gunder Hagen, Mr. and Mrs. Aadna Idland, Knute and Rastus Skartved, A.M. Goff, Mr. and Mrs. Fred Knopp, Carly Voss, Jens Jensen, Pete Hannas, and Mr. and Mrs. John Miller.

Some of the homesteaders proved up* on their claims, then left, looking for greener pastures elsewhere.

We first hauled our grain to Glendive with team and wagon, forty-six miles one way. Those forty-six miles included the climb to cross the Redwater Divide. This took three or four days for the round trip. We tried to travel in pairs in case of trouble.

Generally the last trip to town for the winter would be made a week or so before Christmas, when we'd bring home enough staples (flour, sugar, salt, coffee, and dried fruit) to last until spring.

In the fall of 1916 the Great Northern Railroad laid rails into Richey, twenty-five miles northeast of us. We could make a trip to Richey and back in two days now. On June 2, 1928, the first Northern Pacific train pulled into Circle, just fourteen miles away. Grain hauling was really simplified now.

The school on Corral Creek had its beginning with a three-month term in the summer of 1913 in Ralph Buskirk's granary. Miss Lucille Hennigar, who later taught band and music in the Glendive schools for many years, was the first teacher. Miss Hennigar made a striking picture as she walked across the fields to the schoolhouse, her full, ankle-length skirts billowing in the wind.

Her pupils were four Mahlstedts, three Stones, two Roberts, one Bicha, and my youngest sister and brother. That first day of school Miss Hennigar noticed little Clarence Bicha crying so she asked him what was the matter. Clarence frankly explained, "My mother told me that if I cried, the teacher would send me home!" But it didn't work that way.

That fall and winter the schoolhouse was built on the half section line between the Buskirk and Roberts farms. In October 1924, it was moved to its present location on the northwest corner of the Buskirk place.

The first program, Christmas of 1913, was held at our house, as the schoolhouse was not yet finished. After its completion the schoolhouse was used for Church services and other social activities for a number of years.

The last year school was held at Corral Creek was the 1946-47 term, with Gladys Mullet, now Mrs. Morris Kauffman, as the last teacher.

The old school house, known as the Upper Corral Creek School since the consolidation of school districts, is just an old landmark now. The school presently operating in the district is known as the Lower Corral Creek School.

Before his mother's death, Carl lived with her on the old homestead. One night, after they had retired, a knock came on the door and when Carl answered it he found a stranger on the steps. The man explained that he was from Sidney and had run out of gas. In answer to Carl's questions, he couldn't even say for sure which way he had come, but when Carl asked if he had come through Richey the man said he had so Carl figured he could find the truck and assured him he would help him.

They went to the shed where he kept his gas barrels and were getting some gasoline when four or five horsemen rode into the yard. Quickly the stranger reminded him, "It's Halloween." It was too late to step back out of sight into the shadows because they had already been seen by the horsemen so Carl went forward and greeted them.

It was a group of young men from the neighborhood, and they asked Carl to join them for some 'Halloweening'. Carl was willing, but he explained about

346

he stranger's plight and told them he would have to take him and some asoline back to his truck. They told him to go ahead and they'd wait for him ntil he got back; they'd even catch up his horse and have it saddled for him.

Carl delivered the stranger, and when he returned he found the fellows, all ned up like little Sunday School boys, waiting for him, and his horse saddled, eady to go. They went, but details of the next few hours are lacking.

Next morning Carl started to do his chores and went first to turn on the vindmill. It wouldn't turn on. Investigating, he found the wheel and the tail tied ogether. He began searching about for the ladder that he kept nearby and inally found it – tied to the top of the windmill, just under the wheel.

If he spent time and effort getting that prank undone, it was nothing to vhat lay ahead of him. He had been cleaning barn the day before and had left he first load in the manure spreader instead of emptying it yet that afternoon. Now he found that his pals (!!) had removed the wheels from the spreader eaving the box on the ground for him. He had to unload the load from the preader, with much stress and straining, replace the wheels, then throw the oad back on again. With friends like that who needs enemies!

Sons of the old homesteaders on their dad's farms are George Mahlstedt (with young George about ready to take over), Gene Voss, Louie Undem, Adolph Kirkegard, Jim Kirkegard (on his Uncle Andrew's place) and the Jensen Brothers.

Selma (Idland) Garpestad and her husband live on her parents' homestead and Ruth (Surges) Gasper with her husband and family live on the place where she was born.

A few of the old homesteaders who are still around are Mr. and Mrs. Gust Voss, Mr. and Mrs. Erling Fosfjeld, Mrs. A.M. Goff, Mr. and Mrs. Martin Undem, making their homes in Circle. Mr. & Mrs. Ralph Buskirk spend their summers on their homestead on Corral Creek but go to Mesa, Arizona, for the winters. Soren Jensen lives with son Barney and family on Lower Corral Creek.

Carl concludes, "My mother passed away March 12, 1935. I remained a bachelor until June 1941, when I married Katherine Gaub of Fallon. We lived on the old homestead until October 1963, when we sold the place to Reuben Wagner of Circle. His son LaVerne and wife are living there now. We hope and pray that as the years go by, they will have as wonderful memories of the old home and community as we cherish! They live among fine neighbors, as we experienced it; when help was needed there was help at hand, rain or shine.

"We now live in Terry where we have found more fine people, have made new friends, and always enjoy having old friends stop in. We also enjoy the beautiful town park, the gorgeous lawns, and the flowers from early spring until late in the fall."

Ernest Malkuch

March – April 1968

Ernest Malkuch first ventured west from Medford, Wisconsin in 1905, going as far as North Dakota to work in the harvest. Harvest took a little longer in those days than it does now. Instead of cutting and threshing the grain in one operation, the wheat was cut with a binder, the grain was shocked in the field, and later the threshing crew came.

Not many farmers owned a separator so one rig often served an entire community or even several communities, and threshing might not be completed until late in the fall. Occasionally someone might even be found threshing as late as Christmas. It wasn't that late, however, when Ernest completed his job that first fall in North Dakota.

When the threshing was done, he went back to Wisconsin and spent the winter working in the woods. Many black bears roamed the Wisconsin woods, and he often encountered them but was never molested. He recalled going past one in a hurry, though. The first winter he worked in the woods he wasn't accustomed to being away from home and got lonesome, so after a week or two he decided to go home and visit the folks. As he pedaled his bicycle through the woods he met a man who warned him not to go down that trail because he had wounded but not killed a bear beside the trail.

There was no other road through the woods, and Ernest had made up his mind to go home so, bear or no bear, he kept going. Before long he found the bear. It couldn't get up, but it was making a lot of noise and thrashing around. Ernest wasn't interested in loitering there and pedaled on by as fast as he could. Just as he got past the wounded animal one of his bicycle tires blew out, but he didn't stop. He kept going as fast as he could until his tire was all gone.

Another time when he was afoot in the woods a bear started toward him, but he stood his ground and the bear stopped. They stared at each other for a time, then Ernest started to walk away. The bear made no attempt to follow him so he kept going.

He was well satisfied with his first harvest experience in North Dakota so in the fall of 1906 he returned for another season. He recalled that at the first place he had worked in North Dakota he was pleased to see a Bible lying on the table when he entered the kitchen where they ate their meals. He commented to the housewife, "I like the sight of that Bible." She didn't say anything then, but after supper when he expected to go to the barn and sleep in the haymow as the other crew members did, she told him he was to share a bed in the house with the oldest son. That was where he slept all the time he worked there. As Mr. Malkuch thought back over that experience he remarked, "If everyone would look into the Scripture and take it to heart, it would do them a lot of good."

He went back to Wisconsin again the second fall after he worked in North Dakota, but when he came out in 1907, he found a job in northeastern Montana when harvest was done. Len Burns had a horse ranch twenty miles northeast of

Fairview, and Ernest hired out to him to break horses. By this time homestead country was opening up, and there was a great demand for work horses so he spent the winter breaking horses.

He got along fine but in the spring he heard that they were hiring men to work on 'The Ditch' – the Lower Yellowstone irrigation canal between Intake and Sidney, paying $2.50 a day. That was more than he could expect to make breaking horses, so he went to work on the ditch, driving horses instead of breaking them – although sometimes perhaps there wasn't too much difference.

As Ernest Malkuch began working at his new job on the Lower Yellowstone Project the boss watched closely and observed that he knew how to handle horses. Before long he gave Ernest a pair of white mules to drive. The mules were troublemakers, and without exception other drivers on the project were willing to let someone else have them. Among their many offensive habits was that of stopping in their tracks about half-an-hour before dinner time and starting to bray. The wrath of their driver did not budge them, nor did the wrath of other drivers whose teams were held up by the balky pair. There were twenty or twenty-five teams at work so if the mules happened to be at the front of the line when they decided to halt, they really held up the works.

When Malkuch found himself assigned to the rebels, he asked for one line about six feet longer than the other so he could 'flank' them – hit them between the legs until they moved. They learned. No more holding up the line at noon! For mastering the mules Malkuch's pay was raised to $2.75 a day.

That summer when the weather was warm, the fellows often went swimming in the river. A dozen or so of them would line up along the bank and jump into the water, but one Sunday when a bunch of them dived in, the best swimmer in the lot failed to come up. After a desperate search they found him in a little eddy about two miles downstream from their swimming hole.

Autopsies weren't so common then, and they never did know for sure what happened to him. The water where they dived in was twelve or fifteen feet deep, and there were no rocks so injury from diving seemed to them to be ruled out. The boss figured he must have had a stroke. Whatever the cause of death, it was a sobering experience for all of them.

In the fall of 1908 Ernest's father, seeing Ernest's frontier fever, came from Wisconsin to work in North Dakota's harvest fields (eastern Montana didn't have very many harvest fields in 1908). Both father and son were interested in homesteading. They worked until October, then both were ready to file.

The stage, carrying both mail and passengers, left Fairview at eight o'clock in the morning and reached Glendive at eight o'clock that evening. After sixty years, Mr. Malkuch still remembers the name of the stage driver. Harvey Mitchell piloted them over the trail. He kept the horses on a trot all the way and changed teams twice – once just south of Sidney and again at Savage. Remembering that ride caused Mr. Malkuch to exclaim, "My, that road was rough!" No oiled highways in those days.

With the exception of Thirteen Mile Valley, not many homestead claims had been staked when the Malkuchs were ready to file so they could about take their pick of locations. They chose adjoining quarters twenty miles straight west of Glendive. Later when the law was passed allowing each homesteader a half section, they each filed on another quarter in the original section.

They returned to Wisconsin that fall where Ernest's father sold his little farm. Then in the spring they loaded an immigrant car with some furniture and livestock and headed for their new home in Montana. It wasn't much of a home yet – just 160 acres of Montana prairie without any kind of improvement on it. They immediately set to work to remedy that situation, however.

Ernest's mother, six sisters, and three brothers had come along that spring. Mother and the girls stayed in Glendive while the men folk built the 20'x26' house, living in a little tent 'on the scene'. When the family was settled in their house they built Ernest's little 12'x14' shack on his claim.

Although Ernest was a bachelor homesteader he was in no hurry to get married just to find a housekeeper as might be suspected of some of the bachelors. His folks had built across the line that separated their homesteads, and his mother cooked for him as she did for her other boys. The time came, however, when he changed his mind about the desirability of having a wife. In the spring of 1916 he bought twenty-five head of cattle south of Miles City and had them shipped to Fallon, then trailed them overland to his ranch. He didn't have his saddle horse so he set out on foot with them. He reached the Hohensee ranch about nightfall and noticed they had good corrals for keeping cattle so he asked permission to stay overnight. Permission was readily granted (after all, this was the frontier) and thus he first met Dora Hohensee. The family had already eaten supper, but they quickly put on some more for their unexpected guest.

Ernest was impressed with the good bread and asked Dora if she had baked it. Assured that she had, he complimented her on it, but he didn't say anything about the cookies. According to the stories his daughters have heard, the cookies were so hard they almost broke his teeth, and Dora took refuge in the pantry to hide her giggles while he chewed.

His mother had always told him that if a woman could bake good bread she would make a good wife so perhaps the cookies didn't have much significance. At any rate, fifty-one years later he affirms that his mother was right about the good bread – good wife.

He was definitely interested in Dora and began calling on her now and then. The calls became more regular, and a little more than a year later he asked her to be his wife. She consented, and they were married June 28, 1917 in the Woodrow E.U.B. Church, about four miles north of his homestead.

As the years went by their house filled up with children – six girls and six boys. Twelve children kept things lively for them, and there was no predicting what might happen next – except that when Dad and Mom went to town it might be anything.

One of those days when their parents were gone, they harnessed a yearling colt and hitched it to a two-wheeled cart. Biggest sister was supposed to be holding him, but he managed to get away, and by the time he stopped buggy pokes were scattered everywhere. They didn't tell their folks about that episode until a couple weeks later!

Except for one boy the three girls were the oldest of the children so they had plenty of opportunity to help on the farm. They even recall helping dig the well. Dad, down in the hole, would fill a bucket with dirt, then the children would haul it to the surface with a windlass. Sometimes they would accidentally drop a rock on him, then anxiously check to see if they had hurt him. Mom, the girls report, often wondered why they built up on the flat where they had to dig for water instead of down along the creek near a spring, but Mr. Malkuch points out that they really had good water up there.

Another advantage, they could certainly see the 'Big Sky' from the flat. Now that they've moved down closer to the river, he complains that he can't see the sky well enough to predict the weather as he used to do because there are so many trees. There are so many trees he can't even see where the moon comes up. Out on the homestead their building site was 700 feet higher than Glendive, and they could see far in every direction.

Once one of the boys was unfortunate enough to be in one of the outbuildings when some of the other boys, not realizing he was there, started target practicing with a 22. The little fellow came flying out in a hurry, chattering, "You didn't get me!" He was scared, but he wasn't the only one when the rest of the family realized what a close call it had been.

Another time their dog, Bimbo, tried to kill a skunk, but suddenly the skunk grabbed him by the mouth so Bimbo came running to one of the girls for help. One rock carefully aimed dislodged the skunk, but as soon as Bimbo was free he ran for the car where Mary had forgotten to shut the door, and in he jumped. What an odor permeated that car!

To the early settlers the horse was automobile, tractor, and Honda combined — not to mention friend. The Malkuchs know what it is to be able to depend on a faithful horse. On one occasion Mrs. Malkuch and two of the youngsters had ridden horseback about five miles from home to visit some neighbors. On the way home they were caught in a snowstorm, and as the snow swirled about them they became hopelessly lost. Without realizing it they were trying to go north instead of east, but one horse kept neighing and trying to go the other way. Finally they let her have her head, and she took them directly home through the blizzard. When they arrived home, they were cold, but they were happy to arrive safely.

However, another horse another time went a different direction. They had just bought a horse from Lorance Hogmire, a neighbor to the west, and one of the girls was assigned to ride him home. Darkness overtook them, and patches of snow all around confused her so that she lost her sense of direction. As she rode on her surroundings looked strange, but not until they reached a gate did she realize just what had happened. The newly purchased horse was taking her back to Hogmires. At least he didn't leave her wandering over the prairie.

Not all their horses always performed commendably. Mr. Malkuch bought a team, Jack & Billy, from Donahue, and picked them up at the Northern Pacific stockyards. They put halters on them in the yards, then tied them behind the wagon for the trip home. By the end of the twenty miles, the horses were pretty well halter broke.

In time they turned out to be a good enough team, but it took awhile. Not long after he bought them Mr. Malkuch started to Glendive with them for a load of lumber with just the running gears of the wagon. As he left the home yard the horses began to run. The prairie was rough, and suddenly the front holster pin flew out, leaving the driver sitting on the hind running gears while his team kept right on going. Chuckling at the memory, he exclaimed, "I can see them yet, after all these years!" They didn't stop running until they were about four miles from home. There he caught them with Shorty, a gentle work horse, and brought them back to start over again.

'Dad' wasn't the only one who had 'runaways'. The youngsters used a little cart mounted on the front runners of a bobsled to drive back and forth to school, and on this outfit, too, a bolt came loose, and the horses started to run. Realizing she couldn't control the team, the driver (Mary) told the other children to jump out so they jumped – all but cousin Louise.

"All these years," Mary commented, "I thought she was so brave to stay with me. Then just recently she told me she was too scared to jump!" They had a zigzag ride while the horses threw snowballs with their flying hooves, but she was finally able to stop them.

A couple of the girls had quite an adventure when they decided to break a horse. They snubbed the bronc to the horn of a saddle on another horse, then each girl mounted one of the horses. They were going along fine until the rear horse started bucking and broke the cinch on the forward saddle. Both girls were off in a hurry – the rear by choice and the lead of necessity. The girl from the uncinched saddle landed almost under the feet of the rearing steed but managed to escape his hooves. Then the bronc took off on the run with Uncle Frank Malkuch's saddle bouncing along on the end of the rope. To the dismayed girls it seemed that the saddle was bouncing twelve feet into the air, but as frightened as they were, they admit they were hardly qualified to judge very accurately. They were greatly relieved when they caught that horse again.

Toby, now, behaved much more honorably. Mr. Malkuch and one of the girls found themselves involved with a prairie fire so 'Dad' tried to plow around it with the tractor. The tractor, however, got stuck so wasn't of much use. Daughter was riding Toby, and "you should have seen how wonderful he was when the fire was coming on both sides of him." She jerked the saddle blanket off him and used it to fight the fire, then when it was over put it back on her horse. He started acting strangely so she checked and found the saddle blanket still smoking. Evidently a section of it was burning when she put it back on Toby.

Horses and more horses. The men folk were getting tired of rounding up horses and branding them so one day when the men were all in town Aunt Netty (Mrs. Malkuch's sister who lived on a neighboring farm) decided to finish the job. The youngsters were glad to join in the operation so they helped corral about thirty head.

One by one, Aunt Netty roped the horses, then one of the older Malkuch girls held the rope while Aunt did the branding. She did a beautiful job too, in spite of the victim's struggles to get free. The other children contributed their bit by keeping the irons hot.

Perhaps when your late model car is no longer the latest model, you look forward to trading it in on a newer, but with a horse – well, with a horse it's different. Malkuchs raised Dick from a colt but then traded him to one of the neighbors. The neighbor's boy, however, was afraid of him so Dick was back home again, and one of the girls started riding him to school.

One day she didn't ride him but left him on a picket rope at home. When she returned from school that afternoon, Dick was gone so she lost no time inquiring about him. The bottom dropped out of her world when her mother told her, "Carl sold him to Clarence Giles." Crying didn't bring him back, but she cried anyway.

One day on the way to Glendive she saw 'her' horse pasturing near the sand and gravel pit west of town on Highway 10, and she couldn't resist calling to him. His head went up, and the next day he was home. Soon Mr. Giles came after him and led him all the way back to Glendive – nineteen or twenty miles behind the car, but in a few days he came home again. That was enough to convince the elders that some other course of action was advisable so Malkuchs traded a cow and calf to Giles for Dick. And those fast friends, girl and horse, were once more united officially.

Inevitably horses in time gave way to mechanization, and Malkuchs bought a big gray Buick. The Buick was faster and smoother than a team and buggy, but wagon trails weren't always entirely satisfactory for automobiles. Grades – gravel – pavement – all were in the future and more than once they stalled in mud or snow. Mr. Malkuch observed, "Each and every winter was a battle to get over the roads. I hate to think of it."

Another thing – horses didn't stall. They might balk, but Mr. Malkuch knew how to handle balky horses. Balky cars were something else again. One time the Buick stalled in very severe weather, and they had to walk about two miles. Fortunately the children weren't along, but Mrs. Malkuch froze her legs severely.

Another time when they got stuck in the mud with the same Buick the children were along so they all piled out and started to push – all except one, that is. He was too small to do much pushing, but he wasn't too small to find the shotgun that was lying in the back of the car. He pulled the trigger and really peppered the back of the car. He scattered the family in a hurry, too.

But when the roads were dry, that Buick could really go. One morning when Mrs. Malkuch was expecting the threshing crew for dinner, she found her larder lacking some necessities so she dispatched one of her daughters to town for supplies and sent along strict orders to be back by dinner.

One who is accustomed only to paved highways can hardly appreciate making haste on some of the early country roads. On the way in she managed sixty miles an hour on 'the old coal mine road' and somehow made the curves. On the return trip she decided to take a short cut across the neighbor's pasture.

Concentrating on getting home in a hurry, she forgot all about an old trail until she hit it crosswise. The early trails weren't 'laid out'; teamsters just followed what seemed to be the most convenient route, and when the ruts from the wagon wheels became too deep, another trail was started alongside. Hitting the trails with any speed could result in anything from broken springs to broken necks, but she was lucky and nothing broke. Groceries flew but she reached home with the whole order, and 'Mom' was so happy to have the groceries in time for dinner she didn't ask any questions.

During World War II five of the six Malkuch boys were in the Service, and all five came home. Said Mr. Malkuch simply, "God was good to us." The sixth son worked for Boeing Aircraft Company, and three of the daughters also worked for Boeing during the war.

Mr. Malkuch spent fifty-five years on the homestead. For forty-four years he was a school trustee in District 107, Sunrise School. (If anyone in the county exceeds that record, we'd like to hear about it.) With twelve children to educate, Mr. Malkuch surely had an interest in the school system!

In 1963 they sold their farm to Kenneth Edwards and bought a place on Deer Creek, closer to Glendive. Mr. and Mrs. Malkuch spent four years there together before she passed away last summer – August 18, 1967.

Of his wife, Mr. Malkuch asserts, "She was a fine mother, cook (good bread baker – good wife), doctor, farmer, and rancher. She was a better farmer than I," he continued. "She farmed her own land, had her own tractor. In the spring she'd get through before I (of course, her acreage was much smaller), and then I'd look to see where she was going. I should have known she'd come help me."

She started using mineral on her land before he did on his. She had a little phosphate left over – enough for about ten acres – so she put it on some of his land. That plot made ten bushels per acre more than the rest of his crop so he was convinced.

Mr. Malkuch could tell many other experiences – from breaking up a fight between two high-priced stallions belonging to Len Burns to escapades of his children. The children encountered many cuts and bruises, but not one of the twelve ever had a broken bone. They made pets of everything from horses to weasels. One of the girls saw a weasel go down a hole so she poured some water down, then quickly put a fruit jar over the opening. When the weasel came up he found himself in a jar. She had quite a time getting the cover on for weasels are strong for their size, but she made it.

Now Mr. Malkuch says he just appreciates what he has and enjoys using electricity, gas, lights, and running water. All of his children, though scattered far and wide, are still living, his daughter Mary with him. Again he expresses himself, "God was good to me."

Jack McNaney

January 1965

Glendive's Jack McNaney is the only son of one of the most colorful and illustrious pioneers of eastern Montana, James McNaney. Jim McNaney was born in Philadelphia, June 22, 1860. He was employed by the United States government as a teamster, and in this capacity he came to the Custer Battlefield the year following the Custer massacre, working with others to clear the carnage from the field. He spent the next winter in Denver, then went to Laramie Plains, Nebraska, where he joined a trail herd coming up from Texas and helped bring them on to Montana. Those first years in Montana he lived mostly in the vicinity of Miles City, working on various ranches in the area. At one time he was under-sheriff of Custer County. Later he also operated a ferry across the Yellowstone near Miles City.

A story from the files of the Dawson County Review, relating an incident that occurred while he was running the ferry, reveals much about the character of James McNaney. According to the Review story:

When the late James McNaney, guide, buffalo hunter and ferryman, operated a ferry on the Yellowstone River about two miles west of the old town of Miles City, he became the principal in an incident that produced a classic in speed.

When groups of pioneers gather to talk over the old days, the ride of James McNaney is referred to with a degree of pride that betokens the enduring qualities of the performance. He was a modest individual. The exploits in which he engaged were all in the work of the moment. He expressed no desire to boast. He operated his ferry on the river as a cold-blooded business enterprise. His reward was for services performed.

One bitterly cold night in December 1898, the wife of a rancher living twenty-four miles west of Miles City was taken suddenly ill. Miles City was the nearest point from which a physician could be summoned. A cowboy was dispatched on horseback to ride with all haste possible to the city. Arriving at McNaney's place he awoke the ferryman and informed him of his errand.

Crossing the River

The channel of the river was filled with slush ice. The crossing involved the encountering of possible perils in the deep darkness of the cloud-filled night. There was no hesitation. The life of a wife of a friend was at stake. The ferryboat was loosened from its mooring. "Cowboy, you take that pole and keep the ice out of the way and I'll put her over," McNaney informed his companion.

They came to the east bank of the river safely. McNaney built a fire of some cottonwood tree bark while the messenger proceeded on foot to Miles City, a distance of two miles. Waiting there patiently in the light of the fire, keeping himself warm by replenishing the blaze with faggots and milling around it, listening all the while, he

355

heard within the lapse of a reasonable time the livery team coming across the Tongue River bridge. It was coming on a keen run. The messenger and the doctor were transported safely to the other side of the stream.

The distance of twenty-two miles stretched away in a dreary distance to the home of the rancher. The silence of the ominous night seemed to challenge the stamina of man and beast. The snow-filled trail ahead lay over the river bench land, down in the depressions and over the hills. It was difficult for a rider on horseback to undertake the trip. The cowboy brought no extra mount. It was no time to hesitate.

McNaney Hitched Up

McNaney owned a pair of exceedingly longwinded race horses. The ponies were his pride. No argument was necessary. He hooked them to a light buggy. Up hill and across the flats they sped. The doctor remarked: "Jim, you'll kill your horses." "All right," said McNaney, "you just hold on to that medicine box. If the ponies play out we will stop somewhere and get some more. We are going to the Corry Wilson ranch. His wife is sick. There are plenty of ponies."

The doctor's statement is that the time consumed in making the trip of twenty-two miles on that cold December night was one hour and thirty minutes. The life of the wife of the rancher was saved. When asked, "How much do I owe you, Jim?" the ferryman replied by saying, "Send me word that your wife is better and I am paid."

Shortly following the episode when this classic of speed was enacted, one of the ponies of the McNaney team, known far and wide in the Miles City region for endurance, was accidentally probed with a pitchfork that incapacitated it for further service and subsequently died.

Tribute From Wilson

In appreciation of this exploit on the part of his friend, Mr. Wilson, in speaking of Mr. McNaney, said, "Whilst we are prone to believe it is better far to speak in terms of praise by word and with pen of those worthy while in active life, than wait until they have departed, still I feel a brief mention of some of the commendable qualities of James McNaney, who passed away near Glendive some time since, might tend to act as a blazer along the trail of life for others leading to the goal of more noble traits."

Mr. McNaney came to eastern Montana when quite a young man. He spent the major part of his life in and around Miles City. He was familiar with its earliest traditions. He came to know the solitude of the hills and where the buffalo and deer browsed. By nature he was a gentleman. He possessed those qualifications and characteristics that fitted him for any undertaking, no matter what the hazards might be. He inherited a kindly disposition yet was ever ready to plead his own case or protect a friend by word or action. He possessed a noble bearing and a fine appearance. His courage was unquestioned and his bravery tested under circumstances when his 'nerve' never faltered in times when difficulties arose that required quick action on the trigger. He scorned to boast of his achievements, and rarely related any of his exploits *unless there was something amusing created and which had a bearing on any affair under discussion.*

McNaney gained much local fame as a ferryman. His labors however, were not confined to this occupation during the long period that he spent in eastern Montana. His prowess as a 'crack shot' with the rifle is also remembered.

Tenderfoot Goes Hunting

Miles City, in the halcyon days of its youth, had many visitors. It was then the new west. Buffalo roamed the plains. Deer grazed on the succulent grasses in the valleys. As the menace of roving bands of hostile Indians decreased, so increased the number who would go out and exterminate the wild game. One autumn a young student from one of the leading colleges in the east came west to Miles City. He was well informed in the old dime novel literature of that day. Apparently he was eager to perform some 'heavy' act in the western wilds that would give him a place in history along side of Buffalo Bill, or some other famous frontier character.

After spending a few days in the city to become familiar with the conditions this young man arranged for Mr. McNaney to accompany him and his party on a buffalo hunting trip. They arrived up in the Big Dry Creek country. Off in the distance they caught sight of a band of buffalo. Maneuvering in order to approach the band with the wind the hunters came within striking distance. Addressing the young easterner, McNaney said, "Young man, there is one kid looking right at you. Shoot him in the head and when he falls run quickly and cut his throat."

The young man raised his gun and fired. The quarry went down and remained stunned long enough to allow the highly tensioned tenderfoot to get to him. A surprise awaited him. Instead of being pierced by the bullet from the rifle of the young man, the animal recovered from the impact and arose to his feet. A run for life ensued in which the hunter became the recipient of several snow baths. The race was settled in favor of the easterner by a well-directed bullet behind the left fore shoulder from McNaney's high-powered rifle.

Farmer Takes a Plunge

It was in his capacity as a ferryman, however, that 'Jim' McNaney is better remembered. One day in the month of June when the Yellowstone River was running 'high and wide', a farmer arrived at the ferry. He had some eggs in his wagon. He expressed a desire to take his team and wagon across the stream that he might drive on to Miles City with his farm produce. The necessary arrangements were made. When the team stepped on the apron of the ferryboat the rope that held the craft broke and it moved away from the bank. The farmer and his entire outfit went catapulting into the surging water.

Taking quick note of the situation, McNaney plunged at once into the deep water. He reached the struggling animals and cut the traces. The horses then swam back to shore. In the meantime, the farmer was seen drifting down the stream holding on to his case of eggs. Coming up on the bank McNaney loosed his small skiff and started in pursuit of the farmer in peril in the swiftly moving waters.

Rescues the Eggs

"Crawl in here old hand, that is a poor way of getting a divorce," said McNaney to the farmer, who released his grip on the case of eggs and complied with the order. Taking him to the shore, McNaney then struck out after the eggs, which had drifted about a mile farther down the stream. He picked it up and turned back to shore. With the recovery of the wagon the farmer's outfit was re-assembled and the second try at ferrying him across was successful.

The greater difficulties were encountered in the fall of the years that McNaney operated the ferry. The river ran heavily with slush ice. In emergency cases a skiff was used to transport passengers from one side to the other. The passenger usually was required to stand in the bow of the boat to keep the ice out of the way to make it easier to row the craft.

'Jim' McNaney and his ferryboat on the Yellowstone River in the vicinity of Miles City stands in a picturesque silhouette against the background of the romantic history of the early day of Milestown.

"Mr. McNaney has made a valuable contribution to the history of the west. Aside from his life, which reads like a pioneer's romance, he has given valuable assistance to historians and to various museums in their attempts to preserve the history of the old west. He was a very close friend of W.T. Hornaday of New York City, with whom he traveled in 1886, at which time Mr. Hornaday was gathering specimens for the Smithsonian Institute."

Hornaday in his book, <u>A Wild Animal Roundup</u>, devoted considerable space to Mr. McNaney. In this book, Hornaday explains that when he realized, with a shock, that the bison millions were not only going but gone, he promptly contacted his superiors at the Smithsonian Institute and was instructed to arrange immediately an expedition to the West to see if somewhere there might still be some unkilled bands from which specimens might be taken and preserved for the museum for future generations.

The Smithsonian would meet the expenses and would also ask the Secretary of War for all help possible from the nearest Army post. Some preliminary fieldwork in May and June of 1886 convinced them the bison specimens might be obtained in the area north of Miles City so they returned in late September to the Big Dry country* for the actual hunt (shedding animals in the spring were not suitable for mounting).

Hornaday had engaged Irvin Boyd as 'foreman' of the expedition, and Boyd in turn had engaged Jim McNaney and L.S. Russell to help with the hunting. They planned, if possible, to obtain "twenty skins of males, females and young, ten or fifteen skeletons, and pick up about fifty skulls." By the end of October they had killed ten of the desired twenty.

"Jim McNaney" (writes Hornaday) "is a splendid shot and a genuine Buffalo hunter with a record of about three thousand three hundred head, slain for their hides in three years, killed five of the ten head." At the close of the hunt he wrote, "Jim was the best shot and champion hunter of our outfit, and he killed as many buffalo as all the rest of us together, just half of the whole number."

In a later chapter Hornaday wrote, "Jim McNaney was with me on the historic Smithsonian buffalo hunt of 1886, even unto the day when we found and killed the big bull whose lordly portrait now adorns and illumines the face of our new ten-dollar bill. There is little question that that is the same buffalo that appears on the buffalo nickel."

According to Hornaday, Mr. McNaney's talents were by no means limited to hunting, and he describes how after supper, "Jim brought out his mouth-harp...." Besides being a fine shot and a skillful hunter, Jim enjoyed the unquestioned reputation of being the champion mouth-organist of Montana.

Several years after the buffalo expedition Hornaday returned to Montana for a hunting trip with Jim McNaney and two other men, but a few days out of Miles City a hard-riding messenger brought word early in the morning that "Maggie's been took awful bad. The doctors say that there is going to be an operation right away.... It's at four o'clock this afternoon." Maggie was Jim's wife and the mother of little Jack.

Jim was confident that his horse, 'Bull Pup', would take him the seventy miles to Miles City by four o'clock, and he did. Later he reported to Hornaday that "Bull Pup took me to Miles by half past three — and he never turned a hair! Blamed if I don't believe he could have brought me back again to the Little Dry by midnight!" The operation was successful and Jack's mother recovered.

After the Smithsonian buffalo hunt Jim went to work for the N Bar N (the Home Land and Cattle Company), one of the richest outfits in the 'North Side'. He was one of their line riders* during the rugged winter of 1886-87. About two years after the buffalo hunt, while Jim and Hank Kusker were rounding up horses for the N Bar N, they came upon four grizzly bears.

Both had put their guns into their bed rolls on the pack horse that morning, and even their knives were in the pack so the only weapon they had was Jim's little two-bladed, pearl-handled penknife. But, of course, they had their ropes so they decided to rope the grizzlies. Hank roped his around the neck, and the rope pulled so tightly that the bear choked, but Jim's bear still had considerable fight in him. Hank decided to try riding Jim's grizzly and managed to get astride by slipping up from behind. The reaction of that bear was like nothing Hank had ever before ridden.

Bruin was in no mood for a rough-riding contest and instead of trying to throw his rider when Hank dug in his spurs the bear reached up with both hind feet and clawed at Hank's legs. Hank was more than ready to quit and scrambled off in a hurry, but not before the bear had torn his trousers to shreds and deeply scratched his legs as well.

That was about enough so they choked that bear also since they had no other way to dispatch him.

McNaney, known as 'Cheyenne Jim' to his friends, came to the Glendive vicinity in 1906. Jack recalls helping his father haul hay to Camp La Mesa at Intake, government headquarters for the Lower Yellowstone Irrigation Ditch, and selling it for three dollars a ton. In 1915 the old ferryman began running the ferry at Intake and operated it until his death (from heart failure) in April 1926.

Jack still has the original copy of the telegram, which Mr. Hornaday sent to him and his sister upon receipt of word of Mr. McNaney's death. It reads as follows:

"New York, N. Y., April 28, 1926

Jack and Clara McNaney,
I deeply regret the passing of your father, James McNaney, my comrade in Montana field work and through forty years as beloved friends. His name is written often in my book and particularly in history of the last days of the wild buffalo in Montana. His fine services to the Smithsonian expedition for buffalo in 1886 contributed greatly to its success and now are known to millions of Americans. See my last book Wild Animals Roundup. If possible please order flowers at my expense to represent me.
W. J. Hornaday"

Jack received his schooling in the Savage and Intake areas and mentions that only two of his old school chums, Oscar Larson and Slim Graves, are still around. He noted the coincidence that he and Larson were in the third and fourth grades together, then fifty-five years later (last summer) were elevated to a higher degree of Masonry together. He observed that any mention of Slim would be incomplete without at least a reference to his skill as a bronc rider.

In the days before Savage existed, the school Jack attended was located at Tokna, about two miles west of the present town of Savage, on Dunlap Creek. Tokna was one of the stops for the Glendive-Sidney stage and one of the places they changed horses. The stage route could be seen from the school so instead of automobiles whizzing by distracting attention it was the arrival of the stagecoach each day that provided a brief break in the monotony. The stage at that time was operated by two brothers, Johnson and Johnson. One of their barns was located at the foot of Coal Bank Hill, a short distance beyond the Adams ranch.

At that time the Post Office also was located at Tokna and run by August Frederickson, father of R.J. Frederickson of Glendive. As the town of Savage began to grow the school was moved to Savage, and in order to go to school Jack stayed in Savage with Mrs. Joe Hart – a very fine lady, he added.

Another post office that has changed name and location is the Marko Post Office, operated by the gentleman of that name which preceded the Intake office and was located about three miles below Intake. Jack cherishes memories of many of the area's residents – among them Bill Willett, the George Rice family, and the Tom and Howard McPherson families, all of whom he holds in high esteem.

Jack's only sister, Clara, lives in California, but Jack, with his wife, Virginia, has chosen to stay with his father's 'old stomping grounds'. He retired last summer from the Northern Pacific Railroad where he was working even before he enlisted in the Army at the start of World War I.

They 'get around' though; visiting with their children takes them almost from coast to coast. Their only son, James, lives in Norfolk, Virginia, where he works for the state highway department, since his retirement from the U.S. Navy in 1962. Their only daughter, Mildred (Mrs. Tom Nicholson), lives in Vancouver, Washington. The McNaneys are planning a trip to the East Coast this summer, and Jack says he plans to spend about a week 'just looking' at the Smithsonian Institute where his father's prowess lives on.

Herman Ullman

June – July 1965

Spinning, weaving, candle-making – to most of us these represent some era in the remote past, but when they are still linked with the childhood memories of some of our senior citizens, perhaps the era is not so remote after all.

Herman Ullman has spent most of the last sixty years in Glendive, yet his earliest recollection is the spool going 'round and 'round on his mother's spinning wheel.

Herman was born on a farm in Wisconsin in 1881. The family's flock of sheep supplied the wool from which his mother knit the socks for the entire family. Since there were ten children in the family that was no small order. The socks are long gone, but Mr. Ullman still has one of the linen towels which had its beginnings in the flax fields on the farm. He recalls how they soaked the flax in the creek, and how they combed and combed the fibers, preparing it for his grandmother to spin and weave. Even now he can just about feel the roughness of those towels when they were first used. The children would almost cry when they dried their faces with them, but the towels softened as they were used and laundered until they were much kinder to tender skins.

Kerosene lamps supplied the best artificial light for the Wisconsin farm, but candles performed their share of duties, too. His mother made their own candles, using a form with six tubes. A wick, suspended from a wire across the top, was threaded through the middle of each tube, then the hot tallow was poured in.

When he was about thirteen years old he started working on a neighboring farm and was paid $9 per month for six months. A lot of farmers wanted a kid to help with the chores – milk cows, take the milk to the cheese factory, and so forth. His dad told him he could work out, and his wages would be his own, but he would have to buy his own clothes. Then during the winter he could go to school.

At the place he worked the man's parents lived with them. The old man did like to fish. Sometimes he would ask the boss if Herman could go with him, and that always made Herman happy. Near the river where they fished was a crossroad. The old man would always give Herman a bottle and twenty-five cents and let him off there with instructions to go to the nearby grocery-saloon and get the bottle filled. Even though Herman was just a lad, the grocer always filled the bottle with whiskey and handed it back to him with ten cents change, asking no questions. Then Herman hurried to the river to join his friend. The old fellow fished the middle of the river and usually hadn't caught any fish yet. Herman thought it was better to fish near the shore where the fish fed.

When his six months were up the farmer still had a little work he wanted done so he asked Herman how much he'd want to stay a few more days. Herman said thirty-five cents a day, but the farmer thought that was too much so Herman went home.

362

Grain binders had come into use by that time, but on his father's farm they always started harvesting a field by cutting a swath with a cradle* around the outside so the horses wouldn't trample any grain. One of the older brothers would cut the swath (Herman was about 'in the middle' of the family and the worst place to be, he says), then one of the 'middlers' would tie the grain into bundles by hand. The remainder of the field was harvested with the binder – a while before the day of self-propelled combines.

About 1900 he went with his brother Will to Minnesota to work in the woods. On that job they'd get to the tall timber while the stars were still in the sky and stay until they came out again in the evening. The first winter on that job they were paid $26 a month, the second winter $30 a month, plus room and board.

The day the camp closed in the spring of 1902 a pain in the side overtook Herman. Earlier he had bought a hospital ticket, good for one year, for the sum of $4 so he was promptly admitted to the hospital in Stillwater, and the doctor announced, "Appendicitis." That scared Herman. He was in the hospital five weeks, but he recovered satisfactorily, and he figures that $4 ticket really saved him money.

Harvest that fall found Herman and his brother Will in the Red River Valley making wages of $2 per day plus room and board. Their drifting was ever westward, and after harvest they moved on to the vicinity of Dickinson, North Dakota, where they each found a job. They could get board and room in the hotel in Taylor for $16 a month.

In January Herman took a job at a ranch near Halliday for a bachelor named Charley and moved out on a beautiful day, the ground bare of snow. He soon found that wasn't the norm. Charley had a brother John living about twenty miles from him so the first time he sent Herman to Taylor for groceries, he gave instructions to go as far as John's the first day, then on to Taylor the next. He got to John's just fine, but the next morning a blizzard was raging so John didn't think he should go on to Taylor – he might be there the rest of the winter. He started back for Charley's, but what little trail there had been was obliterated. No fences to follow, no dwellings – nothing but whirling snow between John's and Charley's. Mr. Ullman explains, "It sure was not comfortable to sit on the high seat of a lumber wagon facing a blizzard," so he went back to John's. When John asked where he had been, he could only answer, "Nowhere." The next day John still didn't figure it was safe to start for Taylor but sent his boy along as a guide to Charley's. The boy was familiar with the terrain, and found a trail where there was none so they arrived safely at Charley's, albeit with frostbitten faces and fingers.

At Charley's the wind was so strong it blew the tops off the haystacks. The haystacks were prairie hay, full of hay needles. One of those needles worked through his sock and into his ankle, causing an infection, so he had to use a chair for a crutch for a number of days.

After Taylor they moved farther west. Brother Will was already working in Glendive, and wanted Herman to join him so the next move was – Montana.

363

Herman Ullman hadn't been in the Treasure State long when he made the acquaintance of a 'spooky' iron gray mare. He got a job with Jack Stewart putting up hay, and when that iron gray mare was hitched to the wagon, somebody had better guard the reins. The hayfield was punctuated with bushes and brush so when Jack, walking beside the wagon and loading hay, met some brush on his side of the wagon, he passed the lines behind the horses over to Herman. A little slack was all the iron gray needed – and her teammate was right with her. As the horses started, the corner of the wagon hit Herman in the back and knocked him down. Jack yelled, "Hang onto the lines!" Herman had every intention of hanging on, but about the time he collided with a big bullberry bush he let go and the horses bid farewell. That time they had the good judgment to run to the barnyard and stop at the haystack so when Jack and Herman straggled in, tied for a poor second in that race, they unloaded the jag of hay that was already on the rack and went back to the field.

Jack made up his mind the horses weren't going to pull that trick twice so when they went back to loading, he stayed on the wagon. All went well until they had about half a load on; then the horses took a notion it was time to get going. As they started Jack hollered, "Whoa!" and jumped for the front of the wagon to grab the lines, but the horses weren't listening. They didn't whoa, and before he could get the lines, the rack tipped over and spilled him out. This time the horses headed for the Yellowstone River, and when the men caught up with them, the horses were straddling a tree and had just two wheels behind them.

The stagecoach, making its daily run between Glendive to Mondak, changed horses there at Stewart's place, and one day they left an order to have two of the horses shod. They gave assurance that one of the horses had been ridden so Herman, delegated to take the horses to blacksmith Boschard below Crane, figured he'd ride that one and lead the other one.

He got the one horse saddled and climbed aboard, but if that horse had been ridden, he must have forgotten about it. It was soon plain that both horses were broncs so when Jack suggested, "One at a time is all you can handle," Herman thought that was sure good advice and headed for the road. There was no checking the speed – 'sawing' on a straight bit just had no effect – so all he could do was hang on, and he made the trips to the blacksmith shop and back in record time.

When the haying was finished he came back to Glendive and started working for Dan Sutherland, mixing concrete (by hand) and making the blocks for what is now the Brost building*, known for years as the Sutherland apartments.

The next year he worked with the paint gang on the Northern Pacific, but by then another attack of wanderlust (actually it was gold fever) was coming on so when the paint job closed down, he headed west again, this time on a pass as far as Billings. There he met a fellow by the name of Herman Tronson who was also interested in prospecting so they decided to throw in their lots together. The other Herman thought Idaho more promising than Nevada, where Ullman had intended to go, so they made it Idaho.

There they both worked in a placer mine camp called Tyson. The gold was mixed with gravel so it was run through sluice boxes with water, and the riffles in the bottom of the sluice boxes would catch the gold. Next he went to a mine near Mullen, operating the ore cars in a tunnel. One of the ore cars was equipped with a brake, but two were not.

One day as he was ready to take the ore from the tunnel he found that he had the two cars without brakes loaded. He hesitated a bit about trying to go out with those two but thought he could hold them back so they wouldn't run into the horse that pulled the cars along the track, and he started out.

It didn't work the way he figured. His 'holding back' had no effect whatever on the cars. The horse pulled the cars by a twelve-foot chain, and as the cars began to pick up speed, so did the horse, to keep out of the way. As the horse plunged through the mouth of the tunnel, running for his life the chain caught on a tie and wrapped around it, stopping the cars. As Herman emerged from the tunnel, the boss exploded. Herman fully expected to get fired, but he didn't.

Another time as he was riding the cars back into the tunnel he came in contact with the splice where the electric wire that had been extended back into the tunnel had been spliced but not wrapped. The next thing he remembers he was sitting between the rails.

The next winter he was employed by the Standard Mine at Mace, down in a deep, narrow canyon where for one month the sun never reaches. On the night of February 27, the windows in his room started rattling, and he heard someone yell, "Snowslide!" He jumped from his bed and saw that he was on the edge of a snowslide that buried the little mining town. He quickly joined others who had been spared and began digging through the snow, trying to rescue those who were entombed. The mine superintendent's house was one of the many buried.

They dug until 3:00 a.m. to reach him, only to find him dead, but his lifeless body had protected his wife enough that she was spared and recovered. One daughter also escaped, but his two other children were among the many casualties in the tragedy.

The following summer while Herman worked at the placer mine at Tyson, he found out first hand what it was like to be buried alive. Here, in his own words, is his description of that experience:

One morning when I got on the job, the bank, about fifteen feet high, was sticking over pretty far. The object is to undermine it with the stream of water we call piping. It just would not cave in so I let the stream from the pipe run on one place up about ten feet from the ground during the noon hour.

After dinner I tied seven sticks of dynamite together and put in a long fuse, ready to set it off. Looking at the situation, though, it did look too risky to me to go in there. As I was not making headway, though, it seemed the only thing for me to do so about three p.m., I told my helper to take this one-by-three (sixteen feet) and push the dynamite in the hole when I got on the ladder. This bank had hung there since morning so I figured it was not going to come down.

365

When working underground in the Coeur D' Alenes, a miner said, 'Before the ground caves in there always is a warning; the dirt starts to trickle along the seam where it lets go.' Well, when I stood on that ladder, a long seam appeared at my right. A quick turn and jump and when I hit the ground my feet were tangled up in the loose dirt already so I went down and found myself completely buried.

The ground under me was muddy and soft so there was no pain, but all that weight on top of me made me wonder just how long I could take it. Well, it did not take long for me to pass out, and it sure was a surprise to me to wake up again. They had me almost dug out. They put me in the wagon and took me to the Milwaukee R.R. line along the St. Maries River. There was only one train a day and we got there just in time, and I was taken to the hospital at St. Maries, Idaho. My ears, nose and eyes had a lot of gravel in them, but no bones were broken. For a couple of days I could hardly move. It sure was a surprised bunch when I came back a week later. One fellow said, 'I sure thought you was a goner.' Another said, 'I would not want to have been in your place for Rockefeller's millions!'

That old ladder, of course, was all busted up. When I asked about it later, one of the men said he saw some kindling wood go down the sluice boxes. The dynamite had been tossed in the clear. I was off the job for two weeks.

Herman's brother Bill was still living in Glendive so when he wrote and asked him to come and work for him in his greenhouse, Herman decided to come. This was entirely out of his line, as he mentioned in his answer, but Bill assured him that he would be around at all times, and they always had been close together so Herman decided to come.

None of the present greenhouses was there yet – just some window sash on some frames, a one-room building for living quarters, and a cellar for the furnace. Cut flowers were kept in the basement.

One Sunday forenoon they had a big rain (six inches) and the basement filled up with water. The cut flowers floated on top of the water so they weren't damaged, but he had to dip all that water out of the basement. The next Sunday it was the same thing all over again.

That first Sunday a man who lived a short distance from the greenhouse drowned. He, too, had water in his basement so he had decided to walk to town and get a pump. As he cut through Perham Field he got off the path a little crossing the creek just below the present East End Texaco Station*, and stepped into a hole with nine feet of water in it. It was nine o'clock that evening before they recovered the body. Soon after this the first greenhouse was put up and some remodeling done so there was no more flooding. Mr. Ullman found out there is a lot to learn about plants and bugs and greenhouse work and says there is a lot he doesn't know yet. Like all jobs, some of it was easy sailing and some was not so easy. Making up designs and layouts does not come naturally to everyone, he says, and he didn't like that part. Brother Bill was busy doing carpenter work and the greenhouse in those first years barely made expenses, but it developed into a thriving business.

366

Mr. Ullman worked at various other jobs during his years in Glendive, including some time with the Northern Pacific Railroad and a short period in the post office. He has done much to help make Glendive a more attractive place through his yard and plant work, and when this city undertook its 'Beautification Project' some years ago, it was Mr. Ullman who planted the trees and bushes along Merrill Avenue from the 'Hill' to the depot.

With a weak heart Mr. Ullman has to take things rather easy, but he still manages to get around in spite of his eighty-three years.

J.B. 'Bennie' Dawe, Sr.

October 1965

All his life Bennie Dawe had wanted to be a cowboy, and he hadn't been in Montana long until he figured he 'had it made'. Bennie had been brought up in Michigan's timber country where his father cooked in a lumber camp. When the timber was cleared out, the boss changed his operations from timber to farming and changed location from Michigan to North Dakota.

Two of Bennie's older brothers had been chore boys around the camp so when the boss shipped his horses to Jamestown (that was in 1888), the boys came along and continued to work for him. They stayed with him several years, then in 1892 they both moved on westward to Glendive.

One of the young men found a job at the McCone Ranch on Burns Creek, the other for Merrill and Libby on North Fox Creek. By the time his parents (and Bennie) came to Montana in 1894, Lossie Dawe had started a ranch of his own. In 1894, Dawson County had not been surveyed so prospective ranchers didn't bother with the formality of buying land; they simply 'squatted' on the location that suited their fancy and let their livestock run at large.

Lossie met his parents in Glendive when they arrived from Michigan, and as they visited enroute to his ranch he mentioned that he and several of the other Burns Creek ranchers needed a line rider. There were many southern cattle, belonging to the big outfits, ranging the country, and the local cattlemen wanted someone to keep their cattle within reasonable range and the southern cattle out. That sounded like the job Bennie had dreamed about so it didn't take much negotiating until the ranchers had their line rider, and fourteen-year-old Bennie was a 'cowboy'.

There wasn't much to Glendive when the Dawes came, but what there was of it was – rather rough. No water system, no sewer, no sidewalks, no paved streets – and six saloons. The Jordan Hotel was a two-story frame building. The town's wells had one thing in common: soda water. However, good drinking water could be hauled from a spring west of Glendive.

Dawe soon found a location to his liking on Fox Creek about six miles below Lambert so he 'squatted' there and went into the cattle and sheep business. Dawe had arthritis, so even though Bennie was just a young fellow he assumed a good deal of responsibility around the ranch, and in time he became a partner of his father. While two of his brothers had preceded their parents to Montana, one brother and one sister had remained in Michigan, and they came a few years later.

In the fall of 1894 the government closed Fort Buford* and held an auction to dispose of surplus army goods. Dawe took advantage of the opportunity to acquire some top-quality supplies. Among other things he bought a Sharps 45-70 rifle with two boxes of ammunition (those boxes were each about eighteen inches square and eighteen inches deep, which provided a lot of shooting!) a couple mattresses (Bennie used one of those mattresses on the roundup several years and found that it provided good sleeping), and some harnesses. Those harnesses had chain tugs* covered with leather piping and were the finest quality throughout. The wooden hames had hooks on them so that the harness could be adjusted to fit a large or small horse. Then, as now, "Uncle Sam bought only the best."

When the Great Northern Railroad came through, a Glendive real estate agent, E.C. Leonard, laid out a townsite about one-and-a-half miles from Dawe's ranch and called it Gettysburg. About all the town ever boasted was an elevator, stockyards, and a little shack for a depot. One freight a day came through. Now it's all gone.

Bennie spent two summers as line rider for the Burns Creek ranchers. During the winter he attended school at Tokna (near the present town of Savage), working for his board and room at Dunlaps. Dunlap had a daughter named Tokua, for whom the Tokna post office was named. When the application for post office was sent to Washington, D.C., the 'u' in Tokua was mistaken for 'n' so the post office became Tokna instead of Tokua. Tokua is a Sioux word meaning 'where'. Her father thought she was appropriately named because she was always riding around the ranch, and he was always wondering where.

Neither Sidney nor Savage had anything to offer as a trading center when the Dawes located on Fox Creek so they did a good share of their buying at O'Brien's General Store at Newlon, located near Sidney's present site. A general store then handled just about anything you might need from groceries to harnesses.

If Bennie Dawe may have been somewhat of an amateur when he took on his first job as cowboy, he became a seasoned puncher. He rode for the HS Ranch two summers on roundup. The HS ran two wagons and would start on Bad Route just north of Terry. From there they would work north covering all the territory from the Big Dry to the Yellowstone and as far north as Fort Buford (or the Missouri River).

When he rode for the 'Pool' wagon four Burns Creek Ranchers paid him. Many of the smaller outfits wouldn't find it practical to run a wagon of their own so a number of them would 'pool' their resources and men to join the roundup. Each of the four ranchers sending him furnished him with two horses and paid him fifty cents a day to gather the cattle that belonged to him and his father, too. Roundup was hard on horses, and each rider needed at least eight horses in his 'string'. He'd change horses twice a day (sometimes more, if the riding was extra hard), then after making the 'circle', he'd get his cutting* horse for separating or 'cutting out' the cattle for the different brands.

An automobile can travel the fifty-five miles from the Dawe ranch to Glendive in a little more than an hour now, but sixty-five years ago it was a day's ride horseback or two days trip with a loaded wagon. Mr. Dawe remarked that he'd ride all day to get to Glendive for a dance, dance all night, then ride all the next day to get back home.

Once when a hanging was scheduled in Glendive, Bennie and another young fellow took to the trail horseback, with the intention of coming to Glendive to watch it, but on the way they stopped to rest a bit at Dunlaps, Bennie's old friend. Mr. Dunlap, who had been in California "in the days of '49" and had witnessed hangings, urged them to change their plans and forget about watching such a scene. "You'll never be able to get it out of your mind," he told them. The boys respected his judgment and decided to go back home instead of coming on to Glendive.

Twelve years after his own introduction to the Treasure State, Bennie sent a one-way train ticket, westbound, to a girl he knew back in Michigan and introduced her to Montana, too, And very shortly he was introducing her as Mrs. Bennie Dawe. They had to go clear to Miles City to get married because she wanted a Methodist minister to perform the ceremony, and the nearest one was in Miles City.

Bennie's own father was a Methodist preacher but not an ordained minister so he couldn't perform marriages. Mr. Dawe explains that the difference between a minister and a preacher is that a minister gets a salary while a preacher just gets a little salt pork or 'what have you' now and then. His father pioneered not only in ranching but also in Sunday School work with a Sunday School at Tokna and another on Burns Creek near the Jack Martin place.

But in Montana they didn't have Methodist camp meetings like they used to have back in Michigan. Hundreds of people would come, some by excursion train, some with their own team and buggy, some even walking, anyway they could get there for the week of meetings. They would go out into the timber and cut away the brush, then set up their tents around the edge of the clearing and erect the tabernacle tent in the center, ready for a week of fellowship and worship. This was a time for the entire family to enjoy, and it was at such a meeting that Bennie first met the girl who later became his wife. They also attended the same Sunday School for some time before he said goodbye to Michigan for Montana.

They were married in the fall and the next spring his parents moved to Glendive, leaving the newly-weds to run the ranch. Two years later his mother passed away, and one of his brothers died that same year. Both were buried in the Glendive cemetery. The cemetery then didn't bear much resemblance to the present. At that time it was unkempt, and the road leading up to it was just a rough wagon trail winding up the side of the hill.

Bennie and his wife stayed on the ranch until 1918. Their nearest neighbor was eight miles away, and there was no school for their growing family so they solved their problem by selling their livestock and moving to Sidney.

After leaving the ranch Mr. Dawe worked for the county. At first he did road work, but after the county courthouse was built in 1927 he became Justice of the Peace and served in that capacity until about a year ago. During those thirty-seven years he performed over 1200 marriages (for couples a little less selective than his wife had been). In later years occasionally a couple would come in and would ask him, "Remember my folks? They were married here, too." Another of his responsibilities was to act as coroner when there was no elected coroner, and he was also police judge.

His wife passed away twenty-one years ago, but all of their four children are still living, and now he has grandchildren and great-grandchildren as well.

Other old timers may talk nostalgically of the 'good old days' but Mr. Dawe realistically asks, "After knowing modern conveniences who would want to go back? I wouldn't sell my memories," he declares, "but I wouldn't go through it again for a million dollars!" To illustrate his point he described the trips they used to make to Glendive. When they went with the wagon they took the most direct route, heading for Murphy Table and down toward the river to the mouth of Thirteen Mile Creek, about where Intake is now. There they camped for the night before continuing on to Glendive. Some nights there would be as many as ten or twelve campfires.

He recalled one trip, though, when they didn't get to Intake to make camp. It was after they had one little boy. They decided to go to Glendive for the county fair so they started out across country as usual, but when they reached Murphy Table, they found some changes were taking place. FENCES were making their debut! No longer could they cut across sections just any place they chose. It was a frustrating experience trying to dodge those fences, and darkness overtook them before they reached the edge of the Table. He walked ahead of the horses and led them, but soon they got into the breaks so there was no choice but to camp for the night. They had plenty of blankets with them so Mrs. Dawe and the baby slept, but he didn't attempt to go to bed, and as soon as day began to break they started on their way again.

Go back? Now when he has to shop he gets into his car and in a few minutes he can be at the super market. He picks up his mail at the post office and in just a short time he can be back in his little home again with its electricity and natural gas. Go back? He's satisfied, and sums it up with, "God and Montana have been very good to me."

As I Remember . . .

Glossary of Terms and Landmarks

Anderson's Department Store – 107 North Merrill

B. & B. Gang – Bridge and Building railroad gang (as opposed to track building gangs)

Bachelor's biscuits – Baking powder biscuits, a main staple of early bachelors

Bamber Hill – About two miles north of Glendive on the old Sydney Highway

Bayou – A marshy inlet of the (Yellowstone) river

Beanery – Northern Pacific Lunchroom at the depot

Beasly block – 300 Block of North Merrill

Big bone – Large dinosaur bone discovered summer of 1967

Big Ditch – Lower Yellowstone River irrigation project, starting at a diversion dam at Intake, MT.

Big Dry country – The wide open area of East Central Montana near Jordan named for Big Dry Creek

Bismarck Grocery – At Kendrick, Valentine & Douglas, later First National Bank, later Public Library

Break a horse – Tame or make obedient (a horse)

Break sod – Plowing sod to prepare as a field

Breaking Plow – Plow used to break (plow) sod

Broncpeeler – One who breaks horses for riding

Brost Building – 420 South Merrill

Buckboard – Four-wheeled open carriage; Seats rested on the floorboards

Bum lamb – An orphan lamb or a twin rejected by the mother

Buttrey – Now Albertsons in West Glendive

Callboy – Railroad employee who would go to the home of an employee to call him to work

Chaps – Leather trousers without a seat, worn over ordinary trousers by cowboys to protect the legs

Charivari – A mock serenade with kettles and drums to a couple on their honeymoon

Chinking – Plaster or similar used to fill chinks or cracks in walls

Cloverleaf Cafe – Cafe on Douglas Street

Coast to Coast store – 112 South Merrill

Congregational Church – 120 West Power

Corned – To preserve or pickle with salt granules or in brine

Coulee – A gulch or ravine, usually dry in summer

Cradle – A frame attached to a scythe so the grain can be laid evenly as it is cut

Custer's Battlefield – Now known as the Battle of the Little Bighorn

Cutting – Separating livestock by owner, for example during a roundup

C.Y.A. Hall – Catholic Youth Association Hall on Douglas, later Knights of Columbus Hall

Delco lights – Generator powered electric lights (32 volts DC) used by rural families 1900 to 1935.

Dinky – Combination freight and passenger train between Glendive and Sidney

372

Dion Block – 100 Block of South Merrill featuring brick buildings from 1886

Divide – See Redwater-Yellowstone Divide

Douglas Meade – Large general store at 119 1/2 North Merrill

Drag – Six section drag – farm implement used to uproot weeds in a corn field

Dutch – Pennsylvania Dutch, a German dialect of the Amish

East End Texaco Station – 1023 North Merrill

El Centro Motel – 112 South Kendrick

E.U.B. Church – Glendive Evangelical Church, Kendrick & Borden

Fallow – Plowed ground, typically seeded every other year and allowed to lie unplanted in alternate years to conserve moisture and help control weeds

Fellow – The rim of a spoked wheel

First National Bank – Kendrick & Valentine, later the Public Library

Fort Buford – U.S. army fort at the confluence of the Yellowstone and Missouri Rivers

Fresno – A type of horse-drawn road scraper

Gangplow – Plow with a number of shares side by side to make several furrows at the same time

Gate City – Glendive's nickname

Glendive Machine Works – 110 West Benham

Goose (the) – A short line train between Sidney and Richey

Greyhound Bus Depot – Across the street from the city hall

Guelff's Lumber Yard – Clough & Power Streets

Gumbo – A fine, silty soil which becomes sticky and nonporous when wet – and very slippery!

Hagenston Hardware – 103 North Merrill

Hilger garage – 301 North Kendrick

Hobble – Hampering movement of a horse by tying hind feet together

Homestead – Land given to settlers by the government in exchange for living on it and making improvements

Honeyockers – The disparaging term ranchers applied to the homesteaders

Hungry Joe – The rugged hills towering above Glendive on the east

Immigrant car – Railroad boxcar used by immigrants to transport belongings to their new location

Kampschrors – 606 North Merrill

KXGN studios – 210 South Douglas (formerly on South Pearson)

Lean-to – Makeshift shed or storage area for food supplies

MDU – Montana Dakota Utilities, 113 West Towne

Meissner's Meat Market – 114 South Merrill

New York Cafe – A Chinese cafe located in the 200 block of North Merrill

Phoenix Block – An apparent reference to the Dion Block, rebuilt of brick in 1886, 'rising from the ashes' of a major fire

Picket pin – Stake driven into the ground as a hitching post for animals

Prove up – Satisfy government requirements to own your homestead

Pumphouse – Building (sometimes a residence) along the railroad housing a pump, often for the purpose of filling a water tower etc.

Quanrad, Brink and Riebold Auto Parts – 400 North Kendrick

Rawleigh Wagon – A peddler's wagon, selling spices and extracts – and candy for the kids

Reach – See Wagon Reach

Redwater-Yellowstone Divide – the dividing line between the watersheds of the Redwater / Missouri Rivers and the Yellowstone River.

Repping – Each ranch would send a representative to the roundups to claim their Livestock

Riprap – Reinforce the river bank

Rodman – A person who carries the leveling rod in surveying

Roustabout – An unskilled or transient laborer

Rumley – Also Rumely; Large tractor produced by the Rumely Company, forerunner of Allis Chalmers

Sad iron – Used for ironing laundry and heated on the stove

Scorio Road – A road graveled with a red, cinderlike lava

Scraper – A wide scoop pulled by horses, or other sources of power, to remove dirt

Section – One square mile, 640 acres (quarter section = 160 acres)

Separator belt – Belt to drive the gears on a threshing machine

Shivaree – Same as charivari

Shocks – Bundles or sheaves of grain

Slip – Same as a scraper

Sou – Former French coin similar in value to a penny

Speedcar – Small vehicle designed to run on rails and used to transport workers

Squatted – Established residence on land without legal formalities

Stoneboat – A flat bed on homemade sled runners

Subway Husky Service – 322 South Merrill

Sulky – Carriage with a seat for only one person

Sulky plow – Plow with seat for riding (instead of walking behind the plow)

Summer fallow – See fallow

Tender – Horse's feet sore from walking; also weakened from hard work without grain

Treasure State – Montana's nickname

Trulock's Service Station – Intersection of White Chapel Road and old Highway 10.

Tug – Heavy strap connecting the harness to the crossbar of a wagon

Wooden mold-boards – Curved wooden board attached to a plow for turning soil

Woolworths – 113 North Merrill

Wagon reach – A pole joining the rear axle to the forward part of the wagon

Windlass – A simple winch used to lift a bucket out of a well

Zion Lutheran Church – Sargent & Riverview

List of Interviews

Following is a complete list, in alphabetical order, of the interviews Mrs. Kauffman conducted between 1964 and 1975.

Andrew **Anderson**
Dave **Anderson**
Harry **Anderson**
Felix **Andorno**
Earl **Baggs**
Walton **Baker**
Mrs. Percy **Baldwin**
Mrs. C.A. (Mary Kelly) **Banker**
Irvin **Bawden**
Mrs. George (Helen) **Beeler**
Mrs. Frank (Entonie) **Benes**
Joe S. **Beres**
Mr. James **Bidwell** &
    Mrs. George (**Bidwell**) Pierce
Bill **Blue**
Mrs. H. B. **Boehmer**
Pete **Boje**
Mr. & Mrs. Glen **Borntrager**
Mrs. Albert (Ivy Fluss) **Brubaker**
W. A. **Brubaker**
Mrs. Linda **Bryan**
C. A. **Buller**
Mrs. Grace **Buttelman**
Noel **Carrico**
Carl **Colbrese**
Mrs. George **Coryell**
Mrs. Joe **Crisafulli**, Sr.
Mrs. Bert **Crockett**
Mrs. Forrest **Currens**
DCHS Reunion 1965
DCHS Reunion 1970
DCHS Reunion 1975
Floyd 'Gobbler' **Davis**
J. B. Bennie **Dawe**, Sr.
Nick **Degel**
Arcy **DeLapp**
John **Diercks**
Harry and Fred **Dion**
Edna (Miller) **Doane**

Steve **Douglass**
Mrs. G.P. (Aurilla) **Drowley**
R. R. **Durfey**
Bert **Ekland**
Louie **Elliot**
Russell **Evans**
Mrs. Moore **Eyer**
Mrs. Ludvig (Annie) **Field**
Mrs. H. L. (Gertrude) **Finkle**
History of **First National Bank**
Mrs. Lucy **Fisher**
Erling **Fosfjeld**
Robert J. **Frederickson**
Mrs. Frank **Fritsch**
Mrs. Olive **Garfield**
Mrs. Monica **Geiger**
Don **Gibson**
Charles **Grandey**
Harry **Green**
Mrs. Earl **Grow**
Mrs. Fred **Grulke**
Mike **Guelff**
Jim **Haggerty**
Archie **Hamilton**
Peter **Hangs**, Sr.
Ed **Haskell**
Mr. & Mrs. Frank **Hasty**
Ole **Helvik**
Karl **Hepperle**
Mr. & Mrs. Conrad
    (Lydia Dickhoff) **Hess**
R. J. (Bert) **Hilger**
Gene **Hoffstot**
Mrs. Nancy **Hollenbeck**
Joseph **Holling**
Mrs. Leone **Hubing**
Mrs. Paul **Jarvis**
Jens **Jensen**
Mrs. Charles **Johnson**

Mrs. Mel (Jeanie) **Johnson**
Elsie **Jones**
Eivend **Kalberg**
Mrs. Andreas **Kalmbach**
Joe **Kelly**
Mrs. R. J. **Kennedy**
Mrs. Adolphus
(Margaret Henry) **Kent**
Frank W. **Kinney** & Sons
Art **Kitchen**
Mrs. Henry L. **Klope**
Mrs. Ed **Lamphier**
Mrs. Andrew (Grace) **Larson**
Mrs. Ella **Lineweaver**
Mrs. A. J. **McCarty**
Mrs. William **McGaughy**
Jack **McNaney**
Ernest **Malkuch**
Fritz **Massar**
History of **Methodist Church**
Francis **Miller**
J. F. **Miskimen**
Dr. P. J. **Moe**
Mrs. Jens (Birgette) **Mortensen**
Mrs. Menno
(Ora Chaney) **Mullet**
Mr. & Mrs. William **Muir**
John **Nadwornick**
Mrs. Desmond J. **O'Neil**
James **Osborne**, Sr.
Mrs. James (Marie) **Pechar**
Clifford **Pierce**
Mrs. W. B. **Pomeroy**
Rev. A. E. **Plummer**
John **Quick**
LuLu (Knapp) **Quick**
Mrs. Peter **Quilling**
J. K. **Ralston**
History of **Red Cross**
History of **Red Top**
Fannen **Reece**
History of **Richey**
E. H. **Rigby**
Mrs. Kathryn (Cruikshank) **Rigby**
Maude **Ritchey**

Mrs. H. V. **Robinson**
Fred **Rong**
Mrs. Retina **Rust**
Sam **Sampson**
Percy **Sawyer**
Mrs. Nick **Scabad**
Jens **Scarpholt**
Lenus **Schloss**
Art **Schrumpf**
Mrs. Anna (Manning) **Schultz**
Jean **Sellers**
Amos **Shrader**
A. O. **Skillestad**
Mrs. Grace **Skillestad**
Jacob **Stangeland**
Randal **Stewart**
Anna Caldwell **Stiefvater**
Mrs. Joe (Fanny Hostetler) **Stoll**
Bernie **Storm**
Mrs. John (Meta Hafele) **Sura**
John **Syversen**
Ernest **Temple**
Angelo **Tomalino**
Nils J. **Trangmoe**
Helen **Trocinsky**
Mrs. Ernest (Myrtle **Tusler**)
Kirkpatrick & Sheldon **Tusler**
Herman **Ullman**
Osmund **Vashus**
P. L. **Vine**
Carl **Volpp**
Gust **Voss**
Mrs. Perry (Annie) **Walker**
Mrs. Harold **Waller**
Mrs. Eva **Wester**
Mrs. Henry (Mary Barber) **Wienke**
Mrs. Virginia **Wing**
E. A. **Wolff**
W. W. (Billy) **Woods**
Isabelle Kierzek / Mr. & Mrs.
John **Zabrocki**
Mr. & Mrs. Henry **Zimdars**